# ENGLISH TRAVELLERS ABROAD

# ENGLISH TRAVELLERS ABROAD

## 1604–1667

*Their Influence in English
Society and Politics
(Revised edition)*

## JOHN STOYE

Yale University Press
New Haven and London
1989

First published by Jonathan Cape in 1952
This edition © 1989 John Stoye

Library of Congress Cataloging-in-Publication Data

Stoye, John, 1917–
    English travellers abroad, 1604–1667: their influence in English society and politics/John
  Stoye.
      p.     cm.
    Bibliography: p.
    Includes index.
    ISBN 0-300-04179-9. — ISBN 0-300-04180-2 (pbk.)
   1. England—Civilization—17th century.  2. England—Civilization—European influences.
3. British—Travel—Europe—History—17th century.  4. Travelers—Europe—History—17th
century.  5. Europe—Description and travel—17th–18th centuries.  6. Great Britain—
History—Stuarts, 1603–1714.  I. Title.
DA380.S76  1989
941.06—dc20
                                          89-9186
                                            CIP

Set in 11/12 Ehrhardt by Best-set Typesetter Limited, Hong Kong,
and printed and bound in Great Britain at The Bath Press, Avon.

# CONTENTS

# LIST OF ILLUSTRATIONS

# PREFACE

'I wish to record my gratitude to my three colleges, Christ Church, Corpus Christi and Magdalen, for their generous assistance in the course of these enquiries; to the Marquess of Salisbury, Mr. John Evelyn and Mr. J. Cottrell Dormer for allowing me to search among family papers; to the authorities of the Bodleian Library, the British Museum, and to Mr. Lamb of Sheffield Public Library, Mr. Urry of Canterbury Cathedral Library, Mr. Hiscock of Christ Church Library and Mr. Drage of Hatfield House for courteous and expert assistance; to the Rev. Professor Claude Jenkins for his patient scrutiny of the following pages; to Miss Mary Coate, Professor Wernham, Mr. Gough, the Provost of Oriel and the Rev. R. Trevor Davies for encouragement and corrections; to Professor Billanovich, Mr. Cuthbert Andrews, Mr. J. N. L. Myres and Mrs. I. M. Brown for help of various kinds; to my father and my wife for making the index; and, finally, to Mr. Eric Falk and Mr. Francis Codd for their hospitality at all times in the shadow of the Public Record Office.'

My acknowledgments were dated 31st December 1951, and nearly forty years later I recall the origin of these pages. A college prize happily enabled me to buy at Blackwells many books I wanted. With a little money left over, I took a makeweight of which I knew nothing. It was an old worn volume with a crowded titlepage, dated 1705. Parts of the title ran: 'Familiar Letters Domestick and Foreign; upon emergent Occasions...'. 'Emergent' was a word new to me, and caught my fancy. I forgot the book for six years, and in 1945 found it again. I then started to speculate whether the jumble of dated, undated and misdated letters written from abroad by the author, James Howell, 'one of the clerks of His late Majesty's (Charles I's) Privy Council,' could be put into some sort of historical framework; and so I began, with a great deal of help and encouragement recorded above. Howell almost disappeared as I was led to the mixed pasture and desert of the State Papers.

Of course it was history as a mode of travel. One looked at maps to find where the travellers went. One went to pleasant places to see what they saw. It would do a modern tourist good, I still maintain, to look through the eyes of *my* travellers at the Louvre and the Pont Neuf and the piazza of St. Mark's, or compare his own flight of a few minutes over the Alps with the experience of those who rode, walked, or were carried across them a long time ago.

As to the history the topic proved worthwhile. Not a runaway success like the gentries found rising or declining under Tudor and Stuart rulers, or the persistently elusive nature of the seventeenth-century 'scientific revolution', the study of travel and travellers of that period nonetheless finds favour and makes progress. Lists of the relevant books get longer. Professors confer. Old texts are better edited. New ones appear. Footnotes, I have to confess, get swollen. But little by little our concept of the past appears to gain from acquiring a collective notion, a sort of group portrait, of those who travelled from England to the continent in this period. It can be placed alongside studies of the extraordinary impact on England and Europe at the same time of overseas voyaging east and west.

What did I not understand forty years ago? Perhaps not clearly enough that in the Elizabethan period there was a distinct idea of travel as an 'art', to be practised by a properly taught young man in order to complete his education. The idea had been spelt out in the 1570s, in new books published both in Latin and English. In particular the thought of the great publicist and teacher Ramus, who died in the Paris massacres of St Bartholemews Day in 1572, was used to support this idea. He would be echoed by the even more influential author and teacher, Lipsius. Accordingly, when and where the often disturbed conditions in Europe allowed, a certain number of Englishmen were being sent abroad by their families. They must, in most cases, have gone with several other ideas in mind as well, but the notion quickly became a commonplace which could be used to counter the arguments put forward against such a risky and expensive procedure as foreign travel. These young men went from place to place and resided abroad; but they did not at first' tour' in the seventeenth-century manner which will be described in my pages. I should also have explained that the English travellers were part of a bigger movement. Not only did *they* go on these extended journeys for education and pleasure, but Dutch and German, Austrian and Hungarian, Bohemian and Polish — even Count Mazeppa from the Ukraine a little later — and Scandinavian nobles, gentry and urban patricians, with their governors and servants, were doing the same thing at the same time. Universities, entertainers of all sorts, welcomed and depended upon their valuable custom. It seems possible that fewer Italians, Spaniards and French attempted this sort of educational travel to other parts of Europe, but instead France and Italy were the principal 'host' countries. Large parts of Italy and the Netherlands were also Habsburg territory; it was commonly the military and diplomatic service of the Habsburg kings which took Spaniards as far afield in Europe as anyone else.

In England the attractions of foreign travel were an aspect of notable changes in education. From the early fifteenth century some of the sons of noblemen, gentry and prosperous townsmen had been going to Oxford and Cambridge; their numbers in residence seem generally to have increased until 1640. They wanted to come, and the universities welcomed this chance of attracting extra fees, fresh endowments and additional patronage. Collegiate foundations were already tending to supersede the older halls of residence in the universities. A college system for teaching and maintaining discipline, for the supervision of scholars intending to qualify for university degrees, was being developed. It did not prove too difficult to extend these arrangements so that more and more fee-paying commoners could be admitted to the colleges, and taught by the tutors. Some youths from the propertied families stayed at the university long enough to take degrees; others, whether they stayed for several years or departed rather quickly, did not do so. The system was flexible, and college teaching and college discipline must have been considered worthwhile by large numbers of people. There seems no doubt that the ancient syllabus of the university faculty of 'arts' could involve a good grounding in logic, the study of Latin and Greek authors, and practice in rhetorical speech. The tutors were sometimes gifted men pursuing interests of their own, theological or literary or even scientific; sometimes they gave their pupils guidance in topics outside the normal exercises. It was possible, but not usual, to study French. There is mention of outside teachers to be found for dancing and fencing and lute-playing. There were other, ordinary diversions. But two possible drawbacks in university life had to be considered. One was college discipline, restraints which might be felt oppressive after a period of time; and the second, not surprisingly, was that the commoners were auxiliary to an overwhelmingly ecclesiastical regime. The university clergy, many holding college fellowships, were busy maintaining the new Protestant establishment. Younger men in orders made ready to step into their shoes and the air resounded with theological debate. Although the commoners had been brought up to share the normal concern in church affairs, few of them wanted to attempt graduate courses of study (including law and medicine). They differed from the ordinary scholars benefitting from college endowments, most of whom hoped in due course for academic and clerical preferment. The commoners were to some extent strangers in societies of churchmen. No one would have said so then but this small world of the Oxford and Cambridge clergy made the two universities more provincial in atmosphere than they had been earlier. The English, in repudiating Rome, ran the risk of becoming insular.

These direct and indirect arguments favoured travel abroad after not too long a stint in college. In the seventeenth century travel often became the alternative to university residence among families of rank and wealth. The attractive 'art of peregrination' was the novel syllabus acceptable to parents or guardians. Therafter, fathers who had travelled in due course sent their sons along the same track but daughters, or in relevant cases the very youthful wives, were left at home.

In earlier centuries fighting men, traders, artisans, pilgrims, clergy and students were often on the move in Europe, in contrast to the more static elements of society. In the seventeenth century this circulation continued; as before there were many kinds of traveller; but some of them experienced a novel kind of shock. When English Protestants reached Italy or Catholic France, they had to come to terms with what they had been taught to condemn. There was another, equal novelty for the English Catholics who went abroad. In Paris or Rome or Padua they ceased to be members of a church exposed to persecution; there was a temptation to stay. The members of both groups took with them to the continent the beliefs which they had absorbed beforehand at home, but the possible effects of experience abroad on their church loyalty was for several generations a worry of contemporary government and society. When the zeal of propagandists or the simple acceptance of local practice in a foreign country converted an English Protestant traveller to the Roman obedience, the news, reaching the court or the countryside of home in England, was another characteristic tremor of the period. One reasons for it was that the travellers, Protestant or Catholic, were not easily distinguishable from political and religious exiles who would not or could not come home. These people would be waiting patiently on foreign ground for better times, or waiting impatiently and conspiring for a new regime. The Protestant monarchy, the Commonwealth, the Protectorate and the restored monarchy all confronted their malcontents across the Channel. They had to distinguish between gentry and students on their travels, and dissidents. This was never easy and in the mid-seventeenth century the reader will confront, as governments did, a bewildering medley of intermediate types of person. There were those who preferred not to take sides during the Civil Wars and went abroad, others with decided loyalties who went because they preferred peaceful arts and occupations to warfare. Some preferred residence abroad to living under an oppressive government, while for others punitive taxation simply made it difficult to keep up appearances at home. There is accordingly a link between my subject and the great upheavals in the 1640s, in 1660 and again in the 1680s. Dissidents became tourists. Exiles wrote guidebooks and became tutors to tourists. English domestic history in the seventeenth century took place, in certain aspects, on foreign ground.

The Stuart court increasingly appears as the patron or protector of English Catholics, including returning Catholic travellers. They were well received there. That protection had not existed under Elizabeth, it was occasional and discreet under James I, but after 1625 Queen

Henrietta Maria's household gave it more effectiveness and notoriety. In Rome, at the same time, the welcome given to English Catholics and Protestants alike became all the warmer. Then, with civil war and royal defeat, the court itself and its Catholic component moved abroad and remained in exile for many years. They had been forced to follow the example of those English Catholic schools and other foundations already settled in Catholic Europe. But Henrietta Maria and her sons, the royal travellers who were the most important of the exiles, returned home to Whitehall at the Restoration; and there would be a second, final period of Stuart exile after 1688. The normal stream of educational travel in Europe had been swollen in the 1640s by several tributaries, but the enforced travels of the court in foreign lands would have a bigger political impact on Restoration history than any of my groups of tourist.

Fortunately the divisive elements in this story were counterbalanced by a richly composite legacy, from the countries visited, to the travellers returning home. In these pages I tried to given some account of their total experience, and of what they learnt in France, Italy, Spain and the Netherlands about arts and sciences, about foreign habits and skills, foreign political and social structures, and the appearance of foreign cities and landscapes. There are some large gaps. I left out Germany in the Thirty Years War. I left our gardens, but garden history is moving fast at the present time. I left out what the travellers ate and most of the new clothes they wore. I left out illness, and medicines. On the other hand I restored to memory certain historical figures, forgotten men who were travellers looking for jobs in the seventeenth century, and that seemed research worth doing.

The text has been revised, in some places corrected, extended or shortened. The notes now refer to a good deal of the recent literature. The bibliography lists first the sources consulted up to 1952, and second some of the authorities which would be useful if I started afresh on the subject at the present time.

It is a pleasure also, on this second occasion, to thank my colleagues and friends who have helped me with their enthusiasm and expertise to create an amended version of an old book: Sonia Anderson, Gerald Aylmer, Lawrence Brockliss, Peter Burke, Edward Chaney, Francis Haskell, Richard Luckett, Hugh Macandrew, Angus Macintyre, Richard Ollard, Peter Russell, Keith Thomas, Nicholas Tyacke, Blair Worden, Robert Baldock and Ann Grindrod. I am also grateful to the Trustees of Olive Countess Fitzwilliam's Wentworth settlement, the Trustees of the will of the late Major Peter George Evelyn, the Trustees of the British Library and of the British Museum, the Curators of the Bodleian Library and the Librarian of Sheffield Public Library for permission to use material in their charge; to the staff of those libraries as of the London Library and the Codrington Library, and to Jasper Scovil of Magdalen College Library, Mr. Wing and Mrs. Bradshaw of Christ Church Library, and Mrs. Martin of the Fine Art Library of the Ashmolean for great assistance at various times.


Magdalen College
Oxford
1989

# INTRODUCTION

'To praise Peregrination according to its worth and dignitie were the labor of a longer time and the Arte of a more Industrious braine; the flowers of this large garden will not uppon the sudden be knit up into one Nosegaie.' So wrote a modest, anonymous author; and certainly the task of describing English travellers abroad, and the influence of continental travel upon Englishmen in the seventeenth century, may seem too vaguely defined to present a tangible problem for study. At first, however, it was for the purpose of surveying a particular source of manuscript material — the State Papers Foreign of the early seventeenth century in the Public Record Office — that this enquiry began, and the very deficiencies of these papers limited the field.

During the reign of James I reports from resident ambassadors and agents accredited by the King to various princes frequently mention the names and activities of English travellers passing through foreign countries. It was a part of the vigilant paternalism of Tudor and early Stuart administration to keep an eye on such men, potentially servants of the English crown or dupes of foreign interests or even wilful traitors. Robert Cecil, first Earl of Salisbury, who supervised the ordinary diplomatic correspondence until his death in 1612, also concerned himself with the whereabouts and the welfare of his numerous relatives on their travels; and we shall see the younger generation of Cecils and Howards wasting their substance on the mainland of Europe, as we shall likewise catch glimpses of their servants and tutors who by faithful attendance on patrons in foreign parts hoped to pave their own way to preferment. This side of the enquiry, therefore, involved much preliminary searching in many volumes of the old diplomatic reports which came to Whitehall from Paris, Brussels, Valladolid, Madrid, Venice, Turin and other cities, and provided a rich opportunity for observing travellers moving from point to point in Europe. Such men may be mentioned, for example, as passing a few weeks in Paris. A correspondent in Lyon writes that he has news of their approaching arrival in that city. Then the English ambassador in Venice reports that the same travellers are being entertained by Duke Charles Emmanuel in Turin. They come to Venice itself. Then, possibly, another traveller from Naples or a secretary at Madrid or the agent in Brussels will refer to the same people as they pass through Naples, Madrid or Brussels. A number of these itineraries can be traced through the State Papers of James I's reign, together with a varying amount of incidental evidence: the names of a traveller's companions, his scale of living and his debts, his acquaintance with foreigners and attitude towards the English ambassador. An ambassador might become a useful patron to a promising young gentleman touring the continent, and the friendship of a great nobleman's son prove equally useful to an ambassador eager for promotion at home. Then there are also records of people who travelled with an official embassage, either as attendants to enrich with the lustre of their titles and equipage a diplomat's train on the ceremonial entrance into foreign courts or, more serviceably, as gentlemen intending to remain permanently abroad as members of the diplomat's household. Men of family often welcomed a chance of enrolling their sons in the following of King James's ministers, for it was a simple extension of a very ancient practice, education in the household of powerful or accomplished dignitaries, which had originally no connection with foreign travel. Finally, many papers deal naturally with the diplomats themselves, their journeys to foreign courts, accidents and incidents in the course of residence abroad, and their hopes of rising in the hierarchy of the King's government after this apprenticeship.

Such are the foundations laid by official records for this type of enquiry, and the following chapters attempt to set out some of the information about English travellers in western Europe which may be drawn from the State Papers Foreign. The division by countries is explained by traditional classifying of the records on the same principle; for, in fact, to order them otherwise would have eliminated too much valuable detail. When they are supplemented by a host of contemporary letters and books the result is a general picture of our travellers abroad at that date and, further, a study of the ties of patronage and clientage linking one Englishman to another even while in foreign countries. This affected their future careers and, in this sense, their importance and influence in English history. By way of detailed illustration, separate biographies have here been written round one profession or calling — that of the nobleman's tutor — in an attempt to show what can be gathered for this purpose from the evidence about an Englishman's travel.

It is clear that this evidence has severe limitations. First, the very useful memoranda and addenda about travellers in diplomatic correspondence, usually the final paragraph in long reports from Carew, Cornwallis, Wotton or Carleton, appear less frequently as time wore on. The death of Lord Salisbury marked an epoch in this, as in many more momentous developments, for he seems to have insisted on such incidental intelligence concerning the movement of individuals; while after the death of James I that form of evidence becomes rare indeed.

The change is a simple indication that during the first half of the seventeenth century the historian seems to be moving steadily away from a period in which public and private affairs were hardly distinguishable to the government and the dominant classes of society and into a period in which the distinction was accepted. After 1625 the State Papers Foreign become more exclusively official, comprising significant and insignificant political documents or mere newsletter reports on current affairs. Ordinary individual travellers and their friends no longer preoccupied the politicians, perhaps partly because there were now so many of them. In the same way politics lost their attraction for the traveller. The notion, which underlay so much didactic writing on travel between 1570 and 1630, that its chief justification was to educate trusty and well-informed servants for the State, and that the prime means to this end was the study of Cosmography and Policy and Oeconomy abroad (with mastery of foreign languages an important but subordinate instrument for this purpose), appears less and less frequently. The traveller was beginning to move out of the purview of government and, consequently, out of view of the State Papers.

Secondly, these official records, though they reveal something of the personal relationships and political affiliations of certain travellers, give little help in elucidating the subtler consequences of travel abroad: the intellectual or artistic effect of impressions gathered in foreign courts, churches, cities, what men saw and what they felt in an alien world. The limit of Lord Salisbury's interest in such matters was the possibility that young travellers would succumb to the power and charm of Roman Catholic religion, or the sad tendency of his relatives to neglect their more serious studies.

For these reasons, another type of record invited scrutiny: the numerous manuscript diaries of English travellers still in existence, many of them in the Bodleian Library and the British Museum. Most of these have long been familiar to the devotees of travel literature, though it has usually proved difficult to employ them except as illustrating or explaining one another, or to bring the valuable scattered evidence (which they undoubtedly contain) to bear on the general history of the English people. These autobiographical fragments admittedly make weary reading, sometimes a bare record of distances traversed and cities seen, sometimes a serried array of descriptive detail about churches, palaces, fortifications, 'rarities' and ceremonies; nevertheless they are the best available record of the seventeenth-century gentleman's tour of Europe and its importance as a part of his education, and they form the second main type of document which these pages attempt to explore. Their conventionality and monotony, so dissimilar from the sprightly eccentricity of early 'peregrinators' like Coryat and Lithgow who leapt into print, are very valuable from a historical point of view and build up the picture of a great number of ordinary men, representative of a whole class of their contemporaries, visiting the same towns, receiving the same impressions, bringing back to England the same memories or images, learning to share the same stock of historical commonplaces about the scene of great events and the doings of great men in Europe's past. Such diaries, naturally, unlike the continuous series of State Papers, were written by chance individuals and survive by accident. Who kept diaries, though educational theory at this period recommended the practice, and were they always the most intelligent travellers? How many intended to keep them and forgot them a few miles south of the Channel, then as now? Sometimes, doubtless, little pocket books amply filled were tossed aside or lost or burnt soon afterwards, or they were preserved and then destroyed by subsequent generations. If there is a ratio between the number of travellers, the number of diaries kept and the number that survive, no man can discover it. Instead we may only say that the great period for the study of such documents comes after 1625, after the State Papers have lost their value in this respect. A particularly valuable group of diarists with John Evelyn in the forefront wrote between 1635 and 1665; and for this reason a devotee of the subject is led long past the death of James I and into the reigns of his son and his grandson. It would be folly not to follow the trail left by these papers, especially with regard to Italy, for they reveal the origins of the Grand Tour in its fixed and conventional form.

These, then, are the two principal sources for this essay, together with a miscellany of letters and printed books and pamphlets. But what was the historical situation of which they are relics?

Great changes were undoubtedly taking place, as intelligent contemporaries realized. With the discovery of the west and the plantations of America and Ireland, with the Reformation forcing exiles both Catholic and Protestant over to the continent, and a development of old and new commercial links between England and various European and Mediterranean countries, there emerges to view, gradually and in outline, a movement of the English away from their native land. They were in process of dispersal over the known world just at a time when the notion of a sovereign state at last became rather more precise and rigid and coercive. Even if all this did not involve a permanent departure, as in the case of factors and sailors who returned home, the sphere of their activities had been enormously enlarged. Similarly, the seventeenth is a century of great Scottish and Irish migrations, when they rivalled the Swiss as the best mercenaries in Europe, and the Scots also extended their stray settlements in Sweden, Bohemia and Poland. The inhabitants of Britain, therefore, were among the most widely travelled peoples of the age. If Dutch and Spaniard surpassed them in certain directions, the subjects of the Stuarts, the loyal and the hostile and the indifferent, were unrivalled in the diversity of sites they visited or explored. They were scattering, to a degree not always appreciated, and it will never be easy to recall distinctly to memory and range in order the different groups into which they fall: the state and commonwealth of England itself, the colonies and the plantations; exile colleges of priests, nunneries, and communities of Separatists; bands of neglected soldiery, ships and crews at sea, factors and their servants in foreign parts; the ambassadors' households, the gentry learning languages in Siena and Saumur, and even individual wanderers, scholars, musicians and jewellers. At home, the landscape altered slowly, the economy a little more quickly; among the inhabitants, however, to a much greater degree than before, there were likely travellers who would one day hasten away beyond the near horizon.

Against such as expanding background the records of those men who used only the well-known routes of western Europe may appear somewhat insignificant. Beside the venture of pioneers to America or Asia their actions were still parochial. Giving 'boldnesse to your Factors to fetch exotique rarities in a new division of the world'[1] by journeys overseas, sounds more grandly than humdrum entries in Privy Council registers noting the passport issued to a Thomas Dalton Esq. 'to goe to the Spawe for recovery of his health, and from thence into France or some other partes beyond the seaes for his better experience and knowledge'; or to Mr. John Camber of Essex and John Russe, M.A., and one servant 'to continew beyond the seas for their experience in the languadges', a former licence having lapsed.[2] Nevertheless, these easy journeys for prosaic reasons or pretexts wove one strand in the connection between England and Europe which, in spite of great movements further afield, remains a phenomenon of enduring historical importance. For this connection has never been simple, it cannot easily be defined, yet in the very nature of things contributed most powerfully to the making of English history. Its character has varied from age to age. At an earlier period the interests of island and mainland had been interlocked in a remarkable way, by the authority of Rome and other institutions of the Church, by the necessity and opportunities of trade, by the structure of government and society in the Angevin empire. Mainly for these reasons, numbers of the English king's subjects were in the middle ages scattered over parts of Christendom as churchmen, students, pilgrims, soldiers and buyers or sellers of goods: while a ruling aristocracy held lands and offices on both sides of the sea. However, the Angevin empire was dissolved, and two centuries later a series of attempts by the English crown to conquer France, which still involved long years of military occupation in foreign lands by English armies, ended in failure. Another century passed, and with the Reformation the King in parliament renounced the authority and then the doctrines of Rome, after a lengthy preliminary period during which that authority had been gradually circumscribed. The old links were snapping. If growing economic interests and new political developments made unlikely an isolation which the facts of geography seemed to forbid, by 1558 (when Calais fell) the connections between England and Europe were much altered and, from the point of view familiar to earlier generations, they were rather less substantial. The constitutional struggles of the next century, with their revolutionary consequence, set England to one side of the trend towards absolutism in the state. The Catholic counter-reform was profoundly successful in many parts of the continent but its efforts in England ended in conspicuous failure. The reception of Roman Law, of French literary standards and the Baroque styles of art was either hostile or, at best, incomplete in England. On the other hand, with the desire for independence was mingled a desire for intimacy. There followed the development of that curious, half friendly, half disdainful attitude which was to characterize our exchanges with the general civilization of Europe for several generations. The island neglected the mainland at its peril, and sensible men came more and more to see that the requirements of politics and a general need to educate themselves to the level of the best in Europe made aloofness an impracticable attitude. 'The people of Great Britain', wrote Sir Thomas Palmer to Henry Prince of Wales in 1606, '(of all other famous and glorious Nations separated from the maine Continent of the world) are by so much the more interessed to become Travailers.'[3] The highest importance may therefore be ascribed to the activities of an influential and ambitious class of educated laity, who took the place of the mediaeval clerks, and crossed the seas. Diplomats went out to the courts of Europe, and gentry sent their sons away for a while to learn something of the languages and customs of the European people. Their work was complementary to the 'foreigners' who came over to England. If the water of the Channel could not be bridged by this expedient the travellers at least were messengers and witnesses from abroad, and their experience potentially significant. Also, fortunately for them, the seventeenth century commenced under favourable auspices.

In 1604, when the English ministers signed a treaty of peace with the dominant empire of the western world, they naturally initiated a new phase in the history of England's relations with the continent of Europe. This was obvious in matters of state, perceptible in the affairs of private men. Sir Thomas Bodley now sent his agent to Seville, as well as to Frankfurt and Venice, in order to purchase books for the Library at Oxford. English merchants long resident in southern France crossed the Pyrenean frontier to reopen or develop their Spanish trade. The Catholic Low Countries were opened to English travellers, and English seamen served on Spanish ships to the dismay of our government and in defiance of its proclamations. All this, with the pacification and increasing prosperity of France under Henri IV and the restoration of regular diplomatic relations with Venice, emphasized that a peaceful continent was now once again, after many difficult years, England's more or less friendly neighbour. Englishmen were able to travel abroad in the comfort of relative security.

This was not in itself a startling development and had no immediate consequences. Throughout the most difficult period of Elizabeth's reign when the Spanish war was at its height, Englishmen were found abroad in foreign cities and universities, men who were neither official envoys nor exiles defying the government. It was assumed that a young man like Fynes Moryson, future author of a ponderous Itinerary, who desired to study the Civil Law, could do so best abroad and in due course become useful to government as intelligencer or diplomat. This was the case with Henry Wotton and his friend Lord Zouche, Sir Thomas Chaloner the younger and a number of others. They were allowed to leave England, and occasionally given instructions to send reports on specific questions, when a little discreet enquiry at different points might prove helpful to authority in London. Their own motives for going were various: an inability to keep up appearances at home owing to poverty was one, in certain cases. Fynes Moryson himself, it may be noted, obtained permission to travel from his college, Peterhouse, in 1589 and left England in 1591, a critical period indeed, but he never thought it necessary in his book to justify departure by any other reason than the sheer love of travel; and there were also others who appear to have been sublimely unaware of any special mission abroad: an Earl of Northumberland studying astrology and gardening in Paris, patients taking the waters at Spa, medical students at Padua or Basle or Montpellier, even a musician like John Bull the organist touring the greater European cities amid enthusiastic applause. However, these men were probably exceptional and it is clear that they lived under severe handicaps. They were threatened continually by the suspicions of foreign peoples and governments, and by those of their own, which tended to fear the conversion to Rome or bribery by Spain of every Englishman abroad. When James I became King and the stresses of war were gradually exchanged for the slackening implied in nominally peaceful conditions, the traveller became less of a suspect and more of a student or tourist.

One grave difficulty, which was also a stimulus to the more sensitive, persisted. This was the question of religion. The fundamental fact which confronted an English traveller after a few months abroad in the seventeenth century was the predominantly Catholic character of the mainland. Usually himself a Protestant subject of the church and state of England he might visit with added pleasure the Protestant centres, Holland and the Huguenot towns of the Loire, and Sedan and Geneva and Heidelberg, but the general atmosphere elsewhere was Catholic; and the novelty of this he experienced in vivid contrast, as men always do in foreign lands, with the traditional (the newly traditional) associations

of home. In particular, the recent changes in France, when Henri IV
forsook the religion of his party to secure the crown and restore the unity
of his kingdom, had been of high importance in this respect. The forces
of Catholic revival were now triumphant to a degree which was making
impracticable the ideals of radical English Protestants in a previous
generation; the hope of a final and decisive war between Catholic and
Protestant leading to the victorious domination of the latter, entertained
by Walsingham and Sir Philip Sidney and their circle, was fading
gradually away. England continued to exploit from time to time the
secular rivalry of Bourbon and Habsburg, but France except for the
Huguenots, and Spain, and Italy, which between them taught so much
that was worth learning and possessed so much worth visiting, and
were not only chief guardians of what visibly survived from a classical
past which still exercised such sway over the minds of men, but also
gloried in the pre-eminence of their contemporary courts and arts and
literatures, these countries remained Catholic lands. The Protestant
traveller of the period who desired to share in this civilization without
recognizing its principal ecclesiastical authority necessarily believed that
the dilemma involved a real problem.

The difficulty, of course, had been most acute during Elizabeth's
reign, and a slow decline in the importance of the subject in the minds of
men, during the next two generations, is perceptible. They learnt in time
to set languages, arts, sciences and political information on one side and
questions of religion on the other, but before this division of interests
became complete, references to the attractiveness and the repulsion of
the Roman Church for Englishmen occur throughout the whole range
of evidence about seventeenth-century travel. They will meet us again
and again, as we move from country to country, and from one group of
travellers to another. The extreme cases are simple enough. Clearly, the
survival of Catholicism depended on contacts abroad, the movement
backwards and forwards across the Channel by priests and schoolboys.
Clearly, most Protestants found what their faith taught them to find,
innumerable instances of idolatry and superstition on the continent.
Such men did not return to England more sympathetic to the recusants
or to a Catholic party at the Stuart court, and they distinguished sharply
between 'superstition' and the good things to be seen and heard in
Catholic Europe. However, there were exceptions and certain travellers
of Protestant upbringing succumbed to the power of the Catholic
Church while abroad. It was a proselytizing age, and no one could know
who might respond, nor what would be a convert's influence in later
years if he came back to England and aroused the sympathy of other
Englishmen. The whole problem of these religious influences was followed with a passionate attention to detail by the men of that period and,
as it will be seen, permeates innumerable documents. It provided the
chief objection to foreign travel.

In diplomacy and politics the case was clearer. Certain circumstances, among them the character of the Stuart court and Stuart dynastic interests, encouraged selected individuals to seek experience abroad. Round the family of the ruling house hovered many courtiers, politicians and others who knew the continent. Elizabeth's unwillingness to marry, whatever her motives, meant that the court never took to itself any appreciable and permanent foreign element. After many uncertainties she did not accept an alien prince bringing in his train alien servants, advisers and churchmen. There were foreign influences in literature, art, music and dress; there were French and Italian and German crafts-men and servants, but the court as a whole remained 'mere English'. Things were very different under the Stuarts. First came the Scots who often owed much to a French education, and then the French themselves. Dynasticism demanded marriage alliances and these in-volved a more intimate contact with foreign courts. It did not necessarily lead to political action; by comparison with the Elizabethans Stuart England stood aside from the crucial international crisis of the day. It implied, however, an exchange of courtesies, the despatch of many messengers of the courtier type, particularly to and from Paris, the polite encounter of certain groups of the English aristocracy with the nobility and princes of the continent. As a result there flourished in Whitehall that cosmopolitan and courtly life which upset conservative and Puritan opinion in England. Men criticized the extravagance at court under James I and Charles I, rather unjustly in the latter case, and made unfavourable comparisons with Elizabeth. But the Stuarts in due course created in Whitehall an imitation of contemporary European practice. In that respect Elizabeth had been parochial, a maiden lady busy with purse-strings. Strict economy partly explains her successful statesman-ship during much of her reign but on the other hand liberality built the Banqueting Hall and organized the great masques and purchased the Lumley Library and encouraged Van Dyck. Now to fit a gentleman to rise in this artificial, very treacherous society, it was advisable to send him first to survey the courts and cities in which its standards flourished in their purest form: it was advisable to travel on the continent.

A classic example of the success of this training is the career of George Villiers Duke of Buckingham. His ability by no means equalled his courage and ambition; that ability, such as it was, came from his careful training and one element in his education had been the period of his youth spent in France. James I, it seems, admired qualities which he did not himself possess.

Although a single individual often played both parts in the course of his career, the diplomat can be distinguished from the courtier. By 1600 permanent diplomatic representation in foreign courts was not yet common practice, but a growing need for it arose from the pressure of prolonged negotiations; and in spite of day to day controversy the special rights of a diplomat and his staff in foreign countries were now fairly well defined and admitted. The diplomat was, or tended to be, a great traveller. Experience abroad as a youth, bringing with it a knowledge of languages and affairs, fitted him for a diplomatic appointment and the appointment led him back to the continent, to Venice, Paris, madrid, Turin, the Hague and, less commonly, to other cities, taking with him his 'family' of secretaries, chaplains and servants, including more young men who were thus entering the lower ranks of his own calling. Here again, travel often moulded the careers of those who rose to greater importance, occasionally becoming high officers of state. Alternatively, it kept such claimants far from the centre of patronage in London and the court, where the struggle of interests finally decided the contest for these appointments. Also worth mention is the way in which these men tended to divide into opposing groups. Those who travelled backwards and forwards between Madrid and London were needed for the conduct of Anglo-Spanish diplomacy, and they usually supported such a policy precisely because it made them indispensable. Such were Francis Cottington, John Digby, Walter Aston and Endymion Porter. Another group, on the Stuarts' behalf, dealt with France: James Hay, Thomas Edmondes and Walter Montagu. They generally, though not so consistently as the others, preferred a French negotiation because in this case they became the effective architects of foreign policy. The direction of men's travel, like the direction of trade, was never without importance.

Political conditions therefore required men to visit the continent as diplomats and courtiers. Together with their servants and companions they undoubtedly formed an important group of travellers, brought into existence by the needs of the time, well informed and influential. They were no more than a fraction of the total number that travelled, however. From the classes of substantial gentry there were elder brothers and cousins and friends of the diplomats and secretaries, who came from and returned to assured properties in the English countryside. There were younger brothers, and other cousins and friends, who visited the continent sometimes as gentlemen-servants, and then went back to seek employment in England. Probably as numerous were the miscellaneous travellers of middling or lower standing, clergy, soldiers of fortune, merchants and merchants' factors. The most exalted in rank were of course those rare birds of passage the younger nobility, who travelled increasingly. Yet a substantial part of this army of folk tended to divide naturally into small groupings, which cut across without disregarding social differences, and became a very characteristic and significant institution in English society: the travelling gentleman or nobleman surrounded by servants, governors and companions moving slowly through France and Italy along a predetermined itinerary. He, like the King's ambassador, was leading a tiny mission to the continent.

It may usually be said that all men of any property who were not going on business, particularly the youths, went abroad for what was then called 'experience', education in the widest sense. The procedure was justified by a quiverful of high principles, many of them concealing the ordinary human desire for a season of adventures, and curiosity to see the world. On the basis of an idea that Experience by Travel completed the process of academic education in school and university the sixteenth and seventeenth centuries raised a formidable literature which finally overbore conservative opposition. Some of it was printed, but also many amateur compositions, a page or two of apophthegms quoted and adapted from published books, may be found in family manuscript collections. Parents believed like Polonius in the saving virtues of a few wise words to young men about to travel. They will refer the novice to Moses who sent messengers ahead to spy out the land of Canaan, and to the Queen of Sheba travelling so far to hear the widom of Solomon, and survey his glorious kingdom. They aver that what is learnt by the eye makes a more lasting impression than book knowledge, and is more accurate than hearsay. They claim that the difficulties of travel brace the moral fibre of a man; while gathering true information about the world belongs to the service of one's country. These arguments certainly helped towards general acceptance of a belief in travel and formed an apologia for the fashion. But this belief in travel arose, not only because it justified ordinary human impulse nor because moralists were happy to manipulate rational arguments to this end, but out of the historical situation itself in England during this period. A laity which had sufficient wealth and desired education had come into existence. It made its way increasingly into the Universities and Inns of Court, institutions which in spite of extraordinary powers of adaptation remained fundamentally schools for churchmen and lawyers. Increasingly, therefore, it tended to invade fresh spheres of action. Certain circles were evidently accepting the view that while diplomats undoubtedly, and also courtiers, needed training abroad, it was nearly as difficult to complete a gentleman's education without adopting the same practice.

What substitute was there at home for learning and becoming acquainted with the amenities of life in France and Italy? Conservative gentry had a ready answer to such a question: foreign practices were dangerous, heretical and immoral, but in course of time they spoke with less and less conviction on the point, and their sons were less disposed to believe them. Books, it might also be said, remained the ordinary way of transmitting knowledge, and the majority of literate men had learnt from them at home what they knew of languages, the ancient world, the arts and science. There were professional foreign teachers for a variety of subjects resident in London. But travel seemed to provide a new method of education, more attractive and more extravagant, distinguishing its pupil (as it were) from others who could not afford the time or money.

Further it provided parents with an answer to an age-old question, How to dispose of their children before they grow up? As a result, young men were sent abroad to complete their education by travel, but also they were increasingly sent abroad as children, and given tutors responsible for the whole of their education in academic subjects. For this reason, the tour of western Europe came to be preceded by long periods of residence in a foreign city, sometimes lasting for years.

All these circumstances contributed to the character of English travel in western Europe in the seventeenth century and they are sufficiently important to tempt an enquirer across the seas, for his own 'better experience', to follow in the travellers' footsteps. Since the quality and quantity of surviving evidence must partly determine the nature of our journey, there will undoubtedly be gaps in the itinerary; great men remain tantalizingly obscure while lesser figures have to do duty in their place, but it is hoped nevertheless that the reader will venture over historic ground in pursuit of these travellers, to gather in what the evidence allows. First, France (1604–30) and Italy (1604–67) are visited, for these countries were on most counts by far the most important. The kingdom of Henri IV is described as it struck the traveller of that day, and a group of young noblemen and their tutors are accompanied as they tour round, after which we scan in detail the later careers of the tutors in their struggle for advancement when they tried to turn to account their experience abroad. It Italy, the cities usually frequented in the early decades of the century are described, and honorable mention is made of the ambassador's household at Venice, which helped materially to transmit some of the elements of Italian culture to England. The ambassadors themselves, here and at Turin, are meanwhile working and waiting for promotion at home, hindered rather than helped by absence abroad, as the correspondence shows. After 1630 the diarists come forward, and in a further chapter individuals threading their way from city to city finally weave the conventional pattern of the Giro d'Italia, a development encouraged by the friendly relations of Rome with the Stuart court. In this way, by taking a circuitous course through the wilderness of papers it becomes possible to analyse both the social and political world in which these travellers moved and also the general influence of travel upon them.

The Low Countries and Spain are then explored (1604–67), another biographical study of a gentleman-servant and tutor is attempted from the Clarendon manuscripts in Oxford, and a further visit is paid to France (1630–67). In the Low Countries, despite noteworthy descriptions by individual travellers, the important matters are rather different: the way in which genteel travellers from France and Italy here tend to become military volunteers, joining forces with those Englishmen for whom the wars between Dutch and Spaniard constituted the only valid reason for going abroad to gain experience; the incessant coming and going of many other classes and types, a very old phenomenon and unlike the ordinary interchange between England and France or Italy; finally, the influence of English people who travelled to the Low Countries on English ecclesiastical history. Spain, on the other hand, had few visitors and was not included in the ordinary itineraries. It must be left to the State Papers to throw a fitful light on official or semi-official travellers in James I's reign who attempted to maintain Anglo-Spanish relations on an intimate footing. The very difficulties and discomforts of travel in the Peninsula roused a few bold eccentrics, and a few commercial men with a literary turn of mind, to keep a record of their journeys. Finally a return is made to and through France, the greatest of England's neighbours, growing more influential as the century grew older.

Perhaps the anonymous writer, who found it so difficult to gather together the flowers from his garden in praise of Peregrination, would still be dissatisfied by the varied nature of these enquiries; but, as someone commented in 1628 on the flyleaf of the same manuscript:[4] 'Three things chieffly increase wisdom, Much Observation, Much Meditation, Much Doubt. *Frequens interrogatio est clavis sapientiae.*'

# I. ENGLISH TRAVELLERS IN FRANCE, 1604–1630

Can'st thou Dance, Child?
Ouy, Monsieur.
Hey-dey! French too! Why sure, Sir, you'd never be bred at *Oxford*!*

* taken from George Farquhar's *Sir Harry Wildair*, act 3, scene 2.

# 1. THE YOUNG NOBLEMEN AND THEIR TUTORS

First, wind, weather, the sea, the itinerary, and time taken, all the conditions of a journey to and through northern France after 1600; these simple, physical factors are important.

A man travelled from London to Calais and back in a mid-summer day between dawn and sunset to win a wager in 1619, but this was rare speed.[1] Usually the journey took several times as long, adverse winds might keep the traveller a week at Dover or Rye before blowing him over to one of several French ports, which was not always the starting-point on the continent he himself preferred. An average journey from Paris to London is probably described with the words: 'I praise God, albeit the wynde was awhyle contrary, yet I gott to London in eight daies.'[2] Thomas Coryat in the summer of 1608 reached the French capital in eight, Prince Charles, travelling incognito in 1623, in four days. Both had good reasons for haste. From Calais the important itineraries ran along the coast, either north-east to Dunkirk, Ostende and Bruges, or southwards to Abbeville and up the Somme to Amiens and so to Paris. English Catholics knew best the roads inland to their centres at St. Omer, only a few miles distant in Spanish Artois, and Douai. From Dieppe the way led south to Rouen and up the valley of the Seine to Paris. At this period Sully, Henri IV's grand commissioner of highways and public works, was improving communications in France, and various means of travel were usually available.[3] Some men rode the horses they brought with them, some hired post-horses, sometimes and in some places it was possible to purchase seats in a public coach. A few went on foot, and there was also traffic by water up and down the Seine and the Somme. Men nearly always travelled in company, an elementary precaution. An English gentleman customarily took with him several followers or servants, and travelled together with other gentlemen whom he met either casually or by arrangement, sharing with them their impressions and experience of foreign custom.

An even larger gathering of Englishmen would be assembled by an ambassador moving forward to Paris, with numerous attendants. In 1617 Sir Thomas Edmondes returned for a few weeks to a post where

*Nauiere ordinaire qu'paſſe de Douure a Calais.*

1.   Crossing the Channel: the Florentine Stefano della Bella went by sea from Calais to
     Amsterdam in 1647 and published his maritime views in 1656.

he had previously spent many years and wrote to Winwood, giving the
details of his journey. At Dieppe, where he landed, and at Rouen,
civil and military officers came to salute the ambassador and special
accommodation was allotted for his use. Taking the ordinary road along
the right bank of the river he reached Magny where he found his
secretary who had come out from Paris. And then, Edmondes continues:

> M. de Bonseil was sent forth with one of the Kinges and another of the
> Queenes Coaches who mett me betweene St. Denys and Pontoyse. And as I
> drewe neere to Paris I was mett by the Duke of Mombazon who was
> accompanied with his brother the Marquis of Marigny, the Vicount d'Anchi
> and diverse other principall gentlemen which made to the number of 150
> horse; the which troop was besides much encreased by a good number of
> Englishe gentlemen, and sundry others of my particular frends which did me
> the favour to meete me, and as we found a great concourse of people as we
> passed throwgh the towne, so I may speak it truly to his Majesty's honour and
> comfort, that they expressed publiquely a great joy for my comming for that
> they were confident that my errand was to doe all good offices for the
> establishment of the peace, saying I was *l'oiseau de paix.*[4]

The causes of this outburst of popular enthusiasm were unusual. James I had sent Edmondes to mediate between Louis XIII's new ministers and their enemies after the assassination of Concini, but as a description of an important envoy's journey from the coast to Paris it is a characteristic account. Dieppe, Rouen, Pontoise, St. Denis, the welcome from various civic authorities, the gathering of large numbers for a public entry into Paris: these names and incidents recur again and again.

At the other end of the scale was the single traveller. If he had a quick eye he soon noticed unfamiliar things in the landscape. Thomas Coryat, going to Paris in 1608, observed from time to time the tokens of what was to him a strange and, above all, a Catholic country. Crossing from Dover to Calais, after a rough passage of seven hours, he went with the other travellers to have his name entered in the register kept for the Deputy Governor of the town. After a night's rest he set out on foot, alone. At Boulogne appeared 'the first monks that ever I saw', then a wheel for torture and excution, then at Montreuil a chapel with a holy picture, and people praying to the picture. Between Abbeville and Amiens he met a friar, a good Latinist with whom he discussed the adoration of images. From there he took his seat in the Paris coach, reaching Breteuil twenty miles on in five hours. 'In that space I observed only these two things, a village exceedingly ransacked and ruinated, by means of the civil wars. And about some few miles on this side of Breteuil, certain vineyards which were the first that ever I saw.' The prevailing richness of the Ile de France soon struck his attention, the avenues of walnut trees, and the fine country houses of Parisian lawyers. He reached the capital in time to witness a pompous celebration of the feast of Corpus Christi. Lodging with a Huguenot landlord in the Faubourg St. Germain he went sightseeing, poking about the bookshops, bearded the great scholar Isaac Casaubon in his study, observed the confessing of a lady by a Franciscan friar 'which I therefore mention because it was the first shrifting that ever I saw'. His journey to Italy had started well, he was on his way. Tom Coryat was very alert, noticing much that other travellers appear to have missed, perhaps exceptional, an odd character of genuine ability.[5]

Very similar were the impressions of another scholar, Peter Heylin, who spent a few weeks in France with a friend during the summer of 1625, travelling to Paris by way of Dieppe and Rouen, to Orleans, and from Paris to Amiens and Boulogne. He unfortunately attempts humour by dint of jocular exaggeration; one must treat his comments with caution, but many of his remarks are valuable. First, there was the wonderful fertility of Normandy and the Île de France, a commonplace with all writers on the subject: 'In my life I never saw Cornfields more large and lovely, extended in an equall levell almost as far as eye can reach.' Between Étampes and Angerville 'many a beautiful field of corn', between Pontoise and Paris 'the Vines yet green; the Wheat ready for the sithe; and the cherries now fully ripened'. At Mantes, on the Seine, he had seen his first vineyards, planted like English hop-gardens. Heylin, like Coryat, quickly noted the outward signs of Catholicism. *Quos antea audiebam*, he wrote, *hodie vidi deos*. He saw the Host being carried about the streets of Dieppe by a couple of priests ushered by torches, a company of boys and old people attending, 'before it a Bell continually tinkling'. Then he studied with interest a different manifest-ation of idolatry, adoration of the Virgin, and enumerated the images he found and the various kinds of clothing with which they were draped. *O impudentia admirabilis et vere Romana*! Next, there were examples of supersititon, holy water, censing, the continual burning of lamps before the altars, false relics and the trumpery myths of innumerable saints. It is interesting to observe how a young man who became one of the most popular Anglican apologists regarded the Catholicism of France in 1625.

A rather different point emerging from Heylin's account is the military character of the area between Paris and Calais, and the signs of this in the landscape must have been evident to the most casual of travellers. Amiens, Abbeville, Montreuil, Boulogne and Calais were fortresses in frontier territory; and to a hardly lesser degree this was the case elsewhere in France and on the continent. South of Paris the semi-independent Huguenot towns zealously maintained their defences in good order. It was a land of garrisons and walled cities; with guards set and the gates closed every evening. As Heylin found at Abbeville, travellers ran the danger of being locked in or locked out at nightfall. The importance of cities as military strongholds, either preserving their own liberties against the surrounding countryside or contributing to the power of their governors, was an aspect of European affairs at this period which naturally impressed the traveller, whom it directly concerned.[6]

Somewhere between the Ambassador Extraordinary, and the scholars who went abroad alone or in pairs, may be placed a more conventional class of traveller. The orthodox approach to Paris was Sir Edward Herbert's; when at the age of twenty-five, after his marriage, he says,

> Coming to court I obtained a licence to go beyond sea, taking with me for my companion Mr Aurelian Townsend, a gentleman that spoke the languages of French, Italian and Spanish in great perfection, and a man to wait in my chamber who spoke French, two lacqueys and three horses. Coming thus to Dover and passing the seas thence to Calais I journeyed without memorable adventure until I came to Faubourg St. Germain in Paris where Sir George Carew, then Ambassador for the King lived; I was kindly received by him and often invited to his table.[7]

Herbert travelled, and spent his time, according to custom. He made himself agreeable to the French nobility. The Constable of France, the duc de Montmorency, invited him to stay the summer as his great castle of Mello, where Herbert composed some thorny satires and sonnets, fought duels, hunted and took riding lessons with the best French masters. He returned to Paris and practised fencing, singing and the lute, all 'according to the rules of the French masters'. Sometimes he appeared at Court. It was an ideal training for the future English ambassador in Paris.

Naturally, none of these travellers approached a foreign country without preconceptions, and later on their judgments and knowledge were never simply the result of first-hand observation. Many things could be learnt from books before a journey, during a journey and after a journey. One of Peter Heylin's most successful works was his first, *Microcosmus*, a 'little description of the great world', printed in 1621 and subsequently expanded in the course of numerous editions. Its earliest form had been a series of lectures given in Magdalen College, Oxford, when the author was only twenty years old; for the descriptions of France he had relied on some of the standard geographers, the great historians, Bodin, and even Robert Dallington's View of France, published fifteen years earlier. In 1625 Heylin himself visited the country, and in order to compose his own *Survey of the estate of France*, fused the knowledge gathered earlier with the comments and observations of his travel-diary, interlarding them with further material from contemporary pamphlets. The result was primarily a work of academic learning gleaned before and after travel and in this is embedded his diary; the dates and the days of the week which he mentions correspond perfectly with a calendar for 1625, a fairly exacting test for something which he published a generation after the completion of his journey.

Or, as an instance of composition and study in the course of travel, Dallington's View, used by Heylin, is important. This little book by a future Master of the Charterhouse has frequently been quoted for its information on the motives,the expenditure and accomplishments of the Elizabethan or Jacobean traveller, but in many ways the most interesting point is the manner of its composition. He himself says that it was originally intended for the private use of 'an honourable gentleman', 'the patterne of a method how to discourse of the Cosmography, Policy and Oeconomy of such other Countries wherein you shall travaile'. In fact, to judge from his remarks, Dallington was a young man's tutor in France.[8] Without stopping long in Paris they had spent the summer and autumn of 1598 at Orleans where he first began to draft the book. His patron was evidently superior at tennis and dancing, the tutor stuck to his desk and consulted authorities. For example, they had not been able to visit the French court on their way through Paris and it had come once only, for two days, to Orleans: 'howbeit out of that which I there saw, which I have heard of others and read in Authors, I will adventure and relate concerning the Officers of this Court'. The literary authorities were, as usual, Caesar, Commines, Bodin, Haillan, de la Noue and also the *Guide de France*.[9] Dallington thought it helpful to mention incidents which took place during their stay in France. On an expedition which they both made down the Loire valley they wished to see one of the chateaux but were mistaken for officials, and their reception was in consequence unfriendly: this illustrated the pressure of the royal tax-collector on the French nobility. Or he recalls the gallant 'of whom ye told me the other day' and analyses the quarrelsome nature of Frenchmen 'of whom ye had already seen 2 or three examples'. The rest is an academic exercise, learned and sensible. Dallington was fusing his observations with current reading, thus forming specifically 'the pattern of a method' which his pupil should learn, enabling him to apply it for himself to Italy and the Italians 'whom ye shall in your travells shortly observe'.

The monumental instance of additions made by an author subsequent to his travels was Fynes Moryson's *Itinerary*. He journeyed abroad between 1591 and 1597, keeping diaries and memoranda. Thereafter the reading of a lifetime was piece by piece assembled round the original observations, gradually taking the form of the great folio published in 1617; but the folio again was only a part of Moryson's projected work, which may best be described as an overwhelming conflation of authorities immuring his own very valuable experience.

The routes southward, then, were tolerably secure; and a few select travellers advised their friends or the public of the advantages to be gained and the risks to be run. Naturally, not every traveller was bent on compiling a book, least of all the young gentlemen of good family who were sent across the seas at this date. Nor did they necessarily benefit, to judge by any perceptible token, from months or years spent abroad. Yet the lands of the French monarchy, its history, customs, treasures and character, opened out before them as they travelled; whatever the fears of prudent men at home, the experience was also an opportunity.

For many years after 1603 the two pre-eminent family interests in England were the Cecils and the Howards. Under the aegis of Robert Cecil Earl of Salisbury, Thomas Howard Earl of Suffolk, and Henry Howard Earl of Northampton they annexed the privileges and the profits of government, under the crown. The withering away of their power in the second decade of the century and the consequent rise of George Villiers and his satellites to supremacy was one of the striking phenomena of James I's reign. The causes of this decline centred largely in particular intrigues at court; their landed property appears to have survived substantially intact. Failure depended also on the absence of any real ability in the next generation of these two families; and for that reason it is relevant to observe their young men travelling about Europe, especially in France, between 1603 and Robert Cecil's death in 1612, learning to grow up; but they became courtiers or noblemen who were unable to make real use of an exalted hereditary status. In a sense, most of them justified contemporary moralists' jeremiads on the inanity of frittering time on foreign travel. The earlier representatives of a great family founded an extraordinary, if precarious, state of wealth and power. Their successors could do nothing with it, and a manifestation of this, common throughout a long period of English history, was their life in pleasant places on the continent, supported on rentals from English property transmitted overseas by the ordinary machinery of exchange.

With peace and prosperity in France during Henri IV's later years, these young men came over in fair numbers. The relative pacification of that country is of cardinal importance, in English as in French history. Probably before this date it would not be possible for an enquirer to assemble such a group of noblemen engaged simply in peaceful travel as William Lord Cecil, Theophilus Lord Howard, who afterwards became Earls of Salisbury and Suffolk, the Lords Essex, Roos, Norris and Clifford, all intimately connected with the same family interest by birth or marriage, and all in France during the first decade of the century. Nor did they come alone. With them travelled friends, tutors, servants, and if continental experience profited the Cecils and Howards remarkably little, their companions found ways and means of taking better advantage of the opportunity, learning what they could of foreign custom and politics. Moreover, this mingling and meeting of different classes of Englishmen abroad is important for another reason. The 'conversation' — as it was called — of the representatives of great families with the English ambassadors and their staffs, and with their own travelling companions, shows that the struggle for patronage was going on in foreign courts and capitals as well as at home; and the struggle for patronage determined the struggle for preferment. We shall later be concerned with a number of lesser men whose careers illustrate the connection between the foreign travels of the English gentry and this struggle for preferment. One of them will be Lord Clifford's tutor. But first, the young nobles must make their entry.

In 1603 the English ambassador in France reported that Lord Howard de Walden, heir to the Earl of Suffolk, left Paris on 25 October on his way south to Italy;[1] it was desirable for the Secretary of State to have intelligence of Howard's movements because his company of followers, and the people with whom he became acquainted, were not all reliable. Sir Edwin Rich, half-brother of the Earl of Warwick, for example, figured as one of his principal attendants and Rich subsequently joined Sir Antony Sherley when this adventurer led a political mission from the Emperor Rudolf to the rulers of Morocco. The

English government always mistrusted Sherley. While in Paris Lord Howard met Thomas Morgan, formerly a servant of Mary Queen of Scots and a professional plotter of twenty years' standing. Morgan tried to tempt Howard, and through Howard Cecil himself, into negotiations with certain Catholic families in exile, particularly the Dormers and Jane Dormer Duchess of Feria. Morgan's friends reported Howard's presence, first at Rouen, and after Paris at Avignon and Turin. Cecil also learnt of the young man from Sir Antony Standen, who had likewise been engaged in the seamiest side of politics for many years and was just then returning from a mission into Italy, ostensibly on James I's behalf. Standen wrote from Paris:

> My jorney owtwards was by way of Lorraine and Swytzerland, and my retourne homewards by the Mediterrane from Genova to Marseilles, from thens through Avignon and Lion...neere Lion I met in his peregrination and left in perfect helthe the Lord Howard of Walden and his company, who wysshed I would signifie to his Lord Father and Lady Mother no lesse, and so I humbly beseche your honor to favour me with the delyvery hereof to hys honorable parents the Earl and Countess; I did assure hym that he should receyve all kindes and courtesies in all parts of Italy wythout exception sucth ys the love and regard borne to our Prince and Soveraigne there.[1]

Howard wintered in northern Italy and during the spring of 1604 Cecil learnt through Thomas Morgan that he had spent three days at Rome on his way to Naples. Later, he is said to have been present at the spring celebration of the miracle of St. Januarius. That autumn, travelling homeward through Lorraine he visited the court at Nancy where Duke Charles gave him a letter of compliment for James I.[2]

A great and influential career lay open to the young man, who was then in his twenty-first year. In February 1605 Dudley Carleton wrote to Winwood that the King had gone to Royston 'with his crew of merry hunters, which is the greater by one by the return of my Lord Howard from his travels'.[3] In the same autumn Cecil wrote imperatively to the electors of Maldon in Essex, and although an excellent local candidate had already come forward he secured the place for Howard who took his seat in the House of Commons.[4] Thomas Campion addressed to him some hopeful and significant verses:[5]

> The course of foreign manners far and wide
>     The Courts, the Countries, Cities, Towns and State
> The blossom of your springing youth hath tried
>     Honoured in every place and fortunate;
> Which now grown fairer doth adorn our Court
> With princely revelling and timely sport.
>
> But if the admired virtues of your youth
>     Breed such despairing of my daunted Muse
> That it can scarcely utter naked truth;

How shall it mount as ravished spirits use
Under the burden of your riper days
Or hope to reach the so far distant bays?

This promise for the future quickly faded. Before Howard's return to England it was thought that he might supplant Lord Pembroke in the King's favour, but unfortunately (wrote a correspondent) *minuit praesentia famam*. He lived until 1640, and throughout James I's reign was prominent in society, negligible as a politician. Untiring as cupbearer and pallbearer on great occasions, as a tilter and masquer and duellist, he held a variety of remunerative offices. Between 1614 and 1635, with one short interval during his father's disgrace at the end of 1619, he commanded the band of Gentlemen Pensioners.[16] A year of travel in France and Italy, and a few months of desultory campaigning in 1610, can have contributed little to his moderate capacities but they gave him a certain acquaintance with courtly life in different cities: a type of experience of definite value at that period.

In 1605, the year of Theophilus Howard's return to England, a number of his relatives including his brother Thomas accompanied another Howard, the Earl of Nottingham, into Spain and with them went Francis Lord Norris and his secretary Dudley Carleton. The one was a nobleman of much ambition and wide estates in Oxfordshire and Berkshire, twenty-six years old and married to the Earl of Oxford's daughter, Robert Cecil's niece. The other was of the Oxfordshire gentry, able and ambitious, formerly secretary to an ambassador in Paris and then to the Earl of Northumberland. His salary was £50, with a gratuity of £200 promised later. A party including Lord Norris and Carleton, Lord Willoughby and Sir Lewis Tresham decided to travel home overland from Valladolid; and their passage through Bayonne was reported to Cecil by an English merchant there in July 1605.[17] On arriving in Paris Norris fell desperately ill. Anxious letters from Carleton to Salisbury and to his personal friend Chamberlain described the progress of a dangerous fever.[18] Carleton also secured a quittance from his employer for the £800 which he had spent on his behalf during the journey into and out of Spain. On instructions from England he attempted to discover whether Lord Norris had drawn up a will, in which, naturally, his wife's uncle was keenly interested. A little later he obtained Norris's proxy for his vote in the House of Lords, which he forwarded to Cecil. For greater comfort the patient was then lodged in the ambassador's house where the King of France's physicians attended him. He slowly recovered and in due course appeared again in England, only to renew a long and bitter quarrel with his wife and allow an ungovernable temper to thwart his ambition in affairs of state.

This unexpected interlude in Paris, however, had important consequences for the career of one statesman of the period.[19] Dudley

Carleton spent the time pleasantly enough during his patron's illness, buying books and trinkets among other occupations,[20] not knowing that the official enquiry after Gunpowder Plot was just then questioning his own connection with his previous employer, the Earl of Northumberland. It was alleged that as secretary to the Earl he had rented to the conspirator Thomas Percy the cellars under St. Stephen's Chapel. This in itself required an explanation, but Carleton's long absence from England simply increased hostility. He felt tempted to remain out of harm's way, to the detriment of his prospects. As he himself wrote: 'And yet went I not upon sure ground for my own innocency as I presume on, in so barbarous an attempt, it were not a good phrase should draw me in such post out of a place of security into the midst of danger.'[21] The Council peremptorily ordered him home. After eleven days' detention at a house in St. Martin-in-the-Fields and a scrupulous enquiry he was acquitted of the charges against him; but the connection with Northumberland, aggravated by his long delay in Paris, seriously damaged the prospects of this able young man. As a result the Dudley Carleton who ultimately became Lord Dorchester and a Secretary of State did not receive any preferment until 1610, when James I appointed him his ambassador in Venice. It is a curious illustration of the dilemma which faced travellers of this kind: to go abroad 'for better experience' was judged essential, not to be away from court where appointments were made and intrigues launched against the absent, was also an essential. Diplomats, especially, found the answer to this exceedingly difficult.

On his journey home from Paris Carleton mentions that he met 'the young Lord Ross going thither, with intention to travel three years', another nobleman on the road south. Already on the 26 May 1605 an official had drafted for William Cecil Lord Roos, a copy of his licence to travel. He was fifteen years of age, a grandson of the Earl of Exeter and therefore a great-nephew of Robert Cecil. The names of his tutor and companions are not known. He evidently reached Paris safely. When the new English ambassador to France, Sir George Carew, made his entry into the city a few days later he was met between Pontoise and Paris by 'divers knights and gentlemen of our nation, so as the train was indifferent great'; among them rode Lord Roos. On 28 December Carew had his first audience with Henri IV and, after compliments, and conversation on the late conspiracy in England he introduced Roos to the King, and the King gave Roos his high opinion of Salisbury, which in due course the English statesman formally acknowledged and Henri reiterated.

The young man remained in Paris for some time. In the following summer he wrote to Cecil giving an account of the courtesies he received, the King's kindness, dinner with the duc and duchesse de Sully at the Arsenal, and his own deep affection for the duc de la

Trémouille's widow, a daughter of William of Orange. He begged Cecil's assistance in wooing this lady and explained that he came to know her by 'my curiosity in acquainting myself with the better sort of those of the Religion (where your name is in so great respect)...she is a foreigner but Protestant, and so depending of our State'. A year later Thomas Morgan reported that Lord Roos was in Lyon, but degraded by a poverty that hardly suited his rank. Then, for an interval, we hear no more of him. Probably he returned home before setting out on a longer journey to Italy and Spain in 1609.[22]

Another member of the family interest of Howards and Cecils soon appeared in France. In 1607 Robert Devereux, third Earl of Essex, at the age of sixteen married Frances Howard, elder daughter of the Earl of Suffolk. Little more than a year afterwards he was in Paris. The common custom by which noblemen married while very young and then departed for education and travel on the continent had in this case tragic consequences, since it undoubtedly contributed to the motives for the scandal of Frances Howard's second marriage, to the Earl of Somerset, and Sir Thomas Overbury's murder. On 24 November 1607 Henri IV interviewed Sir George Carew at the Louvre and, after conversation on more important topics,the ambassador presented to him 'my Lord of Essex who beeing lately arrived to Paris came with me to this Audience, whom the King in short speech used gratiously and his Lordship defended himself in French very well for one that hath been no longer in Fraunce, and for his manner the Princes and noblemen sayd to those that came with mee, il a bonne façon, il sent son françois, which in theyre understanding is the greatest commendation that can be given and the top of all perfection'.

It was a satisfactory report, but the stay in France of yet another member of the family grouping concerned Salisbury much more closely. His son and heir, William Lord Cranborne, married Catherine Howard who was Suffolk's younger daughter on 1 December 1608, and left England immediately afterwards. Or, as a correspondent put it, 'the young Lord Cranborne is going into France before Christmas but yet shall marry privately before he go; Dr. Lister and one Finnet, a traveller of no note or account but only preferred by Dr. Wilson, are to be his guides'. Sir Thomas Wilson, who was Salisbury's experienced adviser, must have approved both of Mathew Lister and John Finet. The first had taken his medical degree at Basle in Switzerland; the second became a punctilious Master of Ceremonies at Charles I's court. Already on 15 December Cranborne's company was met between Montreuil and Abbeville, in bad weather, on bad roads, by travellers returning to England.[23]

The winter was spent in Paris. Salisbury, while wishing that he heard more often from his son, did receive certain items of news. Cranborne was in good health; he was learning a new style of handwriting; he sat up

late one night at the Queen's ballet, and visited the court at St.
Germains; and he went riding every day. But once the spring came it
was decided to go on to Orleans, chiming in with the father's constant
fear that his son ran the risk of making unsuitable friends, French or
English, if he stayed too long in one place. Apart from Lister and
Finet Cranborne was accompanied by his brother-in-law, Sir Thomas
Howard. They went first to Fontainebleau in response to an invitation
from the King. Carew came with them, an infant son of his, and William
Becher a member of his household, who had already been brought to
Salisbury's notice as a useful young man: we shall watch him rise from
the level of messenger to that of tutor, to ambassador's secretary, to a
knighthood and a clerkship of the Privy Council. Owing to Henri's
indisposition Carew waited a few days, pausing to inspect the excavation
for a canal which would join the Seine to the Loire; these important
works were attracting attention at the time. Cranborne and his friends
meanwhile dined with the Dauphin and went badger-hunting — which
they did from the Dauphin's coach. They then set off for Montargis and
Briare and along the Loire to Orleans, where servants and baggage had
already arrived. Carew was interviewed by the King and returned to
Paris with Becher, who had been told to forward letters sent to and from
Carnborne's company on their travels. The young man was not to be left
wandering about in France, out of all touch with his father.[24]

The courtesy of Henri IV and other Frenchmen to the heirs of the
Cecils and Howards was again very marked. From London the French
ambassador had written to the Archbishop of Tours, recommending
Cranborne. At Paris Rohan, Vitry and Villeroi offerd their services.
The King capped this by issuing a passport addressed to all French
officials:[25]

> Chers et bien amis. Le Comte de Cranbourne, fils du Comte de Salsbery,
> grand Trésorier d'Angleterre que nous désirons gratifier, pour certaynes
> bonnes considerations, s'en allant voyager en divers lieux et endroits de ce
> royaume, Nous voulons et vous mandons que, passant en une ville vous ayes
> à luy fayre tout bon et favorable acceuil, l'assistant et favorisant de tout ce
> que vous dépensera de vous, comme personne que nous estimons. Et vous
> nous fîtes service très agréable.
> Donné à Paris le 3 jour de Mai 1609.                          Henry.

On 15 May Carew wrote that a servant of his, passing through
Orleans, enquired for Lord Cranborne only to learn that he had gone
for three or four days' journey to visit certain towns in the neighbourhood — 'I am told he profiteth more in his studies there than he did
at Paris'. Two months later there was news of a man who had brought
the travellers fresh horses out of England, but we know nothing further
about them until in August they began what Cranborne calls 'mon
voyage du tour de France'. He kept a diary in French, describing his

itinerary and recording a few details about what he saw on his journey.[20]
It is a modest piece of work but probably the earliest surviving record of
the *tour* — which, with few variations, became the route normally
followed — written by an English traveller. His father delightedly
regarded it later as a testimony of his son's ability to write French and
of a duty performed.

2. A handy map of France: in 1634 Christophe Tassin first published *Les Plans et
Profilz de toutes les principalles villes et lieues considerables de France*.... They were
conveniently compact in size — about 7″ × 5″. After this general map the collection
dealt with the French provinces and their towns. It was reprinted many times.

Cranborne's journal tells a story of uneventful sightseeing. Dinner was
here and sleeping there, and the pace was fairly fast. He stayed two or
three days in a few towns, and ten days at La Rochelle where he suffered
a relatively mild attack of smallpox. Otherwise they moved on every
morning; and he set down the names of one place after another, with a
short note about each. He admired chateaux and bridges, ports and

'modern' fortifications. He tells us where he crossed the Loire or the Garonne, the Durance or the Rhône in the course of his itinerary. Certain things struck him as worth a comment: he liked the alleys and trees in the garden of the chateau at Blois and the grand stairway of Amboise. At Saumur he called on the governor, that famous Protestant leader Duplessis-Mornay, but the great man was absent; he admired instead the library and the armoury in the castle, the defence works and artillery guarding the town. Several stages further the travellers reached Blaye on the Gironde, where they had to catch the tide early on Sunday morning for their journey by water to Bordeaux; while on the way from Bordeaux it was at Moissac that they had a clear view of the distant Pyrenees. More often Cranborne's sense of geography was political or religious: Montauban was a strongly fortified Protestant town but Toulouse — entered two days later — was Catholic, with a profusion of relics ('comme ils le disent') of apostles and saints on display. Montpellier and Nîmes were predominantly Protestant, but then one entered the different world of Papal Avignon (where the Jews were tolerated), Marseilles and Aix. Along the whole stretch of his homeward journey from Geneva to Paris the Huguenots received no further mention. As for the pleasures of travel, he enjoyed the hospitality of the duc de Guise at Marseilles, and the view of its marvellous port[27] He admired, perhaps dutifully, the remains of antiquity at Nîmes and the Pont du Gard and later at Orange.[28] He also learnt something of the commercial and financial importance of Lyon, as of the formidable military defences protecting Geneva, but the majority of his comments were brief and bare. He would have liked to have gone on to Switzerland and Germany, he says, but autumn weather in mid-October convinced them that it was time to return to Paris. When they arrived back, their horses were not surprisingly 'overharried with this long journey,' as William Becher remarked. They had covered 416 leagues in all, an estimate with which Cranborne ended his diary.

The winter was spent in Paris. Interviewed by the King to display his French, Cranborne was called upon to act as interpreter when an Englishman came with a gift of fishing cormorants for Henri from James I. He also took riding lessons with officers of the royal stables. His father meanwhile was sending over men and supplies to enable him to accompany the King of France on his projected expedition to the Rhine, but in May 1610 Henri was assassinated and the whole fragile structure of French administrative and political unity seemed threatened. A servant of Lord Cranborne, provided with a special permit and letters from Villeroi, attempting to hurry home, was stopped at the gates of Paris by nervous officials. He himself arrived in England shortly afterwards.[29]

English noblemen continued to come out to France despite the political uncertainty. Carew was recalled but Becher had been left in Paris as 'agent' in the absence of an ambassador, and in September 1610 he went to St. Denis to meet Sir Thomas Edmondes, the ambassador newly appointed. With Edmondes was Henry Lord Clifford,[30] recently married to Salisbury's daughter, Frances Cecil. Becher became Clifford's governor or tutor, sending home regular reports to the ever intrusive father-in-law; meanwhile Edmondes employed his own servants to act as secretaries for his diplomatic correspondence, a setback for Becher. John Woodford was described as the 'second secretary, that keeps registre of all such letters as passe to and fro whether sent or receyved'[51] Like Becher, he would play a modest but useful role in the conduct of Anglo-French diplomacy during the next ten years.

Clifford followed Cranborne's example on one point, but carried it further. In doing so, he too was an innovator and set a fashion for Englishmen in seventeenth-century France. Cranborne had told his father in 1609 that he saw the King every day when he went riding in the Tuileries. He continued to take riding lessons on his return to Paris, but Becher reports in the following year that Clifford was joining M. de Pluvinel's Academy,[32] something never said of Cranborne. This meant that Clifford would receive regular instruction in the art of dressage at the riding school attached to the Manège or Stables of the royal palaces. Antoine de Pluvinel, a highly gifted cavalier with an eye to business, had associated the teachers of other subjects with his own tuition; at his Academy, it could be claimed, the manners, dress and decorum of a good horseman were those of a good courtier. Making his offer to an aristocratic public, de Pluvinel, 'premier écuyer du roi', assiduously used Henri IV's patronage to attract custom. Lord Clifford proved a good client and took the whole matter very seriously. He even refused an offer of hospitality from the duc de Guise in order to rent a house at £80 a year which was next door to M. de Pluvinel.

He hired a man and a room inside the Academy where he attended for his exercises in riding, fencing, dancing, the lute, mathematics and philosophy. He looked for outside instruction in French, Latin and history. As Becher described it, the arrangement was a compromise: 'My Lord is to lodge out of the Academy notwithstanding he hath a chamber there because the gates of the Academy being kept very strictly, his Lordship will be more at liberty in his own house, and it were to no purpose to distaste him with unnecessary severity.' Becher reckoned that the Academy, the house and tuition would cost £150 a year. The expenses of his household, liveries and horses brought the total up to £500, leaving £300 of Clifford's allowance for clothes and other payments. In this connection it was a pity that Clifford arrived in Paris with entirely unfashionable clothes, 'all gentlemen of quality wearing now black which they say will continew yet this yeare and this half'. For economy's sake he bought a horse cheaply which proved inferior and unsuitable. For economy's sake he soon gave up his house and moved into the Academy.[32]

Clifford settled down to a studious life. Others were not so conscientious. Lord Cranborne passed through Paris again, accompanied as before by Finett and Dr. Lister and also by Henry Howard, another brother-in-law, bound for Italy. Then came Sir Dudley Carleton, appointed ambassador to Venice, bringing with him as far as Paris Sir Thomas Puckering who was nineteen years old and a son of the late Lord Keeper. He joined Clifford at the Academy. Other Englishmen appeared from the Low Countries where they had taken part in the siege of Juliers. From Paris William Becher reported the recent arrivals to Salisbury:[34]

> Though I never knew yet any Englishe noblemen or gentlemen undertake this cours of the Academy before, yet my Lord's example hath already brought one more which is Mr. Puckering, who came over with Sir Dudley Carleton. Here is likewise come out of Cleves my Lord Chandos, Sir Thomas Somersett, Sir Henry Riche, Sir Jhon Sheffield and Sir J. Radcliffe the most part of all which have an intention to come to learne of the same Rider, though not to enter into the Academy, but I trust that eyther by dissuasion or theyre owne change of resolution they will take some other course.

Of all these men Sir Henry Rich, then twenty-one years old, became the most important. He played a great part in the negotiations for the Anglo-French marriage treaty of 1625 and was raised to the peerage as Lord Kensington and, subsequently, as the first Lord Holland. Meanwhile, Becher soon reported that Sir Thomas Somerset had left for Orleans, and Lord Chandos for Blois.

A new representative of the class of Becher and Woodford now appeared in Paris, the Rev. Thomas Lorkin who was Sir Thomas Puckering's tutor. On 1 November 1610 he had reached Dieppe, where he stopped to write one of those newsletters which afterwards became a regular feature in his life.[35] Lorkin set to work supervising Puckering's education, as Becher supervised Clifford, but he also carried out certain instructions of a semi-political character. His patron, or at any rate his superior, was Puckering's brother-in-law Sir Adam Newton, the tutor to Henry Prince of Wales. The Prince had asked the ambassador in Paris to send him periodical reports on the political situation and when Edmondes demurred, nervous for his credit with Salisbury and declaring that such reports should go first to the Lord Treasurer, Newton suggested that Lorkin while in Paris should arrange for such political intelligence to be sent direct to the Prince. It was a sign of the conflict of interests which might be expected to develop between the heir to the throne, now growing of age, his personal advisers, and the King's principal minister. With £80 of Henry's money Lorkin therefore purchased the services of an agent at the French court, arranging to send weekly intelligence direct to Newton and the Prince. This involved using couriers not employed by the English postmaster, Mathew de Questor; it was believed that anything coming into England by the ordinary messengers would be opened by officials in Salisbury's pay.[36] Lorkin thus combined his vocation as tutor with political spade-work, a type of dexterity which circumstances would force him to practise for the rest of his life. Its climax came, as will be shown, in 1625, but in 1610 he went to work more humbly.

Lord Clifford was much the most conscientious and retiring of the English noblemen in Paris at this date. Salisbury had to order him to appear at the French court twice a week. For this purpose he rented a house once again, which was perhaps as well, for Becher had written in the new year that they observed Lent very strictly in the Academy. On the other hand the times were so distracted in France that he feared the danger of involving Lord Clifford in the personal or political feuds of the Frenchmen who befriended him; for example, the quarrel of the duc de Soissons and the due de Guise; and Clifford was a friend of Guise. In this predicament Sir Thomas Edmondes the ambassador smoothed the way, introducing him to safe but 'courtly company', the marquis Spinola, the maréchal de Lavardin and the Princess of Orange. Another difficulty was expense. It cost more to leave the Academy from time to time and visit Fontainebleau, riding about the countryside with French noblemen. Salisbury sent gifts of money, and a good horse, but Becher calculated that they needed £1150 yearly.[37]

If this was the price of a rather dull-witted obedience, there were others in Paris by no means so scrupulous about family finance or a tutor's good intentions. After a long journey through Italy and Spain Lord Roos had returned; he spent his time in Puckering's company and the two became great friends. When Roos suggested a short tour through the Low Countries, to Thomas Lorkin's horror and annoyance Puckering agreed; the excellent plan of residing in Paris long enough to learn French before proceeding into Italy seemed to be in danger. Lord Roos, Lorkin complained, was an insidious and unworthy friend for his pupil, and already had a sufficiently acceptable fellow-traveller in Toby Mathew, the archbishop of York's Catholic son. But they all left Paris in April 1612, including Lorkin. The company was so numerous that they were forced to divide, the post being unable to provide sufficient horses. Between them they visited Péronne, Cambrai, Valenciennes, Mons, Brussels and Antwerp, where they fell in with Lord Cranborne returning from Italy. What Lorkin feared were Roos's Catholic sympathies, so intensified by his years of wandering in Italy and Spain; and also 'the unsavoury and obscene discourses which my Lord usually fell into, able to corrupt a very chaste mind'. When they spent a few hours in territory of the independent Netherlands Roos expressed his hatred of Dutch and Protestant alike in a very curious and public fashion, while in Antwerp and Brussels the gambling and feasting, the conversation of Toby Mathew and the Catholic writer and plotter Verstegen, the visits to Sir William Stanley and to Carthusian monasteries, the words of the Infanta at her audience that Lord Roos was a true friend of Spain —

all this alarmed the sober Protestant tutor of young Puckering. After returning alone the coast route, Ghent, Bruges, Ostende and Calais, he was relieved to bring his charge safely back to Paris and a steadier way of life. Roos had left them and returned to England for a few months. The northern tour was over, at least for Sir Thomas Puckering.[38]

Later in the same year Lord Clifford agreed 'to make the circuit' of southern France, taking with him William Becher, two footmen and six horses.[39] His page remained behind in the Academy because he was too young. They reckoned to spend £2 a day for ten weeks. He went to pay his respects and say goodbye to the King, and in the Louvre found Louis XIII busy fencing. They talked of hawks and dogs, and Clifford came away. He was granted a special passport by the French authorities but failed to obtain a licence to carry pistols, because this contravened the law. They travelled gradually southwards to Troyes, Dijon and Macon. On 13 August an English intelligencer residing at Lyon as the governor of Sir Richard Smyth's sons — his other business was to report to London from time to time on Genevan affairs — wrote to Salisbury that Lord Clifford was shortly expected there; a merchant had already received letters for him, and some of his baggage had come in by boat down the Saône from Macon; he was possibly visiting Grenoble and Geneva on the way. A little later Clifford made his way across Provence to Bordeaux and up to La Rochelle. There he fell ill with 'a great defluxion in his left eye' and Becher wrote next from Orleans that the physicians advised an immediate return to Paris. At Saumur he himself called on the great Huguenot leader Duplessis-Mornay but Clifford was too ill and asked to be excused the honour of a visit. They had seen very little recently, having only 'rolled' through the country. In this way the tour ended rather gloomily. At Paris he recovered his sight and his health but was forbidden to read or write. In these circumstances Salisbury sanctioned a return to England and immediate preparations were made, Lord Clifford sending messages that Lady Clifford should be in London to meet him. Horses were purchased and an appeal sent home for a final £150. He went frequently to court and after many ceremonious farewells arrived in England early in 1612 by way of Brussels.[40]

Although the records are incomplete, the journeys in France of English noblemen of high rank during the first decade of the seventeenth century followed the course described. All these examples, except for Sir Thomas Puckering, belonged directly or by marriage to the family circles of Howard and Cecil. Travel was an extension of their great, their over-riding influence in England. Their wealth followed them abroad by the familiar operations of the bill of exchange and letters of credit; from the evidence in the case of Roos and Clifford it seems that they spent at least £1000 a year.[41] The status of their families secured them a suitable welcome at the French court and from English ambassadors who looked to their fathers for promotion at home. The same status attracted to their service Englishmen of medium social rank who hoped, after due services rendered, to obtain secretaryships to which a knowledge of foreign languages and affairs entitled them. Below these tutors and companions came the messengers and servants; men posted across France with letters from London, with relays of fresh horses for the restless, travelling young men. In England Lord Salisbury kept a watchful eye on their itineraries and their indebtedness; very youthful wives awaited their return. Exercises at a riding academy, the trip to the Low Countries, the tour round France including Orleans, Bordeaux and Lyon, are elements in the Englishman's foreign travel at this period which will ultimately become a customary part of his education. That is their importance.

After the narrative of these travels, it is worth considering what English noblemen found in Paris, and what they did there.

During the reign of Henri IV they could observe some of those changes which were to make the city the centre of French civilization as it was to be understood and admired later on in the seventeenth century. The old Valois tradition had partially crumbled away; revival and reform were essential, encouraged but controlled by authority both secular and ecclesiastical. The process by which the Bourbons slowly captivated the French aristocracy was receiving visible expression, and new architecture provided a stage for French customs and costume, French styles of dining, dancing and conversation. The Place Royale was rising on the site of an old market place near the Bastille, a 'wonder of a building' as Toby Mathew remarked, with its discreet, delightful symmetry, houses, pavilions, arcades encircling a fountain. Henri IV had also resumed the work of enlarging the Louvre, and English travellers remarked how the Grande Galerie which he was building steadily proceeded to connect the original quadrangle with Catherine de Medici's palace of the Tuileries.[42] They admired the new formal gardens by the Tuileries where Henri's advisers, in addition, grew long alleys of mulberries and kept silkworms to study the possibilities of scientific improvement in this important French industry. They saw the Pont Neuf, first opened in 1603, and walked over the new bridge to the western bank of the Seine where divorced Queen Margaret was building a new palace for herself. Beyond this, and outside the old city wall of Paris, they came to the Faubourg St. Germain, now rapidly expanding in population and importance in this period of greater security. The French nobility, with their civil wars in abeyance and their hopes of preferment in life increasingly centred round the court, were commissioning large houses in Paris, and the Faubourg St. Germain was the quarter in which they very frequently settled.

The English ambassador usually lived there also. Sir George Carew rented a house in the Rue Tournon not far from the Porte St. Germain. When the landlord, a valet de chambre to the King, sold his property to the duc de Ventadour in September 1607, after a fierce dispute the ambassador appears to have moved next door, possibly to accommodation which was later known as the Hôtel des Ambassadeurs; on contemporary maps of the city these buildings and their gardens can be clearly seen.[43] Of Carew's successors, Sir Thomas Edmondes lived 'in the suburb of St. Germain' and Sir Edward Herbert, ambassador between 1619 and 1624, in the Rue Tournon; perhaps he wrote his book *de Veritate* there.[43] It is possible, therefore, to visualize with fair historical accuracy English diplomats and noblemen proceeding from the ambassador's house through the faubourg across the Rue des Boucheries where private travellers in the seventeenth century often found lodging, over the Pont Neuf, coming finally to the great courts and galleries of the Louvre old and new, and the Tuileries. All men of fashion were permitted to attend at court, for the air of comparative freedom and publicity around the French King in Paris contrasted with the regultions which screened the King of Spain, and by invitation they consulted with ministers or, in the case of accredited diplomats, were received in audience by the King himself. Young gentlemen who came to Paris for their education found that it was in the quarter of the Louvre, during this reign, that they performed their 'exercises'. The royal stables ran parallel with the long gallery of the palace, between it and the Rue St. Honoré; the Manège or riding-school was adjoining, and only a little further off on the Rue St. Honoré itself stood the Hôtel de Pluvinel.[45] When Becher announced that Lord Clifford was joining this fashionable institution he mentioned that 'M. Benjamin keeps the Academy' and the name of de Pluvinel's manager takes us a step further. Between 1610 and 1612 the heir of the Yorkshire family of Slingsby went to Paris, and a letter was addressed 'a monsieur Guliaulme Slyngesbie gentilholme Anglois a l'Academie pres la porte St Honoree a Paris'. In Yorkshire, the Cliffords were also in touch with the Wentworths. Young Thomas Wentworth, having married Lord Clifford's sister Anne, was preparing to come out to France and Clifford had been asked to introduce him to M. Benjamin.[46] Even twenty years later this Frenchman seems to have been well known to the Earl of Devonshire and his servant Thomas Hobbes. In 1635, in Paris, Hobbes discussed with Benjamin a horse which the Frenchman had apparently trained and then sold to the Earl of Newcastle. The Earl found the animal unsatisfactory and more expensive than it was worth; Hobbes proposed calling him 'the Superbe' in future, partly on account of the price originally paid.[47]

The influence of this activity in the shadow of the Louvre must not be underestimated. In previous centuries the greater nobility of western Europe had alway inclined to disregard merely local customs, partly

3. Riding lessons in Paris: *above*, M. de Pluvinel stands at the back behind the horse-man while M. Benjamin is in the foreground on the left. *Below*, Louis XIII is the seated spectator. The artist of these plates from the famous *Maneige Royal* (first edition, Paris, 1623) was Crispin Passe, who himself taught drawing in this Academy.

because they had more than local interests. Their property and their connections were scattered about the continent. Their very freedom of movement made them particularly sensitive to alien influence of one kind or another. At this period, however, they looked increasingly to France and they felt that their training, as men of birth, was best understood in France. Italian and Spanish fashions of thought and behaviour, popularly associated with the names of Catherine de Medici, Marie de Medici and Anne of Austria, were being transmitted to Paris and assimilated by the practice and prestige of the French court: there the foreigner might find the best of everything. In the case of England, moreover, schools for noblemen like these riding academies never flourished. A prospectus associated with the name of Sir Balthazar Gerbier states that Henry Prince of Wales had intended to found such a school for the English court, 'that by example of the French (who about 30 years ago had no Academy at home, but went into Italy as we do now into France) our Nobility and Gentry might learn their exercises in England in their youth'; the Prince was prepared to borrow and lend horses from the royal stables for the purpose, and appear himself once a week.[48] The only upshot of all this was Gerbier's academy at his house in Bethnal Green which existed, rather ingloriously, for a few years in the middle of the century; lectures given there on mathematics, cosmography and languages, which supplemented the instruction in riding, were published by the founder as pamphlets; in these, as if parading the alien influence at work, parallel English and French versions of the text are given on opposite pages. English controversialists debated the vices and virtues of such schools but opinion finally decided in favour of the traditional curricula of the two universities and the Inns of Court. Dr. John Wallis, for one, poured out his scorn on the alleged necessity 'of erecting an Acàddemy (as they call it, because it is a new word and of a French sound, better than our Académy) in or near London'. He did not think that riding the Great Horse, dancing, singing, playing on musical instruments were the proper accomplishments of gentlemen at the expense of logic, metaphysics and other university learning.[49] In fact, however, these were what gentlemen went over to France in order to learn. Particularly under the early Stuarts anyone desiring the training of a courtier, in order to appear at home in the society of many of his equals who had already travelled, was well advised to go to Paris or some other French towns where these academies flourished on the model of de Pluvinel's.[50] This motive is one explanation of the fact that travel by young men on the continent came to be accepted as an essential part of their education. It partially explains also why the intellectual range of the universities remained so narrow; and finally, it emphasizes the different standards then applied to men and to women. Young women learnt French and deportment at home.

As an alternative to the academy at Paris French riding masters came over to England. Henri IV sent St. Antoine, another of his Ecuyers, to instruct Prince Henry and Charles Duke of York. He became their trusted friend and was undoubtedly a useful servant to the King of France. Newcastle, who in 1658 published at Antwerp his magnificent folio on *La Méthode et Invention Nouvelle de Dresser les Chevaux* and had been governor and riding-master to the future Charles II, was in his youth a pupil of St. Antoine. A further example of the reputation of these French teachers may be found in a letter from Lord Salisbury to Sir Thomas Edmondes in 1611, requesting him to send him an Ecuyer of that country for Lord Cranborne's riding; he adds, 'I could wish he might be one of the Religion, as most fit for his service, but if that cannot be, that you will be careful to make choice of one that is of civil life, and hath good understanding and is well practised in his profession.' However, the centre from which these masters came was Paris and in Paris itself many Englishmen preferred to acquire the arts of the Manège.[51]

Another subject that occupied men of this stamp, taking much time and toll of lives, was the practice of weapons and, as its cause or consequence, the custom of the duel. Notions of personal honour provided a theoretic justification for this, but of greater practical influence was the sheer excitement of a combat with rapier and dagger according to the most recent and ever-advancing science of the fencing masters. The best of these men had been Italian in the sixteenth century although certain Spaniards, especially Carranza 'primer inventor de la Ciencia de las Armas', enjoyed an almost legendary prestige even in England. Italian experts taught in London during the later years of the century but after James I's accession they were no longer prominent. In fact, men who desired to excel learnt their weapons in Italy itself and in France, where the vogue for duelling grew alarmingly in Henri IV's time and consequently the native masters and styles of swordsmanship gradually gained prestige.[52] In England the duel was always considered a French custom, something for which neither the Italian nor the Spaniard could be blamed; and the classical authority for the influence of France upon Englishmen in this particular is the writing and the character of Lord Herbert of Cherbury. An erratic and incalculable man, the Autobiography reveals his steady determination to be not a whit behind the most peremptory French swordsman in affairs of honour, and explains how he learnt from the best French masters.

Our ambassadors in Paris complained bitterly of their countrymen's brawls and duels there. One account, of a proposed duel between two Englishmen in January 1609, vividly describes the men and manners brought to the attention of young Lord Cranborne soon after his arrival in France. Carew wrote to Salisbury:[53]

I am still much troubled here about the quarels of the young gentlemen of our Nation. Understanding of late that Sir Thomas Lucy and one Mr. Helmes were gone out into the fields to fight, and not knowing the place I

sent as many of mine owne household as I had horses for, to seek and stop
them. I sent likewise to those of our nation who lay neere me and had any
horse to go out to the same end. Among the rest I sent to Mr. Finnet to take
paynes in that behalf. But my Lord of Cranbourne (though I purposed not to
trouble his Lordship therein), hearing of it by chaunce, very honourably gave
present order to send as many of his people abroad as he had horses for and
those were the first who founde them, and stopped the mischeif at that
present. When they came out of the field Sir Thomas Lucy, on my sending
to him, came to me whom I required not to proceede any further in that
quarrell; and withall entreated my Lord of Cranbourne taking to him Sir
Thomas Howard and Sir John Sheffield, and to stande behind them Mr.
Finnet, Mr. Grimeston and one Captain Stafford (who is in howse with me
and whom I have often used in stopping these tumults), to heare and
compound theyre quarrell. But Mr Helmes, though I sent unto him thrice,
requiring him upon his allegeance to come unto me, refused flatly to doe it.
Thereupon I went to the Lord Chauncellor here praying him to lend me
some officer to apprehende him...[this was done]...I caused him to be
mooved by some of my folkes and a kinnesman of his owne to have his
quarrell accorded, which he might the better doe bycause Sir Thomas Lucy
was the Chalenger, but he persisted stiffly that he would not have it ended
otherwise then by fight. Whereupon I required Sir Thomas Lucy (doubting
to finde the like stiffness on his side also) to hasten his journey which he had
long before purposed towards England, in regard that he was the Chalenger;
and have taken Mr. Helmes into mine howse, to stay him till the other may
be past the seas that they may not at this time fight in Fraunce...Since that I
understood that Sir Thomas Lucy, a litle before his parting hence, sent
another letter to Mr. Helmes to let him understand that he would stay some
dayes at Rouen for him. Whereon I sent to the Mareshal de Fervacques, who
is Lieutenant of Normandy for the Dolphin, to take order to have Gards sett
on him, to hinder him from fighting and to accompany him till he embarque
for England, at Sir Thomas Lucy's charge, which he hath promised me to
doe but I thinke will advertise the King of it first.

Sir Edward Herbert completed the narrative when he wrote that, having
taken leave of the French court in January 1609:

Myself and Sir Thomas Lucy (whose second I had been twice in France,
against two cavaliers of our nation, who yet were hindered to fight with us in
the field where we attended them) we came on our way as far as Dieppe in
Normandy, and there we took ship about the beginning of February.[54]

In such a world of quarrelling swordsmen, so thoroughly in tune with
prevailing French fashion, a newcomer quickly followed suit. The
affront, giving the lie, the challenge, involving both principals and their
seconds who also fought: these things might easily come the way of the
Englishman travelling abroad, and occasionally they travelled abroad for
the sake of these things.

Horsemanship and skill with weapons attracted the young men most, even though other accomplishments were judged necessary. All or nearly all seem to have taken lessons in dancing or lute playing. Furthermore in the academies drawing and elementary mathematics were taught as a decent prelude to the science of fortification and the practice of siege-warfare. The kind of instruction entailed can be seen from a manuscript of slightly later date, a 'Receuil des Méthodes et manières de fortifier reguilerement plus uscitées en l'Europe', compiled by P. Jourdain 'arithmeticien' and dedicated to the fourth Duke of Lennox at Saumur in September 1631.[55] It is in effect an exercise book in geometry with rules and diagrams for designing fortifications according to approved French, Dutch and Italian practice. But tutors and parents, no doubt, were more concerned about the staple fare of French, Latin and history, for many of the young men abroad were hardly more than boys and often they were boys. The standard of industry and learning which was secured must have varied enormously from pupil to pupil as well as from teacher to teacher. Most Englishmen, after a sufficiently long residence in the country at an early age, probably acquired a smattering of French; accredited professors of the language like Charles Maupas of Blois who dedicated his grammar to George Villiers Earl of Buckingham in 1618 as an apt and successful scholar of his, did their best.[56] In the case of Sir Thomas Puckering the general picture of his education in Paris was epitomized by Lorkin his governor:[57]

> Our dayes therefore are thus divided. In the forenoone Mr Puckering spends two houres on horseback; from seven to nine one morning; from nine to eleven another. Two other houres he spendes in French, one in reading, the other in rendring to his teacher some part of a latine author by word of mouth. A fifth hour is employed in learning to handle his weapon which entertains him till 12 of the clock, when the bell warns him to dinner where the company continues together till two o'clock, either passing the time in discourse or some honest recreation perteyning to armes. Then they are warned by one bell to dauncing which houlds him till three, when he retyres himself into his chamber and there employs with me two other houres in reading over some Latin author; which done he translates some little part into French, leaving his faults to be corrected the morrow following by his teacher. After supper we take a brief Survey of all.

It may be asked, what did Puckering gain from this and his years of travel abroad? The uneventful story of his career seems to show that throughout his life he interested himself in the course of political events both at home and in Europe. He instructed servants and agents to send him periodical reports of which even the surviving portion amounts to an enormous mass of mediocre historical material. He evidently understood French since certain parts of this correspondence came from Frenchmen on the continent. On the other hand his familiarity with fashionable Parisian accomplishments and his knowledge of current affairs never tempted him to play a part as courtier or member of parliament.

One of his greatest contemporaries in France and England made much more of the opportunities given by education abroad, and thanks to the fortunate survival of his notebook we can watch him at work.[58] Thomas Wentworth, later the first Earl of Strafford, who was assured of a good reception by M. Benjamin through the kindness of Lord Clifford, arrived in France in December 1611; Salisbury had also written to the ambassador about him.[59] After spending two months in Paris he travelled on to Orleans and entered a pension on 29 February 1612. Five months were passed at Orleans and the remainder of the year in making a tour of France south of the Loire, following the routes previously taken by Cranborne and Clifford. But in this case evidence is there to show that the young traveller did not waste his time. A list of books, inscribed by Wentworth on the opening pages of his precious diary, gives the titles (and the cost) of at least sixty volumes purchased in France; while notes, also in the diary, show that some of these books were studied with real care. Their subject matter is wide enough: a French dictionary, French comedies (highly recommended by contemporary writers for learning a language), the tragedies of Robert Garnier, the Decamerone of Margaret of Navarre, a *Silva Nuptialis*, a *Dialogue Rustique, Nouvelles Recréations* and *D'Urfée*'s Astrea; a large number of ecclesiastical and theological works both Catholic and Protestant, *les Ordonnances de Genève*, Calvin on Relics, *le Catéchisme des Jésuites, le Catholicon d'Espagne*, various writings of Pierre Dumoulin and everything he could find by Duplessis-Mornay. Unlike Cranborne, Wentworth found him in his castle at Saumur, 'a little man, old, great ills, purblinde, malancholly and hath had a red beard' but the interview made an impression for he noted in his book-list: 'At Saumur I bought as many of Mr. Plessis' writings as cost 6 livres which wear all except those I then had and one discours de l'église written in Latine.' Another substantial category were books on French history, mainly recent history: *Les Antiquités de France*, the commentaries of Montluc, Bodin's Republic, the *Relation des Dernières Troubles*, the *Mercure François*. There were also Polybius, Martial, an Apology for Herodotus, not to mention such stray titles as Guarini's Pastor Fido, the letters of Lipsius and certain *Observations par la sage femme de la Reine*.

The historical value of these entries is that they provide a clue to Wentworth's activities and his reading while at Orleans. Matthieu's Relation des Dernières Troubles, for example, an account of the last wars of the League by Henri IV's Historiographer, underwent sustained scrutiny. Possibly he learnt his French from it. A very great number of judgments and aphorisms are taken from this work and copied, either in their original form or translated or partially translated into English, into the diary. The general argument that unity is the great desideratum of the French monarchy, and that popular disturbance consequently requires drastic handling, was perhaps acceptable to all thinking men at that time; possibly it appealed rather positively to a young man who was already, quite clearly, a vigorous character. Without pressing the evidence too far, those pages of the diary in which Wentworth groups together selected aphorisms from the Relation, Tacitus, the Astrea of d'Urfée, and Duplessis-Mornay, summarize the general principles acceptable to an authoritarian character. The events and tendencies which were forming the dominant French political tradition of the period, justification of absolute monarchy, were firmly embedded in Wentworth's mind. When he had finished, in the course of travel, his survey of the great castles of the Loire valley where many of the more catastrophic incidents connected with the religious wars had taken place, when he had seen the bristling fortifications of Saumur, La Rochelle and Montauban — the Huguenot strongholds — it may be that his political convictions were not very different from those of his greatest contemporary as a statesman: Richelieu.

He was, of course, not simply a student of books and his diary is our second description of a journey which was becoming a convention, the secular pilgrimage in France performed by visitors after acquiring enough of the language. It was not feasible until the great pacification of Henri IV's reign, but after 1598 became a common custom dear to foreigners. With little variation the itinerary and the routine were fixed. Cranborne, Wentworth and a host of other travellers looked at a prescribed list of things worth seeing, and made similar comments.[60] The whole procedure, according to its apologists, familiarized men with the ways of the world and with the historical events which took place in cities through which they passed. They looked at military fortifications, sought information about the forms of municipal and royal government, about commerce, crops and industry. It was their duty to take notes as they travelled, and every evening to incorporate them into a diary. 'By day use your writing tables: at night your book. Sleep not before you have cleared your tables and charged your book with anything remarkable.'[62] Of all this Wentworth provides an example.

By the end of July 1612 his long stay at Orleans was coming to an end. During that period, apart from notes on books, he seems to have put little on paper except to record certain dates, when he saw a star of the first magnitude in the sky, when he began eating apricots and damsons and mulberries; another entry reveals the fact that Richard Marris, for many years afterwards his steward, was with him already at this period.[62] Orleans he found a busy, Catholic city where the cathedral was being restored after its destruction by the Huguenots; and Wentworth usually condemns the activities of Catholic men and women as superstition and their attitude to strangers as unfriendly.[63] But now that the season for travel was at hand the ordinary entries in his diary, interrupted since

February, began again. He made a leisurely progress down the great
valley where the landscape appeared to him one continued garden.
From Orleans to Blois he kept to the left bank of the Loire, from Blois to
Saumur to the right except for the stretch between Amboise and Tours.
He visited castles and admired gardens. At Blois were many more
Protestants than in Orleans and consequently he judged them a friendly
population. Many Scotsmen and many Huguenot students lived in
Saumur, guarded by its castle and 'the beautifullest stone walls that ever
I saw'. Then he went on to La Flèche where the buildings of the great
Jesuit College made quick progress, and visited the Philosophy school.
At Angers and again at Nantes technical details of the fortification
attracted him most; the people were rude and spoke bad French; a fair
number of English merchants could be seen at the port. Here also, at
Nantes, an unkind fate misdirected Wentworth's party to the wrong
*croix rouge* inn (there must have been two or more) and it proved 'the
stinkingest and losiest loging that ever was layd in'. Having reached the
estuary of the Loire at this point they struck south across country which
first resembled Sherwood Forest and then became fenny and flat about
La Rochelle. Sometimes they passed through Huguenot towns, elsewhere he judged the people 'dogged, ill-natured and earnest Catholics'.
By the end of August he had reached Bordeaux, a very dear place for
travellers, 'a towne very rebellious, very lascivious and luxurious ill
natured and earnest Catholics'. He himself fell ill of a surfeit.

The next section of their journey took them up the Garonne. It was
quiet monotonous going, to judge from the uninteresting details given.
Watermen nearly drowned them at Podensac where, almost opposite on
the other side of the river, was a fine new chateau at Cadillac; aux trois
rois at Marmande was an excellent inn, aux trois trompettes between
Agen and Moissac was kept by a Protestant. At Montauban, the Huguenot centre, he noticed Scotsmen again, listened to disputations by
students and professors, and examined the defences. Everything was
brick here, bridges, walls and houses; and the reddish river Tarn flowed
by. On the 8 September they had arrived at Toulouse where many
churches deserved and obtained a visit. He heard Jesuit and Jacobin
sermons while the mummified, uncorrupted human bodies at the Cor-
deliers gave him 'great contentment'. After three days here they
travelled westwards to Carcassonne and Narbonne, mainly to see the
citadels, 'entring in among the Perenei hills which be not highe but very
barren, ther [is] nothing growing on them but time, juniper, lavender,
margerone and rosemary whearon the sheep feed which be not big but
very sweet meat'; there were few vines, little corn but an olive garden —
'the first I saw'. Near Béziers, on the way back, he had a first glimpse of
the Mediterranean. They spent four days at Montpellier and found a
good deal of interest: the complicated nature of the city's constitution,
the conferment of degrees by the university, apothecary's shops ('we

4. Thomas Wentworth reaches Montpellier, 1612: a letter to his father.

bought things') and the Physic Garden, which the diary describes in overpowering detail. They were now in the heart of Roman France, and the apothecaries at Montpellier and Nîmes kept not only drugs and potions but ancient incinerary urns, lacrimals and little old lamps. It was also the land of the chameleon, salamander and Jericho roses. The traveller felt here that all was going splendidly and wrote home on 15 September sending his love and obedience with an assurance that the whole company had completed forty-eight days travelling in perfect health, and were just then on the point of leaving Montpellier for Nîmes.[64] Through Avignon, chiefly remarkable to Wentworth for the Jewish synagogue and Laura's tomb, through Arles and across country monotonous and stony they came to Marseilles, and discussed the strength of the port, the galleys and the local constitution of government. He went on board the Admiral's galley.

By the end of September they had reached Orange, with talk of scorpions, adders, the Roman theatre and the Protestant temple. Wentworth rested a day here because he felt ill, the weather broke and it took them a fortnight to reach Geneva. The arsenal, a sermon in the cathedral church, an afternoon spent walking round the town with a glance at the bookbinders' shops, satisfied his curiosity. By the 20th he was in Lyon. He still felt ill and he was tired, perhaps consoling himself by the purchase of a Catholic devotional work, *Le Jardin Sacré de l'Âme Solitaire*. The season grew cold. Having sold his horses, he went by post to Orleans and completed the whole tour on 28 October. A week later he wrote to his father outlining his future plans. In January he wrote once more; he was still buying books.[65] By the spring of 1613 he was home again.

In this fashion travellers divided their time in France. 'Exercises' and 'Itineraries' were ostensibly their main concern. Supplies of money, steady servants, intelligent tutors were subordinate to these purposes for the time being. On returning to England the travelled nobleman and gentleman were often faced with an entirely new range of problems, marriage, estates, political affiliations; sufficient for the moment was the enjoyment of a strange landscape and an alien society. Meanwhile some of those who served them faithfully while abroad, particularly the educated men of mature age who acted as their governors, had their own careers to make. For them the distinction hardly existed between halcyon days on the continent and serious business at home. They knew that in their case prosperity depended on a reputation for knowledge and experience plus patronage: here also they had to keep in touch with likely patrons. In their careers both considerations played a part. Let us look once again at Becher and Lorkin, tutors of Lord Clifford and Sir Thomas Puckering.

# 2. THE CAREERS OF BECHER, LORKIN AND WOODFORD

William Becher was a man of great and, within the limits set by the form of society in which he lived, of successful ambition. The son of a prominent merchant whose large-scale contracts for military supplies with the government had brought with them large and complicated debts, he first comes clearly into view in November 1606 when Sir George Carew employed him as a messenger between Paris and London. In the despatch which he carried it was explained to Lord Salisbury that the bearer had been recommended to the ambassador by Sir Michael Hicks, a man always in close touch with Salisbury.[1] It was probably Becher's first introduction to the Lord Treasurer. During the next few years he continued to serve in Carew's household at Paris; it has already been shown how useful he made himself there to Lord Cranborne in 1609. Such private diplomacy went hand in hand with direct reminders of his worth addressed to London. He corresponded at intervals with Hicks, 'by whose benefit I am here'.[2] In May 1609 he wrote to Sir Thomas Wilson, Salisbury's secretary, appealing for help and advice: the only men of influence, says Becher, who knew him and had access to the Lord Treasurer were Hicks and Sir Stephen Lesieur, a relative by marriage, and he begged for the additional support of Wilson's favour.[3] Using different arguments to the same end, he wrote to his father that while Carew remained in Paris he had no intention of seeking preferment elsewhere, but since the embassage was coming to an end he would welcome a word, on his return home, from Hicks to Salisbury. Becher referred to such a recommendation in terms which well describe the factors of personal favour which weighed with a young secretary abroad:

> I doe perswade myself that it were likely to be accepted, both for the interest which the worlde conceaves that Sir Michael Hicks hath in my Lordes favour [Salisbury's] and for the favourable and willing testemony which I presume my Master [Carew] will be willing to geve me to his Lordship and Sir Michael. But herein I remitte myself to his grave judgment and you may assure him [Hicks] that I have some experience of my Lordes good testemony of mee to my Lord of Salisbury whereby I am not unknowen to his Lordship.[4]

To stand well with one's employer abroad, to have relatives who interested great men at home, and by this double recommendation to impress the greatest of all, the King, the favourite or the Lord Treasurer — these were ideal requirements for the possibility of promotion.

Carew was recalled but Becher remained in Paris as James I's Agent to transact necessary business. It was a sad blow when Sir Thomas Edmondes, the new ambassador, arrived there bringing with him his own household, and his own secretaries Beaulieu and Woodford. Beaulieu remarked that Becher left France rather unwillingly. To make amends Louis XIII sped the retiring official with the customary gifts, in this instance a gold chain and a medal of the late King, Henri IV; while Lord Cranborne, on his own return to England, had already promised that something should be done for him. In June 1611 Becher wrote to Edmondes from London fussily demonstrating his zeal in the ambassador's affairs at home.[5] The first phase of his career abroad ended in this atmosphere of slight disappointment.

He was soon back in Paris as Clifford's tutor; often in the English embassy, although not of it. He fought a duel with Sir Walter Chute, escaping without harm. Someone remembered his name in London and toward the end of 1612 a mistaken rumour hinted that he would shortly be appointed a clerk of the Council. On coming back to England he earned a little pocket money by copying and engrossing on parchment the bonds recording old French debts to Queen Elizabeth together with their receipts. Evidently at this period he must have been hoping and scheming for some more promising employment of wider scope.[6]

In 1614 it came his way and proved a disappointment fraught with real hardship. Through Winwood's interest he obtained a position in Sir John Merrick's embassy to Moscow. It was hoped to use Becher's experience as a diplomat in order to mediate between Muscovy and Sweden, then at war; for James I planned to enhance his prestige in northern Europe, with special reference to the Muscovy Company's prosperity, by forestalling the Dutch who were similarly anxious to arrange such a peace. He and Merrick and their company arrived at Archangel in July 1614. The tedium of those endless northern journeys depressed him beyond measure. 'Cossacks' were ravaging the country and cut communications; only after long delays an escort of 600 men under arms brought them to Moscow at the end of November. Here Becher met with another setback. The Russians, among whom Sir John Merrick's prestige stood so high after half a lifetime's acquaintance with them, insisted that he should personally conduct the negotiations with Gustav Adolf and interview the Swedish King at Narva in Estonia. Merrick wrote home: 'I did much desire to have been spared this journey and the rather for Mr. Becher's sake whom I wished might have had this employment. The gentleman is one that deserveth well, and of great efficiency for affairs.' On notice of this decision Becher wanted to return to England, but in July 1615 he was still with Merrick at Narva, on the Baltic coast. He described their journey from Moscow as 'a most desolate and tedious way' with many long halts. He assisted the ambassador in negotiating with Gustav Adolf — his readiness in the French language proved helpful — and was then requested to take certain Swedish proposals back to Moscow, a project which appalled him; with winter coming on again 'I shall be locked in Russia for another year, from which I pray God deliver me'. However, he obeyed, went to Moscow and returned to Novgorod. It is hardly surprising that Merrick, in December 1615, concluded his despatch to Winwood with the words: 'Mr. W. Beecher now returneth for England, being his own desire.'[7]

Becher once again had done creditably without securing particular prestige. For him fortune had to be found at home, or not at all; and yet, it would depend partly on his reputation as a competent man in foreign business.

He was back in England in time to manoeuvre himself into the good opinions of George Villiers, then rising very rapidly to supreme influence in the disposal of offices. It is possible that they had met, some years earlier, in Paris. As a subordinate favourite of the King's favourite Becher now took his revenge on the secretaries of Sir Thomas Edmondes. When the ambassador returned from France in 1617 Becher was able to replace him, being given the humbler status of Agent, in spite of the usual custom which would have allowed Edmondes's secretary to take the post, and of Woodford's protests.[8] He did not stay long in Paris. His business was miscellaneous: a journey to Rouen to settle the difficulties of the English merchants there, reports to London on the whereabouts of Lord Roos, confidential letters to Villiers expressing devotion and thanks, an apology to King James because he, William Becher, chanced to rail against the Spaniards to Villeroi the French minister, words which were reported in London so that the King's anger 'doth make my heart wither within me'. Never was greater discretion required by a rising diplomat. But these smaller problems vanished of their own accord in the tide of increasing ill-will between the French and English courts. On both sides the Agents were called home. In 1619 Becher was knighted. He was moving forward at last.[9]

Three years later he went abroad again, as secretary to Lord Chichester on a mission into Germany. Soon afterwards the sometime tutor obtained the office which he was to hold for eighteen years (1623 to January 1641), a clerkship of the Council. The rumour of 1612 had at length come true. Apparently Sir Albertus Morton, one of the clerks, was not considered completely reliable at this crisis of affairs — he was sent from the Council Chamber when negotiations for the Spanish match were discussed — and early in 1623, before Buckingham and Charles left for Spain, Becher succeeded to Morton's place. He took the oath of a clerk on 2 January. In March an engraver was paid for the new silver seal of the Council entrusted to Sir William Becher.[10]

In the years between 1623 and 1628 his position and favour with

Buckingham made him a man of real importance. The King, Buckingham and the Secretary of State Conway were frequently at Newmarket
or Royston. The Council sat at Whitehall and it was Sir William Becher
among the clerks who transmitted instructions from the Secretary to
the Council, and recommendations and drafts of documents from the
Council to the Secretary. In the mobilization of men and money for
expeditions to France and Germany, Becher, secretary and treasurer to
the committee acting as the Council of War, appeared very prominently.
He corresponded with Conway on the funds to be handed to Mansfeld
or the orders for levying 'volunteers'. He examined officials charged
with receiving bribes to release pressed men. He interviewed the Dutch
ambassadors concerning the Amboyna massacre. It came as no surprise
to contemporaries that such a prominent man should aim for the place
of honour and profit desired by a number of high-ranking dignitaries,
the Provostship of Eton. What did surprise them was that Becher, armed
with Buckingham's support, should at length be set aside in favour of Sir
Henry Wotton. Buckingham's absence in Spain during the summer of
1623 was probably responsible for his failure. Sir William Becher
continued to stand out among the permanent officials of the King's
government.[11]

A combination of these duties with his old trade of diplomat in France
finally brought him, if only for a few weeks, into the highlights of
political and military adventure. In 1627 even French writers struggled
with the name of Bécher, Becker or Baker. Villiers, now the Duke of
Buckingham as well as Lord Admiral, after several disputes between the
courts of Louis and Charles in the two previous years, had decided on
a policy of shielding the Huguenots against the French monarchy by
positive intervention.[12] The preparation of Buckingham's expedition to
La Rochelle and the neighboring Isle of Ré in 1627 secured from
Becher, as a royal servant, his unsparing attention to the business of
assembling men, ships and supplies. When the fleet left Portsmouth he
sailed with Buckingham as his secretary and the secretary of his council;
his journal notes incidents of the voyage, orders sent to the ships,
changes of wind and the chase given to enemy or unknown vessels.[13] On
10 July the English fleet appeared off La Rochelle, but the mischances
which Buckingham and Charles insufficiently anticipated began to
occur. The municipality of La Rochelle was reluctant to welcome a
foreign armada. Patricians at odds with some of their townsmen, they
had much to lose; they were timorous or even royalist, their stocks
were low and the local harvest had not yet been gathered. They decided
to temporise. On the next day, the 11th, they proclaimed a fast and
prayed for guidance. Betwixt sermons, one of their number wrote afterwards, there arrived in a Shallope at the Chain, an English gentleman
called Baker, who desired to speak with the Mayor, who returned
answer that they were in the Churches at their devotions in the celebra-

tion of a Fast and could not that day give him audience; upon which he returned not a little discontented.[14] Sir William Becher's first attempt to parley with the citizens of La Rochelle had ended in failure, and he was rowed back to the English fleet off shore.

On the following day Buckingham tried once more: accompanied on this occasion by the duc de Soubise, who had been the leading emissary of the Huguenots at Whitehall, Becher approached the mainland a second time. When he came to the gate of St. Nicholas the guard again barred the way. The mayor arriving on the scene found Soubise and Becher between the inner and outer gate. Once more they were entreated to return to their ships. The weather was bad, with a storm about to break. At this moment the old duchesse de Rohan, Soubise's mother, came out from her lodging in the city. Brushing aside the mayor with the assistance of her followers she invited them to enter, and at least take shelter from the approaching storm. It was almost the last demonstration of the Huguenot nobility's former dominance over Huguenot townsmen. Thereupon Becher demanded an audience of the city council. He says in his journal that although feeling very ill of the stone he delivered a long harangue, inviting and requesting the assistance of La Rochelle in this venture of King Charles I to protect his Protestant allies in Europe. The citizens still refused to declare themselves. Next day in the afternoon the magistrates came to Becher at the duchesse de Rohan's house and, while expressing their gratitude to the King for his offers, declared that they must first consult with the other Huguenot leaders and cities before giving a decision. Becher answered that he would attempt to satisfy the Duke of Buckingham with this reply although he himself profoundly regretted their refusal to co-operate with the English forces. On 13 July, together with two representatives from the city he returned to the fleet.[15] For his part the Duke had begun the siege of St. Martin, the royal fort on the neighboring island of Ré.

The determination of Richelieu and Louis to revoke the political and military privileges of French Protestantism, Buckingham battering away at St. Martin, the movement of a few volunteers from the town to the fleet and of supplies from the fleet to the town, finally drove La Rochelle into hostilities with Louis XIII. Meanwhile Becher was the man whom Buckingham sent to England to hasten reinforcements, the enterprise on Ré having already run into difficulties. On 27 July he wrote to Conway 'from aboard the Charles entering Plymouth road', begging for the speedy muster of men and stores and £9000 in specie'. In the following weeks of delay and disorganisation Becher fought hard for the essential supplies to be sent to Ré. He attended the King and transmitted his instructions to the council. He went down to Portsmouth to arrange for the billeting of soldiers because the ships appointed to carry them to France had not yet arrived. The whole burden of responsibility during this terrible summer, the anxiety that all was not going well, found expression in a letter he wrote to Conway from Portsmouth:

> But this beeing now the 21 of August it afflicts mee much to heare yet no news of the coming of the shipps with the victualls nor of the money ordered to be sent hither, especially the winde beeing now fayr to bring the shipps from the Downes. I beseich your Lordship to acquaint his Majestie with it and to entreat him that hee will please to hasten away both the shipps and money. Your lordship may bee pleased to put his Majestie in minde of his owne letters, and to doe mee the favour to send your owne, and to call to my Lord Chambrelain for his, and to my Lord of Holland also . . . I doe heare a report here that there is a messenger arrived within these two dayes from my Lord Duke, if it bee so I beseiche your Lordship to give mee part of his news.[16]

The King had written to Buckingham a week earlier, assuring him that Becher and the supplies would soon be sailing, but it was not until 7 September that victuals, ships and money had all been brought to Stokes Bay by Portsmouth, and then unfavourable weather delayed their departure. They reached Falmouth roads on 19 September. A week later, as an English soldier reported at Ré, '13 sayle of shippes laden with victualls and munition for our Army' had arrived at last.[17]

In estimating the contribution of a single official in matters so intricate and uncertain, the large scale of the undertaking must be kept in mind. Becher's ships coming belatedly to anchor off St. Martin were not the only nor the largest reinforcement planned by Charles. On 2 September 2500 Irish under Sir Crosby Pierce and Sir Ralph Dingley had arrived, on 25 September came Becher and Sir Henry Palmer with victuals and munitions. After that the main reinforcement was promised, but it waited in port a month for the south-west winds to moderate. Meanwhile the siege of St. Martin continued, a military issue depending largely on the struggle to feed or starve Louis XIII's force in the citadel; the French sending out craft with supplies from the mainland, the English attempting to stop them with booms and a floating battery. On the island itself there was less activity once Buckingham had dug his entrenchments in August. 'For 4 or 5 dayes nothing don, our soldiers dyed apace'[18] was a fair summary of the first week in October, disease now appearing as a principal in the action. It will be seen, therefore, that the work of one important official was a fragment in this great complication of efforts. Furthermore, we hear nothing of him after his return to Ré; but if credit is due to anyone, in must go to Sir William Becher. In fitting out the original expedition, negotiating with the Huguenots in La Rochelle, struggling to hasten reinforcements during August and September 1627, the evidence shows him to have been a valuable official and spokesman. Had the venture proved to be the serious action of European importance which Cardinal Richelieu, for one, feared as a distinct possibility, the increased power of Buckingham might have influenced proportionately the career of his faithful servant. Buckingham occupying some part of western France, Becher negotiating with the Huguenot cities of Guyenne: it was not a wholly improbable conjecture.

A month later the Admiral reluctantly raised the siege. The remnants of his army and the ships returned home in November and Becher was occupied with the problem of securing money to pay off the troops.[19] These four months had been a climax in his official career. After the murder of Buckingham and Conway's retirement the personal favour which he enjoyed was not sufficient to give him any special employment.[20] The period of military expeditions, for Becher and for the nation, had come to an end. During the period of government without Parliament his work lay along the lines laid down by steady conciliar administration. He transmitted orders to the Council messengers to arrest wanted men. He sent proclamations to the attorney-general for redrafting. He was one of those, in 1633, appointed to make trial of the quality of soap supplied by the soap patentees. He was active in the administration of the ship-money taxes, reporting to the Council on petitions against certain assessments. In June 1637, armed with a Council warrent, he searched Oliver St. John's study in Lincoln's Inn. Meanwhile he grew richer, but his career ended in 1640 when his duties involved him in conflict with the renewed power and privileges of Parliament.[21]

On the dissolution of the Short Parliament the secretaries of state Vane and Windebank signed two warrants (8 May 1640), which they handed to Becher, authorizing him to search the Earl of Warwick and Lord Brooke for incriminating documents. Their 'studies and Pockets' were duly searched by Becher. When the Long Parliament met, the Lords raised the matter as a breach of the privilege of the peers and of Parliament. Becher was summoned to the bar of the House as a delinquent on 10 November, where he pleaded his oath and office as a clerk of the King's Council, refusing to show the Lords those warrants given him in the previous May. After three summonses on that day he was examined on oath. Threatened with punishment as a principal, not an agent, he went under guard to his house to fetch his papers and duly surrendered the warrants. 'He made a little speech', says a newsletter, 'but seemed unwilling to deliver them but rather that the usher should take them out of his pocket. But the clerk was sent down to him and he delivered them up.' The Lords sent Becher to the Fleet prison while they arranged for a conference with the Commons. Two days later Becher sent up a petition acknowledging his error; and the Lords (now busy with the case of Strafford) recognizing his age and infirmities, ordered that he should be released.[22] This affair hastened his retirement, for on 27 January 1641 Richard Browne was sworn a clerk of the Council in his stead. As an unsuccessful candidate for the office wrote a fortnight later, Sir William Becher had made quick work of his place, and he handed it over to a friend: the Brownes of Sayes Court, Deptford, the family into which John Evelyn married, appear to have transacted a good deal of business with Becher in the years immediately following, connected with conveyancing and concealment of assets during the great constitutional storm.[23]

A few further documents mention Sir William in his last years. One is a certificate from a Surrey J. P. that in 17 March 1642 Becher took the oath of allegiance; a doctor's certificate, signed by Sir Theodore Mayerne and certain physicians, states that Sir William Becher's health would benefit greatly from a course of the waters at St. Paul, near Rouen, as they had already assisted him in the previous year.[24] This can only mean that his age and frailty which the House of Lords admitted — together with the unsettled condition of the kingdom — caused the sometime Clerk of the Council to apply for a passport (having taken the oath of allegiance) and to go abroad for health and safety to Normandy. The old traveller was back in the country where he had first acquired the experience of affairs which brought him to prosperity in England.

The correspondence of Sir Richard Browne, suggests that Becher was in Paris between February and May 1643. An informer who appeared before the Parliamentary Committee for Advance of Money testified that he had been Sir William Becher's servant for three and a half years at Rouen, between 1643 and 1645. He accused his master of sending shiploads of armaments over to the King's forces at Exeter and Newcastle, but the committee rejected his evidence. Becher was safe in France, while his property in England survived the period of crisis. In 1644 he was assessed at £1000 for purposes of war taxation, a very high figure, and for the same amount in 1647. He does not appear to have married but left a natural son, and the last phase of his life was passed at home in Putney. He died in April 1651, having divided his possessions: there were legacies, to sisters and their children and to cousins, worth not less than £1250 and probably more; £300 for poor clergy, to be derived from the rents of four parsonages in Surrey and Hampshire at the rate of £50 a year; with the residue going to his son, a younger William Becher, of the Inner Temple. It amounted to a substantial property.[25]

The old man was buried in Putney Church, and on a black stone before the altar a legend was later inscribed:

Hic situs est Guil. Bechers eques auratus, perpaucorum hominum homo, nec-non ordinis sine invidia decus. Qui dum stabat Anglia incolumis, Regnumque vigebat consiliis duobus potentissimis regibus, secretorum conciliorum a se-cretis fuit. Idem in transmarinis regionibus bis publicum negotium egit. . . .[26]

The story of William Becher shows a man of no particular status moving slowly up to a responsible post, and the relevance of service abroad to his preferment. The Rev. Thomas Lorkin, a graduate of Emmanuel College, Cambridge, was less fortunate.

An early letter connects him with the family of Sir Thomas Puckering, a Lord Keeper in Elizabeth's reign. He wrote from Richmond to the widowed Lady Puckering with news of her children, requesting that the young Sir Thomas's quarterly allowance should be promptly paid in order to enable him to purchase the customary New Year gifts for the Prince of Wales and the Prince's tutor Adam Newton, Lady Puckering's son-in-law.[27] Evidently Lorkin was already at this date Thomas Puckering's own tutor and in close touch with the Prince of Wales's youthful companions, among whom Puckering could be numbered. In 1610, as we have already shown, he accompanied his charge to Paris for some years. In 1612 they went together as far as Florence but Lorkin then returned to England alone and entered Lady Harrington's family. He continued in regular correspondence with Puckering who was meanwhile wandering from city to city in Italy and Spain, and expressed a desire to re-enter his service more completely than by the mere despatch of newsletters to a good patron. This was arranged, and Lorkin left England shortly afterwards with servants and horses of Puckering's in order to meet the homecoming traveller at Paris. On 19 November 1614 he wrote from Paris to Puckering at Blois, giving his address as 'aux fauxbourgs St. Germain dans la Rue des Boucheries au Cheval Blanc'. Puckering arrived in due course but immediately sent Lorkin on an errand to Saumur to contract with a jeweller for a signet which he had provisionally ordered. Then they both returned to England.[28]

The next few years in the life of this tutor and letter-writer are very obscure. He lived in London, but in whose household or on what means is not clear. A series of reports on events of the day which he addressed to Puckering, then living quietly in Warwickshire after years of travel abroad, are the only positive evidence of Lorkin's activity; though they say disappointingly little of his own concerns they are a useful illustration of the methods by which news of the world found its way into country districts before the printed Intelligencer entered the field. In this case, Puckering's former tutor became his correspondent on public affairs. Later on, another of his correspondents was John Beaulieu, first secretary of the embassy in Paris when Puckering first arrived there. Experience abroad was obviously a desirable qualification in commentators on current affairs; Edward Rossingham, another and a most prolific writer of this class during the first half of the seventeenth century, was in Sir John Digby's embassy at Madrid in 1611 and had evidently travelled widely.[29]

In 1617 Lorkin himself managed to secure a place in the company of

Digby who was returning to Spain on the business of Prince Charles's marriage with the Infanta. There is a single letter of his written at Burgos on 8 October. He took a very unfavourable view of Spain, of their reception there and of the negotiations. Everything was poor and beggarly, neither friendly nor comfortable. He advised Puckering that the political schemes under consideration would fail, but 'I pray Syr, conceal my letters from all, least some prejudice ensue unto my self'.[30]

In the late summer of 1618 Lorkin fell seriously ill, but on recovering looked round anxiously for prospects and preferment. A number of possibilities filled his mind. He discovered that Digby would shortly leave with another embassage to Spain in order to complete the marriage negotiations. 'It is kept a great secret in the interim', wrote Lorkin to Puckering, 'and so imparted unto me who am offered the condition of chaplain, if I shall think fit to accept it.' Six weeks later he considered a fresh scheme which would take him yet further afield:

> A good friend of mine propounded to me within these few days a condition of going over to Virginia, where the Virginia company means to erect a College, and undertakes for to procure me good assurance of £200 a year and better, and, if I shall find there any ground of dislike, liberty to return at pleasure. I assure you I find preferment coming on so slowly at home as makes me rather incline to accept it...I humbly crave your secrecy.

But in December he still thought of going with Sir John Digby to Spain. His future plans remained vague and contradictory.[31]

Meanwhile he was concerned to arrange a marriage between Puckering's niece and the eldest son of Sir Robert Carey, Master of the Prince's Household. He speaks of his own interest in seeing these families joined in alliance 'between whom my Duty rests divided'. At this period, therefore, Lorkin served in Carey's household and it was this connection which decided his immediate future; for Thomas Carey, the second son, fell ill or was delicate and Sir Theodore Mayerne recommended a summer visit to Spa. The boy's father obtained a passport valid for one year, naming both Thomas Carey servant to the Prince, and Thomas Lorkin. On 9 June 1619 they left London expecting to return in September. As Lorkin had written a few weeks earlier, 'Myself am like to pass the seas once again ere long, so I am born, it seems, to a rolling restless life'.[32]

In 1620 he was back, and paid a visit to his old college at Cambridge. But by July he is to be found in Blois, observing the movement of discontented French nobility through that city on their way south in preparation for another round of civil war. He does not mention the name of his new patron. Early in 1623 he was again in Blois, and still a tutor. On this occasion the burden of his news was the movement of Englishmen going through France to Spain in the final stages of the long Anglo-Spanish negotiation. 'My Lord of Doncaster passed by this towne as yesterday who assured us of what we were before incredulous, the Prince's voyage into Spaine whither he posteth after.' Then came Sir Robert Kerr, Viscount Rochester, Lord Feilding and the Marquis of Hamilton's eldest son. Lorkin was still the observer of other men's actions in diplomacy, not yet a preformer on his own account. He remained as yet a nobleman's tutor and a clergyman without office.[33]

In May 1623, at Blois, he received good news, wrote off to Puckering giving notice of 'some preferment offered by my Lord Keeper at Mr. Cary's suite',[34] and hurried home immediately to view at closer quarters the living of Tolland in Somersetshire which had indeed been proposed for him. The advowson belonged to the Crown. This reward for long service brought no real satisfaction because the living appeared on inspection to be worth little more than half what was promised, and Lorkin wrote that had it not been for news from France that 'my gentleman' was now gravely ill, he would have refused it. If 'my gentleman' died the living provided an income of some sort and might provide useful employment. In any case, the rector of Tolland returned quickly to France; in November he was in Paris, settling his gentleman at the Academy. He wrote to Puckering that if in future another hand sent him weekly intelligence reports they were still to be reckoned a testimony of Lorkin's devotion.[35]

This final surviving word to his old patron, which may indicate that he already had other pre-occupations, was written on 28 November 1623. He had clearly settled in Paris for the winter. The next hint of his activity comes from a very different source.

Henry Rich Viscount Kensington arrived in Paris in February 1624 with an instruction to test the possibilities of a negotiation with the French court for a marriage between Charles and Henrietta Maria. His first despatch from Paris bears the date 16 February. A month later Thomas Lorkin's name appears for the first time in Kensington's correspondence: 'This discreet and honest bearer Mr. Lorkin' brought to London a letter of 15 March and took back to Paris Conway's reply. On 7 April Kensington wrote again, saying that full confidence might be placed in his messenger's verbal report on the situation, and the messenger was again Lorkin. Moreover, this letter from Kensington to Conway is written in Lorkin's hand and signed by the ambassador so that by 7 April 1624 the latter had found a useful secretary, and Lorkin a new employer. Probably the budding diplomat still kept an eye on some young gentleman at de Pluvinel's academy; he once mentions coming to Paris from St. Germains on private business, but if the marriage negotiations continued it was clear that the best prospects for his future lay in the service of Lord Kensington. The position demonstrates effectively the relation of the young nobleman, abroad with his tutor, and the ambassador, abroad on official business and with his own staff of servants, into which tutor attempted to merge. Conversely, the ambassador's secretary could become a private tutor. As a travelled man and practised observer of political affairs since 1610, Lorkin was an expert in his own way. Kensington, arrived in Paris on a confidential mission, could have found no one more suitable to be his secretary and courier.[36]

Lorkin came to London with this letter of 7 April and took back the reply. During May he continued to write out the despatches for Kensington, who signed them, and by the end of the month matters had advanced sufficiently for James to send the Earl of Carlisle to join Kensington for official conversations with the French ministers on a treaty of marriage. Carlisle naturally had his own servants, among them Woodford 'my Secretary'. But Lorkin was still on the spot; on 27 May he added the date and superscription to a letter which Carlisle sent to James I announcing his arrival in France. In June, moreover, Woodford went back to England to present a report on the political situation to the King and although he returned to Paris some time later he fell ill, and his handwriting does not appear again in the State Papers until 2 September. The Rev. Thomas Lorkin was able to step into the position of principal secretary to the English ambassadors at Paris and St. Germains. He wrote letters both for Kensington and Carlisle in addition to some of their joint despatches.[37]

These duties involved a delicate responsibility on occasion. When the two ambassadors disagreed, Lorkin had to write out letters containing information and opinions which would have deeply disturbed the ambassador who was not present. In August 1624 Carlisle dictated to him a despatch for James, advising a firm refusal of the latest French draft of clauses in the proposed treaty, which dealt with the English Catholics. Lorkin brought to Kensington, who had been ill, both the despatch and a copy of these articles, and Kensington set moving a little diplomatic negotiation which was kept hidden from Carlisle. He sent his secretary to interview Richelieu in a secret attempt to have certain clauses modified, so that he might then advise James to accept them. It is one of the minor curiosities of this period that an Anglican clergyman should interview the great Cardinal on the business of Henrietta Maria's marriage, Richelieu treating him with all possibly courtesy, 'would not speake with him (on no termes) till he was covered', and immediately summoning Schomberg and Ville-aux-Clercs to a round-table conference with Lorkin on the phrasing of the French articles. No concessions were made.[38]

Lorkin had originally entered Kensington's service. By the end of the year he was equally a secretary to Carlisle, by far the more authoritative of the two ambassadors. On one of his many visits to London he was also given the task of obtaining the ambassador's arrears of payment and bringing such money to Paris. In this connection Secretary Conway referred to 'your trusty and diligent servant Mr. Lorkin' who used 'miraculous diligence' in wringing money from the Treasurer's officials.[39] He was interviewed by James I, and fully trusted by Carlisle.[40]

A crisis in the negotiations came in October. The two principal problems were, naturally, the concessions which the King of England was willing or able to make in favour of the English Catholics and the support which the King of France was willing or able to give the English design of restoring to James I's son-in-law his dominion in the Palatinate. Regarding the first of these problems, it was not only the extent of such concessions but the method of defining them — as public or secret articles, or as an *écrit particulier* separate from the main treaty, or in the form of a personal letter signed by James or by James and a Secretary of State — which led to fierce bargaining. One side referred to the necessity of satisfying Pope Urban VIII from whom a dispensation for Henrietta Maria's marriage had still to be obtained, the other to constitutional difficulties in England and to feeling among the Puritans. Lorkin, undoubtedly, spent much time on the outskirts of this thicket of argument while his superiors continued the debate. At last, by September, a fair measure of agreement had apparently been reached. James still insisted that the concessions to his Catholic subjects should be drafted in the form of a personal letter but their scope was more or less in accordance with Richelieu's definitions. James had given ground largely owing to Buckingham's advice, and Buckingham's friendship with D'Effiat the French ambassador, a compromising alliance much disliked by Carlisle.[41]

The other problem, what steps France was willing to take in driving the Catholic powers from the Palatinate, naturally came up for discussion at the same time. In the view of Conway, if not of Buckingham, it was of prior importance, and he ordered the two ambassadors to negotiate the proposed agreements interdependently: James I would sign the marriage treaty when Louis XIII signed an offensive alliance with him for the restoration of Frederick to the Palatinate.

On 4 October Carlisle, Kensington, Richelieu and the assistant French ministers entered into conference once more. To their dismay the Englishmen now found that Louis refused to accept James's concessions to the Catholics in the form of a personal letter, or to give more than a purely verbal assurance of his own good intentions in the business of the Palatinate. The whole negotiation, in the opinion of the English spokesmen, was in danger of collapse. Further discussion led nowhere, and it became necessary to inform the government at home immediately of this most serious crisis. So it was, that with this urgent news, with confidential messages for King, Prince, Duke and Secretary of State, with a last special despatch dated 'Friday night late' the Rev. Thomas Lorkin was sent hurrying from Paris to London on Saturday 9 October.[42]

Late on Monday evening, the 11th, he was in London; and the details of his journey are a study in the work of a seventeenth-century diplomatic courier. Lorkin rode hard through France all Saturday reaching Boulogne at nightfall where, he says, he would have continued on to Calais and the shorter sea-passage but the wind being fair and favourable he decided to go aboard ship at Boulogne. After resting five or six hours, waiting for the tide to turn, he left port. They had sailed a little way out to sea when all Lorkin's good fortune turned against him. The wind dropped, and for a further nine or ten hours on the Sunday morning his ship was becalmed, motionless. Unlike ordinary passengers who could resign themselves to such enforced delay, his business would not wait and so, after making signs to a little fishing boat he was taken on board the lighter craft and put ashore again in France. He secured a post-horse and hurried on to Calais. Still the weather was calm and 'the little wind contrary'. He decided to venture the crossing in a very light, slight vessel, a shallop which got forward through such motionless weather and, at length, he says, he arrived at Dover half starved with cold between four and five o'clock on Monday morning. Riding hard all day he reached London as the bells struck three in the afternoon. An hour later he waited on Conway, the Secretary of State, who read the despatch exclaiming: 'Before God, I fear all is spoiled, and that we shall suddenly break upon this difference.' They went together in Conway's coach to confer with Buckingham, though Lorkin was not admitted to his presence until the Duke had read over the despatch in private. Lorkin adds that by then he was feeling very hungry, not havng eaten a morsel since leaving Boulogne. Later in the evening, going home to his lodging, he scribbled the news of his arrival in London to Carlisle and Kensington. It had been an important and a difficult journey. The message he carried so faithfully put the English authorities to the necessity of deciding to break the treaty or make further concessions.[43]

The following month was very arduous for Lorkin, very confusing for the statesmen. He returned to Paris with instructions which prepared the way for new concessions from James but when Carlisle, on 24 October at Richelieu's palace, delivered his proposals to the French he met with a fresh refusal. The Venetian representative in Paris reported that no agreement was yet in sight, his own suggestions proving useless. Poor Lorkin once again set off for England carrying a despatch dated the 28th. Meanwhile the French had their own ambassador, messengers and means of secret diplomacy. They trusted to the influence of D'Effiat over Buckingham and of Buckingham over James, who at length gave way, declared himself satisfied with a verbal promise of assistance in the business of the Palatinate and ordered the marriage articles to be signed on his behalf. Lorkin returned to Paris, arriving late on 7 November. Two hours after midnight news was brought to the Venetians from the English ambassadors that their secretary had arrived with the order to sign the treaty, and early next morning he went to congratulate

Carlisle and Kensington, who set their signatures to the agreement on 10 November. All the heated arguments now brought to a temporary conclusion had been matters of high policy, the tactic of two Kings' senior counsellors and representatives; but one indefatigable worker in the background, secretary, courier, junior diplomat, had certainly done his share — Lorkin, the nobleman's tutor with a knowledge of the continent, was now a useful and experienced servant of the state. He had made great progress in eighteen months.[44]

The negotiations continued, first to obtain Urban VIII's dispensation, secondly to force the French to act in the Palatinate and give assistance to Mansfeld who was to intervene there, if Buckingham and James had their way. Lorkin wrote out the ambassador's despatch of 12 November and another for Kensington (now Lord Holland) on 4 January 1625. A few days later he was the bearer of a report from both ambassadors, in which they requested Conway to given Lorkin 'the same credit which you would unto ourselves'. He soon returned to Paris. He appears to have interviewed Mansfeld at Dover, and brought instructions to the ambassadors requesting them to press for the issue to Mansfeld of a permit to land in France on his way through to the Rhineland with English reinforcements — thus involving France in the coming campaign against the Spaniards. In February he spent some time both in London and Paris; travelling and writing were the daily business of his life.[45]

On 12 March, while in England, the Rev. Thomas Lorkin was inducted to the living of Stoke Hammond in Buckinghamshire; he succeeded John Hacket.[46]

On 24 March Conway wrote to Carlisle that Buckingham retained Lorkin in England so long as 'to assist in the preparation of the Prince's powers [for the proxy], that he may bring them unto you as clear as possible and upon anything that hath been debated here may furnish your Lordship with the arguments...' But by 7 April in London they were already expecting Lorkin's return from Paris.[47]

Less than two years had passed since he had entered the diplomatic service but he deserved promotion. The marriage of Henrietta Maria and Charles (for whom the duc de Chevreuse stood proxy) was cele-brated in Notre Dame on 1 May. Buckingham came to Paris to escort the Queen of England to her new home, and the train of gentlemen, servants and officials, with Henrietta Maria, Anne of Austria and the Queen-Mother, made its way towards the coast, Lorkin accompanied them to Boulogne and then turned back to Paris: he was appointed to reside there as Charles I's Agent. It was his responsibility, in these last six months of his life, to placate Cardinal Richelieu in the difficult period of Anglo-French relations immediately following the marriage, in the absence of an English representative of ambassador's rank. For this he obtained an Agent's usual salary (not paid until after his death) of £2 a day.[48] Such work, at any rate, lifted him well above the old status of a correspondent writing newsletters in a rather abject manner to a country gentleman in Warwickshire. He now negotiated, very respectfully, with the great ones of the world, Richelieu, Buckingham and Conway.

Unfortunately the final phase of Lorkin's career lasted only until the autumn of 1625 when he lost his life, probably in a storm while crossing the Channel on a journey to England.[49] He had entered on his new duties with great zeal, writing to thank the secretary of state for his kindness, sending also a present of books. This offering was followed by a series of insufferably prolix despatches, certainly modelled on the old newsletters to Sir Thomas Puckering, which give an account of his negotiations with the French ministers between June and September. There are also two letters, as obsequious as they are confidential, addressed to Buckingham and replete with political intelligences from Paris.[50] But in October two new secretaries, De Vic and Augier, began writing to Conway from France. They were servants of Lord Barrett, recently appointed ambassador although he had not yet arrived, with their address at the 'fauxbourg St. Germain, rue Tournon à l'hotel de M. l'Ambassadeur de l'Angleterre'. They state that they were writing in the absence of Lorkin who left Paris on 13 September. Then, after a few weeks' silence, Conway wrote that Lorkin must be presumed dead. The supposition that the unfortunate diplomat was drowned at sea goes back to the historian Thomas Birch in the eighteenth century; it is certainly possible that Lorkin attempted to cross the Channel in a shallop once too often, for just at this time a French diplomat ordered to London waited three weeks at Boulogne for lack of shipping in outrageous weather. Neither the instructions telling Lorkin to return to England nor any original instructions to Barrett, the new ambassador, appear to be extant. Whatever the true facts of this mysterious close to a praiseworthy career, on 11 October Conway had given Lorkin up for lost and ordered the dead man's trunks in his lodging at Paris to be sealed up and sent home, for the sake of any official papers they might contain. Certain debts were left outstanding in Paris. His brother John was his executor and received a warrant for £240 owing to Lorkin for service abroad.[51]

On 11 December of the same year, also, a new minister was inducted at Stoke Hammond. The register shows that this man visited his parish more frequently than his predecessor could ever have had time to do.[52] He was not a traveller as Lorkin had been, nor a diplomat of merit. It may be doubted, indeed, whether anyone could illustrate so aptly as the Rev. Thomas Lorkin the relation of young gentlemen and tutors on their travels with the rather primitive organization of diplomacy in this period.

The careers of Sir William Becher and the Rev. Thomas Lorkin, developing partly from a profitable association with noble patrons in

foreign countries, have led us sometimes far afield from the scene of
their earliest labours; but the Englishman's travels in France, with all
that this implies — their tutors and companions, their relation with the
English ambassador's household in Paris, their 'exercises', their 'circuit'
in the south giving them a sight of the Loire valley, Bordeaux and Lyon
— has by now shown itself as a convention of importance. The results
were various: to some men the experience gave mastery of a foreign
language, to another skill with horses or the sword, to another respectable manners, to another better prospects of employment at home
or abroad. So far, the evidence has given us a description of Paris and its
attractiveness for the English visitor, a 'tour' of the country in the
footsteps of Cranborne and Wentworth, and an account of two minor
figures whose experience of France helped them to play some part in the
political history of their time. It becomes decidedly more difficult to
find successors to Cranborne and Wentworth during the next fifteen
years (1615–1630). The state of the country, when unrest in several
provinces developed at intervals into civil war, deterred them. The
Huguenots were usually involved, and the encouragement given the
Huguenots by both James I and Charles I aggravated the other causes of
friction between the two governments. This led ultimately, as William
Becher's career showed, to open hostility. So the private English
traveller kept away while armed forces moved through the landscape.
Instead, a sequence of messengers and envoys sent by King James on
urgent official business made their way into the French provinces.

In April 1611, about a year after the assassination of Henri, IV, the
English ambassador to Spain crossed through France. He reported
that in Poitou Protestant gentlemen and ministers came to him and
vehemently expressed a detirmination to maintain their rights. It was an
omen for the next few years.[53]

In May 1614 James sent a Scottish minister, Mr. Hume, to the
Protestant synod held at Tonneins (50 miles up the Garonne from
Bordeaux) and Sir Thomas Edmondes the ambassador advised him, in
view of the dangers, to travel by way of Brussels and Sedan. But at
Soissons he was stopped and his papers were seized; they were said to
contain a plan for the union of all Protestant churches under the aegis of
the King of England.[54] In the following year an important Huguenot
assembly met at Grenoble, and a spokesman for James assured the
delegates that the King fully understood that their liberties were under
threat and assured them of his support.[55] Shortly afterwards Edmondes
himself was authorised to intervene. Troops of the French crown and
those of the opposition leaders appeared south of the Loire; but a
conference for the discussion of a settlement was arranged, to be held at
Loudun. Here the English ambassador took part and, in the opinion
of the Regent's ministers, took too great a part in the proceedings.
Between December 1615 and April 1616 we find Edmondes negotiating

at Saint-Jean d'Angèly, Chatellerault, Loudun and La Rochelle. Meanwhile his secretary John Woodford remained behind in Paris, receiving
and transmitting the letters sent from London and Poitou. The terms of
a treaty were with difficulty agreed.[56]

Understandably the district between the Loire and Bordeaux did not
attract a peaceable tourist at such a time. He would come later. Loudun,
for example, described by an Englishman in 1647[57] as 'a city in a rich
plain, well-walled, and good buildings of free stone' was often visited
twenty or more years after Sir Thomas Edmondes' appearance there. In
1636 young George Courthop, the son of a Sussex landowner, spent
some time in Paris and then, in order to learn French, spent a year in
Loudun at the academy of Mr. Strachan a Scotsman, which had been
recommended to him by Sir William Champion (whose property lay on
the Kent-Sussex border near the Courthops').[58] In the same year and
at the same place Courthop met Lady Purbeck, the daughter of Sir
Edward Coke. Later on, Lord Willoughby visited it in 1647, Lord
Mandeville in 1649, John Reresby in 1655. Many in England who had
never travelled would have heard of the famous nun of Loudun whose
mysterious stigmata attracted many pilgrims or tourists. Loudun, in fact,
became a place worth inspection by those who wandered round France
— but not as early as 1616.

After a few years more trouble threatened. The monarchy annexed
the old Bourbon heritage of Huguenot Béarn, which up to 1619 had
preserved a semi-independence. To this and other measures a Huguenot assembly at La Rochelle responded with defensive and offensive
plans of their own. Soon troop movements, sieges, and parleys began
again, and into this dangerous world James I sent two not wholly
guideless representatives. They were Sir Edward Herbert, his resident
ambassador at Paris, and following him James Hay Earl of Doncaster.

In May 1621 when war broke out Herbert received instructions to
mediate. The royal army laid siege to the Protestant town of Saint-Jean
d'Angély and here, at the beginning of June, he found Louis XIII. The
issue of principle was raised immediately. The Constable Luynes, who
interviewed Herbert, stated peremptorily that the King of England had
no claim to interfere in the domestic concerns of France, a proposition
which at once involved the ambassador and the Constable in a personal
quarrel. In effect, this ended James's first attempt to mediate. The siege
of the town proceeded while Herbert observed with keen professional
interest the methods of warfare used in France, finding that they
resembled Low Country practice. Saint-Jean d'Angély fell to the King
on 25 June and the ambassador followed him south as far as Cognac
where — in a significant aside — he states in his autobiography that he
found accommodation thanks to the kindness of a Huguenot nobleman
who first offered him rooms in his own castle, 'yet I could not with any
honour accept it, since I knew it would endanger him, my business to

those parts being in favour of those of the religion, and the chief ministers of state in France being jealous of my holding intelligence with him'; so, instead, the nobleman secured him lodgings in the town. However, the dispute with Luynes made useless Herbert's attendance on the royal progress southwards and he was forced to return home to England to justify his conduct to James. In this he succeeded.[59]

James I immediately substituted Doncaster for Herbert. He had more talent as a diplomat and previous experience of the French court. He left London at the end of July 1621 with John Woodford as secretary, and in his company Edward Montagu, the Lord Manchester of the English civil war, James Wriothesly, heir to the Earl of Southampton, and Algernon Percy, later Earl of Northumberland.[60] These young noblemen added dignity and importance to the mission by their rank, and for them it was probably as favourable an opportunity of visiting or re-visiting France as could be found at this troubled period.

Louis XIII was now fighting in the Garonne valley. He intended to besiege Montauban and clear his way to the loyal and Catholic city of Toulouse before turning back to settle the score with La Rochelle. Doncaster hurried after him by the usual route. Travelling in the wake of an army, the post horses were too few and the party was sometimes forced to ride six or seven stages without changing them. At Bordeaux the first president of the Parlement and the *jurats* of the municipality met the new English envoy, invited him to a banquet which he declined, and escorted him to the boats made ready for his journey up the river. He went as far as Moissac, a few miles from Montauban. At last he had reached his journey's end, overtaking the King after six weeks' travel; he was just in time to hear the opening thunder of the siege, with Louis on the attack, the Huguenots defending, and his own objective some form of negotiation. It was not a pleasant predicamemt for the English envoy: isolated in the interior of the country to watch the progress of an unsuccessful siege; communicating with Whitehall by expensive special messengers, or more slowly through the English merchants in Bordeaux. Almost worse, great heat had been followed by heavy rains. Fever was decimating the armies, and he himself felt too ill to seek an audience with the King. The chances of mediation were indeed slight.

The fighting went on for two months, Doncaster stayed at Moissac and Castel Sarrasin nearby. The royal officers sent daily supplies of food and wine; but his own cook, who had come with him from England, died of fever as did a Mr. Fairfax of his company. Algernon Percy left them to travel to Italy. Louis still refused the offers of a Stuart mediator. Doncaster sent Woodford to confer with the duc de Rohan, the Protestant leader, who was at Castres another thirty miles east. But by 6 December Louis and Doncaster were both back in Bordeaux. In effect James I's ambassador belonged to the baggage of Louis XIII's army.[61]

Doncaster tried once more. He obtained a pass for Woodford and sent him this time to Royan, a Huguenot town at the mouth of the Gironde estuary: his mission was to put proposals designed to lead to a fresh negotiation. John Woodford now reached, after a long period of service, the climax of his comparatively obscure career. Six years earlier he had stayed in Paris when his chief, Edmondes, went to Loudun and addressed the Huguenots at La Rochelle. It was now his turn. From Royan he too went to La Rochelle, and on 7 January pleaded with the assembly there to send representatives to Louis at Poitiers, on the security of his own passport. They demurred, asking Doncaster to obtain a more comprehensive guarantee for their spokesmen. On 9 January Woodford again appeared before them, this time to ask for a statement of their loyalty which could be transmitted to Louis. From La Rochelle he went to Poitiers where he overtook Doncaster. Nothing came of Woodward's mission; Doncaster made no further headway. Going by the usual route of Blois and Orleans they arrived back in Paris, and the civil war continued.

These long journeys were repeated a few months later, almost stage for stage. Louis and his ministers remained unwilling to compromise, and James received Huguenot envoys in London. He sent Doncaster back to France. and by the middle of May the ambassador was again in Bordeaux, an almost helpless observer of the fighting. Thirty to forty English ships, the wine fleet, had been detained there in order to deprive the Huguenots further down the Gironde of the customs payable. The ambassador sought an interview with Louis. Redress was promised but not given and Doncaster demanded a second audience. Ministers promised one at Agen; at Agen they promised it at Toulouse, to which Doncaster returned for his second visit in less than a year. He settled the dispute over the ships, but little else.[62] His mission had failed, and through a disturbed country — in what a contemporary described as 'these broken times' — he made his way home.

In September 1622 James gave Doncaster the title of Earl of Carlisle in reward for services abroad. His journeys in France had also given John Woodford a chance to do his best and Woodford is certainly a fair example of those Englishmen on the continent, not of the highest rank in status or ability, who were indispensable in the management of affairs. Beginning as second secretary in Paris in 1611, growing in experience, he travelled France on important missions, becoming one of the small body of men who must have passed for expert in the management of Anglo-French affairs. He accompanied Carlisle to Paris in 1623 in order to present James I's explanation of Prince Charles's incognito journey through France on the way to Madrid.[63] He was in Paris again during the months of discussion on the projected marriage of Charles and Henrietta Maria, complaining bitterly of overwork at the end of 1624 in a private letter to Sir Francis Nethersole. It is noticeable, however, that Woodford never secured any substantial preferment, remaining a 'servant' in Carlisle's 'family'. There are no records for his career after 1625; it may be that he died, or was unambitious, or that his status was not sufficient high to bring him into the field for advancement. At any rate he was never directly employed by the crown. In this respect his contemporaries Becher and Lorkin surpassed him; but together they make a trio worth study.

There is of course another reason for describing the missions of James I's envoys in western France between 1615 and 1622. They show very clearly how unfavorable the conditions were for tourists, who wanted study and sightseeing in the towns of the Loire, before following a route which would take them through La Rochelle, Bordeaux, Toulouse and Montpellier on their way to the Rhône valley. So long as the Huguenots (and indeed other Frenchmen) were in arms against Louis XIII, and the English government considered itself directly implicated, the English traveller or student was at risk. In quiet times, the affinity between Protestants of the two states made easier his travel and residence in the areas where he found Protestants; he would be made welcome by Protestant innkeepers, ministers and shopkeepers. Travel in the same areas, in times of trouble, was all the more compromising. Peace in France and peace between England and France were both needed to bring the traveller back. La Rochelle fell in 1629, and Louis XIII and Charles I came to terms in 1630. The way was clear again. In the early history and development of the Grand Tour, moreover, similar political circumstances have a similar importance for the visitor to Italy. It was when the relations of the English court with the Papacy were put on a more amicable basis, also after 1630, that the conventional tour of the Italian peninisula became a reasonable proposition for the travelling Englishman. It is time to follow him over the Alps.

# II. ENGLISH TRAVELLERS IN ITALY

# 3. THE SCENE OF THEIR TRAVELS

Italy, where it will now be necessary to follow travellers such as Lord Howard, Lord Cranborne, Lord Roos, Sir Thomas Puckering, Sir John Harrington and many others, is a country which has always called men south from northern homelands for a variety of good, most solid reasons.

It is difficult to say, however, whether the Elizabethans and Jacobeans harped more constantly on the attractions or the repulsiveness with which they credited the Italian world; and for a few there was also the attraction of repulsiveness. A violent fluctuation from one extreme to another, when Italy appeared before the mind's eye, is one of the most familiar characteristics of their dramatists. More prosaic forms of literature like the essays and reports written by travellers, or 'instructions' to them, serve to show that the feeling of repugnance was accustomed to fix on certain symbols. Individual cities were associated with specific evils.[1] Florence represented a certain type of political activity judged immoral, Duke Alessandro Medici who ruined the Republic, Catherine de Medici who ruined the Kingdom of France and contrived St. Bartholomew's massacre, Machiavel who ruined Europe.[2] Venice represented the evil of licentiousness, the grave of personal virtue, home of the courtesan and homosexual. Above all Rome was England's danger. In the Elizabethan Protestant's blurred image of the Papal city, Jesuits, assassins, Machiavelli's politics, Venetian harlotry, the influence of Spanish overlords in Milan and Naples, all seemed constituent elements in a power menacing the life, liberty and salvation of your Protestant Englishman. Or, if the distinction between separate cities implied more knowledge than was usual or necessary, it could at least be said that the Italians possessed certain generic qualities, common to all or nearly all: a spirit of jealousy and revenge, a faculty for dissembling, a liking for poison. 'Magique is not more publiqlie professed at Cracovia among the Polonians', says one writer who never appears to have left England, 'than is this art of intoxations among the Italians.'[3]

The reverse, the fascination of Italy for Englishmen, was even more important. The renaissance, if mediaevalists nowadays will permit the phrase to survive, involved above all the continuing and increasing reputation of the Italians, in certain activities, in the opinion of peoples further north. 'Report of fashions from proud Italy' still seems the fairest

5.  'Madonna di Loreto': what Protestant travellers saw in Roman Italy.

definition of this phenomenon, and the report undoubtedly weighed
with the rising monarchies, aristocracies and bourgeoisies across the
Alps. In particular, it was essential to the practice of a number of
vocations. The diplomat, the courtier, the poet, the artist and the
physician needed to know something of Italy, or suffer the handicap of
ignorance. This meant that a number of them would be travellers,
in spite of difficulties and dangers. For the English monarchy not to
tolerate such a practical acquaintance with Italy, enforcing its ancient
claim to control travel, or for subjects not to insist on their need to
make this acquaintance, would have been to prepare a closed intellectual
atmosphere, as if hermetically sealed, reminiscent of despotisms in

decay. The English in the sixteenth century were far too vigorous and self-confident to accept such extreme methods of control; and it is well known that traces of their presence may be found in Italy throughout Elizabeth's reign.

Therefore, despite the mounting intensity of the political and religious conflict in Elizabeth's day, and the evils popularly associated with what was alien, distant, heretical and, in a sense, politically hostile, Englishmen still visited Italy who were not themselves exiles. Conditions had altered greatly since th period when mediaeval clerks who were the early humanists crossed the Alps. The sense of ease noticeable in the pleasant Italian journal (1549–1550) of Thomas Hoby, translator of Castiglione, had vanished;[4] but in a discreet way, avoiding the more dangerous cities, taking disguise, avoiding one's fellow-countrymen (old College friends of that generation were sometimes Catholics in exile) and exercising a prudent casuistry about religious observances, the now traditional practice was continued by courtiers, diplomats, physicians and gentlemen from England. Philip Sidney, William Harvey, Inigo Jones are only the most celebrated names.

The popular and religious prejudice against Italy, the importance of Italy for the educated man, the actual journeys there of Englishmen during Elizabeth's reign are elements in the historical background of an English traveller's activities in the following century. Mingling with these was always the undoubted risk to which English people felt themselves exposed by venturing south of the Alps. Spain, at war with England, directly controlled large territories in Italy besides exercising much influence in areas nominally independent. The Roman Church, in the full fervour of courter-reform, regarded the English state and church as heretical, and allied with the ruler of the Spanish empire on this, if not on other questions. An Englishman, therefore, had to show himself a Catholic in Milan, Rome and Naples, or go very warily. In Venice and Tuscany conditions were better but they were never easy. Fynes Moryson enlivens his long narrative with the record of an incident which throws into curious relief the figure of the Italianate Englishman before 1600, an extraordinary contrast with the peaceful travel and residence in Milan, Rome and Naples enjoyed at a later date by John Evelyn and his contemporaries. This example is worth recalling.[5] In 1594, at Voghera in the duchy of Milan an English traveller (a gentleman disguised as a poor man going on foot) reached the inn at evening, and sitting down to a meal found among the company a merchant who said that he was from Germany. On trial of his German, which was wretched, the man explained that he hailed from territory on the frontiers of France; but then, after speaking together in French, which the merchant could hardly manage, they talked again in Italian but his Italian also sounded strange, for in fact both these travellers, Fynes Moryson and the merchant, were Englishmen in disguise. Nor were they alone in their anonymity, with false names and documents. As the century ended, conditions improved. The peace treaties of 1598 and 1604 relaxed the tension all over Europe, except in the Low Countries. A long letter from Sir Henry Wotton ambassador in Venice to Sir Robert Cecil in August 1605 attempts to analyse the changing position in Italy.[6] His own presence there, despatched as James I's official representative to the republic, was itself a sign of the times. Wotton stated that the period when a Protestant's life in Rome depended on a successful disuise or the personal goodwill of Cardinal Allen had gone by. Papal policy was greatly altered since the days of Sixtus V: under Clement VIII 'began not only permission and connivancy, but invitation and allurement of all nations promiscuously'. It appeared probable that this persuasive seemingly-benevolent attitude (in Wotton's opinion so much more dangerous than outright antagonism) was likely to continue. Where Rome led, the rest of the Papal States, and Milan and Naples, would follow. Of course, there were also exceptions to the general tendency, just as at an earlier date during the most dangerous years there had been Englishmen peacefully resident in various cities, but on the whole the times grew milder.

In fact, it is the transition from the uncertain state of affairs depicted by Fynes Moryson, and in the early letters of Henry Wotton, to an era when all Italy, Venetian, Tuscan, Spanish and Papal, was perfectly accessible to the Protestant Englishman, enabling him to make a comprehensive tour of the peninsula, becoming a convention of remarkable fixity — the giro d'Italia — which forms one of the principal topics of the following pages. Associated with it is another, the influence of this experience of Italy upon the traveller, an influence which affected his general education and outlook and in certain cases affected his future career, particularly in politics. The young traveller's Italian journey, his intellectual acquirements, and his career will be our concern. But first, a bird's-eye view of the country and scattered groups of Englishmen to be found there early in the seventeenth century will set the scene. What was this landscape, so fabulous for old men who never travelled, sitting by the fireside with only Stow or Speed in their hands?

Italy is entered either over the passes or though the ports and harbours. The gentry travelled overland, only coming down to the Italian coast cities at their journey's end where they encountered English sailors then in port, and the resident English merchants' factors; at Venice they found·an English ambassador and his staff and after 1615 there was also an official envoy from James I at Turin. They came through Germany and over the Brenner to Venetia, or through France and over Mont Cenis to Piedmont. Occasionally there was news of a traveller passing through Basle, Lucerne and over St. Gotthard to Lugano and Milan, judged a perilous passage where snow waters thundered like the sea, and mules were buried in the snow and the number of fir trees seemed an infinite wilderness;[7] Lord Arundel and Inigo Jones came this way on their famous journey to Italy in 1613, but it was not a popular itinerary. Most commonly France or the cities of central Germany were visited first, and it was simplest to travel due south from Augsburg or south-east from Lyon. Nicholas Ferrar, who like Arundel had left England as one of Princess Elizabeth's company going to Heidelberg after her marriage, spent the summer of 1613 at Leipzig, where he studied the manufacturing activities of that city, and from there continued on to Venice which he reached in November. Sir Edward Herbert twelve months later, after leaving Heidelberg, presumably followed the same route.[8] Lords Howard and Cranborne, on the other hand, Sir Thomas Puckering and Sir John Harrington, travelled through France to Piedmont and Tuscany. We can trace them as far south as Lyon, and their names reappear in the records at Turin or Florence. If they entered Italy by one road they often left by another. Ferrar and Puckering made their way to Spain, Herbert came home through Turin and Lyon, Lord Howard through Lorraine.[9]

The sailors and merchants whom they met at Venice, Florence and Leghorn belonged, of course, to a different level of English society; the merchants handled the bills of exchange which made their journeys possible and the sailors took home the heavy baggage which contained their purchases in Italy. At Venice the most important English merchant at this period was Henry Parvis who described himself as an honest man who had prospered. He lodged young Englishmen in his house who learnt the technique of commerce, and were sent every Sunday to hear the Anglican service in the ambassador's chapel to keep their Protestant faith intact.[10] He transmitted money, stored and shipped goods for travellers, and was in close touch with the ambassador. At Florence when a special envoy from James I arrived for his first audience with the Grand Duke Ferdinand in 1606 he enlarged his company with a number of resident English merchants, Messrs. Aldrich, Tracy, Stock and others.[11] There were more of them at Pisa and Leghorn, where they were perhaps not always distinguishable from the English pirates or renegades whom the Duke had invited to enter his service. Further south, by 1620, a flourishing community of English commercial men also existed in Naples where the factors, wrote James Howell in his exuberant fashion, 'live in better Equipage and in a more splendid manner than in all Italy besides, than their Masters and Principals in London, they ruffle in Silks and Satins and wear good Spanish Leather-Shoes while their Masters' shoes upon our Exchange in London shine with Blacking'.[12] This is confirmed by more prosaic accounts. Fewer English gentry appeared in the south, less accessible than the north, but when they arrived they were by no means solitary in a strange land.

Another class of Englishman in Italy, whom the casual traveller rarely met, were the slaves, usually unfortunates who had been captured at sea, or deserters, or wandering men who failed to pay debts; but there they were, toiling in the harbour works at Leghorn or in the Arsenal at Venice, 'my old profession', said one of them, 'carrying of durt and stone and such like in a basket'.[13]

Much more important for the traveller were the resident English, Scots and Irish Catholics. Their headquarters were naturally Rome but they were to be found in almost every sizeable city, making it their business to become acquainted with itinerant Englishmen out of affection or policy or a desire to earn 'refreshment' for services rendered. The statesmen in London eagerly gathered in any intelligence of such people, and sometimes the information can be checked. It was reported, for instance, that 'at Vicenza there is Doctor Thornton who makes fair weather with his countrymen but I have often been told that he is a close and dangerous spy for the Jesuits and Spaniards...at Bologna, one Thornell and an English friar'. Now an English traveller, Aurelian Townshend the poet, also wrote to Cecil saying that he had actually met at Bologna 'Dottore Thornil Inglese Cannonico di Vincenza' and they travelled together to Florence, lodged together and then went on to Vicenza, the canon explaining that he much wished to come to England, given an assurance of the Secretary's protection. Later on he did appear in England as a Catholic emissary, residing at the Venetian ambassador's house in London.[14] Thus, two dangerous Catholics alleged to be active in northern Italy appear to have been one and the same man, but he at least behaved in the manner suspected of him. There were other such priests and friars at Venice, Padua, Florence, Siena, Ancona, Genoa. When that intractable Protestant William Lithgow arrived in Padua in 1609, and stayed three months to learn the language, he was cheered by the friendship and aided by the tuition of a fellow Scot, John Wedderburn a mathematician; Wedderburn had been a pupil at the Scots College of the Jesuits in Rome.[15] A little earlier a humble English traveller, Tom Coryat, was kindly welcomed at Padua by an old and very senior member of the university, Willoughby, whom the ambassador in Venice described as 'an infectious Papist, of a still and dangerous temper'.[16] When an Englishman died at Leghorn in 1607–1608 a certain Father Sherwood refused to bury him; Sir Henry Wotton likewise reports Sherwood as a priest sent recently to that port 'to practise and corrupt there the servants of his Majesty, to mislead them from their natural obedience under that worn and vulgar pretence of zeal and religion'.[17]

Associated with the churchmen were lay Catholics, usually exiles or converts. The most important of these, in the first decade of the century, was that erring son of an Archbishop of York, Toby Mathew. He took orders in 1614 but before that date appears as a gentleman living on the income derived from estates still held to his use in England and from funds which he had transmitted to the Monte di Pietà in Rome,[18] coming eagerly forward to greet anyone of good family who arrived in

Italy. Between 1606 and 1608 he visited Rome and Naples but lived mainly in Tuscany. He was converted, returned home and spent some time in prison. Coming back to Florence he was soon the principal member of what Wotton called 'a certain knot of bastard Catholics... who with pleasantness of conversation and with force of example do much harm...in that intercepting place among a great confluence of English'. Lord St. John and Lord Roos, for example, reached Florence in 1608 and an English agent commented: 'Mr. Tobey Mathew is also here, the same he was in England, visiteth often the Lords in companie of Mr. Antony Tracy, and specially the Lord St. John'. When Lomax, St. John's tutor, lay dying of fever he was attended by Toby Mathew, Antony Tracy and others of their flock. When Lord Wentworth and his brother-in-law Crofts came to the city they 'were lodged in Lord Roos's house by Mr. Mathew and Mr. Tracy'. Another of these cronies was George Gage, for long Mathew's almost inseparable companion. These two showed Lord Arundel the sights of Rome, and Sir Robert Chamberlain the islands in the bay of Naples. When in 1614 the English ambassador spoke of his countrymen swarming at Padua, among them was Mathew recently arrived with Gage from Florence and Rome. He was, of course, not simply a companionable man; an Italian translation of his friend Francis Bacon's Essays, *Saggi Morali del Signor Fr. Bacono*, first appearing in 1618, contained a dedication by Mathew and he wrote the preface to a new edition of Augustine's Confessions in English.[19]

Compatriots abroad tend to exert an influence out of proportion to their numbers. They are friends and interpreters, sometimes willing to help when difficulties occur. But round the traveller stretched the unfamiliar landscape; strange institutions and unexpected vistas and the babble of foreign speech crowded upon him. There were a host of things, uncommon in England and common in Italy, tablecloths and forks, fans, umbrellas, flyflaps. Little by little they come also to our notice, but here a few impressions will suffice. Descending into the plain of Lombardy, said Coryat, one came to goodly rivers, pleasant meadows, fruitful vineyards, fat pastures, delectable gardens, orchards, woods and what not. One came, said Lord Arundel, from the cold of the Alps to Milan's intolerable heat. One came to many champion and historic cities.[20]

Perhaps supreme among them was Venice, compared by an Elizabethan writer to the jewel-like background of a Flemish picture.[21] The traveller wandered dutifully round the sights, the Piazza, the Rialto, the ghetto, across to the monastery of San Giorgio, up and down the canals; that stately landmark for future generations, the cupola of S. Maria della Salute, was not yet built. A few miles south from the city lay its port Malamocco, 'haven of the great Venetian shippes' as an itinerant Scot remarked, where voyagers by sea were compelled to wait on board a month in quarantine if they came from areas suspected of plague, just as overland travellers waited on the Alpine frontier, like Nicholas Ferrar in 1613, or near Brescia, like the ambassador Sir Dudley Carleton in 1611. Not only ships and cargoes came to Malamocco: sometimes an English gentleman died at Padua or elsewhere on the mainland, and for fear of scandal in using Catholic graveyards his body was brought to the harbour and buried at sea, the English ambassador coming with his household from Venice to help perform the funeral honours. So fared a Yorkshire gentleman, Sir Edward Rossiter in one year; so also a kinsman of the Cecils, Edward Cave, in another.[22]

A few miles across the Lagoons was Murano where the glassworks inevitably attracted purchasers, both tourists and businessmen. Sir Robert Mansell the holder of the English glass monopoly was keenly interested in this pre-eminent rival establishment, and sent an agent (who combined with his employment a good deal of gentlemanly dilettantism) to invite to England Venetian glass blowers.[23] Others frankly preferred the excellent oysters of Murano to its excellent manufacture.

By water, too, men travelled inland up the Brenta to Padua which attracted the gentleman and the scholar as Murano attracted the gentleman and the merchant. The intelligent Erastianism of the Venetians had restricted clerical and Papal influence at this university, to which they had entrusted a monopoly of higher education in the state, fitting it admirably for the reception of foreigners.[24] Perhaps that admiration which the English in the seventeenth century professed for the Venetian oligarchs arose not only from respect for a republican, conservative constitution but also from the fact that the education of the Venetian nobility was compulsory in a place much visited by English travellers. Both learnt from the same teachers. In Padua the English often settled for long periods. The gentry went to fencing masters and dancing schools and when they left, left behind arms and emblems for later generations to identify. Our young physicians appeared in the Anatomy Theatre which had then been recently inaugurated and they studied in the Physic Garden. Other English arms and emblems are still to be seen on the walls of the great university building, the Bò, of which the noble classical façade dates from 1601 — a notable contrast to the Oxford Divinity School where some of the travellers had been previously. In the long arcaded streets it must frequently have happened that one Englishman met another last encountered a few years previously in England. They forgathered in the villas rented by English ambassadors or in their own lodgings. Some came to learn physic, others to consult the physicians and drink the medicinal waters of Abano nearby. There were rich and poor, idle students and conscientious noblemen.

The second great centre for Englishmen was Tuscany. In Florence, there were no schools of law or medicine to tempt the more professional student. The court, though elegant, was considered small and without any marked influence on the diplomatic struggles of the time. Yet the fame and loveliness of the city itself attracted many who desired knowledge or experience which was not exclusively academic or political. 'The beauty and security of the place, and purity of the language' is how Sir Henry Wotton defines the fascination of Florence. In a period of exile, after his patron Essex's death, he succeeded in obtaining permission to read in the Laurentian Library; and he likewise mentions Alan Percy, brother to the earl of Northumberland, who rented a house in Florence in order to take riding lessons from the renowned Rustico Piccardini. 'I live in Florence', wrote Mathew in August 1608, 'in an excellent coole terrene, eate good melons, drinke wholesome wines, looke upon excellent devout pictures, heer choyse musique.' There was the Medici treasury to visit, and the great new chapel the Dukes were building to house their tombs — two of the sights of Florence which in that period monopolized attention to a curious degree. There were pleasant excursions to Pistoia, especially on Lady Day when the Girdle of our Lady was displayed, and the crowds came in from the surrounding countryside, 'whereof we judged one half to have hats\ of straw', wrote one Englishman, 'and one fourth part to be barelegged', confirming his general opinion that the Italian countryside was impoverished by contrast with the splendid cities and suburbs. The same writer, Dallington, also climbed up the steep hills behind Prato and observed how the landscape resembled a chequerboard because the holdings were so small, none above an acre and a half. Or they rode down the valley of the Arno along roads shaded with mulberries to Pisa and Leghorn, or south across the hills to Siena where the noble piazza deserved and obtained a traveller's admiration, and perhaps more important, where good Italian was spoken and good teachers of Italian could be found.[25]

South and east again lay the Papal States, and here it became more difficult. Englishmen who continued on their way were now moving out of territories where it was safe to reside into territory where it seemed safest to keep moving circumspectly. At Bologna and Ferrara and Ancona authority sometimes arrested and detained the traveller. In Rome itself caution was even more necessary, though the evidence about conditions there during James I's reign is conflicting and not always easy to interpret. English Catholic pilgrims, it need hardly be said, had no difficulties. They could find hospitality at the English College, timing their visit for Holy Week and touring the holy places before returning quietly northward; there still survives one anonymous MS. diary of such a pilgrimage, performed in 1622, which derives of right from the most ancient traditions of mediaeval England. Protestants felt rather differently. They tend to betray a distinct nervousness. 'Having stayed four dayes (as long as I durst)', wrote George Sandys in 1612, 'secured by the faith and care of Master Nicolas Fitzherbert who accompanied me in the surveying of all the antiquities and glories of that

Citie, I departed to Siena.' Two or three years later Nicholas Ferrar, whose desire to see Rome was about equalled by his fear of the English Jesuits, travelled there privately on foot. He arrived in Easter week, changed his lodgings every night, and remained ten days. 'What was to be seen in those ten daye he stayed there', wrote his brother, 'he omitted not'. At one extreme of the social scale Lithgow found Rome a very unsafe spot for a man of his robustious temperament. At the other the earl of Oxford, though on friendly terms with the English College, also left the city with all promptness because it was 'unfruitful and unsafe'. John Mole, Lord Roos's Protestant tutor, in 1608 was arrested in Rome where he spent the remainder of his life in prison, a respectable martyr in the thought of many English contemporaries. Other travellers tell a rather different story. Sir Edward Herbert, late in 1614, went straight to the English College, declaring to them that he was a peaceable Protestant who only desired to see the antiquities: they expressed surprise at his boldness, saying that such frankness was without precedent, but invited him to dine. This he politely refused, and then spent about a month quietly visiting the sights of Rome. An essayist and traveller of the same period discusses the whole subject very judiciously, and concludes that while known persecutors or controversialists, and their relatives, should conceal themselves and refrain from speaking English in Rome:

> for others, and especially men of Quality, their coming hither may be with as much freedom as to any other part of Italy. I myselfe have, and have met with divers others that do finde it so, and therefore I beleeve it, whatsoever other men say to the contrary, to grace or make wonderful their own travels.

It was of course wise, he continued, not to visit Roman churches during Mass or Vespers if you wished to avoid the practice of their superstitions. It was wise to observe their fasts and not to go at Easter time.[26]

This view of the question is confirmed by reports from the English ambassadors in Venice. The ideal and reputable plan of action for a traveller, after a period of residence at Padua or Florence, was to undertake a journey, 'aboute all the Principal Townes and Courts of Italie without the Pope's Estate'[27] but this course was by no means always adopted. In the years 1611 and 1612, for example, Sir Dudley Carleton brings up the subject on a number of occasions.

> I hold it my dutie to advertize your lordship, [he wrote to Salisbury] of great libertie taken both by English and Scottish gentlemen who travayle into these parts in going to Rome and there practising in the English colledge, and shewing themselfs publikely in the Courts of the Cardinals. In so much as one Hore, a fellow of Exeter colledge in Oxford and Tutor to two of Sir Robert Dormer's sonnes taking this towne in theyr way homeward (as they are now gon through France) spared not to tell me he had bin with his yong gentlemen to see Cardinal Bellarmin, and were courteously receaved by him.

The ingenuitie of which confession shewes it was done withowt malice to satisfie curiositie.[28]

Carleton says of his own nephew:

He hath taken the comon course (and too comon I must confess for the ill fruits that proceede of it) of seeing Rome in his way to Naples and had there his part of the current of the times (which may seeme not casual but uppon counsaile) and that is to be too well used...yf meanes might be fownd of restraining travellers repaire thether by some more express clause in thayr license, or such other course as may seeme best to his Majestie's wisdome, it was never more needfull then at this present.[29]

Sometimes the case was more serious. The ambassador a few months later reported to Sir John Harrington the suspicious behaviour of one of that nobleman's dependants:

You have a servant which hath spent some time in this city, and is now gone to see more of Italy, touching whom I receaved this advertisement. *Mr. Dearing is at Rome, lodged neere if not in the English Colledge.* I feare he will remaine with them, whether for want of meanes or aboundance of devotion it is uncertaine. That one of these should be no hinderance to his delivery from those temptations, I have taken order underhand to have him supplyed with sufficient allowance to bring him to Florence where I understand your ordinary provision remaynes for him, which if he accept not I shall then suspect the other cause of his abode in that place, and then I suppose you will be at no more cost with him.[30]

It seems true, therefore, that the number of travellers finding their way to Rome was very considerable. Curiosity, the love of a little danger, the prestige derived from classical antiquity for men whose education was coloured through and through by its literature, all conspired to attract them. It was best not to stay too long, awakening the interest of proselytizers or suspicion in London, but a short visit was surely desirable, and if desirable legitimate; and if not permitted, even so worth attempting.

Indeed, a multitude of wonders or beauties or other memorable things awaited the traveller if he came to Rome. An intelligent observer argued that he profited from contemplating them, and the city of Pope Paul V could not but encourage the didactic and sententious strain in a Jacobean Englishman's way of thought. The statuary of Rome, he says, immortalizes the fame of emperors and good men who therefore make the deeper impression upon us. The barren campagna outside prompts to a more vivid remembrance the old truth that ease and 'delicacy of life' are the bane of noble actions. The antique remains illustrate the text of histories. The miracles associated with Rome's great churches, the seven holy places of the pilgrim, lead to a deeper understanding of religion. By them the Protestant is confirmed in disgust, the Catholic and Catholic sympathizers feel their power, while in opposition to both the more daringly philosophic may assert that a common element is the essence of opposing creeds. How revealing it is that for some men the notion of supernatural power depends so simply on the testimony of miracles, that images associated with miracles strike deeper into men's souls than the word of Scripture, that recent Jesuit architecture seems to express an idea that religion is 'a ravishing of men's understanding by sweet music, glorious Altars and the like'! The traveller should also consider the new secular buildings in Rome, the palaces and villas, and the joy and pleasure of great gardens around them, Borghese, Belvedere, Montalta, seeing in them spectacular proof that recreation, properly understood, is an exercise of the intellect's best qualities. In fact, the mind can rise to the level demanded by a great subject when the eye beholds the centre and pivot of the world's history. Such were the loftiest arguments. The ordinary traveller was probably content with a less philosophic or rhetorical enthusiasm, satisfying an ordinary sense of curiosity.[31]

From Rome the adventurous usually proceeded to Naples, which after the signature of the Anglo-Spanish treaty of 1604, was open to Englishmen; a very ancient itinerary involving acquaintance with 'vile hosterias, one mattress, one blanket, no bolster nor anything else'. Here again the ground was strewn thickly with antiquities, diversified by the marvels of nature, in every sense a fabulous landscape: Vesuvius; Virgil's tomb, the Sybil's Cave, Cicero's villa; the Lake of Agnano, the Lake of Lucrinus, the Lake of Avernus. The catalogue seemed unending, and Inigo Jones was one who carefully examined the classical remains during his visit with Lord Arundel in 1614.[32] For the nobleman Naples had an added attraction as the centre of a highly aristocratic society, presided over by the Spanish Viceroy. It was 'the only Regal city of Italy', and so Lord Roos hesitated to leave it because 'he loves no place where are no Dons to visit and be visited'.[33] Others must have come for pleasure and stayed to admire the intrinsic beauty of the scene. Lord Howard de Walden, Sir Thomas Puckering, Sir Richard Musgrave (who died there), Lord Bothwell, Sir George Goring and Sir William Cavendish, are all mentioned as residing for a time in Naples.

Occasionally, they went even further. The Bodleian Library possesses some 'Instructions for a traveller, Mr Curzon, going to Malta', dated 1618. Sir Robert Chamberlain, who was in Naples, took a sympathetic interest in his compatriot Sir Francis Verney, the pirate detained by the Spaniards in the Sicilian galleys, and in 1614 went to Malta to reclaim him. Usually travellers as far south as this were of a humbler kind. At least one English Catholic pilgrim from London visited our Lady of Trapani in Sicily. Lithgow walked all the way from Florence through Calabria and crossed to Messina. He climbed Etna which inspired him to compose a shockingly inferior sonnet near its summit, and he met there by chance a Scotsman on his way from Palermo to Venice. Another time he encountered a little party of English and Scots travellers at

Messina. But on the whole this was unknown territory for the leisured traveller unless, like George Sandys, he returned that way from the Levant. Men came to Naples according to a common practice, but having come so far and rested for a month or two, it was time to turn back.[34]

Such was the Italy known to Englishmen in the early seventeenth century, with its possibilities both of enjoyment and danger. But to convey also the sense of movement from one place to another, two or three of these travellers can be followed in the course of their Italian journeys, which will give an idea of a single traveller's general experience.

In the autumn of 1608 Sir John Harrington, the son of Lord Harrington, a young nobleman of sixteen, and a friend of Prince Henry, appeared in Florence with a great company of attendants. He passed on to Siena and there was talk of his visiting Rome, but he refrained from the temptation and, finding his way through the independent principality of Urbino, reached Venice towards the end of the year. By this itinerary he avoided Bologna on the usual route from Florence to Venice where — as Lord Wentworth discovered in the following summer — the Inquisition was liable to detain a nobleman's tutor and send him to Rome. Harrington had an excellent Protestant tutor of his own, Mr. Tovey, carefully chosen by that excellent Protestant Sir Adam Newton, governor to the Prince of Wales, and it would have been embarrassing to lose him. At Venice, the young man took a house at S. Polo, since the English ambassador could not entertain so large a company. In due course there followed the ceremonious introduction to Doge and Senate of an Englishman enjoying such important political connections, Sir Henry Wotton taking the opportunity to describe him as learned, handsome and virtuous. Certainly, Harrington wrote formal letters of courtesy home, both in Italian and Latin and embellished with suitable quotations, while the tutor reported of him:

> his mind was never more bent upon all honorable and virtuous studys, hee cheefly applyeth latin and greek early and late, as at home; the Italian which as they say hee parleth and understandeth indifferently well, hee hath gotten by the way. My Lord Embassador heer seemeth much to joy in him, they have both on Master for Architecture and fortification, they seldom are asunder. Hee is careful of his daybooke to make an account to his highnes of his travel.[35]

With the study of fortification was connected a few days' journey north to Friuli in order to view examples of modern military engineering in the new Venetian citadel at Palma. In this, and other ways, Sir John Harrington passed the cooler months of the year in Venice, but with the heat of summer coming on, he took his departure over the Alps to Prague, before turning home. In 1614 he died.[36]

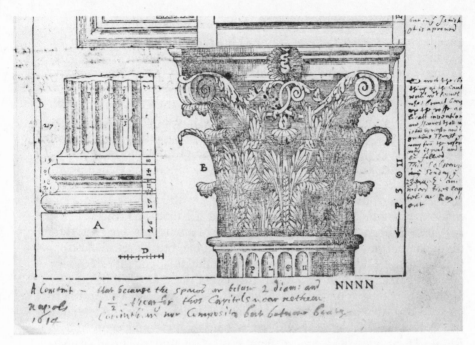

6. Inspecting the ancient ruins, 1614: Inigo Jones commenting on the temple of Castor and Pollux at Naples in his copy of Palladio's *Architecture*. At the edge of the page he wrote, 'This I obsearved Sonday ye 23 March and indeed thes capitels are Exelent'.

7. Inspecting the modern villa and modern garden: in Rome the Papal nephew Cardinal Scipio Borghese was building his villa and assembling its wonderful contents from 1606 onwards.

Lord Cranborne's journey to Italy conformed to the same pattern though he was evidently less educated and by no means a happy young man. Leaving England in the autumn of 1610 with the same advisers who had accompanied him in his earlier tour of France, Sir Henry Howard as friend and equal, Mathew Lister and John Finett as governors, and with his father's strict instruction not to enter Papal territory, he reached Venice in November. The only recorded incident of the long journey, on Venetian testimony, was the arrest of one of his company at Milan where the Viceroy appeared to treat Lord Salisbury's son and heir with studied, and therefore offensive, neglect. In Venice he enjoyed a reception and entertainment easily equal to Harrington's, welcomed by the Doge and lodged in Wotton's house. But Lord Cranborne was not easy to educate, or even to amuse; and Henry Howard fell ill. They moved to Padua and, as Howard recovered, Cranborne fell ill; the physicians diagnosed fever mingled with homesickness. A large number of letters were despatched to and from Padua, Venice and London regarding the patient's illness and ultimate recovery. He resolutely turned down proposals that he should complete his travels, at least visiting Florence; and in February 1611 set out for England.[37]

Sir Thomas Puckering, Thomas Lorkin's pupil, ventured further afield. The patron and his tutor came together as far as Florence at the beginning of November 1612, and Lorkin then returned to England. During the winter Puckering travelled down to Naples where he corresponded intermittently with Carleton, now ambassador at Venice, through whom his money was transmitted to wherever he happened to be residing in Italy. He intended, like everyone else, to visit Venice for himself, but the increasing risk of war in northern Italy made it difficult to plan his journey. A proposal to travel by sea to Genoa, and then across to Milan, was turned down — with Carleton's approval. Ultimately he reached Venice early in July 1613, and spent some time there and in Padua, presumably in an unexciting, conventional and pleasant way, for Puckering was never exciting. One little relic, an odd page of notes which he kept, has the merit of illustrating for us more fully than in the case of Sir John Harrington's meagre surviving letters what was meant by the short tour, which both men took to Palma. (The same had been planned for Cranborne.) It was an easy journey: northwards from Venice to Treviso, and over a number of small rivers, to this site where the technicians had been remodelling the defences for a number of years. Travellers were expected to study and admire the fortifications, deemed a pattern of improved and scientific engineering. From his own words it is possible to see what was in Puckering's mind: these were defences, he wrote,

Very exquisite, consisting of 9 obtuse bulwarks every one whereof hath two cavaliers and two faire sortitas into the ditch, which is drie, and the parepet is 6 braces thick. To every port there shall bee three gates, two whereof, at

# LE FORTIFICATIONI
## DI BVONAIVTO LORINI.
### NOBILE FIORENTINO.
### NVOVAMENTE RISTAMPATE,
Corrette & Ampliate di tutto quello che mancaua
per la lor compita perfettione,

#### CON L'AGGIVNTA DEL SESTO LIBRO.

*Doue si mostra, con la Scienza, e con la Pratica, l'ordine di Fortificare le Città, & altri luoghi, con tutti gli auuertimenti, che più possono apportar beneficio, per la sicurtà delle Fortezze,*

#### CIOE,

*Nel Primo Libro.* Si tratta della Scienza d'intorno alle regole da formare le Piante delle Fortezze, con le sue misure.

*Nel Secondo.* Si mostra la Pratica con la quale si debbe fabricare la Fortezza in opera Reale.

*Nel Terzo.* Si descriuono le diuersità delle Piante, con l'elettione delle miglior difese.

*Nel Quarto.* Si dichiara la diuersità de siti, & come si debbono Fortificare.

*Nel Quinto.* Si tratta delle Scienze Mecaniche, & l'ordine facilissimo del Fabricare tutti gli strumenti & machine artificiose che possono fare dibisogno, si in tempo di pace come di guerra, e come si possano con poca forza dominare grandissimi pesi.

*Nel Sesto, & vltimo.* Si tratta della difesa delle Fortezze, & si mostrano tutti quegli auuertimenti, & inuentioni, con le quali i difensori si possono difendere, con quel maggior vantaggio, che si può desiderare, per la sicurtà della Fortezza; & oltre a ciò si mostra l'ordine del misurare le distanze & leuare le Piante, con altri particolari necessari per effettuare quanto s'è proposto.

### CON PRIVILEGI.

### IN VENETIA.      M DC IX.
#### Presso Francesco Rampazetto.

8.   Palmanova: while English noblemen made an excursion to see these fortifications, Inigo Jones found (possibly in Venice) a splendid volume written by the engineer who designed them.

least, of iron to resist the force of the petards, and loopholes betweene the gates for the souldiurs within to shoote muskets and archibuses, and to throwe artificiall fire scalding water et. ca. upon them that would force the gates.[38]

Part of the journey back could be made by gondola through the Lagoons, and Venice was reached once again after an instructive tour of five days. Carleton had himself intended to accompany Puckering, only to be prevented at the last moment by the sudden arrival of Lord Arundel and Lady Arundel in Venice, greater figures in the eyes of the world than Puckering. In the following autumn, however, he did visit Palma with a number of other Englishmen, among them Lord Cromwell and Sir William Cavendish, who were pleased by the sight of this citadel and the courtesy of its governor.[39] It was thus one of the conventional excursions from Venice.

Sir Thomas Puckering next appears to our view in Spain. For a long time Carleton had no idea where he was to be found; meanwhile most of his purchases in Italy, except a few looking-glasses, were put aboard ship and sent to England. In the scope and scale of his travels he resembled Lord Roos who likewise visited both the north and the south, Venice, Florence and Naples, before setting out for the even less accessible territories of the other peninsula. Sir Robert Chamberlain did the same.

It is important to remember that these young men rarely travelled alone. Tutors or governors were indispensable in Italy as in France, and since they were older and often more intelligent than their patrons, learnt more. Travelled men of middle rank, good 'servants' abroad for great lords or gentry of little experience, they profited most from the journeys of noblemen. Lord Roos's governor Mr. Mole, imprisoned by the Inquisition, Lord Wentworth's Mr. Lichfield who was converted to Catholicism, Sir John Harrington's Mr. Tovey, Lord Cranborne's Dr. Lister and John Finet, Lord Cromwell's Nathaniel Brent, Sir Robert Dormer's Francis Hore, M.A., belong to an important class, because they were intelligentsia. Sometimes they must have had a distinct influence over their social superiors. However, if the records of this period say little enough about the patrons, they say even less about their servants and it is hardly possible to give a connected biographical account of any one of these individuals on his travels in Italy. Indisputably Thomas Hobbes, tutor and secretary of Sir William Cavendish, was the greatest of these men.[40] But a clearer account comes from some letters to and from Thomas Coke, a servant of Lord Arundel and his son Maltravers.

Hobbes accompanied Cavendish on a journey through France and Italy which began in 1614.[41] By September Cavendish was in Venice and, as the English ambassador reported, making 'good use of his travels'. In the course of the following month he and Sir Richard Musgrave and Henry Parvis (the merchant) were said to have gone recently to Naples by way of Rome. Moreover during his stay in Italy Cavendish translated Lord Bacon's Essays into Italian and composed discourses of his own. Hobbes is never mentioned by name, but it seems plain that he too was in Venice, Rome and Naples.[42] Beyond that, we know that he collaborated to some degree in Cavendish's literary ventures, and can surmise that the direct experience of Italian forms of government, the relations of church and state in a novel setting, and the philosophical interests of the intelligentsia in Venice and Padua, must have engaged the attention of so acute and gifted a person. However, his own autobiographical fragment refers merely to the French and Italian tongues which he learnt 'mediocriter' during this first journey abroad.

In the second case, the career of Thomas Coke began with a fellowship at St. John's College, Cambridge, and he entered the service of Arundel's father-in-law, the Earl of Shrewsbury.[43] In September 1608 a correspondent reported that Coke was resolved to travel, and secured 'dismission from his Lordship'. In the following autumn he wrote enthusiastically from Florence, praising the Medici treasures he had seen and the artful relationship of buildings to garden at the famous Medici estate of Pratolino. Later he was in Padua, and re-appeared there during Arundel's visit to Italy in 1612, when the noble lord came to drink the waters and consult physicians. He accompanied Arundel on his memorable second journey of 1613–1614, one of the large company of followers who in due course scattered to a number of different cities, Siena, Lucca, Pisa, Rome. Arundel meanwhile pursued his bent, transforming his mission as ambassador extraordinary to Venice into an educational tour which made him a connoisseur, not just a collector of precious objects, of ancient and modern works of art. Coke was one of the few, like Inigo Jones, who followed him as far as Naples. Whether he also accompanied Jones when Jones examined Roman remains is not recorded, but a later letter gives his notion of Palladio's work after a visit to Vicenza.[44] Then Coke returned to England; only a year later it was anticipated that he would soon be conducting Arundel's elder sons to Padua. As things turned out, Lord Maltravers and his brother did not enter Venetian territory until October 1619, and at or near Padua Coke spent the remainder of his life supervising the young men's education; he found them tutors, he was their secretary and man of business, and reported back to Arundel House. Lady Arundel also reached Venice, surrounding herself with the pleasures of life in the Palazzo Mocenigo and a villa on the mainland. In 1623, in difficult times, she and her sons begin to take their way homeward; but by then Coke himself was dead.[45] His brother John, the Secretary of State, is better known but the career of Thomas has its own interest. In the mixed Italian and English of his letters he writes as if he took a real pleasure in his experiences abroad.

Some travellers, like Coke, never returned. There wss always a chance of death by violence, and the possibility of death by disease or illness. If the rate of mortality was high at home, the risks incident to travel soared proportionately, and no man could be sure of crossing the English Channel a second time. Sir Julius Caesar, Chancellor of the Exchequer, sent his eldest surviving son to study in Padua, and in Padua this wild young man quarrelled with a fencer's usher, whom he tried to waylay in the streets, and was himself slain.[46] William Slingsby, the elder brother of Sir Henry Slingsby who won fame in the Civil Wars, had gone out to Florence in 1612; surviving accounts of the family expenses show with what care his journey was planned, bills of exchange and the right clothes purchased, horses reshod and a licence to travel obtained through the usual channels. But in Florence he was slain by another Englishman, and their seconds Sir Edward Peto and a Captain Hill were imprisoned by the authorities.[47] This aspect of experience in Italy, the hostility of one's own countrymen, is illustrated in diplomatic reports. On 19 July 1611 Carleton was writing to Lord Salisbury:

> There was lately an unfortunate meeting at a supper by fower English at Florence, Sir John Hambden, Skidmore, Cartwright and an old traveler Henry Lock, amongst whom Cartwright upon a *querrelle d'Alaman* was slayne at the boord, for which Skidmore (I heare) as the principal actor is to suffer death: Sir John Hambden uppon suspition of assisting (having had a former quarrel with Cartwright) to remaine two yeares in the gallies. Lock fell sick in prison and getting leave to retire to his lodging there died the next day. One Palmer a priest (who was with him) gives owt he died a Papist, which were a sodaine change in an old man. . . .[48]

There was no need to go to prison to fall ill. Fever and sickness were always about, as Lord Cranborne and Nicholas Ferrar had discovered. 'The Lord St. John here lieth still sick of the smallpox and the town is full of that, and the measles, and such like popular diseases', runs a report from Venice in 1608.

Under such conditions it was important to respect the Italian climate. Then, as now, many felt able to disregard the ordinary advice on this point, but by May travellers tended to come northwards. When Venice, 'the most temperate for the summer season' became intolerable, they either left the country or adopted certain other expedients, taking what shelter they could find: in villas near Padua, occasionally appearing on the shore of Lake Garda, or at the worst, 'wallowing in a gondola in this sultry air'. They did not go into the mountains. However, although the climate was a factor encouraging a seasonal movement from one part of Italy to another, there is practically no sign during James I's reign — and this is a point of the greatest importance in seeking to establish the early history of the Grand Tour — that travellers were then following a conventional itinerary according to a more or less conventional timetable, these two things being the essence of the later tours. The Elizabethan practice, going to reside in Tuscany or Venetia and occasionally venturing on a journey south, often in disguise, still held the field. There was now more security everywhere, but the outlines of the later tour are hardly discernible. To see them clearly, it will be necessary to return to Italy after 1630.

Before leaving the earlier period, however, we are bound to recur to our other question, What influence the experience of Italy had upon Englishmen who travelled there at that time? Lord Howard, Lord Cranborne, Sir Thomas Puckering, Sir William Cavendish and their companions trailed across the plain of Lombardy and elsewhere over the hills, and if they survived, returned to their country houses in England

and their seats in Parliament. They certainly regarded the journey as
important, it became a traditional practice in their descendants, but they
themselves put little on record and their early experiences tend to be
forgotten in the press of more urgent historical problems. The foregoing
hints have sketched the scene of their travels, and their movements
across the scene, and those of contemporaries. Is it possible that if they
have left behind them insufficient to answer our question, some of these
contemporaries are more helpful?

# 4. THE EMBASSIES AT VENICE AND TURIN: THEIR INFLUENCE IN ENGLISH SOCIETY AND POLITICS

Since the repudiation of Papal supremacy by Henry VIII and his Parliament the direct political influence of Italy and Italians upon English affairs has never been of dominant importance; at the same time the general influence of Italy upon Englishmen of the ruling and intellectual classes has been very great indeed. Anglo-Italian relations in the seventeenth century, therefore, are a matter of real interest and importance but at the same time rather difficult of approach for purposes of systematic study. The periodical reports of English diplomats resident at Italian courts, by far the most substantial mass of evidence available, yield little by reason of their underlying insignificance. On the other hand, a host of miscellaneous gleanings from scattered books and diaries, with notes on Italian words, pictures, vegetables or manufactures transmitted to England, can only be brought together into synthesis under extreme pressure; for such evidence is supplied by a small army of individuals whose paths cross only too rarely.

In this predicament the question naturally suggests itself, Was there any medium of exchange between the two countries other than the individual merchant or traveller who introduced novelties from Italy to England? Was there ever in existence a group of English people who were not simply a fortuitous assembly of such individuals but a group of representative Englishmen, exposed to Italian influences, and fitted to transmit them to England? It is from this point of view, as well as in the more obvious search for information on political transactions, that a re-examination of English diplomatic reports may be justified in order to study some of the travellers who were, in varying degrees, connected with the ambassador's household at Venice in this period. Such households in Italy were, in a certain sense, peculiar to James I's reign. Before 1603 they did not exist; after 1630 they lost most of their importance, when the English government lost interest in Italian politics. The people concerned were the ambassador himself, his chaplain, his staff of secretaries and gentlemen, his messenger and spies (such as were English) and, indirectly, the Englishmen abroad who made it their pleasure or their duty to visit him in the course of their travels. Political and diplomatic reports have information of value concerning these people which is sometimes more than purely political or diplomatic in content. We may first consider why this should be the case.

Naturally, Anglo-Italian relations depended partly on the character of England's diplomatic representation in Italy during this period; but this involved more than the transactions of official diplomacy.

In the seventeenth century a distinction between political and private business, between travel for offical and unofficial reasons, was well understood. The wording of applications for passports forwarded to the Privy Council bears witness to the fact: to go abroad to recover property or settle lawsuits, to see relatives, to take the waters at Spa for one's health's sake, and to learn languages, were all considered valid reasons for issuing a passport.[1] Nevertheless, just as the documents which later ages have described as public in character were still usually regarded as the private papers of the statesmen who wrote or received them, so this distinction between travel for reasons of state and for personal reasons, while it appeared convincing to the mind, accorded ill with many cir-cumstances of the period; and never more than in the case of the traveller to Italy. First of all the English government, paternal in outlook and suspicious by policy, had recently guided the independent sovereign state and the English Protestant community through a crisis, of which no one could yet judge whether the climax was past; and it still feared the old Church of Rome and the Spanish governors of Italy as grand cor-rupters of an Englishman's allegiance. In consequence, official des-patches to and from Italy testify to the lively interest taken by the government at home in the names and activities of Englishmen travelling there. A titled gentleman in Florence, learning to fence and ride under the best Italian masters, was a relevant item of news in a political report. But the problem which had exercised Elizabethan statesmen, how to gain intelligence of Italy and educate selected Englishmen in the language, arts and finesse of Italians without allowing these emissaries to fall victims to hostile Catholic or political influences, exercised Lord Salisbury after 1603 rather differently. The opening of official relations with Venice on James I's accession, and the despatch of Sir Henry Wotton to reside there, diminished the difficulties and the dangers. Wotton's embassy was a watchtower, much more substantial by its very nature than the lesser lights of secret intelligence in the preceding reign. For this reason, not only reports on public affairs found their way to Westminster but also a good deal of information on the movement of travellers who were private men, innocent of any particular interest in dangerous affairs of state.

In the second place, the nature of an ambassador's household and the messengers by which he communicated with his government likewise militated against any rigid distinction between the official and the private traveller. An ambassador always desired to secure prestige for his master and himself by assembling for his journey to a foreign court sufficient numbers of gentlemen, true courtiers properly dressed with their own fine horses. Especially on extraordinary and ceremonial missions he required the attendance of gentlemen of family who added lustre to his equipage. Many of them never intended to belong permanently to an embassy; and the journey, under the ambassador's eye, was often their first introduction to continental travel. Moreover, an ambassador's assistants abroad, including his principal secretaries, were his own servants: taken abroad by him, and brought home on his own return, they were but temporarily involved in the transaction of matters of state, unless they secured a diplomatic appointment for themselves. Similarly, private gentlemen returning to England through Venice or Florence were frequently the bearers of an ambassador's despatches. Sometimes they had desired this extra responsibility in order to secure an introduction to the Lord Treasurer, the Secretary of State or even the King himself; sometimes it was purely a matter of convenience, and personal or political ambitions were not involved.

All these circumstances mean that an ambassador's preparations, journeys, activities, and the surviving documents which describe them, form a nucleus round which cluster the names of many other travellers; and while the emphasis is primarily political, it is by no means exclusively so. When Sir Henry Wotton, in his retirement at Eton, coined the resounding phrase, 'a College of Travellers'[2] to which a young man should belong, he may have had something of his own Venetian background in mind: a group of people who were sent abroad or who came abroad and took the opportunity to improve themselves and their prospects. There were some, like the ambassador himself and his secretaries, who undoubtedly hoped for political preferment. Possibly an apprenticeship in foreign travel and languages had brought them this diplomatic employment, and now they schemed that their travels and exertions as diplomats would bring higher political employment at home. Others simply desired to acquire polite accomplishments, to fence and ride and dance, or to gain book-learning or an exact knowledge of the language of Petrarch and Tasso. Some desired to see the world with all the vagueness of that phrase; some to intervene in continental warfare. Often they wished to test themselves in all these experiences. But it is important to realize that they were not exiles, gradually discarding their own inheritance. They intended to return to their country, taking with them their new clothes, and profiting by the accomplishments or the influence they might have acquired. They did not expect, at the least, an Italian interlude to prejudice their careers; and the problem is to discover how such an experience was related to their activities in later life.

The itineraries of the ambassadors and their staff to Italy were very

various. Through France and over Mont Cenis to Turin, through
Augsburg and Bavaria and over the Brenner pass to Venetia, up the
Rhine valley by water to Basle and then to Geneva and Mont Cenis; or
along the upper Rhône to the Great St. Bernard (leading again to
Turin), or to the St. Gotthard (leading to Milan) and, finally, from Basle
to Zurich and the passes of the Grisons — all these routes to Italy were
known to the travellers of that period.[3] In the course of fourteen
journeys over the Alps during his life Sir Henry Wotton had explored
most of the alternatives.[4] However, the choice before such a traveller
was usually limited by various considerations, war, diplomacy and public
health. On his way an ambassador might have duties to perform at the
courts of Paris, Brussels or Heidelberg; roads were frequently blocked
by military campaigning or the erratic movement of disbanded troops.
Local quarantine regulations narrowed the possibilities still further.
Fear of infection, indeed, determined the course of a journey to a
remarkable extent. Wotton himself, in a letter from Turin to Sir Ralph
Winwood, describes how on one occasion he arrived at Basle to find
Berne and Fribourg in quarantine, which forced him to go out of his way
and circle round them. Having rejoined the original route on the shores
of the Lake of Geneva he understood that not only the Valais, through
which lay the road to the Great St. Bernard, but also Geneva and the
road to Mont Cenis were barred for the same reason. He was compelled
to cross the lake 'at hazard' and follow a precipitous and dangerous
course (probably the Little St. Bernard) to Turin.[5] At a slightly earlier
date one of Sir Dudley Carleton's household, returning to England from
Venice, found himself obliged to travel mainly at night through the Tirol
and Bavaria, on account of this universal fear of plague; and 'not
suffered to pass through any towne nor so much as a village, but were
faine to seek unknowne wayes and travayle over the fields till both we
and our horses were utterly tired'.[6]

Whatever the nature of his journey overland an ambassador to Venice
was accustomed to send his heavy baggage forward by sea; and when he
sent presents home to his friends or patrons, the pictures and chests of
glasses came usually by sea. The risks of piracy on the voyage were
somewhat less, apparently, than the cost and difficulty of their carriage
overland.

From the state papers of all countries in this period the journeys
of diplomats emerge as one of the normal, and not the least striking
phenomena of the age. The notion that they were *representative* of
sovereignties, when the visible or ceremonial manifestation and the
actual strength of a sovereign power were more closely identified than
we, in the recent past, have considered necessary, gave to an accredited
ambassador a spectacular importance which he was usually careful to
emphasize, even on his journey; and the journeys alone made possible
the continuous process of negotiation and adjustment between the
conflicting sovereignties of Europe. As a fair sample of such a journey,

the occasion when Sir Dudley Carleton, with his staff of friends and servants, went to reside as James I's ambassador at Venice in 1610 — his first public appointment after years spent living down the accusation of complicity in Gunpowder Plot — can be illustrated by the detail of a few surviving letters.[7]

With a company of twenty-four persons he crossed the Channel in September 1610. He travelled provided with two sets of bills of exchange, one of which could be realized in Strasbourg and Augsburg, the other at Paris and Lyon. This enabled him to defer his choice of route until the last possible moment, when he could make up his mind on the basis of the most recent and reliable information. Coming to Amiens 'where the wayes divide' (for Paris or Lorraine) he learnt of soldiers being levied at Strasbourg and French armies returning home-ward from Cleves, and therefore chose to go through France, the longer way, 'rather than run a hazard amongst those straglers'. At Paris Carleton visited the English ambassador, Sir Thomas Edmondes, but limited severely his ceremonial courtesies to members of the French court and nobility, pleading the urgency of his journey. He reached Lyon early in October and a fortnight later they were all in Turin, after a delay caused by heavy rains and the movement of French and Savoyard troops in the mountains. The soldiers, however, had treated James I's ambassador with proper consideration and respect. There was then some possibility of war between the Spaniards in Milan and the powers of France and Savoy. Relations were critical, although the English learnt that with the exception of war-munitions merchandise was still being carried freely across the frontiers. Duke Charles Emmanuel had left his capital and remained at Asti to observe Spanish troop movements more closely. Carleton and his party left Turin and continued serenely on their way, never spending more than one night in any city. His worst obstacles in the Duchy of Milan were neither political nor military but 'the scaffolds and pageants for canonisation of their Saint Carlo Borromeo (whereof the solemnisation was to be the day following), my coaches could scarce have passage'. Indeed, only on the frontiers of Venice did they really meet with any serious difficulty: the rigorous quarantine regulations of that state. These kept the ambassador waiting five days at Crema, not far from Brescia. He was refused admittance into the town, nor even permitted to go and wait for the result of these negotiations by the pleasanter shores of Lake Garda. While the authorities pondered the matter this party of English people were forced to remain outside Crema 'in a palazzo, as they terme it, but in plaine English a pore Country farme with 4 bedds for 24 men and women'. The Venetians found Sir Dudley Carleton *troppo vivace* on that account. Finally, permission came from Venice and they travelled on through Brescia, Verona, Vicenza to Padua, treated on the way to many stately refreshments by the governors of these cities.

They were now close to the journey's end. At Padua it was only a question of treating with Sir Henry Wotton, the retiring ambassador, for the use of his house in Venice, then rather crowded by the residence there of Lord Cranborne, the Earl of Salisbury's son, in addition to Wotton himself,[8] and also of arranging with the Venetian authorities for the new ambassador's formal entry into the city. On that particular occasion all went well. Carleton had 'honestissimum diem for the number and fashion of his company'. The long journey from London to Venice was safely over at last. Its expense to the English crown had been £550.[9] The ambassador and his household could begin to accustom themselves to the Italian style of life.

The personnel who completed this and other such journeys and comprised the 'College' of Englishmen at Venice was remarkably homogeneous. In the case of Sir Henry Wotton's embassy, thanks to rich material and skilful biographers, the character and origins of his principal servants are fairly well known. Wotton sometimes styled himself *Anglo-Cantianus* and it is not surprising to find that in Venice, especially during his first embassy (1604–1610) he surrounded himself with a group of Kentish gentlemen, many of them distantly related to his own family; Albertus Morton his 'nephew', Rowland Woodward, Henry Cogan, William Parkhurst and George Rooke. The chaplain was first Nathaniel Fletcher and then the more celebrated William Bedell. In Wotton's second embassy (1616–1618) his first chaplain was Isaac Bargrave, later Dean of Canterbury, another Kentish man. It would be a mistake to look for any unusual significance in the common origin of many of these men; for naturally an ambassador's, like any other large household of the period, was filled with neighbours and relatives.[10]

For the staff of Sir Dudley Carleton in Venice (1610–1615) less information is available; for the staff of Sir Isaac Wake, ambassador between 1624 and 1630, practically none. Carleton brought with him his old friend and adviser John Chamberlain; his wife, a step-daughter of Sir Henry Savile, Warden of Merton and Provost of Eton; and his sister Alice Carleton. The Wardenship of Merton is a relevant detail because, as the county of Kent to Sir Henry Wotton, so this Oxford college to Carleton.[11] His chief secretary, Isaac Wake, was a Fellow of Merton. His chaplain Thomas Horne was a Fellow of Merton. Later on, Nathaniel Brent, another Fellow of the College, arrived in Venice as tutor to a young peer, Lord Cromwell, but the records soon show him performing the duties of treasurer or steward to Lady Carleton and he was certainly Carleton's principal secretary when the ambassador transferred to the Hague.[12] Again, in 1620, Isaac Wake attempted to secure a Merton Fellowship for one of his secretaries, Wilkinson.[13] Another secretary of Wake's, who died at Coire in the Grisons in 1625, was Francis Greville, Fellow of Merton; and a third was Richard Browne, Fellow of Merton, who attended Wake on his last embassies to Venice and Paris, ultimately becoming English Resident in the French capital between 1641 and 1660.[14] The connection between the English embassy at Venice and Merton College was certainly well-knit.

Their original journey successfully completed, these men naturally lived much in Venice occupied with the business of their embassy. From time to time they carried despatches to England and returned. More occasionally they were sent on special missions to Milan or Naples or Lucca. Venetia, however, was their main province; and for many reasons exercised its influence upon travellers from north of the Alps. At this period no single area on the whole continent possessed an equivalent fascination for Englishmen travelling abroad; on military grounds the Low Countries, Paris by reason of its proximity, had each their claims; but the varied attractions of Venice surpassed them. The contrast with their own land was much more striking, and several circumstances conspired together in its favour. Here was a great port, the historic point of entry for Levantine produce or treasure; a great political centre, where if actual power was in decline current information or intelligence was diligently collected and assessed; a venerable constitution worthy of analysis; the site of workshops making Venetian glass and Venetian paintings, both much in fashion with the more prosperous sections of English society (partly as a result of the enthusiasm of English travellers). Here also, close at hand, was the University of Padua, supreme in the study of medicine and the sciences. In addition, the political relations of England and Venice were of a fundamentally cordial nature, despite commercial difficulties: both were sovereignties bent on maintaining their freedom of action against Spanish influences. In consequence an English ambassador at Venice held a highly esteemed position. Finally it must be remembered that the climate, though difficult enough, was considered less dangerous for the northerner than the areas of Italy further south. As Carleton noted six months after his arrival, 'Here at this present many English come from most places of Italie, finding these parts the most temperat for the summer season'.[15]

Amid these favouring circumstances none was more important, for the educated Englishman, than the proximity of Padua to Venice. The intimate connection between the two places was almost the first point impressed on the mind of a new ambassador. Sir Henry Wotton in November 1610 advised Sir Dudley Carleton, who had just arrived, to give warning to all the English gentlemen and students in Padua, in order that they might be present when he made his ceremonial entry into Venice and appeared before the Doge, because (says Wotton) 'owre nation is in truthe (as I have noted) more defective therein than the Frenche'. The English of Padua rose to this occasion and Carleton did not complain. In general there was constant coming and going between the two cities. The English would appear for the great festivals of Venice.[16] At such a time they enjoyed themselves, occasionally, in their excitement, quarrelling violently in the very square of St. Mark's until the Venetian officials imprisoned them and the ambassador had to intervene to secure their release. After such an interlude 'our English retired to their ordinary garrison at Padua', for as the ambassador says elsewhere, 'our English swarme at Padua'.[17]

If the young men of the University city came to Carleton and Wotton in Venice, the ambassadors reciprocated by renting villas in or near Padua where they preferred to spend the summer months. Not only that, when the embassy's officials came to Padua some of them settled down to study on their own account. Sir Henry Wotton's steward, William Leete, wrote on this topic in August and September 1618:

> Padova, I come to thee and doe embrace thee and am confident I shall have good cause to acknowledge thee a nursinge mother...in summer we live merrily and honestly, lett state businesses goe as they will, we follow our studies hard and love one another...I houlde to my thesis concerning Padova and in ye meane tyme fitt myself for ytt as well as I can, for *nulla dies sine linea*....[18]

On 9 September 1619 Leete was elected a councillor for one of the 'nations' in the University; but unfortunately this young medical student and diplomat's servant died of a fever in 1621. Part of his life in Italy had been spent like William Harvey's, twenty years earlier, in the study of physic; another part of his short career was given, though indirectly, to what he called state-business.

Leete never had the chance to make his mark as a physician. So far as concerns the study and practice of medicine by Englishmen the name of Padua is too often associated exclusively with the work of William Harvey who attended the lectures and demonstrations of Fabricius there early in the century; for the two men are inseparably linked with one another in the progress of those studies which led to Harvey's publication of *De Motu Cordis* in 1628. Already when he took his degree the professors of the university regarded this Englishman as an outstanding pupil.[19] It can be added, however, that English medical students of more ordinary ability, like Leete, had long been accustomed to visit Padua; and the numbers of these physicians on the roll of the Royal College of Physicians in London who had also taken the Padua degree only diminished perceptibly from 1665–1675 onwards.[20] During Carleton's embassy and Wotton's second embassy, covering the second decade of the century, English medical students were found commonly enough in Venetia, preparing to return to their own country after receiving the best instruction then available in Europe.[21] After all, Edward Gibbon's verdict on Padua as a dying taper could not apply to the residence of Galileo. In virtue of his work it was just then the intellectual capital of the world; the English ambassador wrote home in high excitement when great discoveries were announced by the professor, and he enclosed a copy of *Sidereus Nuntius* recently published.[22] A friend to Sir Henry

Wotton was Francis Bacon himself; and another hint of the effect of all this on the mind of a traveller comes from an anonymous diary (possibly written by Sir Thomas Berkeley) which describes a journey through Europe in 1610. The manuscript ends with 'Divers difficile Questions which in the time of my travaile were propounded pro et Contra', containing a detailed discussion of Galileo's recent discoveries, and also the views of his contemporary critics. The scientist with his telescope, it seemed, spoke of the countless stars he had seen in the Milky Way, of Jupiter's planets, and mountains on the moon. The Englishman, travelling through Italy at this very time, was anxious to assimilate what he could of the new learning.[23]

If William Leete's industry is one example of the way in which the leisure activities of embassy officials profited from the special amenities of Venetia, another may be drawn from the papers of Isaac Wake, then Carleton's secretary and later ambassador at Venice himself. Wake was a learned man but, according to Anthony Wood, 'he spent his time more in reading political and civill matters than philosophy or the great faculties',[24] at a later date Wake looked back with something like nostalgia to his studyful of books at Venice.[25] In addition to these, however, and to all his diplomatic duties, copying or writing despatches for Carleton, he seems to have been employed by English patrons to purchase goods and valuables. Lord Roos, for example, was in Venice during 1614 and visited Domenico, son of the great Jacopo Robusti Tintoretto; he commissioned certain pictures. He likewise bought a substantial amount of tobacco; also carpets, torches, candlesticks and andirons. Some of these were then stored in Isaac Wake's room and left in his keeping, but the pictures required time for completion. . .and they required money from Lord Roos. All this was left in Wake's hands. When the latter left Venice, rather suddenly, he turned the business over to an English merchant; it is owing to this circumstance that details survive. Had Wake remained it would undoubtedly have fallen to him to settle with the younger Tintoretto, offering him — on his patron's instruction — 320 ducats for four pictures, a Last Judgment, Mary Magdalene, portraits of the Doge Donato and Lord Roos, to be shipped for England at the first opportunity.[26]

This evidence may be added to the familiar facts of Sir Henry Wotton's and Sir Dudley Carleton's purchase of pictures,[27] sometimes as a speculation, to transmit them to such powerful patrons as the Earl of Somerset or Prince Charles. In due course certain of Lord Roos's valuables came into the celebrated collections of Lord Arundel.

The Venetian product most in request in England was glassware. Sir Henry Wotton considered himself an expert in the selection of choice specimens and Venetian goblets were the current coin of English diplomats in negotiating the favour of likely patrons at the English court. A Privy Councillor (his name is not given) in 1617 received not only lutes and lutestrings and a mango-tree but, says Wotton, 'a chest of glasses of mine own choosing at Murano, wherein I do somewhat pretend and the artificers are well acquainted with me'.[28] Sir Dudley Carleton wrote, with reference to the wife of Sir Walter Cope, one of Lord Salisbury's most trusted advisers: 'My lady Cope hath just cause to except against her drinking glasses for they were not worthie of her but for ordinarie use, and I remember for the commoditie of sending by a goode ship we took such as we could then find, but I will undertake to furnish her better. I pray you prevent by all meanes her sending anything hether for they have many better occasions of pleasuring me then by presents.'[29] Lady Cope is a fair representative of that class in English society which received samples of Venetian ware, whether choice or ordinary, through the agency of the English ambassadors and their staff.

The importation of these things into England found more immediate favour with Englishmen — the fashion for them was more widespread — than the Italian style of architectural design. Inigo Jones, certainly, is a great name but as late as 1660 Sir Roger Pratt could complain that there were still only two substantial examples of such design in England, the Banqueting House at Whitehall and the Portico of St. Paul's Cathedral.[30] Progress was therefore slow in this field, its most resolute expression perhaps Inigo Jones' classic stage-scenery for a long series of court masques. Only as a precursor of latter-day taste in building can Sir Henry Wotton's famous little book, the *Elements of Architecture*, be considered.[31] First published in 1624, the most satisfactory result of his long official residence in Venetia, he points the way to conventional judgments accepted by the later seventeenth century. He speaks of the 'combustions and tumults of the middle age' which uncivilized good literature, thus delaying a proper appreciation of Vitruvius, earliest and supreme authority on the problems of architecture. He despises the gothic arches which 'both for the natural imbecility of the sharpe Angle itself and likewise for their very uncomeliness ought to be exiled from judicious eyes and left to their first inventors, the Goths and Lombards amongst other Reliques of the barbarous age' — and this within twelve years of the completion of Wadham College. His was a book for the critic and patron, based on the philosophical principles of earlier writers, Vitruvius, Alberti and Philibert de L'Orme. He would not have it thought that 'he had spent his poore observation abroad about nothing but stone and timber and such Rubbage'. His practical suggestions are not those of a technician in the craft of building; on the other hand he clearly made a practice of visiting, in order to admire, the churches and villas of the 'High-Renaissance' at Venice, Vicenza and Padua, modern in their challenge to a man from Elizabethan Oxford, faithful (it was believed) to the spirit and dimensions of Roman work: the paradox which best satisfied progressively-minded people in this period. In Wotton's embassy, therefore, besides glass and tapestry and pictures, the architecture which should determine the positioning of these things was at least a matter for serious discussion.[32]

After examining the various opportunities for study and for enjoying or acquiring the luxuries of Italy in Venetia, from the point of view of these embassy servants, it is natural to approach the less tangible problem of the general influence of Venice, Catholic but anti-papal, oligarchic, secretive, upon Protestant Englishmen. Consider, for example, the opinions of William Bedell, the future Bishop of Kilmore, regarding its Catholicism. An early biographer has stated that Bedell 'desired to concoct his knowledge and learning attain'd at home by the observation of travel and the experience of forraign countreys'.[33] With this idea in mind he accepted Sir Henry Wotton's invitation, sent through Wotton's friend and Bedell's patron in Suffolk, Sir Edmund Bacon, that he should become the ambassador's chaplain in Venice. Once arrived in Italy this Anglican clergyman of great learning and intense sincerity soon expressed his sense of a Catholic land in no uncertain terms to his friend and correspondent, Adam Newton. He found idolatry everywhere, he wrote: statues, pictures, relics not only in churches but in private houses and the shops and streets, in the country highways and on the ships and buoys of the lagoons. It was a scandalous display. On the other hand one point he found himself forced to concede. The careful and costly beautification of churches, the grandiose ceremonies of ecclesiastical feasts and services were more commendable than 'our beggary, the scorne of our religion at home'. Most men, of whatever quality, were led more by shows than by substance, he found, and it was this striking contrast between our own custom and the glittering churches of Italy which many account 'noe small cause of the perversion of soe many of our young Gentlemen that come into these parts'.[34]

Venice was therefore dangerous ground for a Protestant even in the period immediately following that state's quarrel with Pope Paul V, the interdict and the wrangle over conflicting jurisdictions. On the other hand these very circumstances might be turned to account; the anti-clericalism of Venice was worth study by an English cleric. Just as the first Librarian of Bodley, Thomas James, desired to collect Catholic editios of the Fathers in order to study and confute the editors, so William Bedell welcomed the opportunity of examining this great ecclesiastical controversy between Catholic powers. He became the principal intermediary between Sarpi and Fulgenzio the theological advisers of the Venetian authorities, and Sir Henry Wotton, when the latter attempted to encourage Venice against the Pope and prepare a Protestant movement in Italy. He was instrumental in demonstrating to another malcontent Venetian churchman, Marco Antonio De Dominis, Archbishop of Spalato, the merits of the Anglican standpoint, and in due course De Dominis came to England. He also studied the oriental languages and improved his Hebrew by controversies with the Jews of Venice.[35] Above all, however, because Bedell was actively involved in affairs of church and state in Italy, he must have gained a more realistic acquaintance with the fundamental questions at issue — as his early biographer remarked — than the bare reading of ecclesiastical history was able to afford.

All this has importance. The work of Bedell, chaplain of the embassy 1608–1610, shows how a fuller knowledge of Venice entered English academic and political circles. His attempts to indoctrinate the Venetians with his translation into Italian of the Prayer Book and other works met with scant success, but on the other hand he himself returned to England with an interest in Venetian topics, and a desire to popularize them for the benefit of the intellectual classes over here, which lasted a lifetime.[36] He translated into Latin from the Italian — a method of popularization — a number of Sarpi's works, including the History of the Interdict and parts of the History of the Council of Trent. He corresponded on these and kindred subjects with influential men, Samuel Ward the Master of Sidney Sussex College and Laurence Chaderton Master of Emmanuel College, and with Sir Adam Newton and Sir David Murray both of court circles. Undoubtedly he contributed in spreading the information and arguments by which Anglican authors became accustomed to support their own stand against Rome with appeals to the example of Venice. It is noticeable how frequently English publishers of the seventeeth and eighteenth centuries produced translations and adaptations of Sarpi's works, and accounts of Sarpi's life. Bedell had in fact been one of those who first transmitted his reputation to England.[37]

Another figure in the English embassy at Venice, whose literary work is complementary to the more numerous publications of Bedell, was Nathaniel Brent. He joined Sir Dudley Carleton in 1614. Anthony Wood simply says of him that he travelled into several parts of the learned world in 1613 and 1614 and underwent dangerous adventures in Italy to procure the History of the Council of Trent which he translated into English.[38] This was almost but not quite the case. He came to Italy as tutor to Lord Cromwell, mastered Italian and then worked for Carleton. In May 1615 he was arrested by the Spaniards in Milanese territory but soon released. Later, in 1618, Archbishop Abbot sent him on a confidential mission to Venice where he arranged for the secret despatch of Sarpi's manuscript to England, and this Italian original was published in London. Brent himself had returned home. He settled down to the labour of translating into English what proved to be a masterpiece of controversial historical writing.[39]

It does not appear, from the evidence of private letters or printed books that the members of James I's embassies made any similar contribution to English knowledge of the Venetian constitution in its secular aspect. A certain interest in the structure of government in Venice dates back to an earlier period. A treatise on the subject like Cardinal Contarini's *De Magistratibus et Republica Venetorum* enjoyed a European reputations; it was known to Philip Sidney in 1573,[40] and was translated into English in 1599.[41] Moreover, the pre-eminence of the Venetian government for elaboration, for secrecy, and for the conservation which results from an equal balance of opposed political interests, had a continuing history in England during the seventeenth century. It was celebrated afresh by James Howell in his *Survey of the Signories of Venice* in 1651 and in James Harrington's *Oceana*. An appreciation of the Venetian oligarchy became an element in the political philosophy of the Whigs. But it is hardly surprising that the Jacobean diplomats should not say or write anything publicly on this subject: such matters were arcana imperii, reserved for the attention of James I and the Secretaries of State; and the despatches of the ambassadors, regularly received in London, prove their familiar acquaintance with the complexity of the Venetian administration.

Before drawing together the different strands of this process by which the Englishman's experience of Italy was assimilated into English society, there is just sufficient evidence to form another biography in miniature, portraying the type of man connected with the embassy and the kind of influence at work upon him.

George Rooke was born in 1580, a younger son of Laurence Rooke, of a fairly substantial Kentish family.[42] His grandfather Thomas left lands in Mersham, Aldington, Kingsnothe and Folkstone when he died in 1553. George Rooke does not appear to have gone either to Oxford or Cambridge but by the age of twenty-two he claimed that he had already been employed on four occasions by ministers of the King to carry messages to England; evidently he was abroad in France or the Low Countries soon after the turn of the century. In 1604 he accompanied Wotton to Venice and Wotton entrusted him with responsible work. In 1605 he was sent to Naples to settle the nomination to the English consulate there. Next he returned to London with the ambassador's despatches only to find himself arrested and detained, his enemies (so he wrote to Lord Salisbury) having misinformed the Council about certain incidents in his past career. He was soon permitted to return to Italy; fell ill early in 1607, recovered and went off to Padua; and was then sent to Pisa in order to present the exile Sir Robert Dudley with Privy Seals citing him to appear for trial in England. Rooke likewise transacted a little political business at Lucca where he happened to make the acquaintance of Francis Windebank, the future Secretary of State, then on his travels, and of Dr. Thomas Whiston, future professor of Physic at Gresham's College. Then we hear of him in Venice and Padua; he is buying song books and history books for a friend in England; on Wotton's instructions he is winding up the affairs of Sir

Julius Caesar's son, slain in the brawl at Padua; he is elected a councillor of the law-faculty in the university there. Towards the end of 1608 he was travelling again. His next surviving letter, written from Geneva, explains that he had originally intended to come home by way of Spa, but now decided to pass through France 'to abide some few weeks to retrieve that little French which I find the Italian accent hath put to a great fault'.[43]

Two years later he was again in Geneva, his business mainly private, partly political; for he had become tutor to the sons of Sir Richard Smyth of Leeds Castle, of the great Kentish family of the Smyths, Receiver of the Duchy of Cornwall, and these sons were young men to whom Rooke was distantly related — but at the same time, while he was their tutor in Geneva he continued to send periodical reports to Lord Salisbury on the political crisis embroiling the relations of Savoy and Geneva. From Rooke's point of view, it must have seemed an open question whether he might finally secure some more substantial piece of preferment, under Salisbury's patronage.

However, when war became more likely in Switzerland Sir Richard Smyth sent positive orders that they were to move elsewhere. Rooke and the boys then came to Lyon where they spent the summer, the tutor still sending his reports to Salisbury. Smyth wrote again, telling them to winter in Italy; and thus it is that one Giorgius Roccho was mentioned a second time as councillor at Padua University, on 18 December 1611, while Sir Richard Smyth transmitted money by bill of exchange to Venice for the use of his sons. Carleton the ambassador kept an eye on them, and formed the highest opinion of Rooke.

Then came an abrupt change of fortune, an alteration very characteristic of the period. George was now the eldest surviving son and his father Laurence was drowned in crossing over to England from Ireland in the course of the year 1612; so he himself came back to England shortly afterwards to inherit a number of properties in Kent. The principal part of his continental experience was over. He settled down as a country gentleman. He married a niece of Lancelot Andrewers and brought up a family. One of his sons became a Fellow of King's College, Cambridge, and another, later on, Sheriff of Kent. He was a grandfather of the more famous Admiral Rooke, of Gibraltar. His friends, meanwhile, considered him the right man to deal with the merchant Burlamacchi in settling difficult problems of currency and foreign exchange. He died in 1649.

What kind of man was George Rooke? Is it possible to gather any impression of the influence which the early years of travel may have had on this representative of the Kentish gentry? Apart from the records already noted, there are two testimonies of some value: his epitaph and his will. The first gives a judgment which his contemporaries considered appropriate in the circumstances and part of it runs as follows:

And when he had deservedly reaped the just reputation of a complete gentle-man by his conversation among strangers beyond the seas, enriched himself with the beautiful esteem of munificent neighbour by constant hospitality at home....

It was therefore believed that travel should have influenced George Rooke in a certain way, given him interests and advantages which otherwise he would have missed. Some proof that this was the case emerges from the study of his will: apart from the usual bequests re-garding clothes, land and money, he gives away his books on astronomy,[44] on geography, 'all my manuscript notes and papers touching the mathe-matics, and likewise one Mathematical brasse instrument with all the appurtinances composed by Gallileo Gallilei, a famous Mathematician of Italy'. It is difficult to resist the conclusion, on the basis of this evidence, that George Rooke acquired certain enthusiasms in Italy which were transmitted to his son Laurence, the Fellow of King's College, Cambridge, and later on Gresham's Professor successively of astronomy and geometry, one of the foundation members of the Royal Society. Education and learning in that family were bound up with the travels of the diplomat's servant and noblemen's tutor, who was himself connected, at some remove, with the development of scientific studies in England.

All these indications taken together lead naturally to a conclusion that the community of travellers in the service of an ambassador at Venice was responsive to the Italian world surrounding them. In David Mathew's work, *The Jacobean Age*,[45] is an account of Lord Arundel's and his companion Inigo Jones on their Italian journey: boldly (the evidence is indirect) it imagines them surveying buildings together, Jones pointing out the grand effects and suggesting, possibly, their imitation in England; and after his return Lord Arundel built the Palladian halls to be seen in the background of his portrait by Daniel Mytens. This is an example of the process by which Italian travel must have suggested novelties to the English mind. It may well be, however, that the more representative character of the ambassador's household was the more sensitive medium for the same process, covering a wider range of interests. In religion, the arts, and fashions of thought, the little 'college' had its different 'faculties'. Each man exploited his experience rather differently from his companions. But unlike the exiles, gradually flaking off layer after layer of native tradition, such as the family of the Anglo-Tuscan shipbuilder Sir Robert Dudley[46] which was to fuse completely with its Italian environment, these men returned to England. Unlike many travelling noblemen, in too much of a hurry to learn or unlearn anything, these men were away long enough to be influenced by their experience abroad. In so doing they maintained and strengthened the connections between England and western Europe, at a time when Puritanism in one, and the triumphs of revived Catholicism in the other, threatened to separate the two to the disadvantage of both.

The political influence of the ambassadors or members of their staff is a different matter, and in this context Turin deserves to be paired with Venice. It is true that Piedmont was of less significance for most English travellers, affording them merely their first glimpse of Italy if they crossed the Alps by the pass of Mont Cenis. It was a country reached several days after leaving Lyon, passing through Pont de Beauvoisin, Chambèry, Montmélian, across the mountains to Susa and down to the capital. It was observed that here the rye ripened six weeks earlier than in England and that travellers should take care in drinking the local wines.[47] They usually remained only a day or two at Turin before continuing their journey eastwards down the Po, or southwards to Genoa and Tuscany. However, the course of international politics linked very closely the diplomacy of Charles Emmanuel, Duke of Savoy and Piedmont, with that of the kings of England between 1610 and 1630; and it involved certain Englishmen who were resident both in Venice and Turin.

Thomas Rowlandson is little known. His name crops up as an English official at Venice in the third and fourth decades of the century but it was apparently in Piedmont that he first rose to a position of some responsibility. He is first mentioned in a letter written on 15 September 1615 by Wake, recently appointed English resident in Turin, to Carleton at Venice. At this time a notorious quarrel between Foscarini, Venetian ambassador in London, and his secretary Muscorno became notorious. Muscorno had been summoned home to Venice and arrested. The Venetian authorities were collecting evidence with which to sift the charges and counter-charges made by the two men, and they asked their representative at Turin to examine one Rowlandson then living there. From Wake's letter to Carleton two points emerge: Rowlandson had been in England while Muscorno and Foscarini were quarrelling because he was a witness of alleged malpractices of Foscarini; and he also had relatives living in Venice, which imposed a certain restraint upon him in giving evidence against a powerful nobleman. This connection with the Venetian embassy in London, taken together with the fact that he had Venetian relatives, indicates that Rowlandson was one of those Englishmen very much at home in Italy. His earliest surviving letter, addressed to an English ambassador, is written in Italian.[48]

In the following year Wake gives a further description of this elusive figure. Charles Emmanuel sent a confidential message to James I and Wake, writing to the Secretary of State, characterizes the messenger as: 'Mr. Thomas Rowlandson (an English gentleman entertained in his service), that from him you may understand the true state of affairs here, whereof he is well informed as having been from the first beginning of these troubles alwaies *in fractione panis* and near about the Duke's person.' By the beginning of August 1616 Rowlandson was back in Turin. Similarly, in the summer of 1618 and described by Wake as a gentleman of the Duke's Chamber, he carried despatches to England returning with the notice of permission to Wake, so long and earnestly requested by the latter, for the English resident at Turin to pay a short visit to England.[49]

Evidently this man was useful in virtue of his curious, intermediate position; and he continued to play a subordinate part in contemporary diplomacy. In July 1619 the Spanish authorities demanded from Charles Emmanuel permission to send troops through his territory on their way northward to Flanders and Germany: a request directly related to the opening stages of the Thirty Years War. The matter naturally concerned the Elector Frederick. Therefore, says Wake, 'I have despatched a gentleman to Heidelberg expressly to warn the Prince Palatine of this danger.' The gentleman was Rowlandson; as Wake remarked elsewhere, suspicion was avoided and the degree of England's interest in the question concealed, by sending a servant of the Duke's rather than one of his own secretaries to the Elector. Rowlandson returned shortly afterwards, bringing despatches for Wake from the Secretary of State transmitted to him by the Earl of Doncaster, then on his ill-fated mission to Germany.[50]

Reward for these services was duly forthcoming. Wake was transferred to Venice in 1624 and Thomas Rowlandson became the ambassador's Italian Secretary, with a special patent from Charles I. He was to receive a salary, independent of the embassy's finances. Lady Wake arrived in Venice to join her husband early in 1625. Her guide had been Rowlandson whom the ambassador commended to Secretary Conway for his care of the Secretary's stepdaughter on the journey; they came by way of Turin where Rowlandson 'took his leave of the Duke', and now, in accordance with a promise given by Buckingham, he demanded his patent of office 'without which he cannot serve cheerefully, and wee cannot live without him'. Wake makes the observation at this point that Rowlandson was a very reliable servant, and that his presence in Venice would in due course save the Crown the expense of keeping a resident ambassador there, thus foreshadowing the diminished importance of Venice for English diplomacy. An observer, a writer of fortnightly newsletters was soon all that would be required; and this became Rowlandson's duty for a number of years.[51]

After Wake's departure from Venice Rowlandson's salary appears to have been raised. In 1625 it had been £60 a year, subsequently increased to £90. In December 1628 he commenced his series of newsletters to the Secretary of State which continued without interruption until 1635; and his salary was now £1 a day, putting him on somewhat more equal terms with other English Residents or Agents. In 1631 he paid a short visit to the English court and the Venetian envoy later reported that the private interests of Rowlandson naturally militated against the despatch to Venice of a fully accredited ambassador. But in 1635 an ambassador at last arrived, Basil Lord Feilding, with whom Rowlandson was unwilling or unable to work. In April 1635 a warrant was sent to the Exchequer authorizing payment to Rowlandson of £500 in satisfaction of his extra charges in the preceding two and a half years. In the November Sir John Coke calculated that the Agent was still owed £1915. In the following year he made a final visit to settle these involved accounts which mark the conclusion of his official career. In all probability he then returned to Venice as a private citizen. For twenty years at least he had mediated between Englishmen and Italians in the conduct of affairs.[52]

How did people use their experience of Italy to obtain preferment in the world of English politics and diplomacy? Rowlandson's is fundamentally a simple case, because his connections with the English court remained slight throughout his career. At one period, while in England, he secured Buckingham's goodwill; at another, a Venetian in London speaks of Lord Arundel as Rowlandson's protector. On the other hand he was probably born, and he probably died, in Venice; his family lived there, his household remained there when he paid a visit to England.[53] He rose to a respectable position as an English official because he had one effective patron on the spot, Sir Isaac Wake. Had Rowlandson wanted to rise higher, or involve himself in England, the chances of preferment would certainly have been complicated by the need for further patronage. We ought therefore to look next at those who achieved greater success, after their early residence abroad. The stages of such an ascent to positions of influence or affluence might be four or five-fold: traveller, ambassador's secretary, 'resident', ambassador, and secretary of state. Exemplifying them all was the great triumvirate of English diplomats in Italy between 1604 and 1630, Henry Wotton, Dudley Carleton and Isaac Wake, and their careers shed rather more light on the difficulties of those who had to canvass the Stuart government and court from a distance.

Wotton has been supremely fortunate in his biographers, Isaac Walton and Pearsall Smith. It is only necessary to recall how his early life illustrated from the first an Elizabethan traveller's mingle of private and public affairs. He was sent abroad in 1590, partly in order to report to the English government from time to time on the political situation in Europe, partly to complete his education. He reached Italy in 1591 and remained there about two years; he was some time in Padua, Siena, Florence; and in disguise visited Rome and Naples. An Italian scholar dedicated a work on Italian literature to him; and Wotton's own written work, as a result of his journey, appears to have been a treatise on the State of Christendom. Between 1601 and 1603 he was once again resident in Italy, on this occasion as an exile, compromised by his association with the Earl of Essex. He divided the time between study in the Laurentian Library and attempts to ingratiate himself with the Grand Duke of Tuscany, who actually sent him on a confidential mission to James VI of Scotland. When Elizabeth died James remembered Wotton favourably as young Englishman with an extensive knowledge of Italy, who had come from Florence to warn him of a possible attempt at his assassination. Wotton also secured the good-will of Sir Robert Cecil. In consequence he was chosen to go as resident ambassador to Venice. His experience abroad, combined with good fortune at court, brought him this first step in political preferment.

So far there is some resemblance between the lives of Thomas Rowlandson and Henry Wotton. They both served an Italian prince and were well acquainted with Italian politics. Ultimately, however, there could be no comparison between the reserves of influence behind the one and the other. Supporting Wotton were his brother Lord Wotton and his old fellow-traveller Lord Zouche, both of the Council; above them, Cecil, and above Cecil the favour of the King himself. For Carleton and Wake, unfortunately, similar evidence is not available for their movements before they became attached to the households of English ambassadors. Carleton had been in France prior to his appointment in Sir Thomas Parry's embassy at Paris, and in 1610 he hints in a despatch that he had never been before in northern Italy.[54] As for Wake, he may have been abroad when he was offered a secretaryship at Venice; more cannot be stated.[55]

The next stage in the ladder of promotion was the ascent from a minor post as an ambassador's secretary to something more substantial. It never concerned Wotton who had become an ambassador himself at one bound, but it greatly mattered to Wake, for whom the evidence gradually becomes more plentiful. He had reached Venice in 1610 and settled down to his diplomatic and other duties; but in 1612 Carleton sent him to England on a personal mission of high importance. The Earl of Salisbury was dead and the ambassador felt uncomfortably aware that he had lost one powerful patron without any immediate prospect, distant as he was from the centre of English affairs, of finding another. He sent Wake for the purpose of strengthening his own position at home. He was charged to participate, on Carleton's behalf, in the confused struggle for position which continued to disturb the English court after Salisbury's death. It was possible, for example, that a newly appointed Secretary of State would relinquish an office which the ambassador at Venice could profitably acquire. For Wake, the satisfaction of his immediate patron might favour his own prospects in a proportionate measure.

At the end of August 1612 the secretary hastened northwards through Germany, bearing a whole sheaf of complimentary letters from Carleton to great personages in England. He travelled by water from Frankfurt,

passed through Amsterdam, the Hague and Rotterdam. He took ship
for Flushing but after spending two days on the water was forced to go
ashore. At Flushing he took ship for Antwerp, and thence continued
overland to Calais where again contrary winds delayed him for some
days.[56]

The difficulties which faced men, partially estranged from England
and the English court circles by residence abroad, are forcefully described in Wake's correspondence with Carleton. First of all, it was
desirable for the ambassador's secretary to present in person the ambassador's letters to the King. Wake delivers a letter from Carleton to
Sir Thomas Overbury; Overbury gives him a letter of introduction to
Viscount Rochester. The court has gone to Royston; Wake follows and
delivers certain papers to Rochester, who suggests that at a favourable
opportunity Wake should present the despatches to James; behind these
interviews is the effort to bring Carleton's name to the personal attention
of James I and his principal confidant. In consequence, Wake danced
attendance at court for weeks, seeking the opportunity of an interview
which in fact was never granted.[57]

Second to this was the problem of finding support for Carleton among
the other great men at court, and in London. Wake visited the Lord
Privy Seal, the Chancellor of the Exchequer, Sir Walter Cope, the Lord
Chancellor, Henry Howard and many others. It was heartbreaking work:

> Some to whom I should goe are out of Towne, and have been since my
> comming hither in which case there is no remedye. Some others I heare
> of, that they are seen about the Citty many times but they have no certain
> rendevous, so yt I can learne no way to them, their dwelling being out of
> the towne in adjoining parkes. Lastly, many whose howses are well enough
> knowen are gone abroad so early and come home so late, yt it is hard
> finding them within, and when they are found then are either so busy or so
> private that no accession be had.[58]

In the end the King decided not to make any changes, for the present, in
the principal diplomatic and political posts; and Wake travelled back to
Venice in March 1613 simply carrying despatches and polite acknow-
ledgements from some of those who had received the ambassador's letter
of compliment. The mission had failed though Carleton admitted
frankly that Wake did his best in London.[59]

This journey, in spite of the difficulties, was considered worth-while
in order to press the ambassador's case at court; and Wake simply
performed the service expected of a junior. In fact it may have given him
an advantage denied his superior, a chance of meeting the men of
influence around the Privy Chamber. A great man's word, combined
with the goodwill of an ambassador, could do most to secure promotion
for the younger men employed abroad. As it turned out on this occasion,
James I had a letter sent to the Doge in August 1614 announcing

Carleton's recall from Venice and Sir Henry Wotton's appointment as his successor, and he also named Isaac Wake as the temporary 're-sident', after the departure of one ambassador and before the arrival of another.[60] Wake, but not Carleton, had been able to move up a step. Unfortunately this modest promotion took effect for a bare forty-eight hours. There was an emergency, Carleton returned to Venice two days after leaving it, and Wake continued as his secretary.[61]

The status of resident was not denied him for long. The crisis which had brought Carleton back to Venice was the imminence of war between Savoy and the Spaniards in Milan; and in February 1615 he received instructions to join with the spokesmen of other powers in mediating between Savoy and the Spanish viceroy.[62] Carleton, together with Wake and a retinue of thirty to forty persons, went to Turin in the most bitter weather; soldiers had to be called out to clear the snow and let their coaches pass. The political situation depended partly on the wintry conditions. It was expected that fighting would start as soon as the weather improved. In Turin the mediators had no time to lose. The Duke of Savoy reluctantly showed willingness to give satisfaction on certain points but the Venetian, French, Papal and English ambassadors then failed to agree on the procedure to follow in approaching the viceroy. A solution of the difficulty — approved by Charles Emmanuel — was in fact to send Wake to Milan with a letter from Carleton, stating Savoy's willingness in principle to satisfy the King of Spain.[63] The viceroy replied that he could concede nothing without first receiving instructions from Madrid. Wake returned to Turin; it appeared that the diplomats were helpless. Carleton decided to inform James I immediately, and on 29 March secretary Wake was again on the road, this time bound for England. He carried a number of letters and despatches for the King, Winwood the Secretary of State, John Chamberlain who was Carleton's friend in London, and others.[64]

Referring first to the acute political crisis in north Italy these letters also dealt with another topic. Wake was taking home a recommendation for his own preferment. The warmth of Anglo-Savoy relations, main-tained ever since Sir Henry Wotton had paid a visit as ambassador extraordinary in 1612, made it advisable to have an official resident at Charles Emmanuel's court. Albertus Morton, Wotton's nephew, had been appointed but he now desired his recall and recommended Wake as his successor. Carleton echoed this. The King signified approval, and in June 1615 Wake was able to return to Italy and take up his new post. No emergency cancelled it this time, while a treaty agreed at Asti towards the end of June briefly restored peace to Italy. Carleton returned to Venice and Wake commenced business at Turin in a moment of comparative tranquillity.

In our travellers' attempted ascent to places of honour and profit abroad or at home, the next step was from the level of resident or agent to that of ambassador. Here again, Wake's career is revealing. From July 1615 until October 1623 he was at the court of Savoy, a position of considerable but not the highest importance. He too discovered that it was easier for an ambassador's secretary or messenger to approach at intervals the dispensers of patronage in England than for the ambassador or resident to do this himself. The latter was in danger of a semi-exile at the court to which he was accredited while the phrase *servire et non gradire* would begin to haunt his private letters home. Wake, on the whole and unlike Carleton or Wotton, did not repine. He arranged for his books to be brought from Venice; the Prince of Savoy lent him hounds and hawks for hunting.[65] The weekly routine continued as usual. It was business to correspond with the English ambassadors at Madrid, Brussels, Paris, Constantinople and Venice. It was prudence to correspond with important men in England, the Archbishop of Canterbury, Thomas Murray the Prince of Wales's tutor, Sir Thomas Tracy and others.[66] They might be able to help him. For example, in 1618 Sir Thomas Lake, Secretary of State and Latin Secretary, faced criticism on every side as the party at court to which he belonged lost influence. He felt that he could no longer hold both these offices; and then, on the suggestion of someone whose name is not given 'there was meanes made that he sholde have preferred Master Wake', but after hesitating he selected Thomas Read, a man on the spot, for the second of these posts.[67] However, at the end of the same year the resident at Turin obtained permission to come home on leave. Here was another opportunity. He arrived in London exceedingly confident, almost jovial. He was generally applauded by the Council, frequently interviewed by the King, his allowance was doubled and extraordinary grants were allowed him out of the Exchequer.[68] It seems that he secured a promise of the succession to Sir Henry Wotton. But the scepticism of observers was justified.[69] Although Wotton left Venice shortly afterwards, Wake remained at Turin. The latter court was politically more important at the time but the status of an ambassador continued to elude the hardworking resident.

In 1622 his friends made a further attempt to help. They tried to secure for him the provostship of his old college, Merton, on the death of Sir Henry Savile; and they succeeded in interesting the Prince of Wales on that account.[70] Again the diplomat lost the struggle with a candidate who was already in England, his old acquaintance Nathaniel Brent. But in November 1623 he came home again and married Anna Bray, a step-daughter of Sir Edward Conway Secretary of State. A month later he was at last appointed ambassador at Venice, succeeding to the position held earlier by Wotton and Carleton. The English agents in Savoy and Switzerland were made responsible to him and be became, as John Chamberlain expressed it, 'Ambassador Paramount' in Italy. He returned to the continent in the spring of 1624, 'laying it on with great ostentation, as well in liveries flaunting feathers and the like', apparently at his wife's expense.[71] If Wake had failed so far, at the age of forty-five, to leap the gulf separating service abroad from service and power at court, the post in Venice was certainly an attractive reward for this capable man.

Nonetheless, there is still the difficult final stage in the ascent to be considered. The sometime traveller may become a diplomat but continues to hope for office at home. After many years as ambassador at the Hague (1616–26) Carleton was appointed a Secretary of State in 1628. Morton, whose continental experience seems to have begun in Wotton's household at Venice and continued at Turin, the Hague, Heidelberg and elsewhere, secured first a clerkship of the Council and then became a Secretary of State in 1625. In 1631 some observers believed that Charles I favoured the appointment of Wake to the same office; Lord Treasurer Weston demurred and Wake, by then the ambassador in Paris, died in June of the same year.[72] But a more instructive and striking failure at this level was Sir Henry Wotton's in the previous reign.

Ambassador in Venice from 1604 to 1610 Wotton certainly pleased James and Salisbury by his numerous and entertaining despatches. It was not difficult to allow for his tendency to magnify the importance of Venice in European politics, and the importance of the English ambassador at Venice. Even so, the quarrel which broke out between Rome and Venice over the relations of lay and ecclesiastical authority was a godsend for the ambassador. It could not fail to attract the attention of James; and Wotton soon became one of those who expounded the case for encouraging a closer association, perhaps even a league, between Venice and the Protestant princes of Europe. This led him to make a further suggestion in 1609: if he returned to England through Germany he could interview the rulers of Württemberg, Neuburg, the Palatinate and Hesse on his way, and promote the plan for their association with Venice under James's I's patronage. At the same time, from his distant Venetian outpost Wotton was trying to cultivate the goodwill of Henry Prince of Wales and those round him.[73] He appreciated early that any negotiations for the Prince's marriage would affect, and might enhance, the fortune of the diplomats and others who played a part in them.

In fact he came home in 1610 by way of Turin and Mont Cenis. The Duke of Savoy was just then eagerly looking for support from powers independent of his two oppressive neighbours, France and the Spaniards in Lombardy. Wotton's reception at Turin was outstandingly friendly. He soon associated himself with the idea of an alliance between the courts of England and Savoy, possibly involving Prince Henry's marriage with a Savoy princess, and in this context made one of most his detirmined efforts to win preferment. Arrived back in London the prospects indeed looked excellent. He received a number of minor pensions and offices. His favour with the Prince of Wales was remarked. On the illness of Lord Salisbury it was anticipated that he would secure a Secretaryship of State, in spite of numerous other claimants for what was called 'the bear's skin'. Unfortunately, a few weeks after, Salisbury apparently recovered his health. Wotton left England on a second mission to Turin in connection with the Savoy marriage proposals but when Salisbury collapsed once more, dying on 24 May 1612, Wotton was still away. Critical spectators of the scene continued to stress the strength of his chances. Salisbury, they thought, had recommended him in a last letter to the King. The Queen and the Prince of Wales were for his appointment. His elder brother, Lord Wotton, gave powerful support. Chamberlain wrote on 11 June: 'in the multitude of competition for the secretaryship... the most voyces run with Sir Henry Neville, Sir Thomas Lake and Sir Harry Wotton, and great means and measures made for the last'; on 17 June: 'the likeliest now in the world's eye for the secretaryship of State is Sir Harry Wotton and yt is a general opinion that the place is reserved for him'.[74] On 25 June Sir Walter Cope, a well-placed judge of affairs, regarded the matter as settled. It was the climax of Wotton's career as a politician. An undoubted experience of foreign countries and affairs, and his high favour at home, appeared to be combining to confer upon him, with the King's approval, one of the most responsible positions in the state. From that moment, the end of June 1612, fortune turned against him. The secretaryship was never his. The evidence is silent on the representations that were now made, and the influences brought to bear on James; the favourite, Rochester, doubtless pursued his own ambitions, which would deny those of others, by way of conversation and not in written pleas or reports. He persuaded the King to experiment in handling the diplomatic correspondence himself. Already in July, however, men began to remark that Sir Ralph Winwood, ambassador at the Hague, would probably secure the secretaryship in the end. During the long summer recess less was heard of Wotton's chances. He had come back to England with Savoy's latest proposals, with also a Savoyard pension for himself, but the King was turning again to France for a marriageable princess; and it was considered that Wotton's second journey to Turin had done him no good. His mere absence on Salisbury's death had been a misfortune; the negotiations with Charles Emmanuel were losing importance. By November Sir Henry Wotton was thought to be 'down in the wind'. His famous definition of an ambassador, *Legatus est vir bonus, peregrè missus ad mentiendum Reipublicae causa*, was being thoroughly aired at court, to his own discomfiture and the King's real displeasure. The death of the Prince of Wales was a serious blow to his hopes. Wake, arrived from Venice on one of his missions, gives in correspondence with Carleton an interesting analysis of Wotton's decline from grace; and he links it very insistently with the fate of the Savoy marriage proposals. As an old courtier expressed it, Sir Henry Wotton appeared to negotiate for the petty princes of Italy 'as if Italy were his proper dioces'; and it was a mistaken policy. 'I find both him and his followers much crestfallen', concludes Wake.[75]

After this crisis the ambassador's career lost as much in political significance as it gained in other spheres. He went as ambassador to the Low Countries and twice more to Venice but his upward climb to power was halted and he quickly fell below the level of its maximum success. Up to this date he had spent a full twelve years of mature life in Italy; and he was to spend another five there. It is hardly surprising that more homebred members of the English court and government looked on him as something of an apparition *alla Italiana*. His career certainly demonstrates how difficult it was for one who had passed so much of his time south of the Alps to participate in the politics of Whitehall. It shows also what were the means judged appropriate for achieving this purpose.

In describing the route, set with many pitfalls, by which a group of able men attempted to enter English politics from a base in Italy, attention has naturally centred on their relations with the court. Parliament was not their concern unless and until they became counsellors at home. It is interesting, therefore, to note the reputation of two of them, Wotton and Carleton, in the House of Commons. Wotton spoke in the session of 1614, appearing as a staunch defender of the prerogative, which he maintained against the criticisms of Sir Roger Owen. In the debate on Impositions he drew a distinction between hereditary and elective monarchies: James I must be placed in the former and more absolutist class, he argued, together with the Princes of Italy, the King of France and the King of Spain (except in Aragon), who all 'imposed' as they pleased. To this it was retorted that continental examples were no fit guide for the King and Commons of England, and one speaker uttered a warning against 'the unfit persuasions of some which tell the King they do it in France and Spain etc'.[76] As tempers and ambitions in parliament rose higher, the more radical heard with increasing distaste any reference to the despotisms of the continent. This was especially the case when such a reference came from a counsellor who had been a diplomat, long accustomed to continental practice and neglectful of the alleged liberties inherent in the English mode of government. Sir Dudley Carleton, then Vice Chamberlain, defended the arrest of Sir John Eliot in May 1626 and his expressions horrified the Commons: he advised them not to trench upon the royal prerogatives, otherwise the King would be forced to use new counsels. And what were these new counsels? The destruction of parliament, rule by prerogative, taxation and starvation of men to the limit of their endurance — 'you would count it a great misery, if you knew the subjects in foreign countries as well as myself'.[77] The argument of Carleton's speech was construed, probably unfairly, as a threat to parliament; and he himself was in turn condemned as a willing protagonist of dangerous new counsels, based on the continental models with which long experience had familiarized him. Fortunately, the King raised him to the peerage shortly afterwards and his career in the Commons came abruptly to an end. It is fair to conclude (with Clarendon) that Carleton, whatever his abilities, had lost touch with the customs and character of his own country by continuous residence abroad. Without necessarily sponsoring any novel ideas on the virtue of unrestricted monarchies — after all he had lived mainly in the territories of two republics, the Netherlands and Venice — he still preserved intact the Elizabethan notions of the state which no longer satisfied the more radical members in the Commons; and the same was true of his old rival, Sir Henry Wotton. Their lives had been passed principally in the courts of Europe; their political and personal ambitions depended on the successful management of diplomats abroad and the dispensers of preferment at home. Parliament was still, for them, a side-issue.

Apart from Wotton, Wake and Carleton certain other English statesmen of that generation visited Lombardy, Venetia and Tuscany. Much less is known about their travels, but their experience abroad was equivalent to the earliest stage of Wotton's residence on the continent, as described above. These men, such as Richard Naunton, John Coke, and Francis Windebank were indeed more fortunate than their rivals; bypassing the diplomatic service of the Stuarts they came earlier to court.[78] In October 1595 the youthful Coke was in Siena. Almost a year passed before he came homeward through Geneva, Lyon, and Paris. In the autumn of 1597 Naunton wrote from Paris to his patron Essex, expressing a desire to visit Italy; an unnamed correspondent in England had promised to find the money if indeed he was able to 'go into Italy'. We can say also that ten years later the young Windebank enjoyed a leisurely contiental tour, between 1606 and 1608. In July 1607 he wrote from Lucca to his father in Italian; it was a proof of his industry, so he said. Returning to England he then began work in the Signet office, a place promised earlier.

It seems therefore that the posts which English diplomats in Italy most coveted were frequently held by men who, in their earlier days, themselves travelled abroad but never served as diplomats. The latter, the spokesmen of the Stuart king in foreign courts, certainly tried to use their activity, their role as sponsors or instruments of policy, as a recommendation for further preferment. The experience of our three wise men in Italy, Wotton, Carleton and Wake, shows how difficult and chancy it was to advance from the more distant outposts such as Venice and Turin. At home, patrons were needed, and patience abroad.

# 5. THE GIRO D'ITALIA AFTER 1630

So far, much of the evidence has centred round northern Italy. This is partly for the reason that reports from English diplomatic representatives in Venice and Turin provide the basis of such information as survives, partly because it corresponds with other, more general developments. During the reign of James I, although not so emphatically as under Elizabeth, Protestant English people kept mainly to Venetia and Tuscany. Their journeys further south were in the nature of short expeditions into less friendly country. Then followed a pause, in the third decade of the century. Hostilities reopened on a European scale, involving northern Italy. England attempted to play an active part being finally committed to war with both France and Spain. At the same time the plague caused terrible mortality in several areas of England and France, as in Venice, Milan, Bologna and Piedmont.[1] Civilian travel became difficult, if not impossible. Then, after 1630, after Charles I's peace treaties with the courts of France and Spain while the Thirty Years War continued, a new phase began in the history of English travel south of the Alps. If the travellers themselves were unaware of the novelty, it confronts anyone trying to trace their footsteps. In the first place, the process was completed by which the whole peninsula opened its doors to the traveller. Lombardy, Rome and the Papal States became safe ground for the Protestant Englishman. Fear of detention by the Inquisition dwindled sensibly. Secondly, during the twenty years between 1630 and 1650 war continued in Savoy and Piedmont, for the conflict between Bourbon and Habsburg was as fierce there as along the upper and lower reaches of the Rhine. These two facts combined to alter the nature of a traveller's itinerary in Italy; and they produced the conventional *giro d'Italia*. Instead of entering the country by the pass of Mont Cenis into Piedmont, and confining attention to the cities of Tuscany and Venetia, sometimes diversified by a discreet, almost furtive dash to Rome and a less furtive examination of antiquities and natural wonders at Naples, this tour had its starting-point at Marseilles.[2] From there, in the late autumn, English people were now accustomed to go first to Genoa. They continued on their way to Florence and Rome, where they spent some months. They proceeded to Naples for a short visit, and returned to enjoy Easter at Rome, nearly always a fixed point in their calculations of time and travel. After that they struck across the mountains to Loreto and Ancona and so northwards to Bologna, in order to reach Venice for Ascensiontide; if necessary, they hurried by the direct road to Bologna and onwards, for the great Venetian celebrations at Ascension were another fixed point in their timetable. Thereafter, in the summer months they returned northward through Milan and over the Simplon pass to Geneva; on the conclusion of the Thirty Years War in Germany the route over the Brenner to Innsbruck and Augsburg was also open to travellers again.

For individuals mainly concerned with education or pleasure every variation on this itinerary was possible. Yet the records are sufficiently stereotyped to leave an impression that most travellers adhered to it unless they had some special considerations in mind, public or private reasons. At any rate they were aware that this was the customary practice of their friends.

It is clear that the possibility of a round tour in Italy, including a settled period of residence at Rome, depended on the amicable relations of the English government and the Papacy. This in turn was connected with two other considerations. First, the *giro d'Italia* appears as only a part of the normal pattern of foreign travel. It usually followed a long spell of residence in France and very often preceded another lengthy stay in Paris on the homeward journey. As the century continued all the indications show that the Italian tour was becoming subordinate to the more indispensable element in a gentleman's time abroad — as it came to be considered — his education in France. We are steadily moving away from the period when the men and works of the Italian Renaissance, linked naturally with the history of ancient Rome, dominated the imagination of the educated in northern Europe in secular matters. In some spheres the achievement of Italians in the seventeenth century was as remarkable as ever before, but their general prestige was apparently less.[3] Richard Lassels, for example, in the introduction to his *Voyage of Italy*, printed posthumously in 1670, admitted that he was advocating an unpopular view when he recommended that boys of sixteen should be sent first to Italy for three years to learn the language and other arts, before going to France and Paris for practice in the conventional social accomplishments, dancing, fencing, making and receiving visits, and the like.[4]

The second consideration is less important. Time enjoyed in Italy was sometimes part of a more ambitious scheme, a trip to the Levant. In such cases this might simply mean going to Venice as quickly as possible, and there taking ship. It was the route followed in 1634 by Sir Henry Blount, who on his return from Mohammedan countries wrote a favourable account of their creed and society, by comparison with his own observation of Christian practice: an account which merges into the history of Deism in England, and observations which were sharpened by

Blount's earlier travels in Europe.[5] But there is also the example of George Courthop, from a Sussex family, who after eighteen months in France travelled southward through Geneva, Genoa, Rome and Naples, on his way to Messina and Constantinople in 1637.[6] Towards the end of 1638, in the artist Nicholas Stone's diary there is mention of his patron Mr. William Paston, son and heir in the Norfolk family of that name, who after sightseeing in Italy sailed from Leghorn with three English servants and arrived in Rome six months later, having visited Alexandria, Cairo and Jerusalem.[7] At about the same time, so John Milton relates in a famous autobiographical sketch, he himself felt tempted to cross over from Naples to Sicily and Greece but decided ultimately against such a course,[8] and six years later, in 1645, John Evelyn had already booked a passage and purchased stores for a tour through the Levant when the Venetian authorities abruptly requisitioned his ship, to his grief and annoyance.[9] Evidently these eastward journeys, while not the rule for English gentlemen in Italy, provided for a few of the more adventurous spirits an additional experience, a variation from the ordinary continental itineraries which at their furthest extension were bounded by La Rochelle, Madrid, Naples, Vienna and Augsburg.

Almost every traveller, therefore, visited Italy after residing in France; and a few travellers visited Italy in the course of a longer tour to the Levant. In Italy itself, the journey became a circuit of all the principal cities, including Rome and Bologna in the Papal States. In view of the nervousness expressed by an earlier generation on that very topic, and of the old proviso still incorporated in many English passports that the traveller should not proceed to Rome, how did this alteration come about and can it be observed from contemporary accounts?

The Spanish marriage project of James I had failed. Nevertheless the dynasty in England, if not the English people, came to terms with the Catholic world by the marriage of Charles and Henrietta Maria. After a period of preliminary disagreements this step appeared to help the Catholics in England; it certainly smoothed the way for English Protestants in Italy. Papal envoys, Panzani, Con, Rossetti, came to England. In July 1636 Henrietta Maria's representative, Sir William Hamilton, reached Rome. The Catholic authorities considered the possibility of arranging Charles I's conversion; they approached Archbishop Laud; Cardinal Francesco Barberini, Protector of the English Nation, sent a stream of presents, pictures and sculpture, to London. Prominent English courtiers abjured Protestantism. In such circumstances it became daily less feasible for the Roman Inquisition, or any other authority in Italy, to proceed against travelling Englishmen. The approach to a tactic of reconciliation, first observed by Sir Henry Wotton thirty years earlier, grew daily more evident. All that appeared necessary was the exercise of discretion by the English traveller and the ecclesiastical official.[10]

Some idea of the moderation which now began to be practised

emerges from a soberly written account which belongs to the later
sixteen-thirties and describes the examination of an English Protestant,
a servant of the ambassador at Venice, by the Inquisitor at Ferrara. He
had left Rome and was on his way to Venice by coach. While he and his
companions, who were of various professions and nationalities, passed
through Ferrara they were stopped and the coachman was told to drive
to the offices of the Inquisition. The travellers were examined indivi-
dually and the Englishman's interview took the following course:

> Coming to me the first question was of what Countrie I was, what was my
> name, to which having truely answered, the next was, Are you a Christian?
> an constant question to the Ultramontani who, not holding with the Pope,
> they account no Christians; to which having answered affirmatively, he
> passed to other Interrogatories, as, whence I came, what busines I had at
> Rome, whither I was goeing and what busines I had at Venice, to all which
> having made answere and, as I supposed, to the satisfaction of the Inquisitor,
> the Knave officer or Catchpole standing by said to the Inquisitor, 'Your
> Paternity shall do well to Examine this person more fully, for me thought that
> when he answered to some of your demands he did it in a very slighting
> manner.' Whereupon I took the boldnes to tell him that he falsely accused
> me, that I had truely and with reverence answered the father Inquisitor and
> should doe it againe, if he pleased to comand me, but as for him he had no
> authoritie to meddle with me and that possibly he had a desire to make a prey
> of me. Whereupon the Inquisitor gently corrected me for so speaking to the
> officer and fell againe to most of his former Questions, to which he added:
> '*Siete Catholico?*' Are you a Catholike? without adding *Romano*, to my much
> content and safety, whether on purpose or unwittingly he did it I cannott say,
> but I could honestly and with truth say I was a Catholike, as I did, but not a
> Romane Catholike, that never it came unto me [*sic*]; which yet I think, had he
> added Romane and I denyed it, as I must and should, yet I should have
> escaped by virtue of my Lord Ambassador's Passport which I had aboute me,
> wee Protestants at that time being kindly used by the Papists in respect of our
> Queene; but I was not willing to produce my Passe without urgent occasion. I
> must not omitt that amongst other Picktures that hunge in the roome where
> we were was that of St. Raymondo whose speciall protection at that tyme,
> had I beene a Romanist, I must needes have acknowledged. . . I was in greate
> feare they would have searched my valise wherein I had some prohibited
> bookes that might [have] brought me into some trouble; and thus [I] got me
> out of this Hell whence is said, and hath often beene found by many, there is
> no redemption.[11]

In this account the feverish hatred of a traveller like Lithgow, who states
that his downright Protestantism at Rome in 1609 endangered his life,
appears to have been left far behind. Milton, it is true, when in later life
he reviewed his travels in Italy, believed that an undeviating fidelity to
Protestant opinions while at Rome required from him a distinct measure
of courage.[12] But the fact that he was not molested, together with the
appearance of so many Englishmen in central Italy at this time, suggests

that the moderation practised by the Inquisitor of Ferrara was the rule and not the exception by 1640. The sad fate of John Mole, arrested for heresy at Rome in 1609 and imprisoned there for over twenty years because he refused to abjure, belonged to a phase that was now past.

'In Sienna', wrote a traveller in 1646, 'they have a strict Inquisition so yt we dar'd not go for our morning-draughts to an Osteria without taking our way through some Church, to clense us first with holy-water.' At Reggio, not long afterwards, an Inquisitor refused to look over an Englishman's books, which an officious carrier brought to him for examination: preferring to take the traveller's word for their titles and subscribing a licence on the spot. It was not a very terrifying state of affairs and only a little outward conformity was required to allay suspicion. A traveller like John Evelyn in 1645, or Francis Mortoft in 1659, both good Protestants, had no occasion to mention the subject.[13]

Another aspect of the relations between English people and the ecclesiastical authorities was the cordial welcome apparently always given to Protestants by the English Jesuits, and by the dignitaries of the Church, especially Cardinal Francesco Barberini. Thus, documents belonging to the years 1638–1639 show that Milton dined at the English College in October 1638 with a brother of Lord Falkland and other gentlemen, where he was honorably received; and he was personally welcomed by Cardinal Barberini to a concert given in his palace. Only in an account written after the Civil War does Milton refer particularly to the English Jesuits as men preparing to proceed against him after his return to Rome from a visit to Naples.[14] For polemical reasons he undoubtedly exaggerated the hostility he met with in the States of the Pope. The traveller who was soon afterwards cross-questioned at Ferrara gives an account of his reception by the English Jesuits which supplements other evidence on the subject and is more in accordance with the general tendencies of the period:

> We had an Invitation from the Prefect of the English fold (being Jesuits) whoe was then Father Fitzherbert, a grave and reverend person, and learned as his works show. We had very good and sober Chere, every one his Messe apart, and in the tyme of dynner one of the Novices reading some storie out of the Gospel. We were treated very kindly and civilly, and not a word of Religion till we were taking our leaves. . . [then they engaged in a certain amount of controversy] . . . that we should depart from his Colledge sweetned, the old man invited us to the Musick of a Concord of Violyns, performed by some of the younge students and soone after very kindly dismissed us. These Invitations are done to our Nation certaynely to gayne what they can upon those of our Religion, and soften us as to theirs, and at that tyme our Nation was very kindly used in that place and all lawful liberty given them. I remember desiring one day to be admitted unto an Enterlude in *Stilo recitativo* acted before some Cardinals and persons of quallitie being demanded what Country we were of, to which was replyed *Inglesi*; we were presently bid goe in and had given us very comodious seats.[15]

This was all very much in the spirit of Evelyn's reception at Rome in 1644; he had been 'especially recommended' to a number of English Catholics there, including the Rector of the English College, where he was invited to dine on the feast of St. Thomas Becket, 29 December. A year later, on the same date, another prominent English guest was the second Duke of Buckingham with a large company. An earlier generation of English heretics would not have been invited to the feast of Becket's commemoration.[16]

An English Catholic who later became a decided Protestant, in the course of an apologia which adversely criticized most members of the Roman hierarchy, described Cardinal Barberini as 'more tractable, kind and loving' than the other Cardinals; he had met and talked with him in the spring of 1640.[17]

Other travellers expressed outright enthusiasm. Hugh Popham, touring abroad on an allowance of £200 a year from his father, arrived in Rome during February 1639. He dined at the English College with five other gentlemen on the 27th, and in addition wrote home to England describing Cardinal Barberini's great kindness to him — 'the gallantest gentleman in the whole world, ffor the very next day after I came to towne he sent one of his Gentlemen to see me and after I had wayted on him to kiss his hands, he sent continually to visit me, and withall a present of the bravest wine . . . .'[18]

However, the other princes of the Church were never lacking in diplomacy. Sir George Savile, the future Marquis of Halifax, was in Rome in 1650, a boy of sixteen and a semi-exile; Cardinal Savelli received him with great courtesy, claiming a family relationship. At the same period another young English nobleman who spent the greater part of a year there was welcomed and entertained by Cardinals Barberini, Spada and Capponi: this was Philip, second Earl of Chesterfield. Ten years later again, Robert Southwell, who had been at Queen's College, Oxford, during the Protectorate and afterwards became so influential a figure in England and Ireland, spent many hours of his long stay in Rome in friendly conversation with a number of cardinals, Orsini, Pallavicini, Barberini and Asolini; while during the same winter, 1660–1661, the son and heir of one of the Presbyterian peers in England, Lord Maynard, was received in private audience by Clement IX on the strength of a letter of introduction from Henrietta Maria.[19]

The circumstances of the Civil War and the exile would in any case have led to the establishment of friendly relations between Rome and large numbers of English gentry who sided with the Stuarts. In fact, however, this tacit reconciliation took place many years earlier. The journals and papers of English travellers after 1630 nearly all testify to the cordiality of their reception in central Italy. The roads and the cities were open to them. They could travel in peace through the length and

breadth of Italy. They could make the giro d'Italia. Returned to England
their ideas or prejudices still appeared to cling somewhat tenaciously to
the century-old anti-papal tradition but abroad they were now fortunate
enough to enjoy practical toleration of, or acquiescence in, their inherited
opinion regarding ecclesiastical subjects. It was presumably a phase of
marked importance in the education of the English ruling class; and to
this their experience south of the Alps contributed.

The route round Italy, therefore, was no longer made difficult by
political or religious factors. The weather, the incidence of plague, and
bandits were the remaining hindrances. The first of these simply determined the timing of journeys: in the autumn and winter our travellers
were to be found on their way south to Rome through Genoa, Pisa and
Florence. Naples was never more full of English and others from the
north, merchants and sailors apart, than in the early spring. Venice was
crowded with them by June and in the summer they were returning
homeward again. The second hindrance, plague, from time to time
frightened them away altogether. The great devastation of 1627–1628
in the north has already been mentioned. Again in 1657 one young
traveller, John Reresby, after waiting several months for the infection to
diminish was compelled to leave the country without having seen more
than Venice and Florence. Part of the period which he had originally
set aside for his stay in Italy had perforce to be allotted to the lesser
attractions of Germany. Finally, bandits could be evaded by the precaution of travelling in large companies. Since many travellers were
usually on the move at the same seasons of the year, this was by no
means difficult to arrange. Lord Maynard's son rode northwards from
Naples in March 1661 in the company of at least twenty English gentlemen and their servants.[20]

The point of departure was Marseilles in the autumn: Milton remem-
bered passing through Nice, possibly as early as August 1638; Evelyn
reached Marseilles in the first week of October 1644; John Raymond in
December 1646, another anonymous Englishman who kept a diary in
November 1648, Francis Mortoft and his friends in November 1658.
Thomas Abdy in 1634, even though he had gone as far as Chambèry in
Savoy a few months earlier, retraced his steps and reaching Marseilles in
October, took shipping for Italy. The evidence varies only slightly from
one party to another and it must describe the practice of innumerable
English and other travellers. Next they found their way along the Riviera
by sea or land, or a combination of both. Evelyn hired mules to take him
as far as Cannes since the only vessels available at Marseilles were too
small for safety, in view of Turks and other pirates in the neighbourhood.
At Cannes he continued his journey by sea and in five days reached
Genoa. He so enjoyed the perfume of Italian oranges, citron and jas-

9.   A first glimpse of the Mediterranean: after 1630 many tourists went by sea along the
     coast from Marseilles to Italy. This is another of Tassin's *Plans et Profilz*.

mine wafting seaward that the memory of it recurred to mind when he
dedicated his *Fumifugium* — for the abatement of smoke in London —
to Charles II in 1661. Mortoft, on the other hand, could find no
shipping at all and travelled overland into Italy. His experience agreed
with what he had previously been told: that it was indeed 'accounted by
All Travellers absolutely the worst way in Europe'.[21]

By this route Genoa was the first great city where it became necessary
to admire and examine with care a large number of churches and
palaces: the palaces of the Dorias, the Dinegros and the Doge, the
Cathedral and the churches of S. Ambrogio and the Annunziata; also
the wonderful gardens. It was a commonplace, faithfully repeated by
English travellers, to compare Genoa to a theatre on account of its
situation on the steeply shelving amphitheatre of hills. The analogy is
a reminder that for the generation that was then passing the most
accessible view of Italy and the Italian scene had been the stage perspectives and painting of Inigo Jones for the masques at Whitehall. At
any rate, here in Genoa many Englishmen had their first real intro-

duction to this world of sixteenth and seventeenth-century Italian design; not only in the architecture of palaces and streets but the fountains, the statuary, the furniture and a wealth of ecclesiastical ornament. Here in Genoa, also, most travellers began to listen rather mechanically to the comments of Italian guides, and browse in Italian guidebooks. If they had determined to continue with the diaries they kept in France they continued also to copy down a variety of unassimilated details about the places they visited; and in Italy there was a distressing amount to see. A few, of course, were more sensitive. Evelyn and also Roger Pratt, the future architect, greatly admired Genoa, and later on they supplemented their own impressions by reference to the *Palazzi Antichi e Moderni di Genova*, a folio of plans which had been originally collected by P. P. Rubens.[22]

After a few days they continued southwards on their way, which led through small towns and small villages some miles from the coast, into Tuscany. In passing they visited the Republic of Lucca, a city which all English travellers admired either for its political independence or the trimness of the streets or for excellent music to be heard there. A merchant factor bound from Archangel to the Levant, who spent a day in Lucca, summed up the favourable impression of his more leisurely contemporaries by writing that the citizens 'in their customs are nearest to the English of any'.[23] Higher praise he could not give. For a different reason, the same might be said of Leghorn, the great Tuscan port twenty-five miles further south, simply because the community of English traders there was so large by the middle of the century. Travellers came to Leghorn on the journey to Rome without any specific intention of admiring painting or architecture although at this date it impressed them as a handsome city. Its importance to them was primarily as the resort of English merchants and sea-captains, where bills of exchange or letters of credit were honoured, cases of valuables shipped for England and trunks disembarked from home;[24] where also the hospitality of wealthy English merchants might sometimes be anticipated.[25] Leghorn, in fact, was the cosmopolitan centre where the gentleman traveller collected his funds before proceeding on his journey. The circumstance that the citizens there liked wearing English or French clothes — an important matter to the merchant — hardly impressed those who had come to Italy for what Italy alone could give them. They quickly took their departure and, going from Leghorn back to Pisa which they had already seen, travelled up the valley of the Arno to Florence.

In these two cities the duty of sightseeing was paramount. It was regarded as necessary, then as now, to view the Campanile, the Baptistery, the Campo Santo and Cathedral at Pisa; it was more exacting, but equally necessary to survey the accumulated treasures of Florence. A bare catalogue of the latter, which came to be incorporated into the diaries of many travellers, can have been of little educational value to them; it is hardly more useful to the historian, except as an index of the particular enthusiasms and dislikes of the seventeenth century, its neglect of the earlier Florentine artists and whole-hearted admiration for the more modern masters of the decorative arts. Two general points deserve comment. One was the short duration of the average stay in Florence at this period. Gentlemen making the giro d'Italia, especially on this outward journey, never spent long in northern Tuscany. If they felt sufficiently interested or conscientious they came back in the following summer after visiting Venice, but even so the reputation of Florence as a city where Englishmen settled down for a matter of months appears to have diminished since the commencement of the century. Mortoft spent five days in Florence, and Evelyn not more than ten, on their way to Rome; and both were most scrupulous sightseers. Evelyn, it is true, returned later to remedy the deficiency but in general the pattern of the giro sacrificed this city to the ever-growing prestige, and for Englishmen the newly-won liberties, of Rome. Secondly, it is curious to observe the diversity of rare or beautiful things which appealed to travellers so that their lists of works worth seeing in Florence, presumably a mingling of their own observation with hints from books, are always and above all miscellaneous in character: work in alabaster, pietra commessa, paintings, sculpture, saddles, stables of fine horses and wild animals, tables and altars of jasper, cabinets of medals and diamonds, ivories, 'saints done all in amber, and Persian armour'. The Duke's treasury appears nearly always to have interested them more genuinely than the Cathedral. They dutifully examined the architecture of the Pitti and Strozzi palaces, visited S. Spirito, admired the David of Michelangelo; but treasure, in the literal meaning of the word, justified to them in a more authentic manner the great name of the Grand Dukes of Tuscany.

Siena was the next important stage in the journey. Few could refrain from words of praise for its piazza, and the fountain of Jacobo della Quercia, and for the cathedral with its black and white marble cupola, pulpit and the famous pavement. A few more settled here to learn Italian in a thorough manner, or at least determined to come back for that purpose at a later date. But usually they hurried on, through Montefiascone where the wine was good, through Viterbo and the desolate Campagna, to Rome itself.

Here they intended to stay some time and it was necessary to find permanent lodgings. It was usual to put up at an inn for a few days and then to hire a house or apartment:

We continued at the Gamberi [sic] or Lobster till after the holy days, wrote Mr Maynard's servant, and then my master with the help of the Governor took a Lodging at a Privat house near Trinità del Monte of one Mr Pendrich a Scots Gentleman, in whose house there lodged a worthy Gentleman, one Doctor Gage, who was very good company for my maister the whole winter. We hired an Italian Cooke, one Sebastian, to dress our meat, and I myself was caterer to buy all things that was needful.[26]

In 1638 Nicholas and Henry Stone with two Dutchmen had rented an unfurnished house by the church of Trinità dei Monti for 40 crowns a year. Evelyn likewise lodged near the Piazza di Spagna close by in 1644; and in the following year the Duke of Buckingham took a house also on the height of the Trinità dei Monti. English people were thus accustomed, already in the middle of the seventeenth century, to settle in this part of Rome, which in the course of the preceding hundred years had grown increasingly populous and fashionable. In the Piazza di Spagna stood the Spanish ambassador's palace, and on the south side the Collegium Urbanicum de Propaganda Fide the facade of which underwent reconstruction at the end of 1642.[27]

These travellers found it difficult to give anything but a confused impression of their experience at Rome, so innumerable were the sights and rarities of the city. A diarist who has conscientiously noted everything up to this point in his journey will leave a few blank pages in order to fill them at some later date with his memories or knowledge of Rome: a task which in the end he never attempted.[28] Another gives a short description which he promises to enlarge: an undertaking meagrely made good.[29] Others again plunged boldly in, and with the help of professional guides and printed guide-books burden their pages with profuse accounts of the Seven Hills and the Seven Churches, ancient statuary and modern palaces and pictures. The reason for their embarrassment was clear enough. The vast expansion in architectural and artistic activity in the preceding century, especially the great undertakings of Paul V's and Urban VIII's Pontificates had strained the endeavours of the foreign sightseer beyond computation. He now desired to see so much; unlike Moryson and Lithgow fifty years earlier, who were largely content with a view of the remains of ancient Rome, and debarred by their status as heretics or enemies from any but the most cursory examination of Tridentine churches and modern palaces. Now English travellers were welcomed everywhere and they desired to see everything.

The most intelligent, as well as the most famous of these travellers, whose notebooks have survived, was of course Evelyn.[30] His work has the merit of being not only exceptional in quality but representative in character, his journey conforming strictly to pattern. He arrived at Rome early in November, remained until the end of January, made a short trip to Naples and back, in order to attend Carnival, Lent and Easter at Rome before proceeding to Venice; in most respects his performance

*Veüe du Marché Romain appellé Campo Vacino, dou l'on voit*
*les ruines du Palais Majeur des Empereurs, et la vigne farnese.*        *Prospectus fori Romani aut Boarij Ubi Palatij Imperatorum*
                                                                          *Majoris rudera & villa farnesiana conspiciuntur.*

10.  A corner of the Roman Forum: a tourist coming down from the Capitol to the
     Forum (sometimes a cattle-market) would certainly not miss the old well, the three
     pillars from the Temple of Castor and Pollux, and the new facade hiding an
     ancient Christian church, with the ruins and gardens on the Palatine hill behind
     them.

resembled those of Abdy, Mortoft, Milton, Maynard, Raymond and an
anonymous traveller in 1648, for all of whom there are records.[31] Now
of the three months which Evelyn spent in Rome, the first three or four
weeks were evidently given up to the most arduous sightseeing. From
the 6th to the 14th November 1644 he explored the area lying south of
his lodging in the Piazza di Spagna, and on the eastern side of the Tiber:
the great Renaissance palaces, Farnese, Barberini, the Quirinal, the
Villa Ludovisi, the Villa Medici; the ancient and modern buildings in the
Forum and on the Capitoline and Aventine Hills, an assortment of
churches old and new, the Baths of Diocletian and the Colosseum.
Then, partly owing to bad weather he rested for two days. He visited
next the Palazzo Borghese and its gardens, to the north of his lodging;
and after that, apparently for the first time, he ventured westwards over
the river and spent two days viewing the Vatican and St. Peter's. In the
following week he visited a miscellany of different churches and palaces

in various parts of the city, St. John Lateran, the Villa Aldobrandini and the Palazzo Medici. He began also to revisit the scenes which had already attracted his preference. But it was time to pause for breath and at the end of the month he found that he was 'pretty weary of continual walking' and remained at home for a week, taking lessons on the theorbo with an Italian music-master.

It seems probable that Evelyn saw as much, in the month of November 1644, as any other English traveller at this time. After that he, and they, preferred to take things more easily, going again and again to their favourite haunts, watching the ceremonies and processions of ecclesiastical festivals, listening to music, and in certain cases interviewing scholars or artists.

However, a fortnight's excursion to Naples was by no means to be omitted, not so much for what was worth seeing in the city as upon its outskirts. 'Truly if a traveller Hyperbolize in any part of his voyage of Italy', wrote Raymond in his Itinerary, 'the most fit theame he can take are the Wonders a little distant from Naples.' Here the emphasis was twofold, on the remains of antiquity and the marvels of nature. Men travelled southwards here along the Appian Way, 'so smooth and shining', from the transport of many generations, 'that when the sun shines upon it you may see its glitter two Miles off, like a Silver Highway', past ruins where a single structure reminded the tourist of noble cities long since vanished, past bad inns and bandit-infested areas and menacing customs-officers. Arrived at Naples it was essential to make two excursions: one to the Tractus Puteolanus north-westwards, to see 'Virgil's tomb', the 'house of Cicero', the 'Elysian fields' and all the remains connected with the names of Caligula, Nero and Tiberius. In the same area the grotto of Pausillippus, a long tunnel through the mountain, and the Grotto del Cane, where every traveller was accustomed to watch the experiment of stupifying a dog by the fumes and reviving it in the near-by waters of Lake Agnano, provided a foretaste of the natural wonders which were to be viewed south of Naples. For the second excursion was to Vesuvius; to enjoy the excitement of the climb, and the panorama, and the collection of pumice or other rare mineral specimens.[32]

They made this the southern limit of their travel. To go beyond, to Messina or Malta, would be stepping outside the giro d'Italia, the pattern of this particular convention in the seventeenth century, and harking back to a much older tradition of the Christian pilgrimage to Holy Places in the east.[33]

They returned to Rome by the way they had come. Most of them saw something of Carnival and Lent or at any rate of Holy Week and Easter. It does not appear that any Protestant traveller explicitly refers to the contrast between the succession of these Roman seasons and the

11. St Peters, Rome: as the travellers saw it in 1640, with scaffolding in position for a new bell-tower. Fifteen years later Bernini designed his great colonnade and piazza which would in due course transform the prospect on the right.

Puritan conception embodied in 'the rule of the Saints' during the Commonwealth or Protectorate in England. Only Richard Lassels, who was Catholic, felt moved to argue in the course of his description of Rome that a little merriment in season would have prevented the outbreak of 'flat Rebellion and Fanatick Heresies'. Nevertheless they eagerly followed the amusements of Carnival; they purchased a licence to eat meat during Lent, not a matter of great difficulty; and they admired the Easter ceremonies, the showing of St. Veronica's handkerchief or processions of the Flagellants. In fact they joined for a short period in the life of the city, becoming acquainted at first hand with its mingling of imperial and ecclesiastical tradition. They took the opportunity, also, of viewing what had been neglected on their first visit, particularly the villas and gardens at Frascati and Tivoli; 'this shall be my pattern for a countryseat', commented Raymond on the latter.[34]

At length they prepared to depart, as the summer approached. Most of them travelled across the mountains to the Adriatic coast, for a glimpse of Loreto.[35] This was the itinerary of Thomas Abdy in 1635 and of Banister Maynard in 1661, as of many others. John Evelyn regretted that he could not follow the usual practice in this respect but a mischance in his financial arrangements delayed him and he was forced to hasten to Venice by the direct route to Bologna.[36] Most of these English travellers faithfully recount the alleged miracles connected with Loreto. The general view of educated men was probably Mortoft's, that 'they report many miracles of this Lady of Loretto and some are such great lyes that they make any person suspect the truth of the former'. One genuine attraction was the fabulous treasury, tribute of many princes and peoples. The English saw there the gift of their own queen, Henrietta Maria. It is again worth emphasis that the *treasure*, at Florence, Rome, Loreto and Venice, likewise the *arsenals* of Genoa, Rome and Venice received a measure of enthusiastic attention, in the seventeenth as in earlier centuries, which has long since declined.

Having reached Ancona on the coast the travellers turned northwards, to follow the old Via Flaminia through pleasant country and small cities which never detained them long, as far as Bologna. Here they met English people who had come from Rome by way to Siena and Florence. It was a fine and memorable place, and noted (they learnt) for sausages, S. Caterina dei Vigri — 'as odd a relick as can be' — and paintings by the Carracci. No one stopped here more than two or three days. Going on to Ferrara they went by boat down the Po and arrived in Venice, completing a journey from Rome which usually took them a fortnight.

Here they came into touch with a resident English colony again; merchants and seamen in Venice, students at Padua. Maynard in 1661 lived with our consul, Gideon Jones, and enjoyed entertainment fit for a king both in Venice and in Jones's country villa outside. Evelyn lodged at Signor Paolo Rodomonte's inn, the Black Eagle, as did Robert Bargrave ten years later; but he notes with pleasure the English food given him by Hobson, a merchant, and on board an English ship. As a matter of necessity everyone who came to Venice had made arrangements to obtain fresh supplies of money from the English merchants there. One traveller drew pistoles to the value of £100 on the 27 April 1649 and an extra £50 on the 11 May following. Another, perhaps more economically, exchanged bills for £170 between August 1645 and April 1646.[37] With finances restored, it remained an imperious duty to see the sights and participate in the festivals. If all had gone according to plans laid earlier, most of the travellers arrived at Venice in time for the ceremonies of Ascension Day when the Republic celebrated her marriage with the sea, the Doge at the prow of his great gilded galley Bucentoro casting a ring into the waters, in the presence of innumerable Venetians and strangers in gondolas and other craft, to the salute of innumerable guns. It was a time of Carnival again, of operas, gambling and regattas. Then came the inspection of the city's monuments, an itinerary which hardly varies in the recital of different travellers: the Piazza, the Clock, the Treasury, the Cathedral, all of St. Mark; the Ducal Palace, the Arsenal, the Palazzo Grimani, the statue of Bartolomeo Colleoni; the islands of S. Giorgio Maggiore, S. Cristoforo and S. Michele with their ecclesiastical buildings; the Ghetto; and the glassworks of Murano. A visit, or several visits, was also paid to Padua, possibly for the festival of St. Antony the patron saint (June 13), to meet English acquaintances there, admire the University halls, and in some cases to be enrolled a member of the University. This was a ceremony often without any academic implications but the certificate of matriculation served as a useful passport in the state, and on the frontiers, of Venice.[38]

Then, gradually, the travellers took their departure. The giro d'Italia was all but complete. Occasionally they determined to stay a while in Venice, or go back to Florence and Siena; but in any event the ways home were clear. Usually they journeyed westward through Vicenza, admiring the masterpieces of Palladio, through Verona and Brescia into the Duchy of Milan, and into Milan itself. The dangers which Sir Henry Wotton's messengers had formerly encountered in Spanish dominions were now past history. Evelyn, in a familiar passage, tells how he surprised the Viceroy being shaved as he wandered sightseeing through his palace, and travellers placidly spent a few days looking at the cathedral, the hospitals and other places of interest. Then they set their faces northwards to Domodossola and the Simplon pass, very strenuous travel; still, concludes one writer, 'it is but a trouble for 2 dayes yet I thinke it better passage then by sea'.[39] Thence followed the long descent of the Rhône valley to Geneva. By contrast with the preceding period this was probably the route most commonly followed by the returning traveller in the middle years of the century. Some, however, preferred to turn aside at Brescia and cross the Alps by the more easterly passes to Coire and so to Zurich and Basle; while over the Brenner was the road to Innsbruck and into Germany.

By whatever route they left Italy, their tour of the Italian cities had now been completed; and with due regard to special circumstances, whether shortage of money or plague or the desire to settle down for a few months somewhere along the road, these travellers had been made aware of the great seasonal movement to whch the majority of their contemporaries conformed: the winter journey down the Mediterranean coast, the stay in Rome, the excursion to Naples, the return northwards for Easter, the passage over the Apennines to Loreto and Ancona, and so northwards to Bologna and Ferrara; finally, the climax of Ascension week at Venice.[40] Together with the periodic voyages of English traders across the seas for the purpose of commerce should be reckoned also this seasonal journey of the English gentry into and round Italy: a movement which, based upon many experiments and antecedents, dates in this conventional form from the second quarter of the seventeenth century and persisted for several generations.

# 6. THE INFLUENCE OF ITALIAN TRAVEL ON ENGLISH TRAVELLERS

It was a commonplace of the period to praise travel, the business of peregrination, as a 'Moving Academy or the true Peripatetic School'.[1] It was fashionable in certain circles to laugh at the country gentleman who never saw anybody except his father's tenants and the local parson, never read anything except John Stow and John Speed, and believed that all solid greatness consisted in 'a great Fire and a great Estate'. If education was more than this it might well be propounded, in the phrase of Richard Lassels, that no man understood Livy and Caesar, Guicciardini and Montluc who had not performed 'exactly' the Grand Tour of France and the Giro of Italy.[2] Nevertheless, until definite evidence is forthcoming we are bound to feel sceptical of the influence of this tour upon the travellers; it is reasonable to surmise that the mere journeying from city to city during a short period can have made a relatively small impression. Apart from a more or less vivid awareness of the mainland across the English Channel, what were the solid results of this travel in Italy? The answer lies naturally not so much in the minds of those who conformed mechanically to the simpler rules laid down in guidebooks and other 'Advices to Travellers', as in the richer experience of men who seriously attempted to profit from their journeys, and to look about them. In fact, the conventionalized tour of Italy tends to signify the decline of Italian influences upon Englishmen: it was too speedy, too mechanical, and too commonplace. The transmission of Italian fashions in art or custom into England, therefore, rested with the minority of travellers who desired to improve on a merely fleeting acquaintance with Italy by one means or another, by a period of residence in the country or the intelligent purchase of Italian wares, even by the study or the writing of books about Italy.

This last item, books, is the simplest introduction to the problem; and the most rudimentary form of book was the diary. For example, the anonymous traveller who composed the Rawlinson MS. D 120 was apparently the poor relation of a gentleman whom he calls his 'cousin', and partly in order to satisfy his cousin's mother — 'your ladyship', who provided £1000 for the journey — he kept a record of their itinerary, the cities visited and monuments inspected. Partly, also, he conformed to the current belief that it was right and proper, pertaining to the educational purposes of a tour, to keep such a record. In 1660 and 1661 the servant of Banister Maynard, Robert Moody, made similar notes and, on his return, amplified them into a little manuscript volume, ornamented with an amateurishly drawn title-page and an Epistle Dedicatory to Maynard, in which he expressed the hope that these details would serve to remind his young nobleman of their pleasant, prosperous journey. The real effects of these two literary exercises must have been small. From time to time, however, a hint of more serious intentions emerges from such documents. Thomas Abdy in 1635 gives the same uninteresting details of the conventional itinerary; but there is an interval in the dates between 1 May, when he arrived in Florence, and 14 August. At the end of the diary a single note explains what had happened:

> Lorenzo Franciosino il Maestro della Lingua Toscana in Siena. Entred into Pension at Sig. Franc. at 16 scudi per meze 18 May 1635, give him bon conto 8 scudi.

Abdy evidently settled down for a few months to learn Italian. Or, by contrast with Maynard, another young English nobleman, Lord Alington, was living in Rome in 1652 and for his particular use some Italians prepared an elaborate exercise book, essays and stories in the Italian language with English translations on opposite pages, complete with a large subject-vocabulary under twenty headings. More important students were John Raymond and John Bargrave who on their way south stayed who months in Siena to learn the language, and after spending Easter at Rome, returned to Siena for the summer. As Raymond remarked later, 'I filial my books more with observations of the Languages, than of the people, City or Country'.[3]

His studies had one immediate consequence. Together with his travels they helped Raymond to compose his own book, *An Itinerary containing a Voyage made through Italy in the years 1646 and 1647*, published in London during 1648: a work which would have been impossible without some real knowledge of Italian books and without information supplied by natives of the country. He states in the preface that his travelling companions also greatly assisted him, so that the experiences of Raymond, Bargrave, Chapman (another young Kentish gentleman), and the enquiries pursued jointly by them on their way round Italy, happily resulted in a book which became also a useful guide for the next generation of Englishmen, whether they were travelling to Italy, or, less ambitiously, desired to know something of the country. The second important English book on the same subject, *Italy, in its original Glory, Ruine and Revival* by Edmund Warcup, published in London in 1660, was produced for not dissimilar reasons. Few details now survive of the early life of its author but Warcup too was a traveller. A nephew of Speaker Lenthall, he went to Italy as a young man, he was secretary to the Parliamentary commissioners with Charles I on the Isle of Wight in the autumn of 1648[4] and, later on, well known as a Middlesex J. P. and an active Protestant during the Popish Plot. The dedication of his book to Lenthall illustrates the process by which a knowledge of Italy became part of the intellectual equipment of a representative member of the English gentry; he refers to 'the Itinerary of Italy translated long after return thence, in those vacant hours which I allowed to diversion without further intention than to renew that language by a retranslation (which occasioned my so close keeping to the Italian names and Idiomes) and once more to travell that celebrate Country in this exact description, whither in my earlier years your Lordship addressed me'. Warcup's book, therefore, is not like Raymond's since it is a straightforward translation from the Italian. Only in one passage does he appear to make a contribution of his own, by quoting Edmund Waller's verses in praise of the Professor of Anatomy at Padua, and adding that he himself was in Italy at the same time;[5] but like Raymond and Bargrave he went to Italy, he learnt the language, and he conceived the idea of describing the country for the benefit of English readers.

The Italian original of his book was the *Itinerario d'Italia*, first published in the Latin of Franciscus Schotus during the Jubilee year of 1600 for the particular use of travellers to Rome and frequently reprinted later in a number of European cities, translated, enlarged, and improved by the addition of maps.[6] It was used by the brothers Nicholas and Henry Stone, purchased by Sir Thomas Browne's son Edward a few days after he arrived at Rome in December 1664, and already in Richard Symond's possession before ever he left England to tour the continent.[7] In one form or another it ranked among the most popular travel books of the century.

A contemporary critic said of Edmund Warcup that he depended too much on obsolete geographers, and of Raymond that he had spent too little time in Italy, for either of them to produce a satisfactory work on the subject. The critic, Richard Lassels, prepared his own version of the *Voyage to Italy*, which appeared posthumously in 1670. Lassels was a Catholic priest who spent the greater part of his life on the continent and acted as tutor or guide to a succession of English noblemen and women on their travel, and they also were presumably Catholics; but his book on Italy, first published both in Paris and London, enjoyed sufficient popularity in England to be reprinted a number of times.[8] Its detailed description of the sights of Italy, together with occasional gleams of wit, must have made it acceptable to every English traveller. Here again, the work of Lassels owed something, not only to his varied experience of travel in Italy, but also to an extensive knowledge of Italian books. He concludes his description of each important city by referring the reader to Italian works on its history and antiquities, and some of these he must have used himself.

Occasionally the travellers of an older generation also furbished up their acquaintance with the Italian language and literature to profit from the popularity of Italian subjects in England. In 1650 James Howell published his History of Venice, a series of translations and adaptations interspersed with his own direct reminiscences: his description of the glass-works at Murano in the seventeenth century is one of the most vivid and circumstantial of all the accounts given by English writers;[9] for he himself had negotiated with the glass-workers there on a professional basis in years gone by. In 1654 Henry Cogan who had once acted as secretary to Sir Henry Wotton in Venice and was now an impoverished Cavalier gentleman in Kent, produced his *Directions for Such as shall Travel to Rome*, a translation of Martinelli's *Roma Ricercata*, one of the most recent, most reliable of the guides to Rome. Cogan takes the English sightseer, in his native language, round the city in ten days' hard walking, pointing out the chief monuments of interest. In 1673 Sir Robert Honywood, by then a very old man, published a translation of Nani's History of Venice, giving the English reader a full account of Venetian history between 1613 and 1660; though in this case it cannot be proved from other sources that Honywood himself had ever travelled south of the Alps. In 1675 appeared a new English translation of Machiavelli's writings (the first was published in 1636) which was the work of Henry Neville, a Berkshire landowner who had spent two long periods in Italy (1642?–4, 1663–7), with a phase of involvement in Commonwealth politics between them. The fluent Italian of Neville's correspondence and his familiarity with Italian history are in fact more impressive than the colourless Venetian nobleman of his dialogue *Plato Redivivus* (1681) who tries to comment on the proposals of 'an English gentleman', Neville himself, for reforming the English constitution. His friend James Harrington was also at home in Italy, and equally steeped in the writings of Machiavelli.[10]

Finally, the *Painter's Voyage of Italy* may be mentioned, translated by W. L. from the *Viaggio Pittoresco d'Italia* of Giacomo Barri and printed in 1679; for it introduces the questions of Italian artistic influences in England. W. L. was William Lodge, a Yorkshire gentleman of independent means, of Jesus College, Cambridge, and Lincoln's Inn, an amateur artist of merit. He spent some time on the continent, in France and Italy. In 1670 he accompanied Thomas Belasyse, Lord Fauconberg, who was sent as Ambassador Extraordinary to Venice; he explained to the ambassador, in the dedication of his work, how he began by making 'collections' of his own on the principal paintings to be seen in Italy. Afterwards he discovered this book of Barri's, apparently rare in Venice and unobtainable in England, and decided to translate it for the benefit of the English public. He added also his own catalogue of a fine collection in Milan together with a few illustrations, likewise his own work, etched portraits of the great masters, Raphael, Cortona, Veronese and others. Here was another traveller who improved the occasion by study, revealing the Italian world to English readers. At a later data Lodge prepared etchings of certain famous scenes in Italy, of Gaeta, Pozzuoli and a view of Rome from the Appian Way.[11]

The production of English books and translations indicates a very fair degree of popular interest in Italian subjects. But this type of knowledge, although growing ever more widespread, probably resembled the fashionable Giro of Italy in its influence. It was widespread and commonplace, just as the Giro tended to be superficial and hasty. Both the information thus acquired and the journeys thus performed had lost all singularity. The one was no longer esoteric or exciting in any way, nor the other difficult and adventurous. They were simply part of the ordinary education and experience of the educated classes, stored in their libraries or their recollections, without leaving any overwhelming impression. They are not less noteworthy, at least to the historian, for this familiarity but it seems necessary to emphasize the contrast between the intense enthusiasm or the equally intense hatred of the Elizabethans for Italy, and the easy acceptance by Englishmen of the later seventeenth century of this knowledge of Italian cities and books and arts. There were exceptions to the general tendency but an impression of it does emerge from a broad survey of the period. It is a long step backward from the diaries of Evelyn and Mortoft to the scattered notes of such a man as Sir John North, who lived in Italy between 1575 and 1577, and on his return kept his accounts and even described his ordinary journeys in East Anglia and the Midland countries for at least two years in the Italian which he had learnt in Venetia.[12]

Books are a simple form of evidence on the subject because they are readily available, ranged on the library shelves.[13] The larger subject of the influence of Italian journeys on the taste of Englishmen in the arts and in music is more elusive. Broadly, such journeys provided material for contemporary judgment in favour of 'modern' art (the epithet was contemporary also) and for judgment against what was 'Gotique' or 'barbarous'. John Evelyn, for example, compares two Roman ecclesiastical buildings:

> The church of the Tre Fontane (as they are call'd) is perfectly well built although but small (whereas that of St. Paul is but Gotique) having a noble cupola in the middle.

He compares the Vatican Library with a building which he remembered as a student and visitor to Oxford:

> The walls and roofe are painted, not with antiques and grotescs (like our Bodleian at Oxford) but emblems, figures, diagrams and the like learned inventions, found out by the wit and industry of famous men, of which there are now whole volumes extant.

In the Palazzo Farnese he admired a ceiling carved in wood,

> which as I remember was in cedar, as the Italian mode is, and not in poore
> plaster as ours are, and some of them most richly gilt.[14]

In Venice he learnt to distinguish between the sections of the Ducal
Palace which were 'plainly Gotique' or 'much more Romanlike'. Evelyn
was particularly sensitive and well-informed in these matters. John
Raymond, on the same subject, contented himself with the observation
that the cathedral at Milan was more like the English cathedrals than
any he had seen elsewhere in Italy.[15]

Without constant reminders the memory of such a lesson in architectural styles would soon evaporate, except in the mind of enthusiasts;
and probably those who purchased expensive folios on the subject were
few in number. Travellers, however, are unwilling to leave a country
without suitable mementoes, and in this case these often took the form
of engravings, illustrative of the monuments ancient and modern, sheets
which poured from the Italian printing-houses at this period. Large
numbers of these were purchased by English travellers and consigned to
Leghorn or Venice for shipment to England. It is unfortunate that
precise details of subject and artist are usually omitted from the inventories. A miscellaneous set of these engravings, portraying buildings in
or near Rome, found its way into Elias Ashmole's great collection of
books and papers, and is undoubtedly characteristic of the period.[16]
They are now bound with works of a rather different character, French
illustrations of flowers, but their titles and subjects are still of some
interest:

> *Disegno et Sito del sontuoso Giardino et Palazzo del ser^mo Gran Duca di Toscana in
> Roma.[17]*
> *Ritratto...il vero sito dell'Horti et Fontane che con ingenuosissimi adornamenti et
> maraviglie si vedono nella villa in Tivoli...Hippolito Daeste.*
> *Giardino di Belvedere coll Palazzo del Papa in Vaticano.*
> *Giardino del Ill^mo Card. Montalto.*
> *Teatro della Fontana Maggiore del Giardino del Prencipi Lodovisio in Frascati.*
> *Villa Borghesia.*

They are of interest precisely because they illustrate the 'modern'
secular buildings and the gardens universally admired by travellers,
described in every diary and in all the guides.[18] By sending home these
engravings, some of them signed with the names of the most popular
publishers and publishers' artists in Rome, like Greuter or De Rossi, the
Englishman secured a permanent record of the scenes which had
attracted his attention and, possibly, influenced his judgment in matters
of design or decoration.

The same process can be studied in the diary and accounts of Nicholas
Stone, son of Nicholas Stone the elder who designed such a large
number of the elaborate tombs and mural monuments favoured by

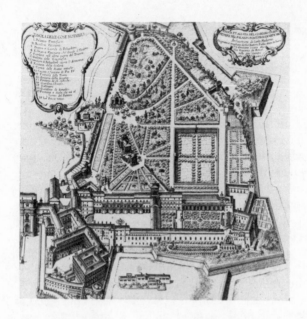

12.    The Vatican: a conscientious tourist duly wandered in search of the library (4), the collection of statues (9), and other treasures. The fountain is (17). The nearby Vatican garden peeps over the wall. Bernini's colonnade is now visible on the far left of the plan.

FONTANA NEL PALAZZO VATICANO
a piedi la scala che va al forno, et auanti la porta che entra in Beluedere Archit.º di Carlo Maderno

English gentry in the first half of the century. In this case it is not so much the manner of a patron's education as that of the artist — the artist who must learn to satisfy his patron — which comes to light. Unfortunately the second Nicholas Stone died while still a young man; but so far as they go, his accounts of purchases in Italy, particularly prints and books, almost tell their own story. He left England in 1638 and travelled southwards by the normal route through Paris, Lyon and Marseilles. On his journey and during a month's stay in Paris his notes of expenses dealt only with the most ordinary items, carriage, clothes and food; also fencing lessons and losses at tennis. But arrived at Florence his purchases mounted rapidly, and their character altered.

Purchases of books, prints and casts were listed from time to time, and it may be presumed that many of them found their way safely to England. Nor were they despatched from Italy merely to lie neglected in a single English country house: Nicholas Stone the elder had instructed his son to acquire examples of Italian workmanship and illustrations of ancient and modern treasures in Italy for the instruction of a wide circle of friends and patrons. A business such as Stone's, which must have both influenced and been influenced by the taste of its clients, was admirably fitted to play and important part in fostering the enthusiasm of the English public for Italian products of this type. Here again the accounts give some useful hints.

A few of the more significant items which had been mentioned by Stone in course of the year 1640 were finally collected together in August of that year, and described as 'Particulars bought in behalfe of my father'; they include the following:

for 2 plaister heads, one of Venus, the other of Cicero
for a book of perspectives of Vignola
for the fountaines of Roome[19]
for 7 prints and a little booke of sights
for a plaister leg moulded from the antique
for a Archytecture of Vitruvius
for a plaister head of Satyre
for a certificate to send to Ligorn
for a Bacchus in plaister
for lute strings to send to Ligorn...
for 113 small peeces of several sorts of marbles to send for England
    according to my father's command

Naturally, therefore, when Nicholas and Henry Stone determined to leave Rome in May 1642 after over three years' residence they had their own purchases to send to England; and their preparations were comprehensive indeed. They bought a great chest, and canvas to cover it, and rope to cord it; inside they placed a large number of smaller boxes, containing books, rolls of prints, basreliefs, models or casts of Christ, Laocoön, Cupid, Apollo, Sybils and Satyrs. The whole consignment was then sent to two English merchants of Leghorn for despatch to England.[20] Immediately afterwards Stone paid the equivalent of six months' rent (at the house where they had been living) for more books, especially the great folio illustrating the statuary in the gallery of Marchese Giustiniani;[21] these also were sent home. He and his brother then departed from Rome and made their way to Venice through Loreto and Ancona.

Some of the drawings and casts were probably the brothers' own workmanship; apart from the gradual impression made upon the English gentry by residence in Italy, and from the shipment of antiquities and modern pictures or drawings to England, there was also the specific training of professional craftsmen. Henry and Nicholas Stone hoped to be ranked among them. This had been the chief purpose of their long period of residence in Italy, and all the evidence left by Nicholas shows that he took his vocation seriously enough. Already in Florence he settled down to study. Ten days after arrival he began drawing in 'Michell Agnolos Chapple' of S. Lorenzo. From Monday to Saturday, 23 to 28 August 1638 he was able to make these entries in his diary:[22]

> I drew after the aforesaid head of Antonino Pio
> The feast of St. Bartholmew
> I drew after a rare head of Cicero; the great Duke came in the gallery; looked one my drawing; told me I was a gallant huomo.
> I drew after the same head; the great Duke came thaire with his brother Don Lorenzo who overlooked all my drawings (in the afternone I waited on Mr. Paston who gave me a case with a knife with an agate halft to give to S<sup>r</sup> Bastian Keper of the gallery).
> I drew after a peice of Carace
> I drew a folliage for memory.

This was a characteristic sample of his activities both in Florence and Rome. He studied the masterpieces of architecture, painting and statuary. He made precise observations, and obtained the measurements of pillars, cupolas, fountains and staircases. In Rome also he had a very memorable interview with Bernini who agreed to instruct him,[23] and it is difficult not to recognize in this encounter a particularly striking example of the influences likely to bear upon an intelligent Englishman in Italy, where all the circumstances conspired to impress him with Italian theory and practice in the arts. Stone's notebooks describe many of the practical hints which he learnt from Italian craftsmen, especially with regard to the working and treatment of marble. Unfortunately, he himself by no means surpassed in native ability the other English artists of this period; and he died very young, in 1647, before completing any original work. Certainly none is known to have survived.

If this was the case, then Nicholas Stone's most useful labours in Rome were the purchases of innumerable prints and books, many of them containing views of famous buildings. But building in England, the development of English architecture, owed much more to another traveller than sculpture did to poor Stone. Sir Roger Pratt, the gifted heir of a Norfolk landed family, on his own testimony learnt in Italy the lessons that enabled him to carry out his work at home. He had entered Magdalen College, Oxford in 1637 and the Inner Temple in 1639, but during the following year inherited his father's estate which was burdened by debt and executors' claims:

> In this very nick of time (he wrote later) comes on the Civil War and twas almost thought a crime to aske any one for Interest money: to avoid which storm, and give myself some convenient education I went out of England about 1643 and continued travelling in France, Italy, Flanders, Holland, etc. till anno 1649, viz about six years and a half, at which time I againe returned after the end of the war and the death of the King.

After this long interlude abroad he continued to live for many years in the Inner Temple and a correspondent congratulated him when his rooms escaped damage during the Great Fire of 1666, since all those 'writings, papers and precious pieces brought from beyond sea' had thus been saved from destruction. A year later, on his appointment as a Commissioner for the rebuilding of London, the same correspondent again congratulated him since the other Commissioners (among them Christopher Wren) would 'get more secrets from your art brought from Rome, and so from Athens, than you from them'. In fact, what did Sir Roger Pratt learn in Rome?[24]

How long a period of travel he allotted to Italy rather than the other countries on the continent is not clear. Possibly he was the 'Mr Pratt' who visited the English College at Rome in February 1644; he was certainly in Padua during January 1645 when he matriculated in the faculty of law at the university; and he was also, if Evelyn's recollections were sufficiently accurate, in Rome immediately before, or soon after, January 1645.[25] In any case his writings prove that he examined with great and loving attention the palaces and churches of Rome, Venice and Genoa. His notes for a book on architecture show also that he insisted on the importance of foreign travel for educating those who intended to live in a good modern building, and those who desired to design them. In an eloquent passage he asserts that acquaintance with the portico of St. Paul's in London, and the Banqueting House at Whitehall, together with diligent study of Palladio and Fréart are insufficient to train the student. He supported, in the specific case of architecture, the old argument of writers on travel: it could not be supposed, he wrote, that 'anything should be in the Intellect, which was never in the Senses'. A man ought to view buildings in their 'full proportions' and observe them in their actual setting in France and Italy. It follows that any man desiring to build a mansion for himself should first get 'some ingenious gentleman who has seen much of that kind of thing abroad to prepare a design of it on paper; for such a person will be superior to a homebred Architect, for want of his daily experience, as is daily seen'.[26] Pratt was convinced that in England theory and practice in building still lagged far behind the best continental examples.

He himself used persistently such phrases as 'the new way of Architecture', and 'modern' churches; and he appealed to a wide range of continental examples for the precepts which he laid down. He decided, from personal observation, that there were three distinct styles of Italian design for the palace, or mansion: *alla Romana, Venetiana*, and *Genoese*; account had also to be taken of the best buildings at Vicenza. In Rome he ranked highest the Palazzo Farnese, in Venice the Grimani, at Florence the Pitti and at Genoa the Dinegro palaces, to which he added the Luxembourg in Paris. This was the selection of most observers at the time. He distinguished between the more ornate exterior of modern French churches, with their scrolls and pilasters between the upper windows of a façade, adorned also with urns and statuary, and the severer manner of the Italian style in this particular. He recommended the cupola as a remarkable innovation which was quite without precedent in the 'old' forms of architecture. In general he leaves the impression, entirely in accordance with his own injunctions, that he had toured the continental cities measuring, criticizing and pondering over all the severe technical problems of satisfactory architecture. His method of study is important because he in fact designed some of the great English houses of the mid-seventeenth century: Coleshill, Berkshire (in collaboration with his forerunner abroad and at home, Inigo Jones), Kingston Lacy near Wimborne and Clarendon House, Piccadilly. The last of these was completed in 1665, and before its demolition in 1683 proved a model for other new mansions erected in London during the Restoration. It is an apt indication of the way in which these classical styles of building should have found favour in England that Pratt designed and constructed Clarendon House in the manner which he had studied on the continent, especially in Italy, while John Evelyn so heartily approved of the performance precisely because he too had performed a similar apprenticeship abroad. Evelyn wrote to Lord Cornbury in January 1666 that the architect, his old friend and fellow-traveller — for they were in Rome together — had successfully completed the finest house in England. It was the highest praise, coming from a discriminating and experienced sightseer who knew the Italian cities as Pratt had known them; the education of the gentry, in this sphere, owed much to their travels.[27]

It is not possible, in a survey of this kind, to distinguish very rigidly between architecture and the dependent decorative arts. The notebooks of Nicholas Stone, primarily a sculptor, have shown how he concerned himself with both architecture and statuary. In fact both were understood as indispensable elements of a single problem, the design and decoration of buildings required by civilized mankind; and so was the art of painting. But emphasis has been laid on the engraved illustrations of temples, palaces and churches, because they were the simplest and most economical form of memento within the means of the average English-man visiting the country. They required no particular outlay, were easily obtained and probably often purchased as a matter of contemporary fashion. Their influence, combined with the traveller's original exper-ience of direct observation, was unostentatious but must have spread widely. In England, stored with the treatises of Palladio, Vitruvius and Serlio in the libraries of men who had once visited Italy, and of those who never had that fortune, these engravings guided contemporary judgment.

They also served to popularize Italian masterpieces in the allied art of painting; to a lesser degree, because great foreign artists came to England and painted for the court, nobility and certain circles of the gentry. The same patrons occasionally desired, and could afford, to purchase original works imported from Italy. Nevertheless, engraved illustrations again contributed to the increase of knowledge on the subject in England, and they more especially concerned the traveller. The ordinary procedure of the Englishman who visited Italy was, first, to admire the masterpieces in Florence, Rome, Bologna and Venice, and then, if he felt inclined, to purchase reproductions. In fact, he usually contented himself with these engravings. An enthusiast like Richard Symonds, an Essex gentleman of moderate means, made a comprehen-sive collection. Under the heading *Stampe comprate in Roma 1650, 1651*, in one of his notebooks, he mentions a bewildering number of pur-chases.[28] First and foremost were the works of Raphael in Rome repre-sented by more than a hundred illustrations. A characteristic purchase were thirty-four sheets of the artist's *Vetus Testamentum*, in the Loggie of the Vatican, which the engravers Lanfranco and Nadobocchi dedicated to their master Annibale Carracci and published in 1607.[29] Symonds was satisfied, on Michelangelo's account, with five large folios of the roof of the Sistine Chapel and of the Day of Judgment, besides prints of his sculpture, Moses, Julius II and the Medici tombs in Florence. Carracci, Titian, Giulio Romano, Caravaggio and Domenichino were all strongly represented. The list ends with a note of the cost: '*Summa Totalis*. All the aforementioned Stampes cast up, I paid 26 crownes, 4 julii and half', some £7 sterling in English money of the time. This collection was latter supplemented by purchases in the Piazza of St. Mark (51 stampe acquired) and on the Rialto at Venice. Other travellers, John Evelyn and Edward Browne, write vaguely of books and prints which they bought in Italy, and Nicholas Stone had copies of paintings by Spagnoletto and Raphael's series of Cupid and Psyche; but in all probability their collections were not more numerous, and certainly not more keenly appraised, than the folios of Symonds who took an avowed and specialized interest in the subject. Symonds' notebook has the merit of showing in detail what a traveller collected if he examined pictures out of more than a sense of duty. In this respect it may be compared with the 'collections' or studies which William Lodge claimed to have made before deciding to translate Barri's *Viaggio Pittoresco*. Both testify to an individual's search for knowledge of Italian painting.

A more ambitious proceeding was to acquire painted copies of pictures. Evelyn found himself so much impressed by a 'Marriage of Saint Catherine' in the Palazzo Barberini that he later procured a copy which he judged hardly inferior to the original.[30] He employed the painter Carlo Maratti to do such work for him, although the only specific example mentioned in the Diary was the artist's rendering, on Evelyn's instruction, of a bas-relief on the Triumphal Arch of Titus.

On the whole the ordinary traveller can have purchased few original paintings. Reliable knowledge, supported by convincing detail, on the subject of Italian pictures which came to England before the end of the century, is still fragmentary. Inventories of the collections in country houses before 1700 rarely appear. Even the contemporary accounts of the King's pictures and the Arundel treasures are far from precise. But it does seem clear, as might be expected, that such paintings were not the concern of the ordinary traveller, whether a nobleman or of lesser rank. At the most, a few pioneers acquired a love of these things while abroad which decided them, in later years, to begin collecting pictures, statuary and drawings. Lord Arundel, early in the century, certainly clarified his view of the part a nobleman should play as a patron of the arts while on his early visits to the continent (1597–1613); in after years it was from Arundel House that orders generally went out to friends and agents abroad to seek out masterpieces of every kind. Later on, Robert Spencer, the second Earl of Sunderland, born in 1640, who founded the great collections at Althorp, travelled in western Europe for a few years before and after 1660. He visited Rome where he had his portrait painted, in classical costume, by Carlo Maratti,[3] but, as far as we know, his purchases began after his return. Here again the experience of Europe had stimulated his enthusiasm but the consequences, though substantial enough, were not direct or immediate.

The purchase of Italian paintings by an Englishman while actually on his travels, as distinct from the influence of such travel during early life in awakening his interest, was therefore a rare phenomenon. One reason why he did not bring Italian pictures with him to England was simply that their value made them essentially the business of the financier, the expert or the politician; and this meant in practice that the supply of such treasure was largely in the hands of cosmopolitan folk on a confidential footing with the princely families and courts of Europe. Italian pictures were presented to Charles I as a part of the conciliatory Papal policy, involving a line of foreign or semi-foreign negotiators and priests, Barberini, Con, Rossetti. They were purchased from foreign artists who were also dealers and diplomats, Rubens and Van Dyck; and also from other sources through the paid services of other advisers, men often of foreign extractions and with special connections abroad, Balthazar Gerbier, William Frizell[32] and Endymion Porter. This severely limits the field of enquiry, so far as Englishmen are concerned.

One group of English people who figured prominently in the purchase of Italian pictures was the succession of ambassadors at Venice. Wotton, Carleton and Lord Feilding, ambassador extraordinary in northern Italy between 1635 and 1638, exerted themselves to satisfy noblemen in England, acting as superior intermediaries or buying and selling on their own account. Wotton and Feilding acquired pictures of their own and some are preserved in the Provost's Lodging at Eton, whither Wotton retired; others, which decorated Feilding's house at Venice, were probably sold to meet expenses when the Exchequer failed to pay the ambassador or his agent after 1638. Sometimes their servants and dependants, travelling backwards and forward between Venice and London, had a direct interest in speculative purchases; with these men financial considerations were paramount. Thus the Marquis of Hamilton, who frequently appealed to the ambassador to find him good pictures in Italy, describes in his correspondence how three servants of the Lords Feilding, Northumberland and Cottington were partners and put down £700 for a collection of pictures recently brought from Italy by Feilding's servant Bashford.[33] Most of them were condemned in London as copies, and the writer estimated that the dealers would lose half their money. Another shadowy figure, one Henry Robinson, informed Feilding in 1639 that he had spent the last ten years collecting pictures which were now for sale, adding that if the ambassador thought of appointing an agent to reside in Florence he might be considered for the post; Robinson evidently hoped to combine a little diplomacy with a profitable search for Florentine art-treasures. So far as the purchase of pictures by Englishmen in Italy is concerned, the careers of men like Bashford and Robinson deserve investigation but reliable evidence is almost wholly lacking. In this very small group Lord Arundel's personal agent the Rev. William Petty stood supreme, both in the range of his activities and the amount of funds at his disposal. Best known for years which he spent in the Levant, securing antiquities and manuscripts for his patron, he was in Italy early in 1633, visiting Milan and Venice. Between the autumn of 1635 and the autumn of 1636 he toured round the whole peninsula. He appeared at Rome in December 1635 after purchasing an important collection of drawings at Naples. He then visited Leghorn and Naples, was in Florence by August 1636 and returned to Rome in October. He was in northern Italy during the spring of 1638. A hostile critic in England observed that Petty sent Lord Arundel weekly advices of all pictures coming up for sale, their prices, owners and likely purchasers.

He added that Arundel was the only English nobleman who employed a permanent agent to work for him in Italy. Other English patrons were at a disadvantage for the reason that 'no Englishman stayeth long in Italy'.[34]

Among Arundel's letters to Petty is one from his son Maltravers, dated 9 September 1636. It acknowledges handsomely what Petty contributed to the collection of Italian drawings, by then a fashionable pursuit for a select group of great men. In the postscript, about a large painting in oils, it also shows us the intermediaries at work while their patrons, between whom there might be the keenest rivalry, remained in the background:

Good Mr Petty,

I receaved your letter 16 August from Florence and I wonder that you had heard nothing of your Neopollitan Collection, I having written unto you of them long since; they proove exceeding well, beeing almost all of Masters' hands: of Zuccari an abondance, and of the greatest Masters' hands above a thousand, out of which there are about 250 of Pollidoro — though not in nomber yet considering theyre goodnesse I hould them almost worth all the drawings of Pollidoro in Ingland beefore — and 500 of Michelangelo (with the blathers and all) and, taking out of my Lord's some 6 choise drawings, I esteeme them as good as all the drawings of his hand in Ingland beefore. You write to have £200 of your owne monney made over unto you to Vennice or Florence, which I have written to William Marsh to doe, though I thinke it will bee the next weeke first, because Mr Rychaut is out of London. I pray you gette mee some good mellonne seedes. So I rest

Your most assured true friende
H. MALTRAVERS.

I have heard that there is a picture of Titian at Vennice to bee sould for five or 6 hundred duccatts. I desire that you would enquire dilligently after it, and [if] you like it, to give earneste for it, for it is for the king although his name must not be used. As I heare it hath some 4 or 5 figures in it, drawen after the life of some of the Nobilitye of Vennice.[35] What you doe must be without Sig. Neeces' [Nys] knowledge untill it bee past, and I pray lette not him knowe that I did write to you of it.[36]

Once only, in the Venetian archives, is there mention of an Englishman of high rank and great wealth, who travelled in northern Italy for the express purpose of admiring and buying fine pictures. His name was variously given as Thomas Bachino, Bachero or Buchers, possibly Baker, and in 1640 he went to Belluno in Friuli where he had heard a good collection might be found. Unfortunately he was arrested and imprisoned on the charge of having loaded pistols in his possession, and only the French ambassador's intervention secured his release. Unfortunately, also, no further details are known of his name, intentions or his travels on this occasion.[37]

In the forty years before the Civil War Italian pictures, therefore, were coming to England. When the war began conditions altered abruptly.

13.  The sculpture of Mr Thomas Baker: it is probable that the same Mr Baker, from Fressingfield in Suffolk, if unlucky in his search for pictures, had previously persuaded Bernini in Rome to sculpt this attractive portrait[37].

Like jewellery and College plate, valuables such as these became the capital on which families and armies had partly to depend. The second Duke of Buckingham for example, lived in exile on the proceeds realized by selling many of the first duke's pictures between 1648 and 1653.[38] A large number of the King's pictures were sold abroad. Arundel had already retired to the continent, taking many of his treasures with him. Painters and dealers continued to trade in the available stock but the amount of the latter can hardly have increased. The age in which a very small number of English noblemen purchased works of art from the mainland of Europe appears to have ended, and with it the role of the ambassadors at Venice and one or two others, especially Petty, as the principal English agents resident in Italy. For the following twenty-five years the scanty evidence only permits a cursory view of another small group: men who desired to gain by detailed examination a genuine knowledge of Italian pictures and the Italian style of painting. William Lodge, the gifted amateur and translator of the Viaggio Pittoresco was in Italy in 1670, possibly for the second time. He certainly knew Venice, Naples, Rome and Milan. John Michael Wright, a successful Scots painter in England immediately before the Restoration and for many years afterwards, probably reached Rome in 1642; he studied, and began to find patrons. At Rome also he had in his possession a number of good things, original drawings by Titian and Raphael as well as rare engravings of Mantegna's work,[39] and they presumably formed the nucleus of the collection which John Evelyn admired at a later date in England.[40] Above all, Richard Symonds, an amateur artist in the old tradition of the heralds, was studying in Rome with industry and enthusiasm. Among his many notebooks one is entitled: *Secrete intorno La Pittura vedute e sentite dalla prattica del. Sig. Giovanni Angelo Canini in Roma, A° 1650, 1651, 1652...non senza una intrinseca favore et amicitia che esso sig. G. A. portava a Ricardo Symonds.*[41] It contains a miscellany of hints for the artist: the preparation of colours and varnishes; advice on the correct placing of the paints on a palette; contrivances for perspective, and the type of equipment required by an artist desiring to go into the countryside to paint. The notes enable the reader to observe Symonds as he watched Canini's technique, while painting portraits or, very differently, covering an enormous canvas twenty four feet by twelve depicting the Story of Cleopatra.[42] This busy student also examined many other types of rarity in many Roman palaces and studios, shells, curios, intaglios, statuary, mandrakes; but his principal loyalty was given to pictures. Not an important artist himself, he was at any rate an Englishman who by travel in Italy had acquired a sound knowledge of the theory and practice of great painters. When he returned to England he continued to seek out pictures with enduring zeal.[43] Too much must not be claimed for him, since in many ways he appears a solitary figure, but the notes of this returned traveller on collections in England have at least been recognized, from the eighteenth century, as among the few authentic sources of evidence on the history of painters and painting in the preceding period.

Unfortunately the work of Symonds only emphasizes the comparative mediocrity of the English achievement in this field. Nor can he be considered entirely representative of the English gentry who travelled in Italy. There were one or two like him. An unnamed gentleman, possibly of the Cavendish family, purchased about forty paintings in Rome in December 1647 and the early part of the following year, pictures of fruit and flowers, classical subjects, and portraits. In the anonymous, and very confusing, inventory appear such phrases as: 'These 9 were bought of

Sig. Giovanni Battista pittore, 2 with frames, the price 40 Crownes at Rome, the 16 December 1647...these 2 were bought by yourselfe of Sig. Girola Marchi living in Strada Condutti (?), the price 36 crownes the 23 December 1647, Rome...una nympha Sopra un' Becco acudi 3 Moneta retoccato dal sig. Angelo Caroselli comprato a Roma Martio 2...un ritratto suo in tela d'Imperatore dal Sig. Michale Wright'.[44] Sir John Finch, residing many years in Padua and Florence, had his portrait painted by the Florentine Carlo Dolci, and there is a companion piece of his friend Sir Thomas Baines. Later on, Finch brought back from Italy sixty paintings which he reckoned the finest collection in any private Englishman's hands, but with a few exceptions these were all purchased during one short final visit to Leghorn and Florence as late as 1680.[45] The usual practice was probably less impressive, and the ordinary collection limited to a number of engraved folios. John Bargrave also commission a miniature portrait of himself and his two fellow-travellers, John Raymond and Alexander Chapman, painted on copper at Siena; and another miniature portrait of himself, on copper, painted by a servant of Symonds' master, Canini; both these little works were brought to England to Canterbury, mementoes of an Italian journey.[46] Richard D'Ewes had his portrait painted, at Venice in 1639, and reported that in the judgment of friends 'tis so like tis the woorse for it'.[47] In general, it must be concluded that a majority of English travellers purchased a few cheap prints, and came away from Italy well content. At the best they had improved themselves by dint of personal observations, like Edward Browne, who wrote from Venice that after making an inspection there he really preferred Veronese to Michelangelo;[48] on the whole they simply learnt to distinguish between the names of Veronese and Michelangelo. It was something.

These reservations and uncertainties do not pertain to another art of which the Italians were supreme practitioners, the art of music. English travellers declared their opinion emphatically on this point by the middle of the century. For some of them listening to music in Italy seems to have been their chief amusement, a distraction from the severer business of examining antiquities and other rarities. Mortoft in 1658, early in the tour, heard his first Italian performance in the church of S. Ambrogio at Genoa not long after entering the country. He and his friends listened to 'the most ravishing musicke' they had ever heard in their lives, a choir with organs, bass viols and trumpets. Ten days later, at Leghorn, he saw his first comedy 'done in Musicke' which gave him almost equal pleasure. While in Rome he went constantly to hear good music. He was present at one of the concerts given every Wednesday evening in the Palazzo Rospigliosi where Queen Christine of Sweden had her residence, he heard the singing of the castrati at Mass in St. Peter's, and frequented a number of churches especially for the sake of their music. Time and again he visited the Chiesa Nuova and after one performance concluded that the harmony was so sweet, 'never the like must be againe expected unlesse in heaven and in Rome'. Mortoft confessed that listening to the music of these churches was much to be preferred to a sight of their pretended relics, and the last visit he paid before leaving Rome in March 1659 was once again to the Chiesa Nuova for a 'sweet and ravishing' performance. His epithets on the subject never vary.[49]

The remarks of an isolated enthusiast would be of no particular value in themselves but contemporary English testimony is unanimous. Even John Evelyn who cared less for music than antiquities and architecture shared Mortoft's admiration for Italian musicians. He too attended with pleasure at the Chiesa Nuova and enjoyed a 'magnificent' opera at Prince Gallicano's, composed by the Prince himself.[50] At Venice he heard at least four operas, in which the perspectives of the scenery and the stage machinery appear to have impressed him rather more deeply than the 'recitative music' itself. In Venice also he was present at concerts given by famous solo singers, one of these performances taking place in the English consul's house.[51] It was assumed, therefore, that the consul's countrymen took some interest in this Italian music. A significant detail in another traveller's diary shows how Banister Maynard's servant Robert Moody, who knew Rome from previous journeys, devised for his master a suitable introduction to the pleasures of the city. They had arrived on 23 December 1660, and on the next day, Christmas Eve, he writes:

> I persuaded my Maister to go to a church called the Apolinario near the Piazza Navona where I knew there would be rare Musick, and truely I was not deceived, for I think my Maister never heard such voyces before nor after, where we continued till next morning and then returned to our Lodging.[52]

It was a suitable distraction for the son of a peer who during the Commonwealth belonged to the Presbyterian party,[53] a party whose more rigid adherents condemned ecclesiastical music. John Milton in Rome confined his very real admiration to secular concerts, an opera at Cardinal Barberini's and the singing of Leonora Baroni whom he celebrated in Latin verse.

The most important of all these travellers, for comments on the Italian music of his day, was Robert Bargrave. A relative of Isaac Bargrave Dean of Canterbury who had been one of Sir Henry Wotton's chaplains in Venice, he touched at the Italian ports on his way to and from the Levant. If he did not belong strictly to the category of English gentleman making the giro d'Italia, his remarks and descriptions conform closely enough to the spirit of their own diaries; and he improved his time in Italy, as they did, by learning the language and viewing the churches and other places of interest. He may therefore be placed together with the overland travellers, among whom were his relatives John Bargrave and John Raymond, author of the Itinerary. Robert was an accomplished amateur musician, and he included in his diary the score of masques which he had composed for certain festival occasions. For this reason his comments in Italy are the more revealing. They illustrate the deep impression made by the virtuosity of Italian musical performances upon a northerner of very fair technical accomplishment himself. The disparity between the level of Italian musicianship, continually improved by popular and professional insistence on the supreme importance of a soloist's absolute mastery over all difficulties in technique, and the more amateur spirit of music-making in England, lies behind much of the later history of English music.

In the summer of 1647 Bargrave left his ship at Leghorn in order to spend a few weeks with his cousin at Siena. While there, his skill as a performer on the viol 'endangered' his playing to one of the Medici princes. He evaded the honour but, instead, the prince's private singers and instrumentalists listened to Bargrave performing, and in return gave a recital on their own account, presenting the Englishman with a copy of some charming songs. At Venice eight years later he went to the opera; his reflections on this experience, unlike other sections of his manuscript, have never been printed, and well deserve comparison with Evelyn's account, which they corroborate:

> But above all, surpassing whatsoever theyr Inventions can else stretch to, are theyr Operas (or Playes) represented in rare musick from the beginning to the end, by select Eunuchs and women, sought throughout all Italy on purpose: whose Persons are adorned as richly and aptly as the best contrivers can imagine: theyr many various Scenes set out in rare painting, and all magnificent costlyness, intermixing most incomparable apparitions and motions in the aire and on the Seae, governed so by Machines, that they are scarse discernable from the reall things they represent: having also most exquisit Anticks and Masking Dances, and whatsoever else beseeming that Art and money can arrive to. One Opera I saw represented about 16 severall times; and so farr from being weary of it, I would ride hundreds of miles to see the same over again: nay I must needs confess that all the pleasant things I have yet heard or seen are inexpressibly short of the delight I had in seeing this Venetian Opera; and as Venice in many things surpasses all places elce where I have been, so are these Operas the most excellent of all its glorious Vanities; and thus the Carnevale and I took leave of Venice both together.... [54]

However, Bargrave's recital at Siena showed that he understood and loved purely musical accomplishment, and not only the additional scenic effects provided by Italian opera. On another occasion at Venice he analysed a famous singer's style with very great attention to detail; and the inference is that he had never heard so masterly a performance before. This Italian virtuosity, first remarked by the English on their travels, would later overshadow English music, and Bargrave's description of it in the year 1655, and his admiration, are therefore the more valuable.

> Here [he writes] is a famous Nunn's way of singing. I observed her excellency above others: first, in a soft stealing Fall from through into 2nd, In Trilling, when usually she made three Offers, and then quick[e]ned her Trillo by degrees, beating strongest upon the higher halfe Noat, and rather slow then quick, in which she seemed to govern her voice by the motion of her tongue. 3rd, in Replicates, singling the first strong, the second Ecchoing, and the third very strong; falling at the close into a soft Trillo. 4ly, After a Pause, shee would rise in a third, drawing the Noat as in length so in Strength, and trilling at the last. 5th, In falling a running Sixth swift and Strong. 6ly, Drawing out a melting Noat from strong to faint. 7ly, In the common close she often trilled, not in but in to end in and would sometimes begin to trill in steale it insensibly into before she closed in Lastly, in expressing of words by singing according to theyr sence: as Morire dolefully, Sospiri sighingly, and Ridendo laughingly.[55]

The triumph of the soloist could at least be appreciated, although not emulated, by the amateur Englishman.

Since Bargrave's enthusiasm was shared by other travellers who came to Venice, and they took home with them the memory of this astounding Italian virtuosity in music, and of the new school of composition which such virtuosity evoked, it is hardly surprising that in the course of time they also welcomed the invasions of the English musical tradition by foreign artists. In a sense the English who had travelled in Italy knew what was coming. To judge from the words of Mortoft and Bargrave they admitted, from direct personal experience, that Italian musical talents were well in advance of anything they had come across previously. Whatever else they condemned in Italian religion, morality, political devices or fashions of dress, for the modern music of Italy they reserved only their praise. Such unmeasured enthusiasm has its historical importance. 'Their Sceanes', wrote Raymond, '(or as they terme them Operas) are Regalios they have not yet fully communicated to us, their other Arts wee daily borrow.' But the time was shortly coming when the Italians would win their final triumph in this sphere also, in music.

By the middle of the seventeenth century the constitutions and institutions of Italy impressed foreign observers very much less than Italian arts and music; but it is necessary to recall the position of the

Academies in Italy at this date, because certain travellers did not neglect them. Richard Lassels in his book raised the subject as soon as he had brought his readers as far as Genoa:

Here is an Academy of Wits called the Adormentati: which together with other Academies of like nature in all the Towns of Italy I would wish my traveller to visit particularly, that he may see how far the Italians excell us, in passing their time well; and how much better, to spend the week in making of Orations and Verses, than in drinking of Ale and smoking of Tobacco.[56]

And then, by way of practical information, he gives the names of these academies in many of the cities through which he conducts his travellers. These were the Intronati at Siena,[57] the Ostinati of Viterbo, the Revocati and Infiammiti of Padua, the Olympici of Vicenza, the Philarmonici of Verona, and of course the Accademia della Crusca in Florence. John Ray, the naturalist, also mentions the societies in his account of a journey through Italy at this time.

On the whole English travellers responded infrequently to this advice. Few of them can have had much use for the literary small talk of an alien people, and most of the societies were concerned with linguistic discussion and the various forms of literary composition in Italian and Latin. Evelyn obediently accepted an invitation from the Umoristi at Rome. He describes how the virtuosi of this society met in their spacious hall, where with proper formality members recited verses and held debate for the purpose of defending the purity of the Italian language. In the hall he observed a portrait of Guarini, the author of *Pastor Fido*, once a member of the society and a famous name to educated men throughout Europe at this date. His impressions must have been favourable; because forty years later he was still deploring, that in spite of an experiment of this kind made by Cowley, Dryden, Waller and himself in the reign of Charles II, no similar society existed in London for the improvement of the English language.[58] Such meetings were also familiar to Milton, and much of the evidence for his tour in Italy centres round his friendship with Italian scholars in Florence, Rome and Naples. He read some of his Latin verse to the Svogliati, a Florentine society, on 16 September 1638. A week earlier, in a letter addressed to Benedetto Buonmattei on the latter's forthcoming treatise, *Della Lingua Toscana*, Milton had examined the very problem which preoccupied these academies: the purification and defence of their mother tongue. He begged the author to supplement his work with hints to foreigners on the correct pronunciation of Italian. Similarly in Rome he enjoyed the society of scholars and poets from whom he received, and to whom he dedicated, Latin verses. At Naples his protector, G. B. Manso, was a patron of the academies of Oziosi and Nobili. Wherever he travelled in Italy Milton introduced himself to this particular section of Italian society. Lassels could only have approved of such behaviour, so natural to the poet, the making of orations and verses, the avoidance of ale or tobacco.

This almost solitary instance of an English traveller who assiduously attended Italian literary societies was by no means without significance, for it was connected with the origins of Milton's greatest work. On the one hand his journey followed the usual pattern of the giro d'Italia. In general he travelled when and where other tourists travelled. His itinerary was theirs, his timetable theirs, except that he returned north-wards rather earlier than was probably usual, missing Easter at Rome, avoiding Loreto, and leaving Venice to reach Geneva by the usual route before the middle of June. It was conventional also, that he should have purchased many books in Italy, and the scores of the best modern composers, Monteverdi and Vecchio, which he sent home by sea from Venice. But while in these respects he imitated the practice of his least important contemporaries, he had other and higher ambitions in mind; and these ambitions were undoubtedly stimulated by his converse with the Italian academicians. In the land of Ariosto and Tasso the tremen-dous possibilities of an epic which he, Milton, should write were given added vitality by the literary discussion he enjoyed with Florentine and Roman scholars. In the circles of these men 'the sheer didactic value'[59] and the principles which governed the forms of heroic literature were endlessly discussed. At the same time the temptation to make Latin his chosen medium of expression in such a venture was rejected, in spite of the applause bestowed by the Italians on his Latin verse; it was natural in a foreign country to respond even more readily than at home to the patriotic element inherent in literary ambitions of this type. So it came about that Milton first explicitly sketched to his friend Manso (O modo spiritus sit) his version of King Arthur repulsing the Saxon invaders. This project, like so much else, was diverted by the political and intel-lectual storms of the following decade, after which it underwent a radical transformation. Yet though the hopes of Milton while in Italy, and immediately afterwards, are hardly recognizable in the completed form and thought of *Paradise Lost*, the stimulus of his journey and of his learned conversation abroad had not been lost. At a later date he recalled the adventure with affection, and respect for the men he met. One feels that the young man,

Missus Hyperboreo juvenis peregrinus ab axe,

brought back from Florence more than a few prized metaphors, allu-sions to the woods of Vallombrosa or to Galileo which he used later in famous verses, and from Naples more than the present of a rich cup given him by Count Manso: he also added something to the width of intellect which was to distinguish him from the other great Puritans, from such as Cromwell and George Fox, who both knew little of the continent. The society of a few chosen Italians contributed, however indirectly, to his thought on the writing of an epic, its form, language and moral justification. Milton was the greatest Englishman to visit Italy in this period. Its influence upon him could hardly be negligible.[60]

Besides these Italian literary societies, to which Lassels was to direct the travellers' attention, there were also the academies with an interest in experimental philosophy, and the scientific studies carried on in Italian universities. The majority of English travellers hardly concerned themselves with either the relatively modern type of academy or the mediaeval universities, but undoubtedly large numbers of medical students still came to Padua. The select group of well-known and prosperous doctors was naturally of marked importance in English society but unfortunately few details survive of the journeys and studies which some of them made abroad in their youth. Even in the celebrated instance of Sir Thomas Browne direct evidence of a physician's foreign apprenticeship is lacking, except for the bare record of matriculation at Leyden. If by a study of *Religio Medici* we may realize that the religion of this doctor owed much to experience of Catholic France and Catholic Italy, details of his medical training and experience abroad cannot be gathered from such reading.

The letters of his son Edward Browne reveal more clearly the usual procedure of a medical student in Italy. A conventional tour to Rome, Naples and Loreto during the winter of 1664–1665 preceded Browne's attendance at the anatomy demonstrations given at Padua from the second week of Lent onwards. This course of instruction he found exceedingly useful, in the beauty and orderliness of the methods employed. Afterwards he visited the hospitals, and commissioned a collection of specimens from the physic garden of Padua to take home with him; and a little later prepared to return to Montpellier for further study.[61] More than twenty years earlier other letters and papers show another student pursuing the same course in Italy. one Joseph Colston, who graduated B. A. from Peterhouse, Cambridge, in 1633, left England in September 1641 and in the conventional way visited Marseilles, Genoa, Rome, Naples, Loreto and Venice before settling down at Padua.[62] He appears to have arrived there rather late in the year, about 1 July, taking his degree on 31 December 1642.[63] During the summer his relatives in London expected him back by Michaelmas[64] but he decided to remain on the continent, influenced possibly by the trend of political and military events at home, and in fact toured between Madrid and Rotterdam in the following three years.[65] In the earlier and Italian part of his travels he conformed strictly to the normal pattern; and represents, in rather an interesting fashion, the class of moderately wealthy traveller, townsmen rather than gentry. Coming from a London family which derived its income from house property (and small loans) in the city, he himself had no parents living at this time, and his aunt and his cousin, also a chirurgeon, forwarded him about £100 a year from his estate.[66] A part of this expense was evidently designed to improve his professional status, by sending him to Padua, but to the dismay of the cousin the remainder simply enabled Colston to travel abroad throughout the years of civil disturbance at home. After the Restoration Joseph Colston was enrolled in the College of Physicians, and kinghted in 1669; his surviving papers testify to steady professional activity in later years.

The examples of Edward Browne and Colston are probably conventional and representative. They owed a part of their technical attainments, or at least of their professional prestige, to the experience of Italy. A more celebrated medical student of Padua University was John Finch, the younger son of a Recorder of London; and with him was always linked, in the minds of their contemporaries, the name of his life-long and inseparable friend Thomas Baines. After studying arts at Christ's College, Cambridge, Finch and Baines left England in 1649; for like Roger Pratt or Evelyn they stood aside from political controversy and became none the less valuable as citizens of the world. Finch kept a journal while travelling through France, but it ceases when he reached Italy. Without troubling to make the preliminary giro of Italy the two friends settled in Padua where they lived, a few short trips in northern Italy apart, from 1653 until 1659. They studied for the degree of a doctorate in medicine, which was conferred on them in 1657. Their letters home contain few details which are relevant in this connection but they clearly grappled with the problems raised by the controversies connectd with the names of Harvey, Copernicus and Descartes, and they were on friendly terms with the professors of anatomy and mathematics at the university. Finch indeed won for himself a high reputation as an anatomist and in 1659 was appointed professor in that subject at Pisa by Ferdinand II of Tuscany. Very naturally, also, he became a member of the Accademia del Cimento, the great Florentine scientific society founded in 1657. He came to England in 1660 but soon returned to Italy, where between 1665 and 1670 he represented Charles II at the court of Tuscany.

Finch lived too long abroad to have much direct influence in England, which in later life he visited so infrequently. However, his residence in Italy and the particular bent of his interests made him an outstanding, almost an exaggerated, example of those English gentlemen, linked by family ties with the political circles of the court and parliament, among whom scientific enthusiasms predominated. It is significant, because it is not in the least surprising, that he and Baines should have been among the original signatories of the petition sent to Charles II in May 1660, asking that a properly constituted 'experimental' society should be founded in England. He had come from a country where experiments of this kind, carried out and evaluated at regular meetings of the Accademia del Cimento, were encouraged by the Grand Duke's patronage. It is reasonable to suppose that he appreciated more readily than many of his fellow sponsors the value of such an institution in a well governed state. A knowledge of the best continental practice contributed to the foundation of the Royal Society.[67]

Finch, like Colston, had made medicine his profession, but even the amateur enthusiast John Evelyn speaks of a winter of hard study at Padua, observing the dissections, visiting the hospitals, and collecting specimens medical and botanical, some of which he later presented to the Royal Society.[68] It was a fashionable interest, largely catered for abroad; but here again it contributed to the knowledge and education of a returning traveller. Two of the contributory elements in the development of interest in the experimental sciences in England were the importation of foreign books and the work in England of enlightened foreign virtuosi; and a third element was the foreign travel of the English themselves.

So far it has proved expedient to divide the subject matter of these Italian experiences, and to distinguish the books on Italy written by English travellers, the influence of the arts and music, of the literary and scientific academies. By this procedure it has been possible to organize the evidence for the many points of contact between the English in Italy, and Italy itself. On the other hand, while the latter-day enquirer is bound to proceed along these lines, for the sake of clarity, the travellers themselves never did so, and the records they have left in fact reveal an inextricable mingling of diverse interests and impressions. This confusion and heterogeneity is perhaps the foremost characteristic of the letters and diaries of the travellers. Emphasis was laid, in the preceding pages, on the roughly conventional pattern of the ordinary journey; due consideration must also be given to the mixed character of the ordinary traveller's impressions and memories.

Mementoes of Italy were nearly always a miscellany. Thus, the important general fact about Colston is that he hoped to become a successful doctor; but among his papers he kept only one substantial remembrance of Rome, a page giving the exact dimensions of St. Peter's.[69] Robert Boyle was above all a chemist and in his account of a winter tour in Italy, as a youth, we look eagerly for any evidence that scientific discussion in Florence or Padua first awakened his enthusiasm Apart from a mention of Galileo's death, there is nothing; but instead Aubrey noted that he had 'oftentimes' heard Boyle say that after seeing the antiquities and architecture of Rome he could never appreciate these things anywhere else.[70] Thomas Killigrew, the Restoration dramatist and theatre-manager, was writing plays in Italy in 1635 and 1636, which ostensibly betray a romantic Italianate atmosphere; but at the same time he was in touch with the Rev. William Petty concerning the purchase of pictures for the King; and his travelling companion was Walter Montagu, then engaged in delicate negotiations with the Roman ecclesiastical authorities.[71] Killigrew's impressions, therefore, must have been exceedingly

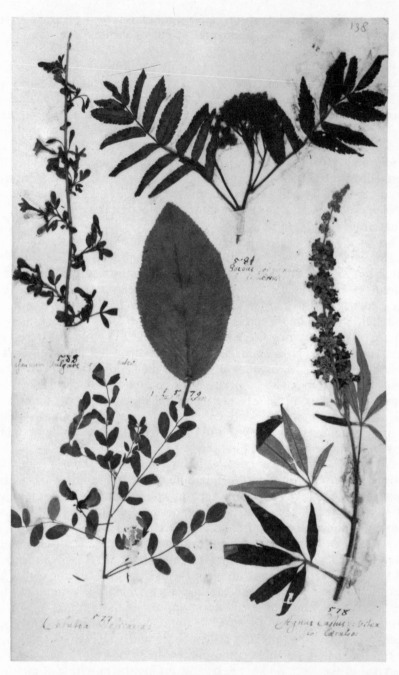

14. John Evelyn's pressed flowers: 'Next morning I went to see the Garden of Simples, rarely furnished with plants, and gave order to the Gardner to make me a Collection of them. (Diary, Padua, July 1646). These same flowers survive in this manuscript volume entitled 'Hortus Eyemalis sive Collectio Plantarum'.

diverse. If this was true of travellers in whom posterity has taken a fairly narrowly defined interest, it naturally colours our view of travellers whose own interests were miscellaneous or many sided, Evelyn, Reresby, Mortoft, and possibly many others of whom the names were barely listed in the Pilgrim Book of the English College in Rome or the university registers at Padua. What a confusion of facts, view-points, encounters, and what a medley of contents in the cases sent home from Venice and Leghorn!

This feature of travel documents, those surviving doubtless representing many more which have vanished, forcibly strikes any reader of John Bargrave's papers.[72] Bargrave, it may be remembered, accompanied John Raymond to Italy in 1646. During the Commonwealth and Protectorate he preferred to live mainly abroad, and though he wandered through France, Holland, Germany and Bohemia, in the course of the years he certainly made four different visits to Rome and Naples. On the first occasion he went with his cousin, on the second he tutored the young Lord Chesterfield and William (later Sir William) Swan; on the third he travelled with William Juxon, nephew of the bishop; while for his last journey in 1658–1659 his companions, if he had any, cannot now be named.[73] During his travels he visited most of the principal Italian cities and, in all, must have spent some years south of the Alps. The knowledge shown in his papers and collections, which he stored up in his mind in consequence, was extremely miscellaneous. On that account it is unfitted for strict analysis, and is simply in keeping with the general tendency of all travellers to amass scattered impressions in the course of a journey, without any conscious design. Yet such impressions or mementoes provide a very useful index to the character of an educated man's thought in that, or any other, period. These bits and pieces are, for one thing, the stock-in-trade of his conversation.

In Bargrave's case the sources for this type of evidence are two, his 'College of Cardinals under Alexander VII', and the catalogue of his Museum, now at Canterbury.

In Rome, in 1658, he tells us, he bought some engraved portraits of Alexander's Cardinals, productions of the printing house of De Rossi, like so many other engravings of the seventeenth century. After returning to England he proceeded to add to them his own annotations, the result of personal recollections of the cardinals at Rome and other adventures in Italy, enriched also by stray reading on the subject. He consulted dubious literary authorities with such titles as Il Nepotismo di Roma and il Cardinalismo di Santa Chiesa, and in certain cases the English translations of these books. The completed result, the annotated engravings, Bargrave liked to lend to friends, saying 'Pray read at your leasure for pass time'. Similarly with the Museum. While in Rome he remarked on the images and coins dug up by workmen when the foundations of new buildings were being prepared, and on the collection of these things by learned enthusiasts, and so he made 'this collection insueing, which I have now, 1676, in a cabinet in my canonical house, at the metropolitical Church of Christ, Canterbury'. This also, we may surmise, was admired by his friends.

From the book of Cardinals, and the Catalogue, it is possible to gather what were perhaps the more ordinary and unexceptional relics in the mind of a traveller returned from Italy. Among them were not, it must be said, any clear-cut distinctions between Renaissance and Baroque art-forms, between polyphonic and harmonic patterns in music, between scholastic and experimental philosophy. They constituted, rather, a jumble of scraps on Italian history ancient and modern. He was extra-ordinarily well acquainted with the highways and byways of papal politics. The rivalry between the French and Spanish factions at Rome, and between the Barberini and Medici families, the importance of Donna Olimpia Maidalchini to Innocent VIII, the repudiation and then the acceptance of nepotism by Alexander VII: these were commonplaces to him. Equally familiar were the social origins, the wealth, ambitions and appearance of most of the many cardinals. The reading of books on the subject, after his return to England, quickly revived the faculty of personal recollection. Cardinal D'Este put Bargrave in mind of the city of Modena where the Cardinal's brother, the Duke, was building a palace when he visited there. Cardinal Mazarin recalled the astonishing history of that family's rise to fame, and spectacle of the Cardinal's father driving in the streets of Rome. Bargrave remembered Bernini 'that famous architect and my friendly acquaintance'; and Crashaw, the poet and Fellow of his old college, Peterhouse, then in Rome and a convert; and Masaniello, of whose rebellion in Naples Bargrave had been a spectator. In addition he remembered certain vivid Italian scenes: the method of executing criminals at Rome; the walk along and under the Roman walls between the Porta del Popolo and the Porta Pinciana on the north side of the city — his 'usual' walk; or uncovering the epitaph of an apocryphal Anglo-Saxon King in a church at Lucca.

Turning from the bric-à-brac in Bargrave's memory to the bric-à-brac of his cabinet the enquirer will find there another collection of curios: such as an image of the infant Romulus dug from the Quirinal hill at Rome, figures of Hercules, Leda, Mercury, Augustus, sometimes ancient but more frequently modern copies, lodestones and minerals, pumice from Naples and crystals from the Rhaetian Alps, a box of imitation sugar-plums from Tivoli, 'a very artificial anatomy of a human eye with all its films or tunicles, by way of turnery in ivory or horn' invented by the physicians of Padua and purchased by Bargrave at Venice, a gold ring from Salerno given him by an English merchant in Naples; also Italian playing cards and relics from the catacombs (later sent to Dr. Plot of Oxfordshire). All these things came from the Italian peninsula and to them were added Indian tobacco pipes, the horns of a goat, the skin of a chameleon and much else besides. Such were the trophies of the pilgrim from Canterbury after his travels in Europe and they rest to this day in the library of the cathedral.

The whole miscellany is from one point of view totally insignificant. It cannot be compared with the pioneer collections of Lord Arundel as patron of the arts, or Ray the naturalist, or Evelyn the enlightened amateur of physic in Italy. But in all probability the minds of less distinguished travellers, whose activities had little enough significance for the grander lines of development in artistic taste and scientific knowledge, resembled the mind of John Bargrave with its collection of stray facts, stray impressions and stray mementoes gathered from the experience of Italy. In that case his evidence has its importance, for it cautions us against claiming for large groups in society an enlightenment perceptible only in the work of their most intelligent members. It means that the usual consequences of the long journey were not, and could not be, spectacular advances to some new point of view in this or that subject, but rather the accumulation of small odd things which were worked into the texture of average thought and became the stock-in-trade of knowledge for many hundreds of unexceptional people — fair representatives of English society in its higher levels — who had visited Italy at some time in their lives. Instead of elaborate paintings, a few engravings of buildings or a miniature portrait on copper; instead of radical scientific theories, a few optical toys for amusement; while there were also innumerable scraps of knowledge about Rome's long history, but no sense of the extraordinary perspectives inherent in such a history. These were the ordinary returns from 'the voyage of Italy'. They were not startling. They filled a proportionate place in the minds of travelled Englishmen; but the unimportant learning and the insignificant collections of a John Bargrave are nevertheless fair warning against the twin dangers of expecting too much for this type of contact between England and Italy, and of distinguishing too strictly between the different topics of interest which attracted a traveller's notice.

This second point, the miscellaneous nature of these Italian impressions, is confirmed by another kind of document, the commonplace book of Robert Southwell, later a secretary of state for Ireland and president of the Royal Society.[74] He was a young man on his travels spending the time between November 1660 and April 1661 in Rome. He says refreshingly little of sightseeing, but evidently enjoyed a many-sided existence in the Papal city. There are signs of his study of Italian, and fair copies of stanzas from Ariosto. There are notes of many conversations on a variety of subjects, on the difference between the English and Spanish schools of acting, on Love, on chemical experiments, on noteworthy books, on bone-setting and grafting, on the circulation of the blood. He visited a number of cardinals who entertained him politely enough; among them was Cardinal Pallavicini, historian and author of a famous Ultramontane counterblast to Sarpi's account of the Council of Trent. It is indicative of the alteration in sentiment over a period of fifty years that an Englishman could now write of an uncompromising Papal historian: 'We told his Eminence that we were sending his Booke home to read it, and that our ambition was to see in presence whom we soe much honoured in fame.'[75] In addition Southwell listened to music, and he describes a noble evening at the Spanish ambassador's when groups of Italian instrumentalists, of academicians who recited prose and verse, and of Spanish singers, succeeded and surpassed one another in entertaining the company.[76] Thus, many topics attracted the traveller and he took from Rome rather a general sense of enjoyment or enlightenment than any specific additions to a single enthusiasm; quite simply it was a general education, and perhaps it raised the standards which henceforth he expected in aristocratic society at home.

After allowing for this difficulty, the natural confusion overlaying all attempts to disentangle the variety of topics which occupied the traveller, certain conclusion nevertheless emerge. Perhaps the foregoing analysis enables us to see in detail what is usually only surmised, so that the following propositions sum up the main tendencies of this, the earliest period of the conventional tour of Italy.

I. From the third decade of the century the whole peninsula lay open to the English traveller, making possible a circuit of the country. The disturbed condition of Germany and Savoy, with the relatively quiet state of France contributed to the mapping out of a conventional itinerary, so that the route led from Marseilles to the western coast of Italy and to Florence, down to Rome and Naples, and then across to the eastern coast and northward to Venice. The date of the great festivals at Rome and Venice, and the heats of summer, fixed approximately the timetable of such journeys.

II. The growth of friendly relations between the English court and the Papacy gave Rome an increasingly important place in the plans of English travellers. The old pre-eminence of Venice in this respect was no longer favoured by political and religious factors, and the balance of interest shifted in favour of Rome. The earlier type of journey, over the Mont Cenis and Brenner passes into northern Italy, where a period of residence was enlivened by a furtive adventure to the south, was replaced by the Giro, longer in mileage if not in the time taken to complete it, in which Rome featured first, and most prominently.

III. The age of the Grand Tour was not the age of the Englishmen Italianate as the Elizabethans understood that phenomenon. The political ideas and practice of Italy no longer disturbed the imagination of the many who stayed in England; the language and manners of Italians no longer attracted so keenly the few who made the journey thither. An increasing store of knowledge about the country in books, transla-

15. Holiday in the Piazza Navona in a jubilee year, 1650.

the name of Italy. In addition, the number was growing of those English travellers who passed annually and rapidly round the country. This widespread familiarity likewise diminished the element of sensationalism in the contact between the two peoples.

IV. Italy was less and less considered the indispensable training ground for those who desired to interest themselves in affairs of state; and since the political importance of the Italian courts declined, except for Rome, while England took a restricted part in European war and diplomacy between 1630 and 1650, our embassies at Venice and Turin dwindled once again to the status of listening posts; nor were they any longer significant colonies of men who in different degrees hoped for substantial preferment at home. At the same time diplomatic reports tions or even pictures gradually diminished or diluted the influence of from these centres cease mentioning the movement of ordinary travellers; after 1630 evidence about them must be sought almost entirely from private diaries and papers. The Giro was therefore free of the political implications which had earlier determined in part the motives of travellers — or were judged to do so by suspicious secretaries of state. It was not associated with the search for information on political affairs, the 'secrets' and the 'intelligence' of states, nor considered one of the direct paths to preferment. It was understood more simply as part of a nobleman's or gentleman's training, whatever the final and fortunate results of such an education in the case of an able young man.

V. The general education of the Giro gave the traveller an opportunity of extending the range of his interests. First, it is true, he consolidated what he already knew by observing for himself the visible foundation of Europe's history in the ruins of ancient Italy: but on this basis he could explore all the arts and sciences practised so vigorously by the Italians of his own and the preceding century. He could learn to appreciate, if not to practise himself, their style of building, of painting, of composing, and in certain spheres, their methods of speculation. Sometimes he returned home with only a few notes or impressions, sometimes also with books, engravings and musical scores, sometimes even with a competent knowledge of the actual technique involved in the arts and sciences. The almost exclusive preoccupations of an earlier generation of moneyed men in England with law, theology and the management of property could not satisfy the returned traveller, who consequently assisted the educated classes in society to extend their intellectual interests. The most striking symptoms of the development were the new town and country houses built in the second half of the century, their decoration, libraries, gardens; and the Royal Society, and the independent activities of many of its members and other like-minded 'virtuosi'. To these activities travellers who had been in Italy certainly contributed in part.

VI. Travellers to Italy (and elsewhere) were the rich and the merely prosperous. The expenditure involved appears to have varied between £100 and £1000 a year. Mortoft, Colston, Symonds and the Bargraves were not wealthy men; and therefore the experience of Italy was by no means confined to a few. It was also open to the middle ranks of society. Merchants and merchants' factors who had been in Italy should be classed with these. Robert Bargrave the factor, and his cousin, John Bargrave the clergyman, belong to the same group of men. Another circumstance contributing to the familiarity of Englishmen with Italy was unrest at home between 1640 and 1660: quite apart from the exiles, certain travellers spent much more time abroad than might otherwise have been the case. Roger Pratt and John Bargrave were examples of this. The institution of the Commonwealth was, in some respects, a defiance of Europe; the travellers, whether neutral or exile, paid court to Europe.

Tracking down the impressions carried from one country to another precludes rigid definition but the evidence and conclusions above reveal the main outlines of the situation. Italy was only a part and the furthermost part of the mainland through which the travellers went. To them, and to us, however, it had a definite character and attraction of its own which justify a separate treatment of its influence, so potent and civilizing in this period of Italian political decline.

# III. ENGLISH TRAVELLERS IN THE LOW COUNTRIES

# 7. MILITARY VOLUNTEERS AND RELIGIOUS REFUGEES: THEIR PLACE IN THE HISTORY OF ENGLISH SOCIETY

One of the most noticeable features of English travel on the Continent during the seventeenth century is that the diaries of the gentry concentrate on France and Italy. The commanding prestige of these two countries imposed on the traveller an almost obligatory itinerary of inspection. 'My Lady Ranalagh's son, who is going to travel with his tutor for some years in France and Italy'[1] or, 'I went abroad and spent about 2 years in France and Italy where I learnt little besides the Languages, partly from my youth and the warmth of my temper, partly from lazynesse and debauchery':[2] these words, of John Dury the Protestant peace-maker and of Sir William Trumbull respectively, derive from a formula universally accepted. The comparative neglect of Spain and most parts of Germany, in the diaries, is understandable; relatively few travellers visited Spain except as merchants or diplomats and Germany was closed by war between 1620 and 1650. But it is strange that they should have so little to say about the Low Countries. While there are several celebrated descriptions by Englishmen who knew them well, the large number of manuscript accounts which in the case of France and Italy testify to the activity of a whole class of travellers are here conspicuous by their absence. It is strange at first sight because few populations were more intimately linked by every sort of common concern, even in their rivalry, than the people of England and the Low Countries. For centuries their trading had been interlocked so closely that it is in no way a matter of surprise to find the younger son of a Norfolk family like the Spelmans, about 1550, working in Bruges as a merchant's factor and then marrying a Dutch wife who lived in England while he spent the greater part of each year in Holland. After her death he settled at Antwerp, enjoyed the revenues of his second wife's landed estate in that city, and with her capital drove a large trade between England and the Low Countries; the wars finally bringing him back to his old home.[3] This intimate connection between neighbouring peoples

16. Bound for Holland: a husbandman, a weaver, and the wives of a felt-maker and a tailor, appear in the passport register for Great Yarmouth, 1637.

appeared part of the natural order. Then, from the time of the Reformation refugees had swollen the movement of population between the Protestant provinces and East Anglia, London and Kent. Finally, war with Spain brought English volunteers followed by English armies into the Low Countries. Between 1585 and 1616 the towns of Flushing (with the neighbouring fort of Rammekens) and Brill were held by the English Crown as pledges for the repayment of monies lent to the States; and there were English garrisons and companies of English soldiers in other parts of the country, according to the fortune of war. Officers and men hailing from England but in Dutch employ became a permanent institution in the military history of these territories in the first half of the seventeenth century; hardly less so were English

Catholics who served the governors of the Spanish Netherlands. It seems probable that for a variety of reasons economic, religious, and political, all the people of English extraction scattered over the rest of the continent hardly compared in number with the English permanently resident in the Low Countries.

The continual exchanges between England and the Low Countries could be shown from the most general historical narrative but another significant proof, relevant to the travellers themselves, is provided by one of the registers of a passport official working at Yarmouth in Charles I's reign.[4] Between Michaelmas 1637 and Michaelmas 1638 his returns demonstrate that 339 passengers sailed to Holland after taking the oath of allegiance before him. Seventy of these were clothworkers of every description, tailors, weavers, woolcombers, embroiderers, feltmakers, cordwainers, glovers who were travelling for a variety of reasons — because their homes were abroad, to collect debts, to visit friends, to find employment, to improve their skill or to purchase goods. Thirty more were tradesmen, tanners, grocers, carpenters, spoonmakers and the like, who gave similar reasons. Twelve were husbandmen, prosperous or improverished. About one hundred were women, frequently wives of the travellers, but some desired to find employment abroad as servants, or wished to visit relatives and friends for a few months. About forty-five men alleged that they intended to serve the States in the wars (this figure including certain entries from the groups already mentioned). Only one titled gentleman appears in the list, Sir Christopher Baynton, who had a special warrant from the King to go overseas. With regard to the prospective destination of all these travellers individual towns in the United Provinces are named in about forty entries. To judge from these Rotterdam, Leyden and Amsterdam in that order, attracted Englishmen most, but the Hague, Haarlem, Brill, Breda and Bergen also had their visitors. Now even if a certain number of these details are erroneous — statements merely designed to satisfy an official by their probability — they show that representatives from many classes in English society were busily coming and going across the North Sea. The single knight who appeared before the passport officer at Yarmouth in one year, while so many of his class favoured the cities of France and Italy,[5] was overshadowed by the shiploads of tradespeople and their wives, folk who profited most from the intimate connection of eastern England with the Low Countries. The mingling of families, customs, even language, rested primarily in their hands.

However, mere numbers of people crossing over the sea bear little relation to the number of diaries kept, because diaries were usually written at this time by a certain class of traveller for particular reasons. The English gentry and their servants were fundamentally less interested in the Low Countries than in France and Italy. There were no great monuments or ancient treasure, universally famed, which every educated man was required to inspect for himself, and the local language and literature were not considered worthy of study.

The result was a relative neglect of these provinces in the documents of travel, in spite of intensive and continuous exchanges of every kind. At the same time some surviving diaries make it easier to understand how the observations of travellers or the experience of English residents in that region could influence contemporary English society.

The most celebrated accounts of the Low Countries by travellers on tour come from the pens of Sir William Brereton[6] and John Evelyn. They both remained unpublished until the nineteenth century.

Brereton, the Parliamentary general of the Civil Wars, belonged to the important Cheshire family of that name. Born in 1604 he matriculated at Brasenose College, Oxford, in 1621 and entered Grays Inn in 1623. Anthony Wood states that he fought in the Low Countires but this cannot be confirmed from any other source. He visited Paris, since at a later date he was able to compare the ecclesiastical vestments treasured in Durham Cathedral with those which he had seen at St. Denis.[7] In 1628 Brereton sat in the House of Commons as member for Cheshire, and although not appearing as a speaker of any importance in the course of its stormy proceedings he cared sufficiently to 'collect' a voluminous diary or record of the proceedings, to which he occasionally added his own annotations.[8] The bias of this document is one of pronounced hostility to the King, the Catholics and the Duke of Buckingham. A speech of the King's Counsel, Sergeant Ashley, was characterized as 'desperate and damnable consequences upon the Resolution of the House of Commons touching the liberty of the subject'. One is tempted to conclude that Sir William Brereton had made up his mind on the crucial questions of politics and religion very early in life.

Six years later he travelled over to Holland. He gives no precise reason for his journey, but apparently desired to consult with the doctors at Leyden about the health of his children, who accompanied him, at the same time taking the opportunity of touring through the country. Towards the end of May 1634 his party left Gravesend in a ship of 50 tons' burden, full of merchandise and with sixty-seven passengers on board. They sailed past Flushing and Goeree in Zeeland and northwards to Brill where they entered the waters of the River Maas. After a short visit to Delfshaven they went by wagon from Schiedam, where Brereton at once remarked the streets neatly paved with brick, to Rotterdam. They reached this city some twenty-five hours after leaving Foreness — a prosperous and speedy voyage.

At Rotterdam the traveller found the following incidents and impressions worthy of note. They visited the English church and listened to Mr. Hugh Peters, a preacher of formidable ability who had

MIDDELBURGH
aen de landtzyde.

17.  Middelburg: the conventional image of a Dutch town, taken from N. J. Visscher's
    *Speculum Zelandiae*, 1661.

left England rather than suppress his Separatist opinions; like all
English travellers Brereton observed with amazement the profusion of
churches and conflicting creeds tolerated in Dutch cities, Dutch,
French, English, Anabaptist, Brownist; on the other hand he was sorry
to see 'little respect to sanctify the Sabbath'. Next, Brereton had his
attention drawn to the fact, or noticed for himself, that the whole
herring-fleet of Rotterdam, save one buss, was absent and away at sea: it
was the aspect of Dutch economic activity which aroused immediately
the jealous admiration of people who had their own claim to the seas
where the Dutch fished. The traveller also saw the state-vessels of the
Prince of Orange, which were then in dock; he saw the statue of
Erasmus in the marketplace; and made enquiries regarding the forms of
municipal government prevailing in Holland, and the arrangements in
Rotterdam for dealing with the poor, the infirm and recalcitrant sections
of the city's population.

After a few days they proceeded south-eastwards to Dordrecht, where Brereton commented on the great manufactories outside the walls, brick-kilns, coppermills, glass and salt works; much of this was of immediate concern to a substantial landowner from Cheshire. Similarly he admired the great decoys for birds in this neighbourhood; another parallel with the local landscape at home. Again they visited the English church and heard the preacher, Mr. John Vincent.

After returning to Rotterdam on 29 May they went northwards by water to Delft and the Hague. Here Brereton visited the English church to listen to 'a very honest, neat sermon' and paid his court to the exiled Queen Elizabeth of Bohemia, with whom he discussed the comparative demerits of witches in Westphalia and in Lancashire; he purchased tulip bulbs in the Prince of Orange's garden. A few days later the party came to Leyden, still a little further north. Brereton consulted the doctors about the health of his children, and certain recommendations were made on their behalf. He heard a lecture in the Botanic garden, and visited the famous Anatomy School. Five days later they were in Haarlem, 'a city much decayed', and on 10 June they reached Amsterdam.

In this, the greatest of Dutch cities, the traveller reveals once more his customary, almost mechanical, concern with religious questions. He attended the Jews' Sabbath at their synagogue. He attended Communion at one of the English churches; the minister, John Paget, was possibly a man with Cheshire connections. Brereton describes carefully and apparently with approval the simple ceremonies of baptism and marriage practised in the Dutch and English churches at Amsterdam. Here, as in the case of Hugh Peters previously, he notes that the English ministers were paid by the municipality for their services, estimating their salaries at £100 and £110 respectively. Likewise, it was 'elders and deacons who govern Church affairs' and provided for the poor: an expedient of government, in ecclesiastical and economic matters, of some significance to the Englishmen of Brereton's generation. His other great concern in Amsterdam was arranging for the despatch to England of all his purchases. These included 180 Delft tiles for fireplaces; there were floor-stones, plaster-casts, certain portraits — including one of the Queen of Bohemia and one of the Prince of Orange — also optical glasses of a type not exactly described; tulips, and turtle-doves. The cost of these things amounted to about 350 gulden, or £35 sterling.

Then the party took its way homeward. It had been a three weeks' journey safely completed. Brereton's account is sober and matter-of-fact, his interests religious and economic. He was not much of a sightseer.

John Evelyn, sixteen years younger than Brereton, visited the Netherlands seven years later. He was a man of quite different character from Brereton although his motives for travelling were not very different. He left England in July 1641 at a time of great crisis in state affairs — unlike his predecessor he represented that type of good citizen who kept aloof from politics. His sentiments as a sincere Royalist were never in doubt, but they were always discreet. He befriended and encouraged active supporters of the King, but was never one of them, refusing to admit to the compulsion of politics in an age of political crisis. He therefore differed from Brereton in opinion and in temperament; though both men came from families of substantial gentry. In 1641 John Evelyn also felt that it was time for a young man of twenty-one to see the world. On 21 July he left Gravesend in a Dutch frigate convoyed and accompanied by five other vessels, and on the following day landed at Flushing.[9]

He desired first of all, he says, to observe the siege of Gennep on the Waal which the Spaniards were defending, the French and Dutch assaulting. At this early stage of his career, therefore, he took sufficient interest in the art and practice of war to follow in the footsteps of many other English gentry who came to the Low Countries in the seventeenth century. He hurried through Middelburg and Veere in Zeeland and reached Dordrecht where he cursorily admired the town-hall, meeting place of the Synod in 1618 which had deeply concerned the Protestants of his father's generation. He drove on northwards to Rotterdam which, like Brereton, he learnt to associate with the name of Erasmus, passed through Delft and reached the Hague where he went first of all to the Queen of Bohemia's court. He visited in quick succession Leyden, Utrecht, Nijmegen — without seeing much of these cities — on the way to Gennep which he reached by 2 August. He was too late to witness the siege; the place had been taken by the Dutch a fortnight previously. Nevertheless he enrolled as a volunteer in one of the English companies, and was alloted a tent and horse. Like hundreds of Englishmen in these parts before him he looked at examples of modern work in military science, entrenchment and scarp and ravine, available for study in the Netherlands; he stood guard and trailed a pike. But Evelyn was no serious volunteer for service as a soldier, finding the August heat by day and the mists rolling off the river at nightfall an insufferable inconvenience. Within a week he 'was pretty well satisfied' with the confusion of Armies and Sieges, and took leave of his new profession and his new colleagues. On 12 August he returned westwards down the Waal to Bummel and Gorcum. These details, few and hasty, describe an experience which attracted other Englishmen, much more than they attracted John Evelyn, to the Netherlands.

The civilian part of his journey now began. He returned to Rotterdam and purchased landscape and genre paintings to send to England. The number and variety of these bought and sold at the city's annual fair filled him with delighted amazement. He revisited Delft and on this occasion paid more attention to the sights of the place, the New Church and its monuments to members of the Orange dynasty, the black-pillared Senate house and the country mansion of the Orange family nearby, at Ryswick. On 19 August he was at the Hague; and he saw Rotterdam again, with Haarlem and Leyden, before coming to Amsterdam.

Here what seems to have impressed him most were the religious services at the Jewish synagogue and the English Reformed church; also the hospitals and poor-houses. In this he echoes Brereton. He says that he changed lodging to live at the house of a Brownist on purpose to observe the sectaries swarming in the city. In his new pension he found staying there the exiled Lord Keeper Finch, Sir John Fotherby, an English Carmelite and an Irish gentleman. In this thriving cosmopolis he was impressed likewise by the multitude of shipping, the inland waterways bringing vessels up to the warehouses of the merchants, even to the back door of their houses; while the streets, shaded by lime trees and trim with stone or brick paving seemed to him clean and sightly; in the air, brimming with the sounds of commerce, resounded the ingenious chiming of the Dutch carillons. Finally, it was satisfying to discover that, in the churches, organs, lamps and monuments had not been swept away by the impiety of popular reformers. The prosperity, the orderly beauty and the relative conservatism of the Protestant Netherlands all made a due impression on the young traveller.

Here at Amsterdam Evelyn bought maps at the shop of Hondius, cartographer and publisher, visited 'cabinets of rarities', and enjoyed himself. After some ten days' stay he went by water to Haarlem, 'a very delicate town', to see the church and the fishmarket. On 27 August he visited Leyden University where he matriculated at the price of one dollar, an expense justified by the consequent freedom from excise duties in the country. He called on Daniel Heinsius the scholar whom he had long desired to see, explored the famous printing-house of the Elzevirs and also the Physic-garden. Above all, he enjoyed the school of Anatomy; and as, previously, he had seen for the first time an elephant and a pelican at Dordrecht, so here he saw anatomies of all sorts from the spider to the whale, remarking how beautiful and delicate the art of dissection could be. His interest in scientific and natural phenomena was probably aroused, and it certainly developed, in the course of this journey through Holland. At Leyden, it may be added, Evelyn was introduced to a false prophet who greatly diverted him by the scope and improbability of his visions; the traveller took the words of the drunken seer more to heart than would have been conceivable in an educated tourist a century later.

Returning through Delft and Rotterdam to the Hague he visited the palace and garden of the Prince of Orange; went next to Dordrecht (observing by the way the decoys already admired by Brereton), in order to be present at the reception of Queen Marie de Medici; thence to 'the Busse'[10] where he was entertained at a convent of nuns; and to Heusdun where he accepted the honour of captaining the watch, and gave the password for one night. It was the last phase of his tour in the northern provinces before entering Spanish territory. Difficulties in obtaining passports, in realizing bills of exchange, and the bad weather, delayed him during the last week of September. The United Netherlands and Spain were still at war and the passage of neutrals from one country to another, though frequent, required care and a measure of good fortune. But by 4 October, after an unpleasant journey between the advanced posts of hostile forces Evelyn was in Antwerp, singling out for admiration among many ecclesiastical foundations the church and school of the Jesuits. A disciplined grandeur seemed to the traveller to characterize both the style of their architecture and the organization of their learning. He saw as much of the citadel as was open to strangers, 'a matchless piece of modern fortification', and also the shop of Plantin the printer where he made purchases of books published there. He described Antwerp as 'a quiet, cleane, elegantly built and civil place'; and though historians of the Spanish Netherlands' recession in the seventeenth century would probably lay stress on the word 'quiet' as the most significant of these epithets, Englishmen of the period always praised Antwerp in generous terms.

After three days Evelyn continued southward to Brussels. The sculpture of the town-hall, the drawbridges across waterways, the city walls and the cathedral attracted his attention in turn as worthy spectacles. He spent some time at the convent of English Benedictine Nuns; and called on Sir Henry de Vic, Charles I's Agent at the Archduke's court. In the churches and palaces he made his first real study of Breughel, Titian and Rubens; and yet one notices how perfunctory were his impressions, by contrast with the overwhelming detail of his descriptions later on, in France and Italy. Soon afterwards he arrived at Ghent, then a half-empty city of great extent. In company with old Lord Arundel he proceeded to Bruges by water. He spent a morning sightseeing and moved on to Ostende, and then along the sea-shore to Dunkirk. He went on board the packet-boat, they sailed past Calais and reached Dover on 12 October. John Evelyn had been three months abroad in the Low Countries, his first journey on the continent; and now he returned to his rooms in the Middle Temple.

These well known descriptions by Brereton and Evelyn of a tour through this part of Europe stand in a class by themselves because they give the outline of a journey from England which was confined to this limited area. The two men were not on their way to Italy, France or Germany. For the time being, the Netherlands contented them. They fixed their attention on its cities, industries and character for a few short weeks, and returned home. In a very similar way two relatives, both named Marmaduke Rawdon, enjoyed a holiday during the summer and autumn of 1662. Crossing to Calais, they visited churches, palaces and gardens in Flanders, and took particular note of the English Catholic foundations. In Holland they made the usual observations on Dutch trade, hospitals, work-houses, and the curiosites to be seen at Leyden. The older man had learnt a little of the language and visited Dutch cities in the intervals of business as a factor, some thirty-five years earlier; but the journey of 1662 was for pleasure or experience only, and then they came home.[11] The evidence provided by these accounts would be detailed enough to indicate what English people most desired or expected to see in the Netherlands; but before proceeding to observe the activities of travellers who left no such comprehensive records behind them, additional testimony can be called from Englishmen who were simply passing through the Low Countries.

In 1592 Fynes Moryson, after a long journey across the continent, sailed by inland waterways from Emden to Harlingen on the eastern side of the Zuyder Zee; the inn where he passed the night was kept by an Englishman. From there he sailed across to Enkhuyzen and then to Amsterdam. He observed how riverways and canals brought shipping to the city, where trade had grown greatly since the blockade of Antwerp; new houses were everywhere springing up; and there also were the imposing almshouses and hospitals which he was to notice in other cities. Coming next to Haarlem, he learnt that it was a centre of linen-manufacture, and less important, that the citizens claimed as their own the discovery of printing, pointing out the old house of Laurence Coster, the alleged inventor. After a short return visit to Amsterdam to receive money sent by exchange from England Moryson settled down at Leyden for the winter, where he matriculated at the University and lodged with a Frenchman in order to learn French. When spring came he set out again, 'purposing to see the Cities of the United Provinces'. It was a land full of cornfields, waterways, mills and, according to contemporary geographers and historians, of Roman remains. At Delft he found a great deal of brewing, one of the principal occupations, and visited the tomb of William of Orange, 'the poorest that ever I saw for such a person'. After touching as far south as Brill he visited Rotterdam, lodging with an Englishman. He, also, had his attention drawn to Erasmus. Then he bent his way south-east-wards to Dort and towards the Dutch armies engaged in besieging Gertruydenberg. Nineteen hours' sailing brought him to Bergen-op-Zoom, garrisoned by English troops in Dutch pay — with the enemy only three miles away; he found an English church. At Middelburg, the staple of English merchants, he was entertained by his countrymen; likewise at Flushing, a few miles off, 'being entertained by my English friends I spent nothing in this city'.

Then he turned again, visiting towns he had already seen, and also the

Hague with Loosduinen nearby — where every traveller of the period learnt the story of the Countess of Holland who gave birth there to 365 children in 1265 — Gouda, and Utrecht. From Amsterdam he took shipping for north Germany and a longer, more adventurous journey to Denmark and Poland.[12]

A quarter of a century later James Howell set out from London on his first continental expedition. Nominally he was employed by Sir Robert Mansel of the glass monopoly to look to certain trading interests but Howell determined to combine business with a pleasurable education. He went by sea to Amsterdam, and lodged with a Frenchman, who was a deacon in the church of the English Brownists, in order to learn French before entering France. In this city he found the commercial activity and the recent building of houses equally prodigious; whole new streets and suburbs were going up; but he came to the conclusion that Amsterdam still could not compare with London in population. A point which struck him was that in Holland 'the generality of Commerce, and the common interest which large numbers of men had in the Indian and other companies produces a strange kind of Equality'. There were few beggars to be seen, thanks to the hospitals and poor-houses. Taxation was excessive; the general cleanliness admirable. Before leaving for France he visited Leyden for the sake of its university which he found less impressive than Oxford both in point of size and of ceremony; while little time, and less study, sufficed to make one a graduate. He saw the Hague, and learnt enough to give a sketch of the character and habits of Prince Maurice; then took his way southward to Middleburg and Flushing, which he found much depressed by the removal of the English staple, and the loss of the English garrison after James I's 'surrender' of the cautionary towns back to the United Provinces; then on to Flanders and Brabant, a more cheerful country and people than the Dutch. The city of Antwerp appeared to Howell greatly impoverished by the catastrophic decline of its commerce; still, it was a stately, spacious place with a noble citadel. His next letter came from Rouen; if the erratic dating of the whole series can be trusted within rough limits, he had been in the Low Countries about three months.[13]

Over twenty years later Peter Mundy, a sailor and merchant, not a 'gentleman', visited Holland. After an adventurous and dangerous passage he reached Rotterdam, which he found a busy, populous place with many English inhabitants wearing English costume. He travelled to Delft by one of the passenger boats which left punctually every hour. Both were clean and pleasant places, with impressive monuments and well-built houses. He went by water to Amsterdam, taking note of the production of peat in this part of the country; at Haarlem he admired the nurseries of small trees which in due course would be sold to the other Dutch towns and gardens. South-east of Amsterdam he visited the old castle at Muiden, and Weesp, where they brewed beer for the great city.

As he went, Mundy made stray notes or jottings on a variety of observations, the difficulties of building in Holland by reason of the marshy land, on the population of Amsterdam, on Dutch burial customs, ecclesiastical ceremonies, the combined facts of religious tolerance with the absence of parochial organization, the church-organs in Holland which played only when people were leaving at the close of a service. He enjoyed the grand prospect from the tower of the Westerkerk in Amsterdam which had been completed two years earlier: observing from afar the cities of Utrecht and Leyden, with the medley of canals and streets closer at hand 'soe long, soe straighte', and the parallel ranks of the trees. He visited the Jewish quarter, tolerated, prosperous and unlike the Jews of Constantinople as he recollected them, allowing and delighting in pictures hung on the walls of their houses. Then, in an eloquent passage, Mundy dilates on 'the general Notion, enclination and delight that these Countrie Natives have to Painting'; he names Rembrandt, and goes on to praise the furniture of Dutch families, their ornaments, porcelain, gilded birdcages and the like. Supporting this opulence was the grandeur and extent of the Netherland's trade. Mundy speaks of streams of ships perpetually ebbing from, and flowing to, the city of Amsterdam, which offset the natural disadvantages and poverty of the country; but like most travellers he was usually immersed in local details and went on to describe church steeples in Holland, the difficult walking in Dutch fields, the pleasantness of their gardens with rare roots and flowers, the fashions in dress and the multiplicity of different coins in current use. The whole of this section of his manuscript betrays an enthusiasm which the writer excuses by admitting that he was himself 'somewhat affectionated and enclined to the Manner off the[se] Countries'. Mundy then took shipping from Amsterdam for Danzig and beyond.[14]

Very different from Mundy in character and status were the English noblemen who, when conditions allowed, passed through the Low Countries in the course of long, leisurely European tours; coming down the Rhine from Italy and Germany, or breaking the monotony of educational exercises in Paris by a short trip into Flanders, or simply returning home to England from France by way of the Low Countries. On the whole conditions did not permit this course, for between 1620 and 1660 war made such journeys generally impracticable, but during the reigns of James I and Charles II there are several instances to record. In the spring of 1611 Sir Thomas Puckering's tutor was upset to find his pupil insisting on an excursion into Flanders, instead of attending quietly to his study of French in Paris and then going on into Italy. The young man wandered about there for several months before returning to France by the well-known coast road, Ghent, Bruges, Ostende, Gravelines and Calais.[15] Half a century later another tutor was very much in the position of Thomas Lorkin. His charges, the two older sons of the fourth Lord Wharton, were residing in Paris in 1665. They grew restless and it was decided to visit the Low Countries, possibly as a stage on the road for Italy. Reaching Brussels in September the party made a series of short excursions but Clifford, the boys' tutor, soon decided that it would be needlessly rash to go on to Cologne, or even towards Sedan; while in view of the Anglo-Dutch war at sea Lord Wharton had forbidden them to use the coast-route to Calais. In these circumstances they returned to Paris by another road and the long letter written by Clifford to Wharton, after they were back, gives an exceedingly clear idea of what this kind of journey usually meant to the English gentry who performed them. Leaving Brussels they went to Enghien, the Duke of Aerschot's seat, 'one of the finest gardens in all Flanders', comparable with those in France for 'statua and handsom contriv'd walks, tho not for water works'; to Ath where they longed to purchase all sorts of fine cloth manufactured in the town 'at very cheape rates'; and Tournai, of which Clifford remarks:

> I never yet saw fewer poor and less richesse than in this town. Never more artificers, nor more diligent in theyr callings: All the grandeur lies in the rich Canons, and magnificent Church, and rare musiques

Then they came to Douai, where the young Whartons were royally entertained by the Bendictines and other English Catholics. Clifford, the servant of a strictly Puritan family and a nonconforming cleric, expressed the deepest admiration for his reception in these Catholic centres. He wrote to Wharton:

> Our journey hither, and to Louvain, I account the most significant of all we have made since we left Paris. Its true in the several stages we have made we have seen strong towns, magnificent buildings, Rich Churches, fine gardens etc. But in these two Universities we mette with learned and intelligent persons, from whom I understood more of the affaires and intrigues of these parts of the world, than from all my other travails. And would the Gentlemen have been willing to it I had spent some few hours more in e[a]ch.

However little he appreciated his tutor, this was part of the education of Thomas Wharton, the notable Whig politician.

At Arras, recently acquired by Louis XIV, the travellers had some difficulty in entering the town, the guard was so strictly kept, and suspicion aroused when it became known that they were English; but after that the way led them peaceably through Compiègne and Senlis to Paris. The tutor concluded his report by a summing-up, and he told Lord Wharton:

> Our journey, I blesse God was safe and exceedingly pleasant, both in regard of the way and weather (excepting one day in Flanders) and of the places we saw, and of the delightfulnesse of the country through which we passed. And tho lying still be commonly lesse chargeable than travelling, yet we saved by

our travils 6 crownes a day of what it would have cost us at Brussels. And since we were commanded not to come at Port townes, the tour we made was the best and shortest. Which way we shall go, or what we shall do next, wholly depends on your Lordships orders, in which we are daily in expectation.[16]

This narrative may be compared with the diary kept by a servant of Banister Maynard, Lord Maynard's son, during the winter of 1661–1662 when that young nobleman returned from Italy and Germany to Paris by way of the Netherlands. Travelling down the Rhine as far as Utrecht they went first to Amsterdam and passed the greater part of the next few months in this city and at the Hague. It cannot be said that they took the responsibilities and possibilities of what the pundits of their time called 'peregrination' very seriously but here again, the quality of the travellers' experience may best be gathered by direct quotation:

> Being safe arrived at the Hague [writes Robert Moody, the servant] and having taken a convenient Lodgin for the winter Season, my Maister went to kiss the Princes hands, where he was received with much respect, and was invited to dine at the Princes table, which he did once or twice a week during his aboad at the Hage, and sometimes at Sir George Downings who was his Majestie's envoy extraordinary, where he very often went for divershion, play'd at Cards and other divertisements with Sir George and his Lady and the other Gentlewomen...Having seen everything in Amsterdam which was most rare, as the Stat haus, the Change, all the best Churches, the Jewes Synagogue, and innumerable of brave Pallaces, and to tell truth I think it to be the most famous Merchant Town in Europe except London, but for neatnesse and faire buildings it goes beyond it...We kept our Christmasse at the Hage where my Maister went sometimes to dine at Court, sometimes to se Balls, sometimes for divershion to se curious Duch Playes.[17]

They began their travels again on 7 February 1662; and passing through Delft and Rotterdam, stopping a week at Dordrecht to enjoy the hospitality of a wealthy Dutch merchant who provided a pleasure-yacht, feasting and music, they spent a fortnight at Brussels. The churches, particularly the Jesuit foundations of Flanders and Brabant, came in for the conventional formulas of praise — they were fair, gracious, very rich — and then young Maynard and servants followed the coast to Calais, and so back to Paris where they found the baggage, safe and intact, which they had left behind them two years earlier on setting out for Italy.

As the last in date, consider the remarks of William Nicolson who was appointed Bishop of Carlisle in Queen Anne's reign, and just before he died in 1727, Archbishop of Cashel. The son of a minister in Cumberland and a poor tabarder of Queen's College, Oxford, he found a patron in Sir Joseph Williamson, Secretary of State, always the friend of humble north country and Queen's men. Williamson put money in Nicolson's pocket and sent him abroad to see the world; in particular he was to spend six months at the university city of Leipzig and elsewhere in Germany. The young man sailed from Gravesend in July 1678 in the

Earl of Ailesbury's retinue on one of the Duke of York's yachts. They entered the river Maas at Brill and Nicolson saw for himself the spot where armed rebellion had broken out against the Spaniards in 1572, now adorned with trees pleasantly shading the bulwarks; but the vessel continued up the river to Rotterdam (the City of Erasmus). The streets, yet another traveller now remarked, were paved with brick and admirably clean. At the Hague, he methodically viewed the principal palaces, churches and hospitals. In particular he gives a valuable description of the interior of the Huis den Bosch, the secluded retreat of the Orange family (before it was modernized in the eighteenth century), the wainscotting of the rooms loaded with ebony and mother-of-pearl, the cedar floors and fine paintings. He went down to the sea at Scheveningen; at Delft he discovered that the citizens boasted of their ability to dispense with the import of English woollen-cloth, manufacturing their own instead. At Leyden where he made a conventional tour of the Library, the Anatomy Theatre and the Physic Garden ('not so big as a fourth part of ours at Oxford') he noted how the Netherlands profited by their connection with the countries beyond Europe, since the catalogue of Leyden MSS. which he was able to transcribe contained 220 items brought-back from the East. He visited St. Peter's Church where great scholars were buried, and climbed the old Burg — said to have been built by the Romans. He went on to Loosduinen, still visited for the monument to the 365 children born there, and Haarlem, still admired as the first home of printing. At Amsterdam, on the other hand, the poverty of the archives seemed to the student to demonstrate how wholeheartedly the citizens devoted themselves to trade, neglecting the duties of scholarship. But unlike Mundy, when he climbed a church-tower to survey the prospect, Nicolson felt convinced that 'a man may reckon more vessels from the top of the Monument at London Bridge than from any watchtower in Amsterdam'; conceivably the slowly changing balance in the trade of two rival commercial nations was reflected in the differing conclusions of two English sightseers, one in 1640 and the other nearly forty years later.[18]

Among the memorabilia of Amsterdam William Nicolson reckoned one which is not to be found, I think, in the more famous English descriptions of Holland. This was the Dutch trade in books purporting to have been printed in other European countries and cities; he lists it third in the sights of the city, after the town hall and the library:

Widdow Shippers print house: where there were 18 hard at work printing, and 6 or 7 setting letters. They print here many English Bibles of all sizes; upon the titlepages of which they sett — *London printed by R. Barker and the Assigns of John Bill* etc. And they were (whilst I lookt on) printeing a small English Bible in Octavo, which they sett printed by the aforesaid, A.D. 1609. They showed me also severall books printed here with the title pages as if at Collen, Leipsick, Mentz etc. whence it comes to pass that you may buy books cheaper at Amsterdam, in all languages, than at the places where they are first printed: for here the Copy costs them nothing.[19]

At Utrecht there was little worth seeing except the pleasant situation of the place. The cathedral had been ruined by a thunderstorm in 1674. The titles of a few manuscripts were worth transcribing; and round about, the countryside appeared to Nicolson much like Herefordshire with its profusion of fruit trees. Then they began to go eastwards and inland where the landscape and cities altered in character. Nijmegen, he found, 'looks old and ruinous, wanting much of the glory of the rest of the cities we mett in the Low Country', and this was only compensated by the prestige gratuitously assured it by the congress of diplomats then engaged in interminable negotiations there. The young traveller was entertained by Sir Leoline Jenkins, one of the English ambassadors, and in consequence he remained longer there than in the more splendid and civilized centres which he had already visited. But by the end of August he was on the road once again, bound for the Library at Wolffenbüttel and the university of Leipzig. He tells us that he left the land of sheets and entered another land, that of the feather bed; for in Westphalia conditions at once deteriorated, and armed with these featherbeds he sometimes slept in houses and outhouses with the cattle on his left hand, and the pigs' sty on his right. He had completed this rapid survey of the Dutch Republic, and his account, *Iter Hollandicum*, like the *Iter Germanicum* which followed, he though worthy of dedicating to his patron Sir Joseph Williamson, who put it with the mass of his other papers and documents.

These narratives, with a few insignificant exceptions, complete the evidence which can give a picture of English travellers surveying the Netherlands in the course of a journey.[20] The comparative monotony of such accounts, when they are summarized in rapid succession, shows how stereotyped were (and are) the impressions and comments of ordinary folk engaged in travel. They saw the same things, learnt what to think of them from books and the local inhabitants, tending to share a common and conventional outlook on the panorama around them; and it is certain that these travellers were representative figures. Such a remark as that of the deputy governor of Flushing in 1606, 'I purpose next week to lead my wife to Holland to take pleasure for 14 days'[21] is given added meaning by the comments of Brereton or Evelyn, who explain clearly enough what Sir William and Lady Browne would have observed on their holiday. In 1611 young Lord Cranborne came down the Rhine from a visit to Italy. At Flushing the Prince of Orange's yacht carried him to Antwerp 'to see the Archduke's Cuntrey'; we now know what he saw.[22] Puckering travelled from Paris into Flanders in the same year; a little later Sir Walter Raleigh's son and his tutor, Ben Jonson, had followed him on that route,[23] while 'my Lord Sheffield's son is come out of France overland by way of Brussels to the Hague and will shortly come this way [to Flushing] and so by Sluys overland to Callis, and from thence to England',[24] again, their journeys have been illustrated by other and more detailed accounts. In fact, by considering some rather scattered evidence, in the light of the larger narratives summarized above, we can describe more fully the general importance of the Netherlands in the minds of those who travelled abroad.

For example, one of the surprising features of John Evelyn's journey, considering his temperament, was its military prelude. He set out, ostensibly, to participate in the wars of the Low Countries; and followed a traditional practice of many gentry in going to seek training and experience, sometimes also a livelihood, in the longstanding hostilities of the Dutch and Spanish armies. Often this involved a lifetime of residence abroad, or it was merely one interlude in a few years' travel as a young man.[25] In this second instance, men *toured* from city to city in France and Italy learning languages and manners, they *fought* in the Low Countries. Thus Sir Edward Herbert, having acquired the language and practised the arts of poetry and horsemanship at French castles and the French capital, was next attracted by the prospect of war in the Cleves-Juliers dispute (1610). He accompanied the fifth Lord Chandos thither, and the unrestrained egotism of his autobiographical writing shows him behaving at the siege of Juliers as a brave, undisciplined spirit, essentially the aristocratic volunteer more intent on displaying his courage, and enjoying the exercise of that courage, than inspired by any sense of the serious political issues that might be involved in the dispute. Moreover, he forced a quarrel upon his countryman Lord Theophilus Howard who, like Herbert himself, had earlier travelled in France and Italy before entering upon this campaign in the Low Countries. There were also further quarrels between Herbert and other Englishmen of the same type and temper, for of course Herbert and Howard were not alone in sallying out from England to play a part in the Cleves-Juliers affair.[26] Sir Robert Sidney, the titular Governor of Flushing, wrote to his Deputy in August 1612 that 'many of our young Gallants are gone into Cleve', and the Deputy reported back on 12 August, that besides Howard and Sir Thomas Somerset, Sir Henry Rich, Sir Thomas Howard and Sir Edward Sheffield had arrived in Flushing on the previous day, visited Middelburg and were intending to go with all possible speed to the scene of action.[27] After the conclusion of the siege, Herbert returned to England by way of Düsseldorf, Antwerp, Brussels and Calais. Four years later he set out again for the Low Countries, serving under Maurice of Nassau who welcomed him to his table; but he took advantage of the military conventions of the time to interview and compliment the opposing generalissimo, Spinola. A truce was then negotiated, so Herbert continued on his journey, to Ulm, Augsburg and Italy where we have already made his acquaintance. On his return north of the Alps he again enjoyed the Prince of Orange's company, and since there was no campaigning that year contrary to his hope and expectation, satisfied himself with lesser activities, horsemanship, chessplaying, making love; and meanwhile raised a troop of horse for service in Savoy. Undoubtedly Herbert would have fought in the Palatinate in 1621, when hostilities broke out again, had he not been appointed to the embassy at Paris.[28]

Or we may take another case of the nobleman who combined travel with a desultory experience in warfare. From time to time stray references may be found to the head of the family of Vere, Henry the 18th earl of Oxford, wandering through Europe in the second decade of the century. In 1614, at the age of twenty-one, he was writing from Paris to Sir Christopher Hatton, his deputy as Keeper of Havering and Waltham Forests. He states that he soon hoped to travel south to Italy, and meanwhile gave instructions for the disposal of offices in the administration of the forests, in his patronage, and confirmed the permission granted to certain friends to receive game from the forest, or to hunt there.[29] Apparently he made his way to Italy the same autumn, for Sir Edward Herbert encountered him at Florence, where he remained for some years practising horsemanship and other noble exercises.[30] In 1617 Sir Henry Wotton began to take notice of him, reporting that he had gone to Rome under the Grand Duke's protection to intercede for a cousin who was in the hands of the Inquisition, to Padua for the advice of physicians, and to Venice where the ambassador introduced him to the Doge.[31] Oxford hoped to raise troops in England and lead them as an auxiliary in the Venetian frontier wars, but it appears that his intended intervention ended where it began. Italy was only a possible campaigning-ground in default of the more conventional theatre of war in the Low Countries, then enjoying a few years of peace. When the affair of the Palatinate blew up, and the Twelve Years Truce came to an end, the Earl of Oxford duly appeared in the Low Countries. He was one of the commanders of the ill-fated English expedition to the Rhineland in 1621–1622; while in the summer of 1624 a correspondent reported that preparations were being made to receive him at the Hague, before another campaign. His wife, formerly Lady Anne Cecil, came with him; in October she was staying at Gertruydenberg and on one occasion entered the trenches to observe the enemy's position. Oxford then began to participate in the different attempts to raise the Spanish siege of Breda. He was seriously wounded, and died at the Hague, in June 1625.[32]

Had he survived he might well have obtained the high military command usually conferred on men of birth and fair military experience at the beginning of the English civil wars. His almost exact contemporary, Robert third Earl of Essex, the Parliamentary general, had passed through a very similar apprenticeship. After two years in France, as we have seen, he returned home by way of the Low Countries; the deputy-governor of Flushing mentions his passage through that town in November 1608.[33] Then came the scandal of his wife's connection with Somerset and the murder of Overbury, and at first he lived a retired existence in the country but thereafter spent every summer for some years campaigning in the Low Countries. The winters were passed in England, says his servant and biographer Arthur Wilson, when he hunted and in the evenings played the game called 'catastrophe'. In 1621 he was at Tournai, in 1622 at Rees, in 1623 at Arnhem, in 1624 at Breda. On this last occasion he wintered abroad, returning to England in July 1625.[34] When the expeditions to Cadiz and the Isle of Ré are added to this list of campaigns in the Low Countries, it may be seen how fairly Essex could lay claim to a senior military command fifteen years later.

We are fast approaching the point when the traveller who completes his experience on the continent by campaigning in the Low Countries merges into the professional soldier. By contrast with the varied career of the Earl of Oxford was the single-minded devotion to the Low Country wars revealed by his cousins Sir Francis and Sir Horace Vere who between them commanded the English forces for almost forty years. Even more striking in this context were the Fairfaxes. Sir Thomas, the first Lord Fairfax of Cameron, fought under the Earl of Leicester and reappeared as an old man in the early stages of the Palatinate expedition in 1620. His brother Charles fought at Ostende and Sluys early in the century. His sons William and John were killed at Franckental in 1621. His grandson, the famous Parliamentary general, went to the Low Countries in 1629 at the age of seventeen. England and France were still at war and it was pointed out to the boy's father that the education usually sought in France could also be had in Holland, combined with a practical training in arms: in Sir Horace Vere's company at Dort his son would learn fencing, dancing and mathematics. Young Thomas Fairfax went out to the army, and his earliest extant letter gives a detailed description of the terrain at the siege of Hertogenbosch where Vere was the senior English commander.[35] After this episode he made his way to Paris and learned French. Then he thought of joining the forces of Gustavus Adolphus; his brother Charles took his place campaigning in the Low Countries, while their sister was at the Hague as a lady-in-waiting to the Queen of Bohemia. The ties were already close, and appropriately in 1637 Thomas Fairfax married Anne, one of the daughters of Sir Horace.[36]

Journeys backwards and forwards between England and the region of warfare along the Maas and Waal figure equally at this period in the record of the Holles family of Lincolnshire.[37] A descendant wrote of an Edward Holles in Elizabeth's reign who 'in his life had been a soldier and trayled a pike' for some years in the Netherlands. Edward's cousin

George also went over there and, became a respected soldier abroad for the rest of his life, but lies buried in Westminster Abbey next to Sir Francis Vere. His brother John, who became in due course Earl of Clare, fought for a short period in the Low Countries. Another brother rose to the post of lieutenant-colonel in the same service and married the daughter of a nobleman from Guelderland: they lived in Delft and his children grew up in Holland; he was buried in Hertogenbosch. One of his sons, George Holles, was likewise a soldier; it was remarked that he spoke French and Dutch rather better than English. He died in 1655 and was buried at Maastricht. Meanwhile Sir Gervase, from another branch of the family, had been a volunteer under the Dutch, and after him his two sons, Francis and Frescheville. Francis' son fought in the Low Countries only to be slain at Newark in 1644. Gervase, son of Frescheville, wished to go on the same errand but, being an only son, this was disallowed by his father; he entered the Middle Temple instead and became a lawyer. His experience of the Low Countries came later when he passed the years of exile in Rotterdam and the Hague, compiling the family history from which the details given above have been drawn. After 1660 he was an M.P. and Mayor of Grimsby. In this way, from a number of families many of the male representatives found their way to the Netherlands. A few settled permanently abroad, others returned to take a part in the English civil wars. They were not travellers in the sense of those who toured round Europe; but for many Englishmen service in the Low Countries was more than a rival attraction to the itineraries of France and Italy. It might be only an interlude; but it was also a profession. For some, also, it was a duty worth performing in defence of the Protestant cause.

This accumulation of personal details serves to show that there were two principal groups of Englishmen who saw military service in the Low Countries during the first forty years of the century: those who were 'a souldier swallowlike, for a summer or only a siege', and the permanent servants of the States. The latter class had the greater historical importance. Monck, the son of an impoverished gentleman in Devon, who lived and fought in the Low Countries between 1629 and 1638, Skippon, whose military experience abroad covered some twenty years' campaigning, and certain members of the Holles family, were all of this type, in due course bringing their professional skill to bear (without much·success) on the issue of the English civil wars. Of the others, men like Henry Vere, Essex and Thomas Fairfax genuinely desired to gain a sufficiency of military experience without in any way transferring themselves permanently to the Low Countries; but the majority were of the stamp of Sir Edward Herbert and John Evelyn. In their case it has been seen how their sojourn in the Low Countries was only one segment of a general acquaintance with the countries of western Europe which they desired to cultivate.

In the same way, contemporaries who had not sufficient means to please themselves in this matter served in the Dutch wars for a season — *Pay day, O pay day, O sweete pay day, come away, make hast* — but swiftly concluded that the life of a common soldier was the most miserable in the world, marching, looting, fighting, starving, and then looked out for something else. Thomas Raymond, for example, of Colonel Packenham's company in 1633, next became an ambassador's servant in Venice and later on a nobleman's tutor in Paris.[38] So he, too, saw something of both worlds.

Meanwhile a similar tradition can be traced in the lives of English Catholics who volunteered for service in Flanders. The records are scattered, their significance less obvious, but here also the connection between early years of travel and later years devoted to campaigning in the Low Countries is clear. The families concerned had often sent their sons abroad at a youthful age to secure for them a Catholic upbringing unharassed by the recusancy laws. When the governor of Dover Castle arrested a man for entering England with suspicious books and relics in his baggage, it could surprise no one that he was the servant of a Lancashire family who had just escorted two of the sons to Douai.[39] In the biographies of Catholics who later became Royalist officers in the civil wars a reference to this first journey abroad becomes almost conventional. Being now between thirteen and fourteen years of age, says a writer on Sir John Digby who was killed at Lostwithiel in 1645, his parents sent him into Flanders, where making his abode three or four years he perfected and polished himself in the liberal sciences, musique and French, in all which he was initiated and wellgrounded before his going. Afterwards, he spent four years in Italy, finishing at Venice and Florence 'the better to enable himself in the perfect knowledge of the Italian tongue and other points of civility and gentilenesse'.[40] Sir John Smith, another Catholic hero of the civil wars, went over to the Low Countries for his education, and later returned there to live as a soldier.[41] Sir Henry Gage had also gone first to Flanders and then on to Italy. About 1618, after his studies in philosophy at the English College in Rome were complete, he decided definitely to be a soldier, not a priest:

> And considering that Travaile did much conduce to that end, to Flanders, France and Italy which he had already viewed he adds Germany and returns that way to the Netherlands.... But least you may judge that of his Travayles he made only a pleasant delight and fed his Curiosity, I must assure you his observation was so strong and punctual that all men did admire the exact account he was able to render of all things deserving serious memory.[42]

According to this author's account Gage then became a volunteer in the garrison at Antwerp. With more certainty it can be said that he was one of Lord Vaux's captains in April 1622, when Vaux, in accordance with James I's policy of balance between opposed forces on the continent, received permission from the Privy Council to take over to Flanders a volunteer regiment to assist the Spaniards.[43] Gage fought at Bergen and Breda. He married a Flemish gentlewoman. When the English officers and soldiers in Spanish service were recalled on the outbreak of war with that country in 1625 he came back to England, but shortly afterwards was allowed to return.[44] Thereafter he lived abroad for many years, becoming colonel of the English regiment in Flanders.[45] He translated a Catholic account of the siege of Breda into English and Vincent's Heraldry into French. He fought and died as a Royalist soldier, and lies buried in Oxford Cathedral. Little is known of his life but the surviving details allow us to know him a little more intimately than his colleagues, who probably had a similar upbringing. Our concern is to note that his active military career in the Low Countries was preceded by a period of travel in Italy and elsewhere. In this respect he resembled his adversaries, Vere and Essex, and his colleague Lord Vaux; for Vaux likewise is mentioned as a visitor to Florence, in 1610, long before he appeared as a commanding officer in Flanders.[46]

After the military connection, a second matter of great importance raised by the travellers' itineraries is the interest which they display in the religion of the Low Countries, particularly in the religious practice of resident Englishmen. Brereton approved especially of the simple worship of the Reformed Churches, stripped, as he thought, of all relics of Catholicism. Evelyn took a more discursive interest in the varieties of ecclesiastical custom which came to his notice. A stout Catholic like Lord Roos, fresh from the congenial environment of Italy and Spain, felt at home among the colleges and seminaries of Flanders as he travelled in Sir Thomas Puckering's company, but on setting foot in Dutch territory expressed the utmost scorn for the heretic.[47] In isolation these indications cannot prove very much, but even so they afford a useful glimpse of the important part played by the Low Countries in the religious history of English society, and also of the considerable movement of English people into these territories during the reigns of Elizabeth, James I and Charles I. Such a movement divides naturally into the migration of Protestants into the northern provinces and the corresponding journeys of Catholics into Flanders, Brabant, Luxemburg and Artois.

The first of these generally concerned a level of English society below that of the gentry. Small farmers and townsmen, with a sprinkling of leaders educated at Oxford and Cambridge provided the personnel of the Separatist churches.[48] The Presbyterians, the larger grouping, appear generally to have been traders and craftsmen. Robert Browne's little congregation at Middelburg (1581–1583), the community of

Merchant Adventurers in the same town, and the Scotsmen with their staple at Veere, also in Zeeland, were the forerunners. Some twelve years later (from 1593) certain followers of Henry Barrow left London, and after a period of preliminary wandering to Campen and Naarden settled at Amsterdam, the 'First and Ancient Church' of the exiled separatists. Another decade passed, and the numbers grew. A Presbyterian church had been founded at Amsterdam, and in 1607 John Paget, whom Brereton heard and admired in 1634, was introduced to the congregation there by the chaplain of a Scots regiment in Dutch service.[49] Then John Smith brought over his followers from Gainsborough and established the 'second' English community of separatists. Most famous of all, the Scrooby congregation, also from Lincolnshire, arrived at Amsterdam under the leadership of John Robinson and William Brewster. In his old age, spent in the settlements of New England, one of their companions attempted to recollect the impression made upon these humble travellers by the unfamiliar Dutch landscape:

> Being now come into the Low Countries they saw many goodly and fortified cities, strongly walled and garded with troopes of armed men. Also they heard a strange and uncouth language, and beheld the differente manners and customes of the people, with their strange fashons and attires; all so farre differing from that of their plaine countrie villages (wherein they were bred and had so longe lived) as it seemed they were come into a new world.[50]

Almost immediately the process of disintegration associated with separatism made itself felt among these congregations. Both the Ancient and the 'second' Churches at Amsterdam were divided by controversy, which led to further wandering. One group, in dudgeon or despair, went as far as Emden. In 1611 the Scrooby congregation moved to Leyden. Here they settled until July 1620 when many of them commenced a longer and more momentous journey. William Bradford, their historian, has related how they went from Leyden to Delfshaven, twenty-four miles south on the shores of the Maas. Friends came from Amsterdam and Rotterdam to say goodbye; and then, with a favourable wind, the *Speedwell* left for Southampton and the Pilgrim Fathers for New England. In time, the English separatists remaining in Holland were merged into the Dutch population — although in Amsterdam at least one Independent congregation and one English and Scots presbyterian church survived during the seventeenth century. In 1701, however, the Independents joined the Presbyterians who always enjoyed the advantage of endowment and support from the municipal authority. A similar development took place in Leyden where, besides assistance from the town, the presbyterians were fortunate in their minister, Hugh Goodyer, heard by Brereton, who led the congregation for fifty years.

In Zeeland the English merchants held their staple at Middelburg until 1620 and they had their own chaplain. After the staple was trans-

ferred, the congregation survived; in 1667, for example, they invited
'Joseph Hill, B.D. formerly Fellow of Magdalene College Cambridge
and then residing as a traveller and student in the University of Leyden
in Holland' to be their minister.[51] In close touch with the merchants at
Middelburg was the English garrison in Flushing till 1616. Here again
severely protestant tendencies, stimulated by connections with the
Dutch and the Dutch war against Spain, are readily perceptible, while
the influence of the military chaplains and garrison preachers bears a
remarkable resemblance to their work in the English civil wars. In 1605,
the Deputy-Governor of Flushing wrote of a minister, Thomas Potts,
who was coming to the garrison from the army: 'Trewly he moves very
much and the soldiers are more attentive than ever I saw them to any
man.' Two years later Potts himself applied to the Governor, Viscount
Lisle, for an assistant; he made three requests: one, that the new minister might be selected from the Puritan clergy who had been suspended
after the Hampton Court Conference, secondly, that the ministers
should be assisted by Elders according to the pattern of Dutch ecclesiastical governance, thirdly, that the garrison church should join the Classis
of Walcheren.[52] Potts does not seem to have succeeded with his plans,
the governor's deputy considering him too extreme a Puritan, but the
nature of his influence is clear enough. He had a brother, who preached
to the merchants at Middelburg; and both these men gave a generous
welcome to Presbyterian exiles from Scotland such as John Dury the
elder and John Forbes who were to spend the rest of their lives in
Holland. The tradition they served persisted for many years, foreshadowing the great Puritan experiment in England. In 1633, the con-
sistory at Flushing determined to send an elder and a deacon to 'visit the
taphouses of the English' and arrange for the reformation of their inmates; also to send the minister and a deacon to call on members who
failed to appear in church on Sundays. These congregations, together
with the Scots' community at Veere, existed throughout the seventeeth
and eighteenth centuries.

There were also other centres. A town chronicler at Arnhem relates
that in 1638 ten or twelve English families settled there, only to merge
gradually into the Dutch population, with their Anglo-Saxon surnames
persisting long afterwards to memorialize the fact.[53] At Bergen, Hertogenbosch and Breda there were similar English communities of which
little is known.

The Merchant Adventurers, on leaving Middelburg, settled at Delft
in 1621 and the opportunity was taken to found a church on the
presbyterian pattern with a minister, elders and deacons. Transferring
their headquarters to the bigger trading centre of Rotterdam in 1635
they confronted another English congregation, which had been led in
the recent past by two remarkable and radical ministers, the comparatively young Hugh Peters[54] and his older partner, William Ames. Ames

was on the move from one place to another in the Dutch provinces for many years, promoting his personal view of Calvinist theology. Peters's career as an outstanding military chaplain in the Parliamentary army was still to come, but during his own lifetime the English church which he left behind in Rotterdam acquired a more presbyterian character; while in the same town the Quakers found a profitable haven.[55] Meanwhile, a church for both the English and the Scots at Dordrecht was joined to the local classis in 1623, and there Thomas Marshall ministered to another, Anglican, congregation during the Protectorate before becoming a notable Anglo-Saxon scholar in Restoration Oxford.

At Utrecht, an important garrison town full of English troops, the authorities made provision in 1622 for an English church; Thomas Scot, author of *Vox Populi* — the famous anti-Spanish anti-Catholic tract of the times — was invited to transfer from Gorcum and maintained a large congregation of a hundred and twenty English families and many English officers, who played a weighty part in the affairs of this church. Finally, at the Hague, besides the ambassador's chapel, an English Presbyterian church was built by subscription in 1627. It was a place patronized, if not always with enthusiasm, by the Queen of Bohemia. In its registers may be found the names of many families of the English gentry, their baptisms and marriages.[56]

The number, diversity and mutability of these congregations of English people resident or semi-resident in the Dutch provinces have their relevance in the context of travel. In other parts of western Europe, gentlemen on tour were constantly made aware of the difference between the Catholic world and the environment at home. They were warned by a suspicious government against what were considered hostile influences of a potent kind, and a certain number succumbed abroad to the Catholic omnipresence; many more simply imbibed something of the culture of Latin countries. In Holland the case was different. It was a territory with a Calvinist church, but where in addition Protestant radicalism was normally tolerated by the civil authority. English and Scottish residents were able to use presbyterian and also other forms of Protestant worship and church government. It was at the same time — with its wonderfully buoyant economy — the resort of numerous English and Scottish traders, artisans, men and women looking for domestic employment, and volunteer soldiers. Whether this hinterland across the sea helped in various ways to tip the balance in favour of the Parliamentary party in the Civil Wars may be open to question; the King also looked for supplies and political assistance from the United Provinces. It seems harder not to concede that Holland was a providential base for experiments in English Protestantism. Many people, having crossed the North Sea, became directly acquainted with forms of worship which at home could only be practised in secret or envisaged through personal study, but were readily experienced in some of the English congregations of Dutch towns. Middelburg, Rotterdam, Leyden, Amsterdam: they protected and moulded English (and American) non-conformity before 1640,[57] and to a lesser extent after 1660.

This Protestant refuge should be visualised alongside the parallel movement of English Catholics to that part of the Low Countries still under Spanish rule.[58] Catholics, when they left England in the seventeenth century, gravitated toward the institutions already prepared to receive them. The English colleage at Douai dated from 1568 and the Jesuit centre at St. Omer, a little further south and east, really commenced its corporate existence in 1593. In 1598 Lady Mary Percy had founded a Benedictine convent for English nuns at Brussels. In addition there were other exiles who attached themselves to the local communities; for example, some English women from Catholic land-owning families entered St. Ursula's, the house of the Austin Canon-esses of Liège, while a handful of Carthusians pursued an uncertain course through Flanders and Brabant, migrating from one centre to another in the later years of Elizabeth's reign. During the following century the movement expanded and consolidated. Catholic men and women, boys and young girls, found their way across the Channel to the Low Countries. In 1605 one Henry Keene, 'dwelling obscurely in Tower Street', London, owned a vessel which transported English Catholics from secret points near Rochester and Sittingbourne to Calais.[59] His name must do duty here for other 'travel-agents' who have concealed their activities from enquiry (as they would have wished); while it seems that a single passport from the Privy Council, in skilful hands, could help several parties of Catholics crossing over to Europe, well disguised, from ports of public embarkation.

On arrival at Calais or elsewhere along that coast a wide choice of towns was available for residence or education, according to the travel-lers' needs. For women the Benedictine nunneries had greatly increas-ed; from the original community at Brussels a little group went to Ghent in 1624, from Ghent others departed in due course to Boulogne and Dunkirk; Cambrai was founded independently in 1623, sending out members to settle in Paris nearly thirty years later, just as the community at Boulogne sent nuns to Pontoise, north of Paris.[60] Or there were the Poor Clares, settling at Gravelines in 1607, and later on at Aire and Dunkirk; the English Franciscan nuns began their corporate life in Brussels in 1621, moving from there to the coast town of Nieuport sixteen years afterwards. Later on they migrated to Bruges and Paris. The Carmelites had their centre in Antwerp, with other settlements in the same neighbourhood. In many of these communities carefully kept records afford a brief glimpse at the lives of those English women who left England and, in most cases, after one rather dangerous journey settled down to the exercise of steady piety, visited by their ecclesiastical advisers, by Catholic friends, and inquisitive travellers like John Evelyn.

The men had an equally extensive choice before them. When they first went abroad, as boys, it was usually to the schools of St. Omer or at Douai for their education. The Annual Letter of the Belgian colleges of the English Province of Jesuits in 1605 relates how three young men were robbed in France while travelling to the school at St. Omer. Usually they arrived in the care of servants or such agents as Henry Keene already mentioned. Numbers steadily increased. At St. Omer, after the first ten years, there were about 100 pupils and in 1605, after the peace between England and Spain, applications for admission were said to be daily received. One young fellow, in the autumn of that year, attempted unsuccessfully to enter there, was forced to go back to Douai where he likewise failed to secure a place in the College, and instead settled down in the town at an Englishman's house with three or four other pupils. At St. Omer there were 200 scholars in 1635, although the numbers decreased shortly afterwards, with the difficulties of war first in the Low Countries and then in England, which made the transmission of sufficient funds exceedingly precarious. In general, great emphasis was laid on the good family of the candidates who came to these centres.[61]

A sketch of the later careers of certain Catholics has been given in the cases of John Digby and John Smith and Henry Gage. Some returned quietly to England. Others again decided to enter the religious orders or become priests. The latter would certainly travel elsewhere in the Low Countries. There was the Jesuit College at Liège which opened its doors in the second decade of the century, after James I's agents had forced it to withdraw further inland from Louvain. When the organization of the society was finally elaborated the candidates would go from St. Omer to the novitiate at Watten, a few miles outside the town, and afterwards spent some years both at Liège and at Ghent, 'the house of the third probation' founded by the wealth and piety of Anne Dacre Countess of Arundel, in 1621; there were also many migrations to Jesuit centres in France, Italy and Spain. A community of English Carthusians resided at Nieuport between 1626 and 1783 — *Sheen Anglorum*, named in recollection of their mediaeval residence; and there were a number of Benedictine centres. The English Franciscans founded a community at Douai in 1618.

Undoubtedly these institutions helped to maintain the English Catholicism. That part of the population which lived in the shadows during the seventeenth and eighteenth centuries while a Protestant House of Commons did its worst and the Stuart monarchy its best on their behalf, owed much to the existence of these centres in the Low Countries. Apart from training the clergy who became part of the Catholic organization in England itself, they likewise provided a stronghold where the English Catholics preserved their distinctive tradition in relative security, and when the French Revolution broke into the stronghold, at a period when a measure of practical tolerance at last prevailed in England, these schools and monasteries moved to the homeland from which their individual members had been coming for two centuries. The critical period in the long history of this movement was in many ways the peaceful period of James I's reign. The beginnings which had been made under Elizabeth were then consolidated. Afterwards nothing was likely to hinder permanently the journeys of young English Catholics into the Low Countries or the journeys of somewhat older men back into England, short of complete elimination of the Catholics in England itself. In the same way, these centres across the Channel maintained the strength of Catholicism just sufficiently to make the possibility of such repression less likely. As a result, the movement of these travellers into and home from Spanish Flanders influenced an important minority in English society. It was a conservative and probably an aristocratic influence, by contrast with the stream of English traders or craftsmen to the Protestant provinces; but the work of the Catholic clergy who were trained abroad influenced the whole Catholic community at home.

This description of the religious activities of the English in the Low Countries has led us some way from the original observations of Brereton and Evelyn, but it is a partial answer to the question, What did these travellers see as they travelled from city to city? It was certainly one of the phenomena which interested them most, because they realized its bearing on the affairs of their own country. Moreover the enquirer is able to see what concerned a very much larger number of travellers who left behind no diaries and few papers, but were none the less likely to exert as individuals some influence on the character of English society, and the opinions of English people, during the seventeenth century.

# 8. OTHER TRAVELLERS IN THE LOW COUNTRIES

Inevitably the political relations of England to the government of the Low Countries concerned economic and religious problems. It was assumed that all these matters claimed attention from prudent statesmen. Even the ordinary traveller, aware that a proper education required some knowledge of this highly diverse territory as of other states and kingdoms in Europe, tried to observe a fairly wide selection of its characteristic features. Nicholas Ferrar, for example, began a tour of Europe by crossing to the Low Countries in the company of Princess Elizabeth on her way out to the Palatinate in 1613. Arrived in Holland his biographer praises him for not wasting time in merely seeing the sights and measuring the height of towers. First he looked into the language and then into the constitution of different cities, the 'humours' of the people in various provinces, the strength of fortresses, methods of shipbuilding, banking and poor relief: very appropriate interests for one destined to fill an important post in the Virginia Company's offices in London before he decided to give himself to the practice of religion.[1]

In some instances, certain men had a specifically political career in mind. In 1610 it was rumoured that George Calvert, a servant and secretary to Lord Salisbury, would shortly be appointed ambassador at Brussels. Calvert, after leaving college, had already travelled overseas and was mentioned as the bearer of despatches from Paris to London.[2] But Salisbury evidently considered that a further period of travel, particularly in the Low Countries, would be useful to the future diplomat. Calvert set out immediately; a cursory employment, said one correspondent, to hold the world *en cervelle* and enable himself for new tasks. Another contemporary letter refers to Salisbury's patronage in paying Calvert's expenses, doing this for his 'experience to entertain himself this vacacion'. A third correspondent agreed with the others that he was intended for a post at Brussels.[3] During the summer the traveller duly visited the Low Countries, Low Germany, Brussels, Marymont and Cambrai, reaching Paris by October.[4] In the end it was decided not to send a resident ambassador to the Archdukes for the time being, and Calvert's career took another turn. In June 1612 he was answering the

Spanish and Italian correspondence in the Secretary of State's office.[5] The experience had probably been valuable in any case; and it is possible to see very clearly from this instance what was considered by Salisbury a useful apprenticeship for an important diplomatic post.

Although no details survive for the actual journey performed by Calvert, or of the nature of his reflections while travelling, their absence can be partially made good by reference to that celebrated work, Sir Thomas Overbury's *Observations in his Travailes upon the State of the XVII Provinces as they stood Anno Domini 1609*. It has sometimes been doubted whether Overbury was in fact the author. The ascription cannot be formally proved but certainly Overbury himself did tour through the Low Countries in 1609; for in May of that year he was writing to William Trumbull at Brussels in a way which shows that he had recently come from Flanders and Brabant, and suggests in addition that he was preparing something like the report which first appeared in print in 1628 under his name:

> In the State House at Antwerp [he writes] I saw the names of the Duke of Burgundy and their wives, being writ by their pictures down to this present Archduke. Being straightened in time I could not write them out. I ask you to take the pains to send me an entire note of them as they are there in Mr Rous his next letter from you. I would be glad to serve my lord [Sir Thomas Edmondes] in any use for England in August. Thomas Overbury.[6]

In the spring of 1611 another of Trumbull's correspondents stated that Overbury was anxious to be appointed ambassador at Brussels.[7] If Calvert went abroad because his superiors wished to train him for a particular employment, it certainly looks also as if Overbury performed a very similar journey a year earlier and shortly afterwards decided that his experiences qualified him for the same post. He had made the observations abroad required of a future statesman. Then, as fortune would have it, the Earl of Rochester his patron was able to set him on a shorter road to power and preferment; or so it seemed, in 1612.

Overbury first summarizes, in his little work, the history of the Dutch uprising against Spanish misrule and the conditions which determined its success: the geographical situation of the provinces, the outcry against Alva and the Inquisition, the opportunities of calling in French and English aid against a common enemy. He notes that in recent years the King of France has gained in influence at the King of England's expense in the United Provinces; an important point for a diplomat to grasp. Then he considers the framework of Dutch government, the States General, the Council of State and the guiding influence of Oldenbarneveldt, the Advocate of Holland. It was necessary to observe that the political influence of the towns overshadowed the gentry, while 'their care in government is very exact and particular, by reason that everyone hath an immediate interest in the State'. This ensured the sound administration of justice and finance. With all these advantages to their credit Overbury still wondered whether the heterogeneous constitution of Dutch government could survive the easier conditions of peace as it had survived in war: this was another problem for the observant diplomat. However, the great economic strength of this people, drawing wealth from the East and the Baltic, from fisheries and the sheer number of their ships, added to a strategic situation at the mouths of three rivers, and the high discipline of their chartered armies, and the tough, slow but inventive disposition of the population ('unlike the rashnesse and changeablenesse of the French and Florentine wits') — these assets contributed to the power of the independent Dutch provinces.

How different was Overbury's impression of the Archduke's country! He has been quoted by the Belgian historian Pirenne as an eyewitness of the contrast between the northern and southern sections of the Low Countries; in the south he found every class of society embittered and impoverished, and the cities ruinous, a description most properly applicable to the area round Antwerp, Lille and Ghent.[8] He has little else to say, noting only the state of the revenue which was partly dependent on the import of American silver, the personnel of the army which was likewise replenished from abroad, and the splendour of Antwerp 'strong and beautiful, remaining yet so, upon the strength of its former greatness'; and he secured statistics about the garrison and the fire-power of the citadel there. Satisfied with this information he then travelled on to France where absolute monarchy provided a striking contrast with the governments previously analysed. It is permissible to argue that George Calvert would not have written very differently had he drafted a report on his journey for Lord Salisbury, in recompense for the interested generosity which made the expedition possible and also desirable.

An instance of another kind was the mission of Sir Gilbert Chaworth to Flanders in 1621.[9] A courtier of long standing under James I for whom he performed the duties of a gentleman of the bedchamber, he was sent to present the King's condolences to the Infanta Isabella on the death of her husband Albert, the Archduke, and in addition to secure her support in the diplomatic warfare then raging on the question of the Palatinate concurrently with actual military campaigning. Buckingham's candidate for this mission had been Sir Henry Rich but, wrote Chaworth afterwards, 'his Majesty wold have me, intending it as a foundation for honor to me'. With some such hopes of preferment in mind he acquiesced in the responsibility and the expense of embassage. His papers contain one of the most elaborate of surviving accounts for the preparation of such a journey in this period, the costs of transport, the purchase of clothes and the selection of suitable companions. The latter included 'gentlemen voluntaries', whom Chaworth took with him, and

the English gentlemen who joined him in Flanders; his servants and
their servants, a cook, interpreter, steward, coachman and grooms; and,
finally, his son Gilbert who would see something of the world before
going up to Cambridge, and his son's tutor who was a Frenchman. Of
the financial details it is worth noting that it cost the envoy £27 8s. in
fees to draw £1000 from the Exchequer, and £106 12s. to pay and clothe
eleven servants.

He commenced his journey on 4 October 1621, and crossing over
from Dover to Calais travelled northwards along the coast road to
Bruges and from there to Ghent and Brussels. His comments on the
different towns were precise and to the point: Calais 'a beggarly extort-
ing town' which would soon be engulfed by the sea, Gravelines a pretty
little place and strongly fortified, easily defensible when the sluices were
opened. He noted the English convents on the route, and the ruination
of the area between Nieuport and Ostende. At the last of these places he
was quick to observe signs of vigorous shipbuilding. He visited the
churches old and new at Bruges and Ghent, while his stay in Brussels
itself was long enough to excite admiration for the Infanta's residence,
especially her 'dayntie oratorie' full of relics and fine paintings, jewels
and medals; and like all Englishmen he admired gardens, and waterworks in a garden, wherever he found them.

The official part of his mission was soon over. The Infanta accepted
the expression of James I's sympathy, but declared herself powerless to
act independently of Spain and the Emperor in the matter of the
Palatinate. In any case Chaworth's presence in Brussels soon became
unnecessary because Sir John Digby arrived in the city on his way
homeward from his more important but fruitless embassage into
Germany. The junior of the two English diplomats quickly made plans
for departure, as a measure of economy sending his staff back to
England via Antwerp, Lillo and the Scheldt, while he himself determined to complete his experience by observing a little more of the
Spanish Low Countries. His notes permit a reconstruction of the
journey he took to Calais. He toured through Courtrai and Lille where
he learnt of the important cloth-industries in those towns, the unwhited
linen, diaper, damask and cambrics manufactured there. He visited
Béthune and Aire and spent a night at St. Omer; and his memories of
the English College in the latter are exceedingly interesting. It was a
shame, he thought, to see 140 English boys being educated as traitors,
but apart from their religion they were 'the strictest, orderlyest and best
bredd in the world'. Chaworth was present, privately, at one of their
dramatic performances but they soon recognized him. The Rector
entered into friendly conversation and the ambassador gave the scholars
a theme for disputation which was at once discussed, elegantly enough,
in Greek and Latin. In St. Omer he found the wine good and food
cheap; and then he took his way northward to the coast at Calais,
crossed the sea to Dover, and so to London once again.

This envoy was never destined to make political history nor do his papers suggest that he brought back, as one result of his visit to Flanders, any pronounced bias in favour of the rulers of that country. Still, he was attached to the Spanish 'party' at the English court during the next few years. He believed that his services over a long period, culminating in this embassy to Brussels, deserved a signal measure of preferment. He desired a peerage and appears to have thought that the Infanta, who expressed appreciation of him, might well employ her influence to move James I on his behalf. Gondomar was on friendly terms with Chaworth who never lost hope until the collapse of the Spanish marriage proposals at the beginning of 1624. After that date the mere idea of manufacturing a peerage at the suggestion of a Spanish princess became ludicrous, Buckingham was always unfriendly to him, and Chaworth made critical speeches in the Commons. At length rewards were offered: an Irish peerage, after payment to the Duke of Buckingham of £2500; promotion which seemed a grievance and an insult to Chaworth in his old age.[10] The history of this transaction depends too much on the reminiscences of a single witness to obtain unconditional acceptance, but certainly the witness was a courtier who hoped, by his journey, to obtain preferment, and with that end in view took his friends and his servants to Brussels. His observations on the country came by the way.

At a later date, but as a younger man, a more gifted observer appeared in the Low Countries. William Temple, after a stay in France, lived and travelled here in 1650 and 1651.[11] Settling at Brussels, we can only be certain that the place took his fancy, that he added Spanish to his other languages and wrote some promising early essays. This enjoyable phase of his youth stood him in good stead later when the Secretary of State early in 1665 chose the underemployed, independently minded Temple for the difficult mission of negotiating with the Bishop of Munster during the second Anglo-Dutch War. Arlington assured him that this was 'an entrance into his Majesty's service and the way to something he might like better'. Although the political purposes for which he travelled to Munster were not achieved, Temple satisfied his superiors and was appointed the English Agent at Brussels in October 1665. Subsequently his name would be more closely associated with the Dutch provinces than with Spanish Flanders: as a diplomat for his role in negotiating the 'triple alliance' of 1668 which temporarily brought together the states of Holland, England and Sweden, and as a writer for his *Observations upon the United Provinces*.

This famous book was written during a period of retirement from public affairs which began before and continued after the commencement of the third Dutch war. The new French alliance of Charles II, of which he disapproved, was being tested in action. The apparent collapse of the Dutch in the face of Louis XIV's invasion of 1672 was so remarkable a phenomenon to contemporaries that it cried out for expert discussion. This Temple gave it. No doubt his embassy at the Hague between 1668 and 1670, and his intimacy with John de Witt, afforded him an intimate acquaintance with the Dutch political system, but it also seems likely that he had been a sensitive eye-witness and traveller. He put to good use what he saw for himself. In northern Holland there were large-scale schemes of land reclamation in progress:

> That part of the Country called the Bemster, being now the richest soil of the Province, lying upon a dead Flat, divided with Canals, and the ways through it distinguisht with ranges of Trees, which make it the pleasantest Summer-Landschip of any Country I have seen of that sort.

Near by was Enkhuysen on the Zuyder Zee; in the Dutch systems of poor relief, celebrated by every traveller, he recollected a visit there to a home for retired seamen,

> And here I met with the only rich man that I ever saw in my life: For one of these old Seamen entertaining me a good while with the plain Stories of his fifty years Voyages and Adventures while I was viewing the Hospitall and the Church adjoining; I gave him at parting a piece of thin Coin about the value of a Crown; He took it smiling, and offer'd it me again; but when I refused it, he asked me what he should do with Money? for all that they ever wanted was provided for them at their House.

Temple also remembered vividly the changeableness of the weather, 'more violent than in any place I know'; when in 1670 he began to suffer from 'Rheums upon his teeth and eyes' he attributed them to the air of Holland.

In fact his exposition was realistic as well as vivid and he gave the reader a firm basis for understanding Dutch history and politics. The sympathetic interpretation of a country's decline, from what he believed to be an earlier period of greater vigour and success, was probably the best account of a European country written by an English commentator in the seventeenth century. One part of the work deserves emphasis, the celebrated chapter on religion. It has been shown how English Protestants and Catholics drew reserves of strength from different areas of the Low Countries, encouraging the survival of a fundamental cleavage between opposed sections of English society. On the other hand the practice of religious toleration diminished the importance of this division; and though the development of a new attitude towards an exceedingly ancient problem was gradual and complex, we are bound to enquire whether the observation of intelligent English travellers in the Low Countries was one element in that development. A man like Brereton simply noted that there were variations between one city in Holland and another. At Dort he finds 'Arminians, Brownists and Anabaptists do lurk here, and also swarm, but not so much tolerated as at Rotterdam'. Temple brought a more philosophic mind to bear on the question. To put the case in its most modest form, he found all his sympathies for toleration of varying religious creeds amply confirmed by a survey of religious affairs in the United Provinces. If it was true that 'Belief is no more in a man's power than his Stature or his Feature', and if men of sense were justified in questioning 'why a State should venture the subversion of their Peace and their Order, which are certain Goods, and so universally esteemed, for the propagation of uncertain or contested Opinions', then the attitude of the ruling authorities in Holland to the religious question deserved approval and imitation. It certainly produced the happiest results. The violence of theological controversy was softened by the general freedom. Immigrants streamed into the country bringing their wealth and their skill. Conversely 'the force of Commerce' diminished the emphasis which might otherwise be placed on religious differences. The result was an equal encouragement of all Art and Industry and equal Freedom of Speculation and Enquiry. Religion, concludes Temple, may possibly do more good in other places, but it does less hurt here. Ultimately, this point of view gained ground among certain sections of English opinion.

Temple's political activities dated from the second Dutch War but already at an earlier period one important group had pleaded for the common interest of the two countries. During the first Dutch war many Independents had done their best to keep, and when this failed, to restore the peace; and the most outspoken of these was Hugh Peters, formerly the minister at Rotterdam. In July 1652 he persuaded the Dutch congregation worshipping at Austin Friars to petition Parliament in favour of negotiations for peace; and a little later urged Admiral Ayscue to leave his command rather than wage war against a Protestant state. His published writings show him a convinced admirer of the Dutch whom he regarded as the Commonwealth's natural allies; and in his plans for social reform in England he revealed most clearly the influence of his experience in the Netherlands. His pamphlet *Good Work for a Good Magistrate* (1651) was one long plea for the imitation of the Dutch in an effort to solve the intricate problems of poverty, social disorder, and maladministration. Such phrases as 'Amsterdam is far advanced herein', 'Amsterdam doth much this waie', 'this will enrich a Nation as we see in Holland', and 'manie such things are done in the Low Countries', are scattered through the work. And what were the many such things done in the Low Countries? Why, the vigilant action of public authorities in considering the needs of the poor; occupations provided for the able, hospitals for the disabled; freedom of residence, and the right to trade, for all foreigners; legal proceedings in all civil cases to be deferred until officially appointed arbitrators have first attempted to arrange a settlement; reduction of 'the Port and Grandeur' of functionaries civil and military ('Lords of the Admiraltie, Burgomasters of the greatest Cities, not one of a hundred have so much as a man or sergeant to wait on them in the streets, yet do the highest acts of Power with as much vigor as the King of Spain himself'); Temple observed similarly that de Ruyter walked abroad dressed like a common seaman. Peters also recommended the fixing of low rates of interest and the foundation of a bank modelled on the Bank of Amsterdam, lending to the state and to individuals; proper insurance schemes against risk of piracy; the rebuilding of English cities, particularly London, according to Dutch patterns with paving-stones in the streets, and roadways cambered, and gutters and side-pavements. He asked for wooden houses to be pulled down, to induce strangers to adventure their goods here with less risk of fire; while in London he wanted to build proper quays along the Thames from the Bridge to Wapping. Hugh Peters' vision of a better England, in fact, was based on his admiration for Dutch practice, and he dreamt of London as Amsterdam transplanted. That kind of radicalism depended on a knowledge of conditions abroad.

Looking back at these examples of men who knew the Netherlands and also had a place in the politics of this period, we again discern the familiar pattern. There were some who made, or hoped to make, experience of travel in these territories an opportunity for entering the field of diplomacy and politics. Others brought back a definite sympathy for the country which influenced their opinions, whether in the matter of international relations or in domestic questions. With regard to the second of these groupings it would be difficult to determine how far they succeeded in persuading their countrymen to accept their opinions; but it is likely, as in other cases, that there were many who visited the Low Countries and developed ideas very similar to those of Peters or Temple; only they had neither the desire nor the ability to put pen to paper on the matter. They would, however, agree with the eloquent or the literate who did describe their impressions and their conclusions.

Certain miscellaneous matters remain. Sir William Brereton brought with him his children to consult the Leyden physicians on their health, but by far the most usual journey for one's health's was to Spa, near Liège, to drink the waters. During the early years of the century before hostilities became general on the continent, a list of the itineraries followed by the English gentry and nobility across Europe would not be complete without a notice of this fashionable rendezvous. The young men might wander through France and Italy, or even Germany and Spain, and the soldiers come and go between England and Holland, but their seniors in age, troubled with ailments, were content with a summer journey to these famous waters. When the Earl of Hertford was sent to Brussels in 1605 to accept the Archduke's ratification of the peace with Spain, Sir Edmund Bacon wanted to take the opportunity of accompanying him as far as Brussels, then proceeding to Spa. His chaplain

Joseph Hall has described their journey, crossing over to Calais and travelling by wagon along the coast road to Gravelines and Dunkirk, then inland to Ypres and Courtrai, and from Brussels to Spa. They returned homeward in June by way of Flushing. Hall, later the famous churchman, had not been interested in the question of health. He was chiefly concerned to satisfy 'the great desire I had to inform myself ocularly of the state and practice of the Romish Church; the knowledge whereof might be of no small use to me in my holy station'. Such an experience helped him in handling religious controversies later on.[12]

The road to Spa, then, led through Brussels where from 1605 the English ambassador had his residence. Members of his household periodically took the opportunity of going to drink the waters. John Beaulieu, one of Sir Thomas Edmondes' secretaries, wrote in May 1606 that he wanted to visit Spa before the season was over, and begged his colleague Trumbull to return from London in time, thus permitting him to go; but Trumbull was detained in London. Unfortunately the same thing happened in the following year, 1607. In 1608 Beaulieu once more feared the worst but on 22 July he was safely in Liège, accompanying Lady Edmondes and two other women. They travelled by coach, spending twelve hours on 'the rugged, crooked way' from Liège to Spa, where another English gentleman had secured them a house for the season. On arrival they probably followed the routine of most other visitors. They rose at four o'clock, drank the waters at six, walked and talked until nearly midday; and passed the afternoons in making and receiving visits. By the end of August the place would be emptying fast; the wealthy burghers of the Low Countries, the Duke of Mantua and his hundred gentlemen, Sir Oliver Butler, Sir Rowland Lee and others were all on their way home. So far as the English embassy to the Archduke was concerned, 'the family at Spa' rejoined the household at Brussels, and Beaulieu turned once more to his official business. Next year he hoped to go again; and meanwhile the ambassador himself was drinking Spa water at table. We hear also of the Archbishop of Canterbury employing a gentleman to fetch him water from Spa, in July 1610.[13]

When the Cleves-Juliers crisis brought large military forces into the neighbourhood many travellers no doubt preferred to keep away from this particular resort, though a soldier like Lord Chandos shuttled backwards and forwards between the camp and the waters. When conditions improved the visitors reappeared. In 1613 some of the nobility, Lord Lisle and the Harringtons, who had accompanied Princess Elizabeth to Heidelberg, left the Rhine at Cologne and came home by way of Spa. Others, Lord Chandos, Lord Southampton, Lady Lumley and Sir Thomas Savage were coming out from England to meet them there.[44] It was June, height of summer and the season; the Prince and Princess of Orange were also at Spa.

Punctually a year later the same theme reappears in Trumbull's correspondence. Lord and Lady Southampton, Sir Thomas Leeds and his wife, Lord Lisle and his sister Lady Pembroke, all wished to go to Spa again, and saw Flushing, Antwerp and Brussels on their way.[15] The names occurring again and again suggest an annual pilgrimage, which must have gone on as long as political conditions allowed. The Calendars of the State Papers[16] show that English people continued to visit Spa in fair numbers up till 1623; there are only a couple of doctors' certificates recommending the cure in 1624, and then, almost complete silence until 1630 when peace was restored with Spain. Even after this few were willing to chance the risks of intermittent campaiging; unfortunately Spa, like war itself, relied on the summer months. In July 1641 Henrietta Maria alleged that she desired to leave England to try the Spa waters, but the Commons protested, and prevented her journey. However, in 1649 and again in 1654 and 1655 a number of passports were issued by the Council of State for travellers going to Spa; but generally English visitors do not appear to have been very frequent. The truth was that after 1620 the journey was no longer comfortable or secure, while thirty years of war gave the cult of the English watering place its first opportunity. In 1663 state papers make their first mention of the spa at Knaresborough in Yorkshire — as a centre of Republican plots.[17]

After Sir Thomas Edmondes was recalled from Brussels in 1610 the most prominent English diplomat who used to go to Spa in peaceful years was Sir Dudley Carleton, ambassador at the Hague. His first visit, accompanied by Sir Horace Vere the military commander, took place in August 1616 when he was anxious to survey all the neighbouring territories whose problems and politics now immediately concerned him. Long descriptive letters report on this journey; and they have the additional merit of introducing another topic of concern to English travellers in the Low Countries — Dutch and Flemish pictures.[18]

Carleton travelled out to the little place from the Hague, going as usual through Liège. On his return he preferred 'to see a new towne and country', inspecting Maastricht which he found poor and desolated though set in rich, pleasant surroundings; then to St. Troyen, where the party had to brave an encounter with disorderly and wandering soldiery. At Louvain they met William Trumbull and Toby Mathew, and went on to Brussels to see the court, in the Archduke's absence; 'the hall and chapell are exceeding faire, and the parke within the walls of a towne is a singularitie; the grotte and gardens very pleasant; the whole house and furniture rather commodious than sutable to a pallace of a Prince'. The travellers next admired Malines and came to Antwerp where the beauty of streets, buildings and ramparts extorted the usual meed of praise; it was probably all the more beautiful for an impression of emptiness and depopulation. The territory of the northern provinces, on the other hand, reflected Carleton as he moved through Breda, Gertruydenberg and Gorcum to Rotterdam, was 'rich and unpleasant'.

Probably the most important single episode of this tour had been a meeting between the ambassador and Peter Paul Rubens at Antwerp. From that time began the strenuous negotiations between painter and diplomat, lasting over a number of years, which involved the purchase and exchange of works of art. In due course some of these found their way to England, and the acquaintance of the two men was one of the significant signs of the growing interest in such matters felt by English noblemen of Carleton's generation.[19] His embassy to Venice had stimulated the commerce in pictures and statuary between Italy and England; now he was extending his sphere of influence into the Low Countries. The ambassador began by attempting to purchase a 'hunting-piece' on which Rubens was then engaged. This was finally acquired by the Duke of Aerschot but during the following months (1616–1617) several English intermediaries, the Catholic exiles Toby Mathew and George Gage, Trumbull the diplomat and Lionet Wake the big Antwerp merchant, were busy on Carleton's behalf, and as a result, one year after his visit to Antwerp the ambassador became possessed of a smaller version of the hunting-piece by Rubens, and paintings by one of the Breughels, Snyders and Sebastian Vranctz for an outlay of £80 sterling. 1618 witnessed a second transaction: a collection of ancient statuary purchased by Carleton in Italy (in all probability for the ill-fated Earl of Somerset) was sent from London to the Hague and then exchanged with Rubens for a number of his own paintings and some tapestries from the Brussels workshops. Carleton declared that his earlier enthusiasm for sculpture had now been replaced by an ever-growing interest in the art of painting, particularly the painting of P. P. Rubens. A little later he was attempting to assist his old friend Sir John Danvers to obtain a picture by the hand of Rubens for the Prince of Wales, since at that time (May 1621) there was only one example of his work in the royal collections. During that autumn the artist received his commission to decorate the new Banqueting Hall, and a little earlier Van Dyck, his pupil, paid a first visit to England. For these developments much may be ascribed to the growing reputation of famous artists, which spread gradually to the English court, but honorable mention is due also to intermediaries and pioneers like Sir Dudley Carleton.

In 1621 another English ambassador, Sir John Digby, commissioned a large painting from Rubens to present to the Marquis of Hamilton. During the same year it is interesting to note the testimony, on this subject, of Sir Gilbert Chaworth who was then on his mission to the Infanta. Passing through Antwerp he admired the galleries of the unfinished Jesuit Church — 'wholly roofed with brave pictures of Rubens' making, who at this tyme ys held the masterworkeman of the world'. And Chaworth well understood the fashion of his day by which paintings were held acceptable gifts; his accounts show these minor entries:

> In Antwerp, for a little picture which I gave the King, of Browgle's
> hand,                                                                     £6–12s.
> Payed for the picture of the storie of Japha which I gave my Lord of
> Buckingham,                                                               £6–12s.
> For an old picture which I keepe myselfe               £3–6s.[20]

In the spring of 1625 the Duke of Buckingham made the personal acquaintance of Rubens at Paris where he had his portrait painted; and on coming to Antwerp in September for political discussions, he was so much impressed by the artist's collection of antiques, gems and paintings, that he began to negotiate for their purchase. In due course they arrived in England, remaining there until 1648.

To revert once more to Sir Dudley Carleton and his tour of the Low Countries in 1616. Shortly after coming back to the Hague from Spa he began another journey through the northern provinces, spending six days at Haarlem, Amsterdam, Utrecht and Leyden. His reminiscences are a commentary on the remarks of Evelyn and Mundy at a later date about Dutch painting; for Carleton was anxious, on this tour, to learn something on this very subject.[21] At Haarlem he became acquainted with the work of Cornelius Cornelisz 'who doth excell in colouring, but erres in proportion', and of Vroom the sea-painter, and of the more famous Goltzius. At Amsterdam there were many good pictures but few resident painters. In Leyden he found that even the inn where travellers were accustomed to dine was hung with tapestries and pictures of the best quality.[22] In this way he began to acquire a smattering of the subject, and in the following years he was able to introduce to the notice of patrons at home Dutch artists of promise and reputation. He was writing to John Chamberlain about the painter Miereveldt already in 1616; Gerard Honthorst who came to England in 1628 was first mentioned by Carleton in a letter to Lord Arundel (accompanying the present of a specimen of his work) in 1621.

Lady Carleton joined in the hunt.[23] Prize goods captured from a ship belonging to the Viceroy of Naples were for sale in Flushing in 1624; and the ambassador received a commission from the Duke of Buckingham to purchases certain goods. His wife hurried in the teeth of the winter weather from the Hague to Delft and Dort, and from there to Middleburg in order 'to make my Lord of Buckingham a wonderfull sumptious present'. She found on view fine silks and camlet hangings, books, candlesticks and pictures, cups and crystals:[24]

> The conselare Hasson hath helped me to by som picturs to day; but heere is
> such keching for them that I know not what to doe, and some times on must
> bye good and bad to gether. I have bought nine today, good and bad, but in
> truth none very bad, without it be one as bige as halfe my hand. They are

sold exstreme deere and yet there are infinit heere. I have some very raire peeces, on of Tisianes, it cost me all most £30. I have another littel peece which cost me £40 and ode. My Lord Willibye is heere, and hee is a great byer. Yet if I have not these picturs, the painters of Antwarp would have given the mony.

In the end she spent £627, and still more valuables found their way into the Buckingham collections. They were, of course, Spanish or Italian in origin and not Dutch.

With this ambitious purchase for the Duke of Buckingham another part of our journey must come to an end. There have been omissions, inevitably. The residence of a Stuart princess and her court in Holland from 1621, first Elizabeth and then Mary, involved constant coming and going of messengers between London, the Hague, the villa at Rhenen and other places. There was the usual correspondence between English diplomats in the Low Countries and the Secretaries of State at Whitehall. There was Sir Richard Weston, the Catholic landowner with property in Hereford and Surrey, who spent some time in Flanders after 1643: his reports on the rotation of new crops in the region north of Bruges helped the cause of progressive farming in England.[25] On these and other topics much might be said; conversely, it is singularly unfortunate that in no case do the papers of any English student at Leyden University appear to survive.[25] From the starting point provided by a particular kind of record, however, it has been possible to survey some of the common interests linking England and the Low Countries, and therefore to account for the movement of thousands across the North Sea during this period. But for the English gentleman, travel in that area was only a subordinate part of his tour of the continent. He passed through, to or from the south. The itinerary never became stereotyped as in France and Italy, mainly because communications between city and city were easy and speedy. Before 1648, when Dutchmen and Spaniards at last came to terms, he sometimes turned volunteer for a campaign, and in this case joined forces with other Englishmen who were long-term soldiers and rarely troubled to travel elsewhere except to fight — like Skippon and Sydnam Poyntz.[27] This was the principal connection between the Low Countries and English travellers from other parts of Europe. It is also clear that exchanges with the United Provinces and Flanders had a distinct influence on the history of English non-conformity and English Catholicism, more especially in the latter case since the Catholics depended on a measure of support from outside for their bare survival. Finally, travellers learnt to appreciate at first hand the crafts and customs of Holland, in many ways the most progressive region in Europe, and certainly the most prosperous. Three hard fought wars, and brutal competition overseas, must not obscure the great debt of the English to the Dutch in the seventeenth century, a debt to which our travellers bear witness.

# 9.  THE CAREER OF WILLIAM AYLESBURY

Reference to the Duke of Buckingham's famous collection of pictures and other treasures recalls to mind the fact that much of it was dispersed again by the second Duke, also in the Low Countries, when he fled into exile after the civil wars. One of his most active agents at this crisis was William Aylesbury, who had formerly travelled with him in France and Italy.

In studying Aylesbury's career we turn once more to the nobleman's tutor. It provides a further illustration of the possibilities of foreign travel of the conventional type, showing how such men hovered on the fringe of political preferment, while in addition the special circumstances thrown up by revolutionary change at home naturally influenced his fortune. Although the materials are insufficient for a formal biography something may be added to what has hitherto been known of him, so that he takes his place in the group of which Lorkin and Becher were representative in the previous generation. He is made more interesting by his share in the English translation of Davila's once celebrated *History of the Civil Wars in France*, regarded in the seventeenth century as a modern classic and familiar to all educated men. He reached the height of his activity and influence in the Low Countries, but an adventurous life took him further afield both in Europe and across the Atlantic.

The son of Sir Thomas Aylesbury, who had risen to importance in the service of two Lord Admirals, Nottingham and Buckingham, before he became a Master of Requests, William Aylesbury was a gentleman-commoner of Christ Church and took his bachelor's degree in 1631. What happened next is obscure. The statement of Anthony Wood, that shortly afterwards he was appointed governor to the second Duke of Buckingham and his brother Francis Villiers and travelled abroad with them, is certainly mistaken:[1] his tour to Italy with the Villiers brothers came years later, in 1645–1646. Since the elder Aylesbury served the first Duke the son was presumably known to the family and may have served it at court; the second George Villiers, born in 1627, was a ward of Charles I and brought up with the King's own children. Possibly also, William Aylesbury at this period travelled on the continent without any particular patron. In February 1638 official despatches from Paris first make a definite statement about him. Leicester, ambassador extraordinary there, reported that Richelieu and the whole world of French society had come to the capital to 'passe in feasting and jollity the fat dayes of shrovetide', rounding off his letter with the remark that Mr. Aylesbury brought fresh instructions from London on the evening of 8 February.[2] These were not unimportant and gave plenty of anxious work to Leicester and his colleague and rival, Lord Scudamore the resident ambassador. They concerned the release of English goods impounded in France, and Charles I's insistence on a speedy conclusion to the treaty of alliance under discussion. During the following year there is no further mention of Aylesbury, nor is his handwriting to be found in the despatches signed by Leicester, whose secretary throughout the period 1636–1640 was James Battyer,[3] or in the despatches of Scudamore whose principal assistant was Richard Browne. Nevertheless, Aylesbury appears to have been a gentleman in Leicester's household; when the ambassador returned to England for a visit on private business in 1639, he was accompanied by Battyer and Aylesbury.[4] Leicester came back to Paris in August of the same year.

Meanwhile Barbara Aylesbury, William's sister, had married Edward Hyde and additional information comes from Hyde's papers in letters written and received between December 1640 and February 1641. Aylesbury was still a member of Leicester's household in Paris when the Long Parliament began, and corresponded with his brother-in-law who lived sometimes in his chambers in the Middle Temple, sometimes at Sir Thomas Aylesbury's house in Dean's Yard, Westminster.[5] An Englishman in Paris naturally longed for news of the constitutional upheaval in progress at home and he appealed for information to one who was rapidly becoming a leader of men and opinions. Aylesbury's political sentiments deferred more to the Crown than Hyde's at this period and he did not restrain the expression of his loyal fervour, though regretting this difference of opinion. However, he needed money. His allowance was nearly exhausted by December 1640 and from the tone of his appeals it seems that Hyde managed the finances of the Aylesbury family.[6] More important than either the general political situation or the remission of a further allowance was the question of future prospects, particularly of a new appointment for the Earl of Leicester with whom Aylesbury's fortune appeared likely to rise or fall.[7] In Westminster and Whitehall a group of politicians headed by Northumberland, Leicester's brother-in-law, had long desired to find him a post at home, first as Secretary of State, a scheme which broke down early in 1640, and then as Strafford's successor in Ireland: Aylesbury, writing of Francis Windebank's escape to France after his arrest, added: 'Looke better to him in the Towre, for it concernes us.'[8]

Again, referring to Leicester and then to his own ambitions he wrote to Hyde on 12 February 1641:[9]

I wonder my Lord of Bedford is not yet Treasurer and whether your other Parliament men shall have the places they are named to, but most of all I hearken what becomes of the Lieftenant and who shall have his place. Wee, I assure you, have butt little hopes of it: if you can give any when you are att leasure to write I pray say something of it. Wee heare that Mr Nicolas is like to succeed Windebanke; if it be soe, you may thinke a freind of yours as fitt for his place as Browne for Beechers and wish it to him. But in all this change of officers I thinke it very strange that my Father can putt in for nothing; my thinks it were possible for him now soe to make use of his creditt with the King as once more to gett into play. . . .

Then he goes on to ask Hyde to send him a finely bound copy of John Donne's Sermons, as a present for Lady Leicester; and his confidential position in the household may be inferred from the fact that Windebank, now in exile in Paris, writing to his son says that Mr. Aylesbury has undertaken to safeguard their correspondence by forwarding letters under the ambassador's cover.[10]

A week later he returned to the problem of his own prospects at this crisis of affairs:[41]

The worst news I have heard since I came into France was yt of the last weeke, that my Lord of Holland is generally beleeved to succeed the Lieftenant for now I cannot imagine any possibility of provideing for us. Therefore with all my heart I wish I had any reasonable provision for my selfe in England, that now I begin to grow into yeares, I may have the happiness to live at home amongst my friends. For my Lord, I beleeve, will be desirous to stay here as long as hee can unless hee might change for a better employ-ment, but what advantage that will bee to mee I know not. Therefore I pray stirr up my father as much as you can to looke about him whilst he may, for if he should faile you know what a condition I shall bee in. . . .

In March 1641 the ambassador and Aylesbury returned to England and immediately afterwards Leicester was appointed Lord-Lieutenant of Ireland. In August he visited Paris for the last time to bid farewell and receive a parting present from Louis XIII. Sir Richard Browne, formerly Lord Scudamore's secretary, succeeded to the post of Charles I's representative at the French court.

What became of Aylesbury? It is not an easy question to answer. The tour abroad with the second Duke of Buckingham, to which Anthony Wood referred, was made some years later on. The Duke was still in England preparing to play a small part in the early skirmishes of the civil war. Nor did the new Lord-Lieutenant of Ireland, uneasily balancing between the rival authorities of King and parliament, find him public employment in his new province or at home. Of Sir Thomas Aylesbury's influence with Charles I, exerted on his son's behalf, there is not a word in surviving reports. In fact he must be found elsewhere. Now Hyde preserved an isolated letter from Aylesbury which was written at Rome on 29 March 1642. It said that 'we' had just come from Naples and were then enjoying the company of Cardinal Francesco Barberini (Protector of the English Nation).[12] In the Pilgrim Book of the English College at Rome, under the date 31 March 1642, a certain 'Lord Sidney' (who would be a son of the Earl of Leicester) was mentioned as a nobleman dining there.[13] Next, among the papers of Sir Richard Browne a single sheet endorsed 'Compte de M. Aylesbery' refers to a debt contracted in Paris in June 1642,[14] and lastly, in the summer of 1644 Leicester ordered his son Robert to come home 'out of France', as he recorded in his diary.[15] These fragments of evidence suggest that when the ambassador left Paris in August 1641 William Aylesbury remained behind as governor to young Robert Sidney, performed the conventional tour of Italy in the course of the winter, came back to reside in Paris, and returned to England in 1644.

This makes it possible to fix more accurately the date of Aylesbury's association with the second Duke of Buckingham. In 1643 the Villiers and Aylesbury families, loyal servants of the crown, were both gravitating towards Oxford. In January the Court of Requests held a session in the School of Natural Philosophy there, Sir Thomas Aylesbury, Master of Requests, presiding in court.[16] In May Lady Aylesbury with her sister, two daughters, their servants, saddlehorses and coaches was given a pass by the House of Lords to go from London to Oxford.[17] In July servants of the Duke of Buckingham were carrying clothes and provisions from London to Oxford.[18] In September Dr. Aglionby died, formerly a master of Westminster School and more recently tutor to the Duke, and was buried in Christ Church Cathedral; at a later period the Duke spoke of Aglionby as the man who led him to follow the king in the war's early stages.[19] These facts, coupled with Leicester's failure in Ireland (he was dismissed at the close of 1643) which made him an unsatisfactory patron, make it plausible to imagine Aylesbury returning to England in 1644, and going to Oxford to offer his services to the family to which his own already owed so much. The Villiers and the Sidneys were, in any case, closely connected at this date: Northumberland, Leicester's brother-in-law, was also guardian of Buckingham's interests in London.

After these preliminaries George and Francis Villiers began their tour abroad with William Aylesbury as their governor. In 1645 the brothers were eighteen and seventeen years old; their most powerful friends, Lord Denbigh, who was a cousin, and Northumberland, moderate parliamentarians, had evidently decided to send the young men out of harm's way while they attempted to arrange a reconciliation with the House of Commons, then engaged in sequestrating the Villiers property. Aylesbury himself was about thirty. He had failed, even with Hyde as his brother-in-law, to secure any official employment and so remained a private servant in a great nobleman's household. How long was spent on the earlier stages of the journey is uncertain. In April 1645 the Committee for Advance of Money in London learnt that Buckingham and his party were then in France.[20] About 1 May Sir Richard Browne in Paris drew up a detailed statement of Aylesbury's debts to him, amounting to 969 livres; part of this sum was money laid out for the dowager Duchess of Buckingham on orders from Aylesbury.[21] By the end of June a correspondent in Venice wrote that the brothers were daily expected in Rome.[22] They travelled in great pomp. Brian Fairfax and Anthony Wood mention their truly royal progress through Europe. Before the end of the year they were in Rome, having rented a house on the Trinità dei Monti.[23] On the 7 December (n.s.) Buckingham, his brother and their tutor were invited to dine at the vineyard of the English College. A few weeks later they dined again at the College with a following of nine, accompanied by others who were musicians.[24] There were a number of Englishmen then in Rome with whom Buckingham no doubt became acquainted. According to Anthony Wood, Abraham Woodhead, Fellow of University College and later a noted Catholic controversialist, who had been touring on the continent with pupils, settled in Rome and taught the Duke mathematics.[25]Richard Flecknoe, who was to correspond with the Duke and became like him an amateur playwright, was another visitor to the English College at the same time,[26] and Andrew Marvell, who afterwards composed a satire on Flecknoe and an elegy on the death of Francis Villiers, probably dined there also in December 1645.[27] Aylesbury, writing to Browne in Paris, remarked that they had now settled down in Rome. He himself felt 'little at ease though much at leasure' — an excellent opportunity for the private labour of translating Davila's great History.

Meanwhile the relation of the travellers to authority at home was far from clear. In 1643 the Commons had treated Buckingham as an enemy, giving orders for money to be raised from the sale of his collection of pictures at York House, excepting that part of the property assigned to the Earl of Northumberland. In 1645, however, it appeared that nothing had yet been done and Northumberland simply paid a man £40 a year to act as caretaker in York House. Again the Commons ordered the sale of the pictures, provided that they were not of a 'superstitious' character, and the burning of those judged superstitious. Again the discreet but powerful conservatism of Northumberland, resisting the demands of more radical parliamentary or Puritan champions, contrived for delay.[28] He was so successful that Buckingham, having withdrawn from the king's service and waiting for the chance of a full reconciliation with Parliament, was able to preserve his property in London and elsewhere and travel abroad under the guardianship of Aylesbury, himself the member of a devotedly royalist family and brother-in-law of Sir Edward Hyde the arch-malignant.

The next little group of the tutor's surviving letters were addressed to the Earl of Denbigh, a son of Susan Villiers the first Duke's sister; for Denbigh, after patient diplomacy in London which aimed at the repeal of the Commons' sentence against Buckingham, had ordered the party to return home, and the tutor wrote to report their progress.[29] On 21 May (n.s.) 1646 the Duke, his brother and Aylesbury set out from Rome on the long journey to England. Aylesbury felt far from well, and suggested that if the business in London was really urgent the brothers would have to go forward without him, though their youth and the summer heat made travelling by post an inadvisable expedient. On 16 June he wrote from Venice; desperately in need of money, and dependent on the goodwill of an English merchant at Leghorn, they continued on their way and passed the Alps. On 21 July they left Geneva and made for Lyon and Paris. Aylesbury again pleaded for a supply of money in order to avoid delay. It seemed to him particularly necessary to hasten through Paris 'especially now the Prince is there', for Prince Charles had arrived at the French capital from Jersey. The special purpose of Buckingham's return homeward, and also its speed, must finally dispose of Bishop Burnet's story that, on his way back from Italy, the young Duke 'who was then got into all the impieties and vices of the age, set himself to corrupt the King, in which he was too successful'. The Villiers cannot possibly have arrived in Paris before the second week of August and they were back in England by the end of September. On 31 October the Duke of Buckingham's petition to have the sequestration order upon his estates removed, was presented to the House of Lords.[30] That day Northumberland and Denbigh and the Earl of Pembroke, another ally, were in their places in the House.

The petition was heard and sent down to the Commons with a request that it should be submitted to the Committee for Sequestration. After a fortnight the Lords reminded the Commons of this business; Buckingham's friends were determined to persist.[31] However, the wheels of government turned slowly, their movement hindered by the confusing currents of radical and conservative opinion, and only on 4 October 1647 was the sequestration formally revoked by order of the Lords and Commons.[32]

A humbler claimant, Aylesbury himself, had not been idle. After all, through Buckingham, he enjoyed similar support; and on 14 December 1646 the Lords, learning that William Aylesbury had translated Davila's *History of the Civil Wars in France* and desired a licence to print his book, ordered the Earl of Denbigh and Lord North to examine it and, if they approved, to grant him such a licence.[33] Early in the year 1647 the Clerk of the Parliament formulated this permission, giving Aylesbury sole rights of printing for fourteen years, and a few months later the first volume appeared.[34] It was work well done, sober and authoritative in appearance. On the title-page a beautifully designed monogram entwines the initials *W.A.* with *C. C.*, those of his good friend Sir Charles Cotterell who had been Master of Ceremonies at court. Many years later when a second impression came out, in 1678, long after Aylesbury's death, the publisher claimed by far the greater share of the work for Cotterell who was still alive. It must be admitted that the latter in his time translated a number of books from Italian and French; but the long periods of leisure spent by Aylesbury in Italy and France with Sidney and Buckingham, the fact that his name was given to the Lords as author, and permission to publish sought immediately after his return from abroad, all suggest that he was a competent linguist responsible for a substantial share of the work.[35] In 1647 his political affiliations were not less suspicious or compromising than Cotterell's, who though a follower of Charles I was living undisturbed at home.

This year, 1647, completed a distinct phase in the careers of Aylesbury and his patron Buckingham, very different though the two men were in status and ability. For the older man, a decade spent in service to the Sidney and Villiers families, on the fringe of diplomacy while Leicester held ambassadorial rank, on the fringe of politics while Buckingham's guardians steered the latter from the court of Charles I to reconciliation with Parliament, had apparently no more solid consequence than the translation into English of an Italian historian. As for Buckingham, now twenty years old, a position of great inherited honour and wealth had been maintained by judicious (and interested) protection. His education, which began at court and continued at Cambridge, was interrupted by the first civil war but then completed by the customary phase of foreign travel. Both men now returned to England at the unfortunate time when differences between King, Parliament, Levellers and the army leaders appeared to pose an insoluble problem. All sense of security had vanished. Poor men suffered from want, unemployment or arrears of pay. Men of property looked with foreboding at the omens of an upheaval more far-reaching than anything which had yet occurred. The bishops' lands were for sale, the future of estates formerly belonging to deans and chapters was hotly debated. Some extremists, it was said, 'began to eye the vast revenues' of the city companies.[36] No wonder we learn of lively dealing in movable assets, and the shipment of valuables abroad. In February 1648 one newsletter, from an Independent, states:[37]

> The cheefest trade now in London is buying and selling of gold which is worth ten pound in the hundred Exchange. This makes us feare that some of our great masters intend to fly from us and leave us in the lurch but I hope better of them. The earl of Northumberlands goods were stayed this weeke going into Holland, whither it is reported that divers of the House of Commons have sent theirs.

The movement of these goods to the Low Countries was naturally connected also with preparations for a renewal of hostilities in England, and here the Duke of Buckingham soon became involved. The opinions, intrigues, well grounded fears and far-fetched hopes which brought about the second civil war were all astir, in conversations going on round him, in letters sent or received. In February 1648 another intelligencer writing from London had heard that the Duke was greatly incensed by recent references in the Commons to the character of his father, while Ashburnham and other royalists were determined 'to set him on something of desperate'.[38] He too now arranged to remove pictures and jewels from York House overseas, entrusting the matter to a faithful and experienced servant. An English copy of a warrant concerning such treasure has been preserved, countersigned by the appropriate Dutch authority in the United Provinces, and bearing the date 25 February; it gave William Aylesbury, English gentleman, permission to transport from London to Amsterdam, and in due course from Amsterdam to any part of England, sixteen chests of pictures belonging to the Duke of Buckingham. Custom or dues would not be exacted, provided that the chests were sealed and no attempt made to sell the pictures in the United Provinces.[39] A new sphere of activity now opened out before the Duke's former governor. At the same time Henrietta Maria in Paris despatched Sir William Fleming and Dr. Stephen Goff to Amsterdam to obtain money by pledging her jewels, in order to purchase equipment needed for a new rising in England;[40] years before, in 1642–3 she had already dealt with the big English banker and merchant of Amsterdam, John Webster, whom Aylesbury was now to approach.[41] In this way, at the commencement of 1648, important reserves were being transmitted to the Low Countries, particularly Holland. Some was for immediate use in the coming campaign. Some was sent over for security's sake by Englishmen still at home, worried men of property with no particular political cause at heart. Some was for the maintenance of royalists abroad; it is well known how Edward Hyde, Lord Cottington and Sir George Radcliffe tried to bring £2000 in money and jewels from Jersey to the Low Countries in May 1648, of which a great part was captured by pirates from Ostende.[42] The treasure of the Duke of Buckingham, in Aylesbury's keeping, served all these purposes in turn.

Such transactions, mixing private finance with politics, demanded secrecy. A number of letters received by Aylesbury during the next two years have survived but it is difficult to unravel a correspondence in which the answers are missing and the signatories were concerned to hide both name and business from hostile scrutiny. However, we are given some idea of the budding financier's activity. He travelled almost incessantly between London, the Hague and Amsterdam, Antwerp and Brussels. He was concerned, first, with the shipment of Buckingham's valuables overseas and raising money on their security. With this was linked the maintenance of the Duke's friends and relatives. He was concerned, secondly, for the well-being of his own family and friends, arranging for the journey of his parents and sisters to the Low Countries and their residence at Antwerp from the spring of 1649; and this brought him into touch once more with his brother-in-law Hyde. Through this connection his correspondence found its way into the Clarendon papers. Thus, for the year 1648 and part of 1649 the few words of Wood and Brian Fairfax on the lives of Aylesbury and Buckingham at this period can be amplified and corrected. After Hyde left the Low Countries on his mission to Spain in the spring of 1649 evidence about Aylesbury dwindles once more to a trickle.

In April 1648 he was in Brussels, during May in London and from there he went to Amsterdam. Letters were addressed to him at Mr. Webster's. The sixteen chests had arrived and Webster, on his behalf, paid for their storage and sent a handsome fee to the officers of the Dutch admiralty.[43] In June, however, Aylesbury began to suspect that after all he had not brought his master's wares to the best market, and in confirmation of this he received a letter from Dr. Goff; that expert on diplomacy and finance stated that he was always of the following opinion: 'Amsterdam would not be the proper place to vent those commodities in, and that all the time spent there is unprofitably lost; without question Antwerp will afford many chapmen, and the Archduke's good success in Flanders will make him prodigal in these curiosities. I should therefore advise the removal of all your cases thither. . .'[44] Aylesbury now began to enquire at Antwerp for a house which he could take on a short lease, and the English merchant Joseph Ashe forwarded details of the painter Rubens' old house.[45] Unfortunately the owner refused to consider letting for less than six months. It would cost 600 guilders for one year, and something more than 300 for six months. Whether these terms were accepted is not stated. A little later Rubens' house was certainly taken by the Duke of Newcastle who borrowed money from Aylesbury for the purpose. The Duchess of Newcastle's testimony should be noted: her husband borrowed Buckingham's money from Aylesbury.[46]

The treasure came to Antwerp and was stored by Justus Collimar, merchant.

At the same time his old patron, Robert Sidney, now a soldier in Dutch service, was answering his enquiry about the possibility of purchasing arms in Holland;[47] Buckingham had determined on his part in the second civil war.

Aylesbury also received letters from Paris, from the Duke's step-father Randal MacDonnell the Irish Earl of Antrim and from an incoherent and mysterious gentlemen called Roberts, another servant of the Villiers family who apparently still possessed a little property of his own in England. Antrim had recently arrived from Ireland on a deputation sent by the Supreme Council of Irish Catholics to Henrietta Maria. His policy was to insist that the royal interest should be linked with the cause of the extreme Catholic party of the Papal Nuncio in Ireland. Privately he even hoped to be appointed Lord-Lieutenant, but was frustrated by Ormonde who obtained the Queen's support. In the midst of these important affairs Antrim found time to write to Aylesbury before he left Paris in June.[48] Reading between the lines of a letter thick with mysterious references and hidden names it appears that he was asking Aylesbury to do all in his power to transfer money from England to France and so make it possible for Antrim's wife, the old Duchess of Buckingham, to come and reside there. For this purpose he enclosed a power of attorney.

'Mrs. Crombie's business' — as the scheme was called — was likewise the principal argument of Roberts' galloping pen. 'Hasten all the supply you can for my mistress, nothing keeps her but that', he wrote on 25 April. On 18 June he wrote again: 'I hope by your good meanes all will go well and that my mistress will be here by Michaelmas and also that she shall have a very noble and good supply.' A week later he was overjoyed to learn that Aylesbury had now obtained £1000 for Mrs. Crombie, 'this is houge service and comfort'.[49] Apart from more important matters, on his recent journey from England Aylesbury had brought over £130 for Roberts himself, who was desperately anxious to secure it. Absolute penury threatened him in Paris; but although it was more economical to transmit money from England to France by way of Flanders or Holland rather than directly, owing to favourable rates of exchange, the war between France and Flanders raised other difficulties before such a transaction could be completed. This was by no means all. At an earlier date Roberts had pawned certain jewels in Brussels or Antwerp and his letters to Aylesbury resound with pleas that these jewels should either be redeemed or the half-yearly interest paid at once; otherwise the brokers would sell. This was somehow dependent on the good offices of the English Jesuits at Antwerp and at last, on 28 October 1648, Father Clayton wrote from that city thanking Aylesbury for his 'diligent care in discharging us of the jewels'.[50] Finally, Roberts often reminded his colleague of other miscellaneous possessions (his own or the Villiers') pledged here or there, a cabinet or a carpet which might be turned into money at Amsterdam or Antwerp. He pestered Aylesbury to send him reliable passports so that they might meet and discuss these great questions. At length he ventured on the journey, and by 28 September was writing from the Hague.[51]

In retrospect, it seems that Roberts arrived on the continent before Aylesbury in order to transfer money from the Duchess of Buckingham's English estates for the use of the lady and her husband, whether in France or in Ireland. Then the Duke decided to follow their example and some of his wealth, under Aylesbury's supervision, was taken abroad. Aylesbury became the principal agent of the Villiers interest on the continent while Roberts went to Paris, preparing for the arrival of the Duchess. The foolishness of Antrim in Ireland, therefore, and the foolishness of Buckingham in England during 1648, had been partially covered by the shipment of valuables or money.

Nevertheless Aylesbury's chief preoccupation was always the position in England, not France, and most of his letters came from London. There political decisions affecting the whole future of ancient fortunes and dignities might be taken in the aftermath of civil war. There stood York House on the Strand — a maze of smaller houses and tenements beside the principal building — the head-office of the Villiers interest. This was the Duke of Buckingham's residence, where his chief steward and receiver of revenue sat at the receipt of custom. Here also the treasures of the first Duke, from which Aylesbury's shipment had been selected, were stored in safety or, as pessimists feared at this time, in the semblance of safety. Here the Duke's friends and dependants congregated, men of very varying types: Lord Holland who led the Villiers brothers to the ill-fated encounters at Kingston and St. Neots early in July, Sir Charles Cotterell who corresponded with Aylesbury and sent him news of the Duke's movements, Lady Cotterell who forwarded clothes to Aylesbury and also the quires of the second volume of Davila then in the press, the work of those good friends W. A. and C. C.; the business men who managed the family finances, Richard Hollins the steward, Trailman who corresponded with Roberts in Paris and appeared more particularly concerned with the Duchess of Buckingham's affairs, Aylesbury himself when he came to London from Antwerp or Amsterdam. There too was Abraham Woodhead the mathematical tutor and several other servants. It was from the assembly of the Duke's officers and advisers at York House that the Duke's special representative in the Low Countries received information in the trying weeks of the second civil war, in June and July; and to them he sent instructions.[52]

Popular anxiety and confusion were at their height. The Kentish rising over, the royalist troops escaped to Colchester. Fairfax began besieging the town on 14 June. Buckingham and his brother remained in London until 4 July when they set out to attempt a diversion against the parliamentary forces.[53] Lord Francis Villiers was slain at Kingston on the 7th and the Duke, with Lord Holland, was finally defeated on the 9th. He escaped and reached the continent, and by 10 August was on board the *Constant Reformation*, Prince Charles' flagship, sailing off the Downs.[54] During this hectic period, when public affairs directly affected individual fortunes and none more directly than the Villiers family, Aylesbury at Antwerp learnt what he could from the letters of his friends.

In June they had been relatively unperturbed. A number of correspondents regretted, or complained of, Aylesbury's unexpected departure from London. It meant that certain creditors were disappointed, a fact which raises in our eyes his status as a senior official, and this is confirmed by Sir Walter Pye, a very substantial man who acted for the Villiers in Herefordshire and the west; he took £100 of the Duke's money for his own immediate necessities and wrote requesting Aylesbury to obtain a quittance for this amount from the steward in London. Then on 26 June Sir Charles Cotterell sent news of the Duke, who was still in town, and of old Sir Thomas and Lady Aylesbury who were negotiating for the purchase of a house in the country. By 8 July matters had grown serious. Abraham Woodhead wrote that the Duke was now declared a traitor by the Commons. A week later he described the position after the defeat at Kingston and referred to the stout rearguard action of the Duke's old friends in high places, Denbigh and Northumberland: 'the procuring of an act of Indemnity for him in his inexperienced youth so much seduced by bad counsell, is much labored, proposed and well accepted yesterday in the House of Lords. The greatest doubt is in the Commons. His goods are inventoried and prized'.[55] The Commons indeed were doubtful. In the following week Woodhead stated that they had not remitted their original sentence, adding however that 'nothing is yet removed from this place'. Buckingham's servants were struggling hard on their master's behalf. Trailman put in a claim for some of his goods which caused a stir in the Committee of Sequestration, and the demands of genuine creditors were another hindrance to the swift impounding of his estate by victorious authority. Meanwhile he had reached Holland and safety.[56]

All this information, public and private, was of great importance to Aylesbury. The collapse of the counter-revolutionary force meant that the exiled Duke must rely in future on assets already available in the Low Countries. In England he was outside the law, and the government was his enemy. This deterioration at home was soon reflected in the letters of his servants. Vallois, a Frenchman who had worked for Buckingham in London, wrote to Aylesbury requesting help in securing payment due for services rendered; his money was ten months in arrears. One Edward du Jardin, saying that he owed his position with the Duke to Aylesbury, petitioned him for an order to the steward from his Grace to settle on account of £93.[57] On 10 October Abraham Woodhead was in despair: 'Sir, it was me Mr. Hollins furnished with £10 and when I have eaten that what shall I do? I am voted out of my fellowships. My Lord hath had little employment for me of late, less, I suppose, now.' He asked his friend to obtain the Duke's consent that he might look for other work, 'going beyond sea or pedanting in some gentleman's house'.[58] His one hope for the present was that Lord Denbigh, always the official enemy and unofficial friend, would not turn him out of York House. Finally, a less pleasant but more useful type of correspondent now put in a word, the attorney who undertook to arrange matters with the committees for sequestration — at a price. Mr. John Pulford told Aylesbury to inform the Duke that he must submit to composition, and promised to advise further as to ways and means.[59]

Both the Duke of Buckingham and his mother were now at the Hague, where Prince Charles was also resident. Roberts had likewise arrived from Paris and was in attendance; with great difficulty he procured a warrant from the Duke which he forwarded to Aylesbury at the end of September, for the disbursal of more money. 'My poore yet most noble and dear mistress' was suffering terribly, partly because the Duke insisted on taking his meals in her house. The expenses were very onerous.[60]

Towards the end of the year Aylesbury turned over in his mind the possibility of returning to England to see for himself how matters stood. One correspondent advised against this. Another, Algernon Sidney, the son of his old master Leicester, thought the idea feasible provided the Duke had done nothing since July to annoy the government. Since in the next few months there are no further letters addressed to Aylesbury from London it is probable that he came to England.[61] Charles I was executed, York House was let to a stranger, and the Villiers interest in England was apparently obliterated for ever.

Lord Denbigh still offered his services. Buckingham, who had followed Charles II to Paris, received news and advice in April 1649 that he had one more chance of compounding for his English estates and saving something. 'My Lord Denbigh beleeves it were not a very difficult thing to bring to bee brought to passe if I now lay hold of this conjecture when most people are admitted to it, but if I make not use of this opportunity it will bee very hard, if not impossible, for mee to doe it herafter.'[62] Denbigh even forwarded to Paris specimen letters which Buckingham was to copy out in his own hand and send to influential persons in England, soliciting their aid in negotiating the composition with authority. The London attorney, Pulford, writing to Aylesbury at the same time, also advised the Duke to compound.[63] He felt that it might be arranged without any particular degradation, comparing his prospects very favourably with those of the old Duchess. She could only compound on the authorization of Antrim her husband, and his political activities were such that the Commonwealth would never negotiate with him. Buckingham evidently took the whole problem very seriously despite a parade of principle, and desired Aylesbury to formulate a considered opinion; Aylesbury presumably sought further advice from London. In the end the Duchess died at Limerick in December 1649, the Duke refused to compound and followed the King. The immediate future, in its material aspect, depended on the treasure in Antwerp.

The working of the new system of ducal finance may be easily defined. It was based on the reluctant expenditure of capital, not income. Instead of the great estates of the Villiers scattered through many English counties, with the local stewards, Sir Walter Pye in Herefordshire and Walter Mercer in Cranborne Chase, for example, collecting the rents and sending the surplus to a receiver-general at York House, where the Duke could satisfy himself that he was one of the wealthiest men in England, a central reserve was now stored in the vaults of Antwerp. Small in value by comparison with the original patrimony but very substantial for these adverse circumstances, its treasures were sold, pledged or duplicated (copyists set to work on the pictures) according to the directions of the confidential adviser, William Aylesbury; while the Duke, whatever the difficulties, could still satisfy himself that he was one of the wealthiest English exiles. 'Pray do me all the service you can. . .', he wrote, 'but be sure not to sell any of the Pictures or Agates'. In practice this meant, Dispose of them as reluctantly and profitably as is humanly possible. The process can be watched in operation:[64]

> Whereas I William Aylesbury [begins the draft of a bond in the Clarendon Papers], by procuration to me made by his Grace, George Duke of Bucking-ham, having full power to dispose of all the pictures and agatts belonging to the said Duke of Buckingham and now in the house of Mr. Justus Collimar of Antwerpe, merchant, being engaged for the summe of thirty thousand gulders to Mr. John and Mr. Lionel Coram and Mr. Thomas Woulters of Antwerpe, with these conditions, that if within the space of one yeare after the date of the said engagement the said summe of thirty thousand gulders be not payd, then the soe much of the said pictures and Agatts beeing sold as will satisfye the debt of the above-mentioned John and Lionel Coram and Thomas Woulters, the remainder are to be restored to mee. William Aylesbury. . . .

And so the balance remained, useful pledges for a further loan.

This simple expedient of raising money on the security of valuables formed the basis of Buckingham's relative prosperity during the earlier years of his exile. He eked out capital until very little was left and it then became necessary, since the problem of political obligation never disturbed him, to make his peace with Cromwell. In 1649 this was still far in the future. At that time he lived abroad and was forced to do so, but his servant Aylesbury continued to visit England, so that in all probability the Antwerp treasure received some small but useful additions even after the great collapse of 1648. This had its political aspect. One reason why the moderate Royalists, like Hyde and Nicholas found it difficult to make headway against rival groups of exiled politicians was the relative wealth of Jermyn, who obtained funds from Henrietta Maria's French pension, and Walter Montagu who was a prosperous ecclesiastical dignitary, and also Buckingham. Apart from other considerations these men were able to outbid more poverty-stricken statesmen for the favour of the Stuarts.

This introduces a further topic, one of Aylesbury's most interesting contributions to the history of his time, his services for Sir Edward Hyde.

Aylesbury's brother-in-law, whatever his opinion of Buckingham (and it was very low), kept closely in touch with that nobleman's treasurer. Early in 1649 Aylesbury returned from a visit to England. Deciding that it was necessary, and would also be possible, to bring over to the continent his mother and father, his two sisters, one of whom was Lady Cotterell, he wrote to his brother-in-law and offered to maintain the whole company for one year, provided that Hyde undertook a similar responsibility for a second year, should that prove necessary. At the time Hyde was extremely anxious to remove from England anyone liable to be treated by the Commonwealth as a hostage for his own behaviour, especially since he had decided to go with Lord Cottington to Spain and request Spanish aid for the Stuarts.[65] He welcomed Aylesbury's remarkable offer and wrote enthusiastically from the Hague on 18 March.[66]

> I have not had so much content these many dayes as I had this evening in the reading your letter, without a date, and I am so abundantly satisfyed with the overture that I do not only promise to discharge the 2nd year for the whole company (which I doubt not I should be able to do) but if I lyve will likewise reimburse you for what you lay out in the first year. For gods sake loose no tyme in getting them over, for which I have another reason, I meane for the speede of it, than I can yet imparte to you. It will be an unspeakable comfort to me, to see all the company together, and truly I beleive they would parte very unwillingly. I wish the Warden [Sheldon, of All Souls] would come with them, for I wonder how any honest man can stay in England. I do seldom omitt writing to my wyfe once a week but the weather or some interruptions in the way, it may be, heaped the letters together. Gods blessing on your travail for this good overture. I pray leave nothing undone that may effect it, by which you will lay the greatest obligation that is imaginable upon
>
> > my dearest Will
> > Your most affectionate debtor and
> > Servant
>
> Hague, this 18 of March. E.H.

By the middle of May Lady Hyde was safe in Antwerp, and Aylesbury had found his friends and relatives a house. Hyde and Cottington set off for Spain and the former saw his brother-in-law for the last time when they said goodbye somewhere on the road between Brussels and Mons on 26 July 1649.[67] The letters which Hyde wrote to his wife during the next few months continued to express the most heartfelt gratitude to her brother and it was only when the year of grace drew to a close that he began to feel anxious. It became necessary to forward money, which could ill be spared, to Lady Hyde. Aylesbury himself had disappeared, he never wrote, and Hyde surmised that he was in England on an occasional visit. Entreaties or reproaches from Madrid produced no response. 'My William', Hyde scribbled on 3 January 1650, 'if you will write nothing else, nor ever again after this tyme, at least tell me what is the reason of this strange, peremptory, unkind silence.'[68] In May he returned to the problem: 'It is strange thy brother should have undertaken that journey without communicating to thee'; he might have raised the family funds for the coming year by selling to would-be purchasers, slightly nervous of the Commonwealth's stability, the genuine titles to property which the Hydes used to own in Wiltshire.[69]

In fact, what had happened to Aylesbury? His relatives were not alone in their mystification, for it is from this point onwards that our usual informants have nothing further to say. Hyde never mentions him again, he never wrote to him, and after his journey to Spain letters addressed to Aylesbury by other correspondents could not be incorporated in his own collection of papers. We appear to be left with the unsupported testimony of Anthony Wood declaring that in 1650, poverty-stricken, he crept back to England and remained there.[70] If so, the silence of Hyde was perhaps the silence of contempt for a traitor to the cause. If, in addition, Aylesbury broke off all dealing with his friends and relatives or refused them further assistance, perhaps Hyde felt as much irritation as contempt. Uncompromising royalist though he was, Charles II's chancellor of the exchequer had a somewhat casuistical notion of the duty of people in England during the period of exile: 'they who strayne their consciences to injoy plenty there, will administer a share to those who keep themselves intyre abroad against that temptation'.[71] He did not like men who rejected the dilemma.

This enigma naturally turns on the relations of the Duke of Buckingham and his confidential servant, and fortunately it is possible to find an explanation in the letters and copies of letters kept by Sir Charles Cotterell, and still in the hands of his descendants. When the second impression of the Davila translation came out in 1678, it will be remembered that the publisher claimed for Cotterell all the credit of the work, at Aylesbury's expense. Similarly, in 1650 Cotterell supplanted or at any rate succeeded Aylesbury as Buckingham's agent in the Low Countries; and in his papers there are several references to his former friend's fall from grace.[72] On 4 April 1650 Buckingham wrote to Cotterell requesting him to forward certain goods to Paris for sale there, and since not more than three months later Cotterell still considered himself 'an utter stranger to my Lord's business' he cannot have taken Aylesbury's place long before the date of this letter. The new arrangement was certainly confirmed soon afterwards, when the Duke himself arrived in the Low Countries accompanying Charles II on his journey from France to Holland en route for Scotland. On 26 May he signed confidential instructions for his other servant Peter Roberts, the original of which was left in Cotterell's safe-keeping. Roberts was going to England on the Duke's affairs, and several clauses demonstrate that Aylesbury and the Duke of Buckingham had at long last quarrelled irremediably over money matters. Both men claimed to be the other's creditor. This was almost inevitable, given the nature of their transactions. Buckingham was never a scrupulous man. It is equally obvious that Aylesbury's ability to help his own friends, and to make loans to such persons as the Duke of Newcastle, was directly connected with his credit as agent for one of the wealthiest Englishmen abroad. Cotterell would hardly have stepped straight into his friend's employment had he not disapproved, in some measure, of his conduct; and this took place only a few weeks after Hyde in Madrid was still wondering what had happened. It is also possible that Buckingham lost confidence not only in Aylesbury's honesty but also in his ability. In November 1650 Dr. Goff declared that 'the great collection of pictures' had already been sold, very unskilfully, at an earlier date.[73] Such errors were to be avoided in future.

The directions to Roberts afford a fascinating glimpse of the Duke of Buckingham's methods of business, and his principal interests, at this period:

> Instructions for my servant P. Roberts going into England. 26 May 1650 o.s....[74]
>
> (3) The rich Suite of hangings in Baynards Castle is to be sent over either into France or into these countries as you shall find best opportunity and speedy notice is to be given me what you have done therein, that accordingly I may give my further orders about them. If they cannot presently be translated some means must be used to remove them from the place where they now are, because Alesbury hath knowledge of them....
>
> (5) The — blanks which are put into your hands must be employed for the uses following and no other, viz: to call Mr. Alesbury to account for the two debts of £200 a peice, using therein such persons as you shall find fittest, allowing them such rewards out of them as you shall agree. To make enquiry after such bedding, Hangings, Household stuffe etc. as belong unto me, and ly deposited in several places in London and elsewhere. To sell such goods as shall not be of use and to transport the rest. To take up such summes of money as you can procure upon my obligation. To take Alesbury's account for £2000 in England.
>
> (6) The statues are to be transmitted into these parts either by meanes of the Spanish Ambassador, to whom you are to repair and desire his assistance by virtue of letters he hath already received from the Archduke. If that way be impracticable you are to enquire what merchant may be found that will do it. And in case Van de Wolfe a Burger of Rotterdam or some factor for him do repaire unto you with orders from me, you make use of him. Let this article be perused with all diligence.

Other clauses refer to negotiations, in which £2000 gratuity was one item, for the Duke's composition; and they authorize the sale of land in Leicestershire, the making and recalling of leases, and the repurchases from Lord Fairfax of Buckingham estates assigned to him by Parliament.

In this way the administration of the Duke's interest at home and abroad continued to function, supervised by Sir Charles Cotterell with occasional expert advice from Dr. Goff in Paris.[75] The Duke himself went to Scotland with Charles II. Aylesbury was in England. One final reference to him, indicating his view of the fatal quarrel, appears in a letter from Goff to Cotterell written on 18 November 1650

> ...Besides the real debts I assure you my Lord Duke was in some apprehension that Mr Aylesbury (knowing his Graces fast engagement in Scotland) might renew again some suit for his pretended debts, for prevention of which I may let you know that I am instructed with full powers to arrest him if he, coming over on this side the sea, gives the least cause to suspect him.

It only remained for Aylesbury to make his peace with the authorities in England. The power which he had helped to build and fortify on the continent thrust him back into his own country. The skill and adaptability formerly employed in moving men and women, pictures, jewels and money across the sea were now required to help him steer his passage home: while others left their fortunes in England as the price of liberty, William Aylesbury, in fear of Buckingham or perhaps tempted by the regicide government, left his friends behind him on the continent.

Nothing further is known of him, except one final scrap of information. In 1655 he joined Oliver Cromwell's expedition to the West Indies, serving as secretary to Major-General Sedgwick. Two letters which he wrote to Thurloe are among Thurloe's papers, and two references by other correspondents conclude with the announcement that Aylesbury died on 24 August 1656, in the course of the expedition, 'late Secretary, a man very well versed in the weighty affairs of state who, in his councills and advice both to army and fleet was very useful; for the want of which we shall have more and more cause to grieve'.[76]

Whatever the inconclusiveness of this narrative after 1650 the evidence over a period of twelve years (1639–1650) has proved sufficient to study the relationship between the two great families of Sidney and Villiers and a well-born, well educated gentleman in their service, to show him hoping for preferment under their auspices and at last, in the period of upheaval, becoming a not unimportant figure as he helped to smooth the path of exile for the Villiers and the Hydes. He was not merely a tutor of noblemen, or a literary figure, or a likely diplomat who failed to secure public employment until the year of his death, he was all three; and his career helps to explain how a certain position in society combined with general experience abroad quite easily placed a man in the midst of important affairs in which the relations of England and the continent were specifically involved. After that, it was not more than a single step from stewardship of the Villiers treasure at Antwerp to 'council and advice to army and fleet' off the coasts of Hispaniola. The reversal of political loyalties implied by such a transition is not more interesting, as a characteristic detail of the age in which he lived, than the fact that the same man was considered, and considered himself, fitted to carry out either task without any special preliminary training.

Aylesbury had been an ambassador's servant in France, a young nobleman's companion and governor in Italy, a business agent in the Low Countries. The last phase of his life brought him into conflict with the Spaniards in American waters. Spain itself he never seems to have visited, and in this omission he resembled most travelled Englishmen of his day; for Spain, the familiar and almost traditional enemy of the Elizabethan and of Oliver Cromwell (or so he was persuaded) appeared to them a remote and inhospitable land. Nevertheless the English travelled there, on business political and commercial, or occasionally for the sake of general experience and to satisfy a natural curiosity. In the early part of the century at least the diplomats were of high potential significance, since an alliance between the courts of Madrid and Whitehall was frequently under discussion. For that reason the Englishmen in Spain next deserve attention; just as their hardships were such that they deserve also a measure of sympathy.

# IV. ENGLISH TRAVELLERS IN SPAIN

# 10. THE RETURN OF THE ENGLISH TO SPAIN

On 16 May 1605 Charles Lord Howard Earl of Nottingham, who had commanded the victorious English navies against the Armada, arrived with his followers before the city of Valladolid. He and this celebrated embassage of five hundred English noblemen, gentlemen and their servants were on their way to witness and accept the King of Spain's ratification of the peace treaty. The Constable of Castile with other great dignitaries came forward to greet the Earl and amid torrential rain that spoilt the splendours of man and costume the elaborate procession hastened into the city. The trumpeters prefaced a new phase in Anglo-Spanish history.

For the past quarter of a century English impressions of Spain had been obscured by war. The experience of diplomats and merchants who worked there before hostilities began, secondhand reports filtering through Italy and Paris, information gathered from spies or friendly Catholic exiles, apart from the misleading contacts of war itself, constituted the sum of English knowledge on the subject. In any case, it was the Spanish empire overseas rather than Spain itself which attracted the curiosity of foreigners. For twenty years merchants of the old 'Company trading to Spain and Portugal' had omitted from their apprentices' indentures the words 'merchant of Spain and Portugal', so that when peace made legitimate commerce with the Peninsula a possibility these younger men had difficulties at law in claiming the benefit of the Company's freedom to trade.[1] Students and gentlemen would be advised to read translations of *Lazarillo de Tormes*, earliest of the picaresque novels, where captions beside the text noted general nastiness and naughtiness in Spanish customs; or to study the attacks of such liberal-minded champions of the American natives as Bishop Bartholomew Las Casas on the cruelties of Spanish dominion in America.[2] The Inquisition, and the proud slow Spaniard, were suitable themes for patriotic prejudice. The Englishman's racial and religious pride was inflamed by the view that 'this semi-Morisco nation as touching its beginning is sprung from the filth and slime of Africa, the base Ottomans and the rejected Jews, and which is more infamous, a great part of Spain unchristened until an hundred years ago that Granada was conquered by Ferdinando and Isabella'.[3] One of the most galling consequences of defeat in war would be the deportation of able-bodied Englishmen to work for the conquerors in the mines of Peru and Rio Tinto, 'to wear out our flesh in their minerals'.[4] Even those who, misguided by conscience, had voluntarily gone over to Spain or Spanish dominions were said to be ill-used; and pamphleteers manipulated this charge to warn all who might still contemplate deserting their native country.[5] Mutual antagonism and mutual ignorance, as usual, fused together. The Spaniard was best known by war on the seas and misrule over other men's territory. There were no authentic reports of his homeland by accredited Englishmen.

The altered situation in 1605, therefore, raises questions of some interest. Would the restoration of peace bring English travellers into the Spanish kingdoms of Philip III? Or their experience and impressions contribute in any way to the formulation of English policy towards Spain? In itself the arrival of Nottingham and his company at Valladolid marked a change. Large numbers of English people, some of them men of intelligence and a few of great influence, were now looking about in a peaceful land and a court which, on this occasion, was anxious to impress. After the mission's return it became a part of ordinary diplomatic routine to exchange envoys with Spain. There was the influence of the Spanish embassy in London, no mean instrument in the hands of Gondomar after 1611, and the influence of the Spanish court on the English embassy in Valladolid and, after 1606, in Madrid. Legitimate trade with Spain began again, and in spite of all sorts of difficulties at the ports and customs-houses, in lawsuits and appeals to higher authority over the interpretation by conflicting interests of the articles of the peace treaty, this trade became an important element in English commerce. Similarly English merchants and factors in Spain selling pilchards, selling cloth, selling both English and European goods, were soon a perceptible element in Spanish economic life.[6] When the rivalries of France and Spain merged openly into the Thirty Years War (1635) this importance was more than confirmed. All these developments must be set beside one of the standing paradoxes in English affairs, the paradox that while popular opinion in this matter well represented in the House of Commons, continued to express an Elizabethan antipathy towards Spain, the so-called 'Spanish faction' in the Stuart court and government was so persistent and so strong. Precisely in that connection the Spanish journeys and experiences in Spain of certain Englishmen repay some investigation. James I's treaty of peace was not purely personal. He was crowned King of England in time to complete negotiations countenanced long before his accession by statesmen like Lord Burleigh and Lord Burleigh's followers; and yet a policy of peace with Spain, which might develop into a more positive alliance, divided the Stuarts from many of their subjects for many years.

The documentary sources for such a study of Englishmen travelling in Spain, whether in printed narratives, manuscript diaries or diplomatic reports soon make it clear that Spain never became a fashionable resort for leisured travellers, as did France and Italy, during the seventeenth century. Englishmen went to that country primarily on business, commercial or political. It will be seen that there were soon significant little groups of English traders in Spain, and a central office or embassy which negotiated on current problems with the higher Spanish authorities. In this respect Anglo-Spanish relations hardly differed from the relations of Englishmen with the other states of western Europe, although the extent and constitution of the Spanish empire involved many peculiar difficulties and also, in the opinion of a few speculators, offered the possibility of greater economic or political advantages. From those engaged in commerce and in diplomacy come several descriptions of travel in Spain; and owing to the relative inaccessibility of the country to foreigners the writings of such men are perhaps more plentiful than for France, Italy and the Low Countries.

On the other hand, the same inaccessibility naturally deterred the type of leisured traveller whose memorials predominate in the evidence for the remainder of western Europe. Some of these people, but only a fraction of the company who saw France and Italy, did in fact visit the country. Various reasons combined to keep the foreigner from entering Spain. First and foremost was the actual discomfort, the poverty, which affected the state of the inns and roads, the difficult climate. Gondomar himself pointed out to Philip III, in a memorandum of March 1619, how strangers agreed that travel in Spain was more disagreeable than elsewhere because there were neither inns nor beds nor meals, amenities noticeable by their absence even on the main roads from the Pyrenees to Madrid and from Madrid to Seville.[7] Then, the Englishman's fear of the Inquisition persisted and, conversely, authority in England tended to regard with suspicion the loyalty of men who desired to visit territories which were Catholic in religion and Spanish by political affiliation. Licences to travel granted by James I's council from time to time include a proviso that the bearer shall not stray into the dominions of Philip III.

Finally, the prestige of Spanish culture hardly equalled the Italian which possessed an overwhelming advantage in the direct classical and imperial heritage of Rome, with which was connected the extraordinary achievements of Italian cities and craftsmen in the more recent past. The Spanish court appeared remote while Paris was close at hand. Educated English people learnt to read Spanish, in the period from Hakluyt and Donne to Samuel Pepys[8] they collected Spanish books which were held in high esteem by theologians for purposes of controversy, by writers of fiction for providing the material of many excellent stories, by sailors and scientists for information on the new world overseas; but it never seems to have been generally assumed that Spanish, unlike French or Italian, was a language that gentlemen should learn to speak, in spite of a few colloquial phrases with which they occasionally flavoured letters, plays and diplomatic reports. In contemporary travel books little argument will be found about the Spanish cities where a pure dialect could be heard, as they discussed the merits of Tours and Paris. Florence and Siena in that respect. Nevertheless this was the period of Spain's apogee, and it would be as serious an error to under-estimate the reputation abroad of Spanish achievement in arts, literature and manners as to antedate the decay of Spanish political power; but such a reputation did not necessarily bring travellers into Spain.[9] A fair number came on business but few came alone with their servants or in small private parties merely to see the country; and very few kept records which have survived. Most of the English gentry who travelled without any specific purpose in mind probably came as members of an embassy, with Nottingham or Digby in James I's reign, with Fanshawe or Sandwich or Godolphin sixty years later. Pride of place must certainly be given to the Earl of Nottingham and his followers, for it seems unlikely that a deputation of representative Englishmen reappeared on such a scale in Spain in the course of the century, the occasion of Prince Charles's residence at Madrid in 1623 excepted.

The welcome received in 1605 was certainly most cordial throughout the long journey from Corunna to Valladolid.[10] The Spaniards who knew and feared the weariness and expense of overland travel in their own country, expected them to land at Santander on the northern coast, about half as far from the capital as the ports of remote, impoverished Galicia. However, the English admiral protested against sailing into the Bay of Biscay when he had no pilots (after so long a period of war) who were acquainted with the coastline and the treacherous harbour of Santander: 'No Master of this Relme hath taken charge of any ships thither', he wrote to Cranborne.[11] After much worry on his part and the failure of certain orders to reach the storeships which had gone on ahead, they all directed their course further to the west. The Spanish authorities warned the Governor of Galicia; and seventy guns from the neighbouring citadels saluted the Admiral's fleet which sailed into Corun-na harbour on a Monday afternoon, 15 April, the storeships having al-ready arrived. The Governor hastily arranged all possible courtesies. There were dinners, tilting, fireworks, dumb shows of the Judgment of Paris and the loveliness of Peace. Doctors of Law, friars and many others climbed up into King James's ships and admired their size and finish.[12] When a drunken English sailor struck a cleric in the town, the Admiral offered to hang him while the Governor asked for his life and had the fellow given a good meal.[13] Some of the visitors observed the multitude of beggars to whom Nottingham in his turn was profuse in giving alms. They observed what difficulty the Spaniards had in securing sufficient transports, mules, coaches and litters for the long journey overland, but everything was done that could be done; the English wars had not been popular in north-western Spain, exposed to the danger of naval attacks. In the end a section of the embassage was compelled to remain behind and on Friday 3 May, to the noise of sackbuts and a farewell salute from their ships at anchor in the harbour, the Englishmen left the town.

Various descriptions of their journey have been handed down. A fair number of Spaniards went ahead, scouring the country for food and requisitioning quarters for each night. Sometimes the towns prepared a civic welcome, with speeches, music and ceremonial alleys of interlaced branches cut from the trees; occasionally there were 'Moorish' dances to watch in the evenings. A thousand mules climbed over the hills with the court cloths and all the other furnishings of an extraordinary embassy on their backs.[14] Among the travellers were the Earl of Nottingham himself, his son Lord Howard of Effingham, his second son Sir Charles Howard and his nephews Sir Thomas and Sir Edward Howard, the family which, for some hostile critics, would soon represent the core of the Spanish interest in England. There was the Scots courtier the Earl of Perth. There were Lords Willoughby and Norris, who had brought young Dudley Carleton as his secretary, very intelligent and very critical of the Spanish scene. Sir Charles Cornwallis, apppointed by James to remain as permanent ambassador in Spain, travelled always in his litter ill and querulous, early convinced of the opinion which echoed and re-echoed through his official reports for many years: 'I hold this estate to be one of the most confused and disordered in Christendom.[15] Not long after landing, according to another traveller, Sir George Buck, Cornwallis had quarrelled with peers and grandees of the party on questions of precedence and remained in his lodging in Corunna while the official festivities proceeded;[16] on his journey he may be imagined going slowly forward in his litter, aloof, and more concerned with political realities than were the courtiers of the party. He was attended by his son William Cornwallis, a young man who later carried despatches for him between England and Spain and was already known as a minor essayist of merit. There were many others also, struggling over the Galician mountains with Nottingham, who compared them with the Scottish Highlands. There were courtiers dependent on the Cecils like Sir Walter Cope, the builder of Holland House, Kensington, and Sir Richard Levison; Sir Robert Mansell the sailor and business man, a Cary, a Killigrew, a Tresham, Pickering Wotton the son and heir of Lord Wotton, Sir Robert Drury, with the chaplains Wadsworth and Palmer, the interpreter Giles Porter, and musicians, grooms and servants of all sorts. At last they arrived at Villafranca across the steepest hills, where it became possible for some of the higher ranking travellers to use coaches.

A Spanish account of this journey hints at a certain diversity of religious opinion among the travellers. A few copies of the Spanish Bible printed in Protestant Holland had been brought by sea to smuggle into the country but officers of the Inquisition hearing of this insisted on a promise that such dangerous books should not leave the ships.[17] On the other hand the Spaniards were gratified to observe that at the Benedictine priory of Cebreros, where a miracle connected with the Holy Sacrament was to be seen, certain of the English paid a special visit 'some for curiosity' and others for devotion.[18] Later on one or two English noblemen took their place in the religious processions at Whitsun and Corpus Christi;[19] and an observer noted that Lord Howard of Effingham made a special journey from Valladolid to Madrid to visit his relative the famous Catholic exile Jane Dormer Duchess of Feria.[20] It is extraordinarily difficult to evaluate these contradictory touches of fact and opinion. All reports agree on the courteous reception of the embassy: 'I must saye to your Lordship', wrote Nottingham, 'that in my life I never saw soe kinde a people of all sortes.'[21] Against this should be set the experience recorded by Sir Thomas Bodley only a few months earlier who wrote to his Librarian at Oxford that the stationer John Bill had recently returned from Seville with a good store of books, but intending to go to other Spanish towns and universities to collect and purchase still further, 'the people's usage towardes all of our nation is so cruel and malicious, as he was utterly discouraged for this time'.[22]

For twenty days they moved slowly eastwards into Castile, through Lugo, Astorga and Simancas. It was the worst of all the routes into central Spain, usually avoided, but in the course of a century many other English diplomats travelled between the Spanish capital and ships in the Galician harbours, and it was therefore an itinerary well known to the English during this period.

On arriving at Valladolid, the court of Philip III spared no pains to impress them. The christening of the King's son, Corpus Christi, and the ceremony in which the King ratified his acceptance of the peace treaty, were the great formal occasions. There was bull fighting, judged by Cornwallis an unpleasant spectacle,[23] and jousting by selected Spanish nobles. Among them was Don Diego Sarmiento, Corregidor of Valladolid and later Count of Gondomar, who would in due course spend many years in London as Spanish ambassador — the first view by many English courtiers of an important figure in their own history.[24] Treswell, Somerset Herald and the official English narrator, praised especially a certain festival evening in the newly built hall of the palace where innumerable candles, on silver standards, illumined a gathering of the ambassadors and their followers and members of the Spanish court while singing and dancing passed away the hours. The Infanta Anna, soon considered as a possible Queen of England in the speculation of diplomats, appeared on the stage in an antique chariot carrying a gold sceptre tipped with the dove of peace.[25] The Earl of Perth and Lord Willoughby joined in the dancing. Such entertainments impressed the

Earl of Nottingham. Dudley Carleton would fasten on the signs of pride and poverty which he found in Spain, writing off contemptuously 'feasts and triumphs enough for Stoes-chronicle',[26] but the Earl of Nottingham was predisposed to admire the conjunction of kingly rule and aristocratic society which he found expressed in the old ceremonial of the Habsburg court at Valladolid. 'The maner of all for the sumtiousnes was wonderfull', and 'truely, my Lord, I doe not thinck that ever Ambassador was more honored for the King his Majesties sake then I am', were two of his comments expressed in reports to Salisbury.[27] Cornwallis wrote also, and his view was that the Spaniards were evidently attempting to woo Nottingham by fair means, if not by bribery. The Earl appeared later on the pension list kept by the Spanish ambassadors in London from 1605, at a figure of £1000 yearly; but his sympathy with the Spaniards, as from one grandee to other grandees is more convincingly shown in the account given above than by any enjoyment of specific rewards. In his unreserved admiration and gratitude for the elaborate official welcome at Valladolid he contrasts vividly with Cornwallis, and even with Treswell who wrote soberly enough on the drawbacks of travel in Spain: they realized something of the poverty, and were not quite so certain of the courtesy, of Spaniards in this northern half of the country. No doubts appeared to trouble Nottingham.

At last on 7 June 1605 the great majority of the embassy made their farewells, Nottingham accepted a substantial parting gift from Philip III and shortly afterwards they set out on the journey to their own ships. A few remained behind with Sir Charles Cornwallis, forming the staff of an English embassy in Spain at a time of open and accredited peace. A few, among them Lords Norris and Willoughby and Dudley Carleton, decided to return overland by way of the Pyrenees and Paris, and over a month later an English merchant at San Sebastian met them passing through that town on their road north-eastwards, and reported the fact to official quarters in London.[29] This route to Spain through Paris later became familiar to English gentlemen touring round Europe and was preferred by diplomats, given sufficiently peaceful conditions in southern France. In 1605, however, Nottingham with his sons and nephews and the greater number of his followers took the shortest road to the coast: to Santander, to which the ships had sailed from Galicia. No one desired to face again the longer journey if it could be avoided. The mules in their hundreds went through Palencia, Burgos and over the terrible Cantabrian mountains, which struck at least one traveller as the worst hardship yet encountered. The English were glad to get to sea and so home on the completion of an undertaking which was hardly inferior in scale to a raid made upon the Spanish coast in the wars of Elizabeth's reign.

To judge from the literature produced on this occasion English people had taken a genuine interest in the embassy. Both Treswell's narrative and the anonymous pamphlet printed for John Ferbrand were published in 1605. The author of the latter described himself as more of a soldier than a scholar who passed the many idle hours of his journey in noting down its main features. Another anonymous servant of Nottingham soon afterwards translated a Spanish account originally compiled by a Valladolid stationer; early in 1607 the English version was apparently doing the rounds at the Inns of Court in London where copies were made, some indication of the interest aroused by the proceedings.[30] In 1605 also appeared a grammar-book, *The Key of the Spanish Tongue*, written by Lewis Owen and dedicated to Sir Roger Owen of Shropshire, Sir Thomas Middleton of London and John Lloyd of the Inner Temple, including as well as grammar intelligent dialogues and a vocabulary. The author speaks of 'having compiled this little Pamphlet at some vacant houres in the Kingdom of Castille', but probably he had been in Spain, in some unknown capacity, before peace was signed or ratified.

Now that peace had been restored the English who came to Spain can be divided into separate groups. By far the most notorious, in their countrymen's eyes, were Catholic exiles, some of whom had already been in the country during the great war; the Jesuit Creswell, particularly, did his best to influence both Spanish politicians and English Protestant travellers in these early years. The most numerous were undoubtedly the sailors and merchants' factors at the principal ports, San Sebastian, Lisbon, Cadiz, Seville, Malaga, Alicante. The most important, politically, were the ambassador and his staff resident first in Valladolid and later in Madrid. The last two of these categories were men concerned with trade, diplomacy and the conjunction of trade and diplomacy in lawsuits for the recovery of debts or property. Through a labyrinth of official papers a number of individuals can still be identified, busily occupied and often travelling from the ports to the capital, or from the capital back to the coast.

Practically nothing is known of the embassy at Valladolid, its diplomatic work apart, except Cornwallis' chance remark that it cost him £350 to set up house there.[31] At Madrid he lived first a little way outside the city, and writing home he mentions his low gallery facing on to a little garden, and the lodgings of his chaplain where the walls were lined with maps.[32] The ambassador shared this accommodation with certain Spaniards but finding them a nuisance, and their coming and going a complication of his diplomatic privilege, he asked for a more suitable residence. The authorities found a large house 'towards the Prado' belonging to the Duke of Maqueda, with a fine garden and a view over the town and the surrounding fields.[33] Here the embassy was able to organize its common life in greater comfort; the ambassador, the secretaries, the chaplains, the servants, the visitors both gentlemen and merchants all forming a curious and alien society in the heart of Spain. The servants were

English and also Spanish, and the ambassador lamented more than once that illness or death forced him to employ Catholics in his household, but Englishmen were sent out whenever possible; in later years Sir Arthur Hopton, another diplomat, declared that the English embassy in Madrid differed from all embassies there in employing only English Protestants who had to be housed in the building, instead of Spaniards who came daily or others who could at least be boarded out in the city. Apart from these, Cornwallis had also a coach,[34] and a man who travelled into the surrounding countryside to buy food, always a problem in seventeenth-century Spain where even diplomatic privileges might fail to obtain meat and bread. Such was the administration of this kingdom, the ambassador complained, that we might starve though corn was plentiful not many miles away. In spite of these difficulties the embassy remained an obvious port of call for all English travellers in Spain, especially for the occasional Protestant gentleman engaged on a leisurely tour round Europe.

Of all the rooms in the Duke of Maqueda's house, the Anglican chapel was first in importance, the shrine which tested each man's doctrine, and even more his loyalty. Cornwallis stoutly averred to the Inquisition that here he had prayers said every day and sermons preached on Sundays, according to the usage of the Church of England. A bell warned the few faithful to attendance and the sound of it scandalized a Catholic neighbourhood. Cornwallis, the secretaries and the chaplain headed this little establishment, the congregation were formed by the members of his family and 'three or four' who might be staying with them. It was a tiny Protestant citadel in the depths of Catholic Europe and from time to time a rabble (headed by English exiles) collected outside the gates crying 'Heretics! Lutheran dogs!' to remind the inmates of their isolation.[35] On the whole, a religious independence was maintained; the last resident English ambassador in Spain, in 1568, had been refused by the Inquisition any right to hold a Protestant service however privately, but the growing acceptance by statesmen of diplomatic privilege allowed Cornwallis to protest successfully, when officials infringed his rights.[36] The chief danger was never the fragility of privilege but the sense of isolation. For the fanatical and for the deeply convinced Protestant, no problem existed; men less opinionated than William Lithgow could traverse all the kingdoms of Spain without adding a qualm to their religion. For others, experience proved very different. They might have come with the Earl of Nottingham because they were secretly Catholic and rejoiced to find themselves in a Catholic land again.[37] They might have been undecided in their minds. They might merely desire to live according to the overwhelming custom of the countries where they found themselves. When many years later, the Earl of Bristol defended himself in the House of Lords against the charges trumped up against him by Charles and the Duke of Buckingham (19

May 1626) he agreed that when he was with the Spanish court he may have observed their custom of kneeling down with 'the Spanish King and Courtiers' when they heard the evening bell toll, but this, he said, was performed over almost all Europe, even in Lutheran Germany;[38] and Bristol considered himself a perfectly good Protestant. He followed the custom of a Catholic country; and many others, men with not quite the same diplomatic balance of mind, preferred in Spain to think and above all to die as their Spanish neighbours. The question of religious conformity abroad was a favourite casuistical theme in contemporary advice to travellers. In practice, the results would be equally various, troublesome and subtle.

This isolation was vividly experienced. Time and again, men surrendered to pervading Catholic influences. The transference of allegiances continued over a period of many years and from the start Cornwallis complained of the desertions from his household. Above all his first chaplain, James Wadsworth, after serving for a few months to the 'great comfort of the little establishment', on the plea of a short visit to Salamanca university left his office never to return. On 8 September 1605 he wrote from that city to the ambassador that he had been very ill and, 'having desire to inform my tender conscience of diverse intricate controversies in Divinity between the Catholics and us', would 'either return an expert and armed Protestant or remain resolved and a converted Catholic'.[39] He remained, and attended the university at Alcalá de Henares for further study. In the year 1610 he arranged for his wife and family to come over from England and settle down in a new country and a different church.[40] Somehow he managed to support them, and on one occasion he seriously alarmed the English Agent by a proposal to the King of Spain to farm the customs on woollen imports at Seville, because he claimed to know how the English traders defrauded the revenue by large scale consignments and inaccurate bills of lading; between them the Agent, and the Spaniards who already farmed these customs, blocked this scheme of Wadsworth to gain favour and add to the family's income.[41] His life was also diversified by a friendly theological correspondence with William Bedell, the loyal Protestant chaplain in Venice; and by a period as tutor in English to the Infanta Maria, for whom he wrote a grammar when the Spanish marriage of Prince Charles appeared likely. His son, a less respectable adventurer, returned to England and with his intimate knowledge of the subject became a poursuivant of the Privy Council, harassing recusant families (1630–1640). His own book, the *English Spanish Pilgrim*, describes a part of this curious family history. The Wadsworths flitting between London, Valladolid, Madrid, Seville and London again, were representative of the undecided exiles, hesitant birds of passage.[42]

Cornwallis bitterly lamented this betrayal by the elder James Wadsworth. He believed that delay in sending out a new chaplain would bring further troubles; and indeed, while he could say in one letter that Pickering Wotton, Lord Wotton's heir, who came with Nottingham, and certain Irish gentlemen, came to his house for service and sermon on Sundays, not long afterwards he announced the death of the young man, given Catholic unction and Catholic burial.[43] In paying the expenses of the funeral, up to £100, he expressed his trust that Lord Wotton would refund him. Another who died in Valladolid in 1605 was Sir Thomas Palmer. He also declared himself a Catholic.[44] For the Spaniards these conversions, the not unduly Protestant character of Nottingham's embassy and the misleading item of news that Sir Charles Cornwallis's father had been a noted Papist during Elizabeth's reign, may well have fortified a conviction that heresy in England was not immovable. And insistently at work, attempting to influence both Spaniards and English Protestant by intrigue and conversation were of course the exiles, layman and priest, the other group abroad.

The secretaries worked harder than anyone else in the embassy, first Hawkesworth who died within a few months, and then Francis Cottington, who began his long political career here, a man whose Spanish apprenticeship influenced a lifetime devoted to the Spanish party in Stuart diplomacy.[45] He was fortunate at this moment in being preferred by Cornwallis to Nicholas Ousely, a master of fluent Spanish and plausible dealing, bequeathed and recommended to the embassy by Nottingham when he left Valladolid but one who speedily made friends with the Jesuits and other English Catholics; and in the end the ambassador would have nothing more to do with him.[46] Still a young man of twenty-six, Cottington was employed in taking down reports to Cornwallis's dictation and inverviewing Spanish statemen and juntas when Cornwallis felt weary or fell ill, as he often did. In particular, he shared the burden of persuading the courts to give a reasonable hearing to the suits of English merchants, men who would travel up to Valladolid and Madrid, sublimely unaware of the difficulties before them, incapable of applying to good lawyers or without sufficient money or desire to pay for the expenses of lawsuit. They too sometimes lived at the embassy and dined at Cornwallis's table. State papers are full of their difficulties, the unwillingness of the Spaniards to solve these and also of the profits which could be made in the Spanish trade. As Cornwallis remarked, 'Howsoever they complayne there, I have gathered from out of some of themselves that their Gaines are great here; but your Lordships and my poor self are only made Partakers of their Oes, not of their Alliluyas.'[47] All these matters, and cross-currents of opinion, it is certain, were discussed over the supper-tables of the embassy. Cornwallis himself would be there, contemptuously aware that he saved rich merchants some of the proctors' and solicitors' fees and arranged for the yearly and continual rewards to the porters, pages and clerks of the Councillors and Secretaries of the Spanish courts, securing repayment with difficulty. Ousely,

until finally turned out of the house 'with some fewe blowes' was both
indispensable and unpopular, skilled in negotiation but apt to annex a
high percentage of any compensation squeezed out of the Spanish
authorities.[48] Cottington never left the mark of any special personality
but that of a reliable official. John Jude, who arrived a little later, was also
employed as a secretary, a man obsequiously polite in letters to Sir
Thomas Wilson, his patron in England, but evidently conscientious; he
knew no Spanish when he arrived but in due course became expert
according to the testimony of a friendly correspondent.[49] Also a member
of the ambassador's family was Dr. Alexander Chapman, who succeeded
Wadsworth as chaplain. Against him were no Protestant complaints and
on returning to England he could safely be recommended for preferment as chaplain to the Earl of Salisbury.[50] Finally, there was one
other Englishman of subordinate status, the outstanding traveller among
them all, an essential link with their own land, Walsingham Gresley,
who from 1605 to 1623 carried despatches and letters from Madrid to
London and back again to Madrid. He nearly always went by way of
Bayonne and Paris and it is impossible to say how many of these trips he
made over the whole period.[51] He was almost the only official English
messenger who left no letters, no bills and hardly a notice except his
name in other men's letters. At intervals he too would be at the embassy,
and was described as a good observer 'though not verie easie to be
broatched'; clearly the ideal messenger.[52]

Madrid, then, was the centre of public affairs for Englishmen as well
as for Spaniards; the ports along the coast of the Peninsula, from which
travellers came or through which they passed, were naturally second in
importance. In particular, a fair amount of English correspondence from
San Sebastian in the north-east has been preserved. The reason for this
is clear: the stretch of coastline from here to Bayonne — the central
section of Biscay — was also important as a route by land past the
Pyrenean barrier, the obvious road from Spain to France and the
northern countries including Spanish Flanders. It was therefore considered advisable by English statesmen to arrange for intelligence to be
transmitted from this vantage point. What exactly was the significance,
queried their man on the spot, of a messenger from Paris who requested
the Governor of Bayonne to delay, on any pretext, another messenger
bearing letters from Antwerp to Madrid who was travelling an hour or
two behind him? so that, while the Spaniard was detained, the man with
despatches from the French court hurried southwards to Madrid?[53] This
kind of question, and speculations concerning them, were of interest to
Salisbury in London. But the coast-road from France to San Sebastian
was also used in the seventeenth century, very naturally, by Englishmen
travelling into and out of Spain. It was the same observer on the spot,
one Richard Cocks, who noted that Lord Norris and Lord Willoughby
passed through the town on their way homeward towards Paris. In fact,

for all Englishmen who were neither diplomats nor merchants, and for many of these also, San Sebastian was the gateway into the Peninsula.

Five hundred miles to the south lay Andalusia; rich in its own right, and official port of entry to the greater riches of America. Seville, Cadiz, and Puerto S. Maria were magnets acting with irresistible force upon merchants and their shipping. The produce of the land, its wines and olives; the demands of the land, corn, fish and timber; the arrival there from America of treasure fleets: all this attracted the English. How many they might be, is a difficult question. At the end of 1605 one of the Earl of Essex's supporters during the late rebellion, Marsham, died far from home in Seville, and the ambassador believed that a hundred Englishmen accompanied his body out into the fields (for he died a Protestant), attending the burial.[54] Such a number may be a fair estimate of the traders and sailors who at that time would have been free and willing to meet together for so pathetic a ceremony. A characteristic example of their kind was young Peter Mundy, who arrived in Spain a little later and spent his first years of restless travel between 1611 and 1617 at San Lucar with an English weaver settled there, at Seville with another Englishman, and sometimes touched at other towns, Ayamonte, Castro Marim and Tavira. He was concerned in the trade of olive oil and pilchards and during this period relates that 'he attained the Spanish tongue'. After 1620 he appeared again in those parts, bringing pilchards to Seville and was involved in the business of a mysterious copper contract, of which no details remain.[55] Somewhat older was a man like Thomas Ferrers, a merchant who while at Ayamonte in April 1608 was arrested by the Inquisition and taken to Seville. He refused to subscribe to a confession presented to him by an English friar. His goods were confiscated and he lay in prison during the summer until the embassy secured his release and the return of his property.[56] By a curious stroke of irony in 1614 he presented to the Bodleian Library in Oxford a Spanish folio of Catholic theology, *Epistolas y Evangelios*, ex donatione Thomae Ferrers mercatoris Londinensis negotiantis in Hispaniam.[52] More important in the eyes of both English and Spanish officials was Neville Davis, of whom Cornwallis thought rather poorly, but he acted as consul and wrote regular reports direct to Salisbury: that English interlopers had unloaded so much corn in Spain and the trade could only continue at a loss, that several English merchants had left the city for a journey to Valladolid on legal business, or that he had been to the Commander of the Galleys with a Spanish royal warrant for the release of the captive Englishmen in his hands.[58]

These unfortunates, men who had been pirates or taken for pirates in European waters and beyond, were subject to no law. Their release was a question of fortune and grace. At the signing of a treaty, the entry of a new English ambassador into Madrid, his departure or the marriage of the King of Spain's daughter, that King as an act of grace sometimes signed a warrant granting their release. During the century, too, a distinction came to be drawn between men captured 'beyond the line' — for them an ambassador could only ask that they be kept from starving, at the King of Spain's charge — and those who were taken for illegalities committed or alleged to have been committed on the eastern side of it.[59] Here the ambassador had a better chance of securing outright liberation. No clear-cut principles of law or treatment governed the lives of these English galley-slaves. Prisoners of fortune working along the southern shores of Spain they formed part of the alien population there, demanding a certain remembrance because they impressed the contemporary imagination; and from 1605 to 1665, every ambassador from Sir Charles Cornwallis to Sir Richard Fanshawe concerned himself with them. Very often, fortunately, conditions were easier than at first sight appear. The haphazard nature of Spanish administration worked in favour of the prisoners. Fanshawe, while a young man, had in 1638 acted as Agent in Spain in the interval between the departure of Lord Aston and the arrival of a new ambassador in Sir Ralph Hopton, and one of his letters describes an odd procedure in Seville which certainly saved from the galleys two men taken in the West Indies, and for the time being imprisoned:

> The Consull of our nation in Sevill hath written to mee that the Judge of those matters there had lately sent for him, telling him that hee perceived the Counsell would take no resolution concerning these poore men, and therefore hee out of pitty of their case had commanded that they should have the freedome of the Prison, even as farre as the Street doore to talke with their Friends, with other such like words which seemd to intimate that Hee was willing they should make an escape and hee would connive at it. This the Consull making use of (finding likewise the Jaylor the same way inclind) gott them out and they are shipt for England. I have been the more particular to your Honour heerein because these men seemed to thinke my Lord Ambassador did nothing for them, and yet there is scarse any doubt to bee made but that the Counsell chose this way to satisfy his Lordship's importunities, beeing resolved (as I conceive) not to declare themselves eyther one way or other in a matter of that nature.[60]

Another incident shows how careless supervision favoured such prisoners as these. In November 1637 when the treasure fleet arrived, more captives from the West Indies were landed. In charge of the Englishmen was George Gage, a priest with money in his pocket, and Protestant doubts, who later published a famous book *The English-American, his Travel by Sea and Land* and was one of the voices influencing Oliver Cromwell's West Indian policy; at this point in his narrative he says that at San Lucar he went to the English Inn, in preference to his official cloister, together with the English prisoners.[61] Clearly, with such gaolers and guardians certain men did succeed in evading the worst of all lives in Spanish ports; even if some were drowned or taken in open fighting with piratical Turks and many more died in their chains, unknown folk for whom nothing had been or could be done.

It is difficult to give realistic account of the little English communities in the other ports. At Lisbon a reliable consul, Hugh Lee, was bullied by Spaniards and intermittently paid by his own compatriots for some fifteen years, 1605–1620.[82] Merchants's factors would be imprisoned on suspicion there and one of them wrote to Salisbury in 1606, with unconscious irony appealing for help 'to you and to your noble Family which ever Flourish in our Commonwealth'. At about the same time Rolles, a Catholic married to a Spanish lady, gave a dinner party at Lisbon and it was reported to the ambassador at Valladolid that sixteen English merchants and factors were present. They acclaimed their host's resolution that the King of England and his ambassador should be whipped for the preposterous terms of the peace,[63] and represented a fairly large group of traders. Of Corunna, on the other hand, there is hardly a mention. A little more activity gradually touched Malaga, Alicante and Barcelona; by 1620, quite a colony of Englishmen greeted the first English fleet to enter Mediterranean waters, at Malaga,[64] and in 1617 there is mention of a consul in the Balearic Islands.[65] These settlements grew as the century continued. For the moment it is sufficient to remember their isolated existence, appearing and reappearing in view as travellers moved from place and place.

One recurring event, rather like the vintage and the harvest, was usually of interest to the tiny groups of the English in Spain, the arrival and distribution of American treasure. News of a fleet's arrival from the Indies, anxiously awaited in the financial and political centres of half Europe, was first known in Andalusia and Castile. For those on the spot, as accurate a guess as possible at the amount of bullion and specie imported on each occasion, and the proportions belonging to private interests and to the crown, were matters of the greatest importance. Year after year the English embassy at Madrid would secure figures, and send copies of the bills of lading home to the secretaries of state. In 1611, annotating these, Sir John Digby argued that the long continued peace between Spain and its neighbours, together with the financial recovery implicit in the movement of so much treasure into the country, made Spain the more attractive as a possible ally. Or if a young gentleman travelled into Spain for general pleasure and instruction, Digby wrote to Salisbury: 'I am now perswading him to take a journy to Sevill that he may see the maner and ordering of the West Indian fleet and treasure.'[66] Nothing in Europe could be more exciting for the traveller, and more instructive. Not only larger political questions, in which differences between the dowry of the Habsburg and other royal princesses affected the trend of dynastic ambition in England and France, but an ordinary merchant's calculation of annual profit and his hopes that a debt would

18.   The fame of Seville: a print produced for an Amsterdam publisher, c. 1650–60.

be paid, might well hinge on the punctual arrival and the size of the
treasure fleet. Hardwon decisions in the Spanish courts providing compensation to English suitors often stipulated that money would be paid
when the fleet came in, or that a third would be paid on the arrival of
three successive fleets, or that interest on such debts was due for
payment annually — when the fleet came in. English traders met with
most difficulty in the early years of the century. The peace treaty offered
a basis for lawful commerce and both sides reverted to what they
claimed to be the current practice, and their rights, enjoyed before the
war. These often appeared obsolete in 1605. The English hardly knew
the market they were now trying to re-enter. Spanish local officials obeyed
sluggishly the orders and decisions on individual cases, emanating from
the central authority, although the ambassador in Madrid might believe
that his representations at court on a particular issue had been successful. In spite of these difficulties official papers leave the impression that

in the longer run the English trading interest prospered. Imprisonment, repudiation of debts, requisitions, and arbitrary fiscal levies became no more than a fraction of the total story. A renewal of the warfare betwen the Habsburg crown, the Dutch, and the French offered further opportunities. Spain acquiesced in, and partially depended on, stable English trading communities at its ports.

When in 1664 Sir Richard Fanshawe and his lady landed at Cadiz, passing through Seville on their ambassadorial way to Madrid, polite groups of English merchants came to greet them. Those of Cadiz presented two silver basins and ewers with a hundredweight of chocolate and crimson and taffeta cloths — all from the Indies. Those of Seville brought chocolate, sugar, napkins, a silver pot and salvers and twelve silver cups. Those from Malaga gave a horse worth £300.[67] Such gifts perhaps convinced a new ambassador that the English trading interest in Andalusia deserved his favorable attention when he reached Madrid. As a response, it must be admitted that the new Anglo-Spanish commercial treaty of 1667 did indeed carry further the protection and encouragement of this interest which was barely formulated in the treaty of 1604. The English merchants of Andalusia had firmly established themselves.

An example of the goodwill which Nottingham's great embassy fostered or revived comes from the history of the Porter family.[68] It is well known that the secret or semi-secret negotiations between England and Spain, and the Prince of Wales's journey to Madrid, are connected with the career of Endymion Porter, the ageing courtier of Charles I so suavely depicted by William Dobson; but his youth and his origins, also, were 'spagnolized'.

In 1605, soon after landing, the Earl of Notttingham noticed the gratifying fluency of his interpreter Giles Porter; and both the Earl and Sir Charles Cornwallis mention him with praise in their despatches.[69] The truth was that Porter had already performed a long Spanish apprenticeship. Before the wars he is said to have been a member of an English embassy in Spain, and he certainly married a Spanish lady Juana de Figueroa y Mont Salve. The middle years of his life left hardly a trace in historical records but, in March 1583, the Spanish ambassador in London wrote home that 'an English gentleman Giles Porter who is married in Seville and a good Catholic and faithful adherent of your Majesty' had made a vow to go to Jerusalem, and the ambassador requested him to observe the diplomacy of the English in the Levant and report to agents of the Spanish Crown.[70] If this was our Giles Porter he later returned to England and in the year of the Armada was living in Gloucestershire, at Mickleton, on the family estate. Since his eldest son Luis spent some time in the Spanish diplomatic service, it is fair to surmise that the latter had grown up in Spain; Luys's sisters Angela and

Lucina came to England. Angela married a cousin, and Endymion her son was born in 1587. In due course, when contemporary writers discussed Endymion Porter they asserted that he had passed his youth in Spain.[71] It seems unlikely that he left England before accompanying his grandfather Giles in the Earl of Nottingham's mission, aged eighteen; with them travelled his younger brother Tom. The family, half English and half Spanish, then resumed a mediatory position between the two countries, crossing the seas and frontiers with indifference to difficulties which made other men hesitate. Giles was in Valladolid in 1605, as we have seen. In July 1607 it was stated in a despatch that he had recently left England again for Spain by sea, and he arrived during the autumn.[72] In January 1608 Giles Porter wrote to his son-in-law describing how he had been two months in Madrid, vainly attempting to hasten a suit in the lawcourts concerning property to which he had a claim through his wife's family.[73] He was being assisted by a kinsman of his wife who, at the moment of writing, had gone away to Segorbe 'where lyttell Thom is with the bysshop' (and the bishop was another kinsman to whom Juana Porter had given a power of attorney). Evidently the Porters were still on intimate terms with their Spanish relatives and a long war had only interrupted this familiarity. In January 1610 the English resident Cottington wrote home that Porter was still following his suit, and every day more hopefully. He thought that the matter would end in a satisfactory compromise between the parties.[74] However, when the new ambassador Sir John Digby arrived the suit was still continuing; 'Mr. Porter and Mr. Cawley, old suitors', were daily in consultation with members of the embassy, as one of their number reported. In March 1612 Porter was living in the ambassador's house; a judgment had at length been delivered, deferring the question of possession to a further trial. The old man made up his mind to return to England, and by 23 May he was no longer in Madrid.[75]

'Little Tom' became a captain in the English navy, often employed where a knowledge of Spanish was useful. He took part in Sir Robert Mansell's expedition against the pirates of Algiers in 1620–1621, when English ships were based on Spanish harbours. He transported Sir Walter Aston the ambassador over to Spain in 1635. When James Howell arrived in that country he soon took the opportunity to write to his old friend Tom Porter: 'I remembered I had heard you often discoursing how you received part of your education there which brought you to speak Spanish so exactly well: I think often of the Relations I have heard you make of this country, and the good instruction you pleased to give me.'[76]

Meanwhile Endymion had passed the early years of his manhood in Spain. When the Earl of Bristol, defying Charles and Buckingham, wished to damage the testimony of Porter against his own conduct of the negotiations for Charles's marriage with the Infanta Maria he sent in a questionnaire, which began by asking whether Endymion Porter had not been a servant of Olivares, and the servant of Cawleigh, a merchant.[77] It is not possible to amplify the bare statement — for in the circumstances Bristol's question hardly permits of a negative response — that Porter must have spent some time in the service of the man who later became the leading Spanish statesman. When in 1629 Cottington wrote to Porter from Madrid, 'I delivered your letters to the Conde and his Lady who were both very glad to hear from you and asked me a thousand questions concerning you all expressing their love and their care towards you',[78] this may have been the usual courtesy between diplomats who had dealt together during the Spanish Marriage episode, but it also refers to a longer and more intimate acquaintance. To the Stuarts Porter appeared indispensable when they wished to negotiate confidentially with the Spanish court; but he was only a nonentity in negotiating with other governments. His early experiences abroad helped to determine his political affiliations.

Regarding Cawleigh, the merchant whom Porter was said to have served in his youth, a few more details can be added. He was one of those business men who spent many years in Mardrid attempting to secure payment for a large contract, cloth for the Spanish armed forces which he had delivered in Flanders. He arrived at Madrid in 1607 when Giles Porter also appeared and, as we have seen, their names were linked together as claimants who required Sir John Digby's assistance in their suits. Cawleigh was suspected of Catholic leanings by the English officials, for he had begun by negotiating with the Spaniards through the English Jesuits in Madrid. Toby Mathew the convert and George Gage, who had come from Italy in 1609, lodged in his house.[79] In the same year Cottington wrote.[80] 'For myn opinione, the poore man ys much gone in Papistry and tells me playnly he wyll not take the last oath [the Oath of Allegiance as worded after 1605], but sayes he intends to goe againe to Church in England at his cuming home.' Cawleigh was evidently adapting himself of life in Spain, as did Cottington himself later on. In the same report Cottington added rather gloomily that he hoped to be no longer in Spain when this particular merchant was finally paid. In fact, a settlement appears to have been reached in 1614 after intervention by Digby and the Spanish ambassador in London.

Such were the lives of Endymion Porter's relatives and acquaintances in Spain, and the background of his own career. After years spent in Olivares' household, or with his grandfather and members of his grandmother's family, or with Cawleigh the petitioning merchant, he returned to England and ultimately found service with George Villiers then rising into favour at court. He brought with him a knowledge of Spain and a predisposition to support an active diplomacy with that country, if his master saw fit: in that direction lay employment and with employment, riches and influence. In 1622, in a ship commanded by his brother, he sailed over to France. The vessel ran ashore outside Calais in a storm and he was injured jumping overboard. But hurrying on to Madrid he carried with him an official despatch setting a limit to the concessions James I was prepared to make for a Spanish match, and a letter from Buckingham to Gondomar proposing that Prince Charles himself should go at once to Madrid, if Gondomar approved of the scheme. It was a responsible mission for Porter. Next year he went again, in company with Charles and Buckingham; and then after the collapse of the nego-tiations, and during the final stages of the Spanish war, it was Porter who travelled to Rome and Madrid to begin the secret discussions for the restoration of peace.

In the following decade he lived as Dobson painted him: portly, affable and refined. He was still corresponding with Spanish friends and Englishmen in Spain, importing wine and swordblades, marmalade and gloves, or reminding officials there of certain enquiries made by Lord Arundel for drawings of Michael Angelo. He sent his own sons to Spain and it must have gratified him to learn from Sir Arthur Hopton that Philip Porter was very well and proved a gallant youth and would be of his father's growth.[81] Certainly in the civil wars the family fortunes declined with the royal cause, Endymion retired to Flanders, his sons were killed or changed sides or turned ruffian; but his own personality had borne the stamp of the family's two-fold origin, and the 'servant' from Spain with a specialized ability in gratifying noble or royal patrons met the need for useful men with this continental experience. He was not a Royalist like Sir Edmund Verney, a more independently minded courtier who had been with him in Spain in 1623. He belonged, rather, to the significant group of people who assimilated from Catholic Europe a notion of absolute princely government tempered both by privilege and the possibilities of court intrigue.

In concluding this study of one Anglo-Spanish family reference can be made to another, whose history is fragmentary but comparable with theirs. In March 1605 Giles Porter received a letter from Sir Thomas Tresham, the noted recusant and landowner.[82] Tresham asked Porter, because of his familiarity with Spanish and Spanish affairs, to keep a fatherly eye on Lewis, Sir Thomas's second son, who was also going to Spain with the Nottingham embassy. Lewis had recently married Maria, stepdaughter of Alderman More of London; Maria's mother was born of the marriage of an English merchant in Seville and a Spanish lady, while her father was a Spaniard Alonso Perez de Recalde; Lewis and Maria Tresham had claims in Spain on the property of her dead father's family. Lewis made the journey and returned with Lord Norris and Dudley Carleton through France,[83] apparently without having won his point in this dispute. Twelve years later he still found it worth while to draw up a detailed account of the claim,[84] and accompanied Sir John Digby on another embassy to the Spanish capital.[85] In 1623 he was again in Madrid. Little enough is known about the rest of his life but it is permissible to rank him with the Porters as a representative of the type most repugnant to Protestant gentry in the Commons. His elder brother Francis had been executed for complicity in Gunpowder Plot.[86] A younger brother William spent many years in Flanders fighting for the King of Spain. A sister, Lady Webb, was killed on the notorious occasion in 1623 when the floor of an upper room collapsed under the weight of an illegal Catholic meeting in Clerkenwell. But Lewis stated that he himself was not a Catholic, though neighbouring J.P.s clearly suspected the opposite.[87] His life was spent partly at court doubtless looking out for small grants or pickings from time to time, partly in Northamptonshire, where in 1615 the ambassadors of Spain and the Archdukes visited him during a summer progress. Gondomar came again in 1620.[88] For Sir Lewis Tresham, at least, embassies to Spain could never be inopportune; and Protestant antipathies held no meaning.

Besides private noblemen and merchants and merchants' servants, whatever they might in time become, there were the acknowledged servants of the state going backwards and forwards between London and Madrid. Travel was not the least arduous part of diplomacy.

In the early seventeenth century, a special messenger on the overland route expected to reach Seville twenty-four days after leaving London during the summer months. In winter he took thirty days. The ordinary post rode from Paris to the Spanish frontier in four an a half days, from the frontier to Valladolid in two days and arrived in Seville four days later. In winter the time was correspondingly longer.[89] These were very rough assumptions. The uncertainty of communications, the fortunate chance of a special messenger or traveller, the expense, the need to send duplicate letters by alternative messengers and routes, were all considerations emphasized in a larger number of official despatches. Meanwhile the ambassadors themselves moved with corresponding difficulty, at a slower pace, to their stations abroad or back again.

In 1609 Sir Charles Cornwallis obtained his recall and on 7 September he left Madrid. A secretary who returned with him described in a letter home how they began the long journey. Whatever the truculent arrogance of the Spanish nobility, he said, there was no denying the good-will of ordinary citizens who crowded into the streets as the ambassador's litter went by for the last time. They had respected Cornwallis and now they wished him health and prosperity, exclaiming that his company were 'gente de paz, muy honrada gente'.[90] All the Englishmen in the city who could come, except of course the Catholics, accompanied the party, some riding and some on foot, as far as the first night's lodging at Alcovendas. Their regrets were the more heartfelt

because the ambassador's residence had been for them a refuge and a
restaurant, the ambassador a man who protected them and fought for
their interests. At Alcovendas they finally said goodbye. The travellers
moved northwards along the normal route to France, and at Aranda
Cornwallis expressed himself as he usually did, cursing the poor lodgings and worse diet, feeling convinced (he wrote) that he was fitter for a
hospital than such a journey. On the 14th they reached Lerma. Ten days
later he was outside Bordeaux and thought it prudent to forward to
England a duplicate of the letter he had written from Aranda, adding an
item of news which interested everyone: 'A Correo sent... in post into
Italy hath here overtaken me who adviseth the arryval of the Indyan
fleete loden with 12 myllyons for the Kyng and for partyculars, and
goeth on purpose to carry the good tydings to Myllan, Naples and
Sycylya.' By 17 October he was at Dieppe, where he remained a month,
delayed by bad weather, but the particulars he had received in a message
from Cottington concerning the expulsion of the Moriscoes — an event
of the highest importance — he forwarded by a more expeditious
messenger to Lord Salisbury; and this messenger was also to discover
from Lady Cornwallis or his son Thomas where the returning ambassador could lodge in England: he would expect their reply in the
posthouse at Gravesend when he arrived there. At last, the embassy to
Spain was over.[91]

His successor Sir John Digby also preferred to travel through France.
With him came his wife Beatrice and her son by a first marriage, Lewis
Dyves, the well known Royalist commander in the civil wars.[92] Among
his servants and companions, many of whom went by sea to San
Sebastian, were John Sanford of Magdalen College, Oxford where
Digby had been a student, and James Mabbe, Fellow of the same
college.[93] In this year, 1611, Sanford dedicated to Lady Digby his new
book, *An Entrance into the Spanish Tongue* — 'a means of conciliation of
love amongst those with whom, for a time, you have to live' — and
distributed copies to other members of the embassy. Mabbe's literary
work first appeared many years later, his translations of Spanish picaresque stories, *Celestina, Don Guzman de Alfarache* and the Exemplary
Novels of Cervantes. The ambassador's steward was Rossingham, who
in 1612 returned to England 'so Spagnolized' that one person at least
failed to recognize him.[94]

Digby duly arrived at San Sebastian on 7 May 1611, some time after
the ship bringing his company and household goods. Then their troubles
began. The searchers and the officers of the Inquisition claimed the
right to search all goods, and while awaiting the ambassador's arrival,
these were stored in a warehouse and guarded by Spanish officials.
Digby, when he came, refused to allow any search or inspection as a part
of his ambassadorial privilege. Everyone settled down to wait for the
King of Spain's order which Cottington, always the faithful resident,

was to forward from Madrid: this would exempt the goods from search. In the meantime Rossingham the steward was travelling toward the court to arrange for lodgings on the way and, with Cottington, for a suitable house in the capital. Digby, at San Sebastian, noticed that the officials there were friendly while the English merchants 'in this place live quietly and without complaint'. The ship which took his letter of 8 May to England was the *Angel* of Barnstaple.[95]

At last the order from the King to his searchers reached the port, and the whole company set out. Then also, the rains began and it rained for a month. Rivers could not be forded at the usual points. The longer the journey the higher the cost of all the mules and carriage. On 4 June they struggled into Alcovendas to learn that the house in Madrid granted by the King of Spain for the use of Digby and his family was still occupied by the Persian ambassador. This difficulty caused further delay until the authorities finally obtained 'a convenient house with a fair garden'.

It is worth adding to this account the bill sent to the royal exchequer for the costs of the expedition.:[96]

> Sr John Digby knight his Majesties Ambassadour resident with the King of Spayne humbly craveth allowance ffor loading and shipping of all his howshold stuff that went by Sea to St. Sebastians.                    £12
>
> ffor the hire of a Ship called the Dewty and her charges to St. Sebastians with divers of his people and howshold stuff                    £72
>
> ffor the charge of horses and Coaches from London to Dover, for the hire of two Barkes, ffor the transportation of his Coache, his horses and people, ffor reward of the Ships that carried over himself unto Deipe. As likewise the charge of horses Coach and carriages from Deipe unto St. Sebastians in Spayne                    £457
>
> ffor the disimbarking of Stuffe, duties at the landing at St. Sebastians. As likewise for the Carriage of all his howshold stuff by Moyles. Moyles of mounture for his trayne which were detayned thirtie three daies betwixt St. Sebastians and Madrid. As likewise for Coach and horses for himself                    £391
>
> Given unto the Kings Officers for duties and fees belonging unto them from everie Ambassadour upon his first Audience                    £38
>
> The whole Summe amounteth unto £970.
>
> [Signed] Jhon Digbye

This money was paid to Digby by the end of the year. His entertainment as resident ambassador amounted to £6 a day £2 more than used to be allowed to men sent into Spain in Elizabethan days before the war. This large increase was warranted by the continuing inflation in the country and the high costs of goods, at which all ambassadors exclaimed. These rates did not alter up to the time of the English civil wars. In addition, Digby claimed £125 for 'intelligence' every three months. But security of payment from the embarrassed exchequer, like the security of communications, was shadowy and unreliable.[97] An embassy, after long and troublesome journeys through distant countries, usually lived on hopes and credit. Routine went dully forward. Life's incidents bordered upon it. The chaplain performed daily service in the little chapel. The ambassador interviewed the Spanish authorities on this or that political question and returned to his house to dictate reports to the secretaries; among them was his cousin, Simon Digby, a man fated to spend many years in spain and a still more distant future as agent in Russia in Caroline times. Lady Digby gave birth to one child, who died, and then in 1612 to a boy who became the second Earl of Bristol. He certainly was brought up in Spain and retained all through his career a predilection for Catholic alliances and monarchical government. Cottington, likewise, remained in Madrid until August 1611, and Digby commented on 'his industry which (to do him right) is as much as I ever found in any'.[98]

The year 1616 found these diplomats once again on the road. Cottington, returning from England complained of a terrible journey in the depths of winter, nine days at sea and deep snow in Spain. He found Digby very ill and entirely ignorant of a previous order for his recall, for with civil commotions in France the overland post never reached Madrid.[99] Moreover, he had no money, having received nothing from the exchequer for over a year. Digby, when Cottington arrived at once went to take leave of Philip III and sent to the English merchants at Seville for credit. He already owed large sums in Madrid. At the end of February he set out, leaving his wife behind to await the spring and easier travelling. No details of his journey survive. Of Lady Digby a little more is known. She left in April and next month some idea of her troubles reached England.

My Ladie Digbie pressing toward St. Anderas over the mountaynes in Austurias, divers of the mules that carryed her stuff fell from the high rock of a great height into a ryver wher her stuff lay halfe a day under water and [much] of it was spoyled to a great valew, wherwith the poore ladie ys much trubled I heare. Some of the moyles died with the falle.[100]

Digby, in future embassies, travelled without his wife.

Sir Charles Cornwallis and Sir John Digby were James I's principal representatives at Madrid. His son entrusted the same post to Sir Walter Aston and Sir Arthur Hopton. What were their arrangements for travelling from one court to another?

From 1620 until 1638, except when the two countries entered into half-hearted war after the breakdown of Charles's marriage project, Aston was the ordinary English resident ambassador at Madrid. A wealthy man of no great distinction, popular with Charles, he filled the post competently. In the end he began to feel tired and ill, and in December 1637 wrote asking for his recall. The King appointed Hopton, who had been earlier in Spain as ambassador's agent and secretary, to succeed him. Such an exchange, over a thousand miles of sea and land, did not prove simple. Hopton began by pleading for the greatest possible despatch, having no desire to travel in the dog-days of summer. He also expressed alarm at a proposal to economise on his allowance, which would reduce it once again to the Elizabethan level of £4 a day. The level of payment had been raised in Cornwallis's time to meet an increase in the costs of living, and now bread and mutton, wine and barley in Madrid cost three times as much again. It would shame the King his master, Hopton wrote, for the ambassador to maintain his embassy in such a beggarly style. While this honest indignation blew into Whitehall, the Secretary of State was arranging for Aston to return on the ship which would first carry Hopton to Corunna in Galicia.[101] Merchants in Lisbon were expressing thanks and gratitude to the retiring ambassador for his labour in their interests. Merchants of London trading to Spain and Portugal petitioned the King, meanwhile, that his new representative should obtain some remedy for their lawsuits pending in Spanish courts.[102] During the month of May both Aston and Hopton made their final preparations. The first carriages and sumpter mules with Aston's baggage were already on their way through Old Castile, on the westward roads to Galicia. He himself was busy staving off a Venetian ambassador and his wife who wished to go to England and share the convenience of a ship returning. He rather regretted, now at the last moment, that he was leaving Spain and wrote wistfully of coming out again if his health should ever mend.[103] On 27 May, everything was ready and he wrote his final letter from Madrid.[104]

> Right Honorable
> This morning abowte 11 of the clock I receaved this king's dispatches; and I am now going to putt myself into my litter, yt I may loose no time in my jorney; though itt be late, my health not verie good and I no great lover of night jorneys. We have as yet no news of Sir Arthur Hopton's arrivall so yt although my stay hath beene longer in this court then I expected I hope it wilbe without prejudice or any detention of his Majesty's Shipp. God-willing I hope to be in the Groighne within 30 dayes, which beeing what I have att present to advertise unto your honour, leaving all other occurents to Mr. Fanshaw's relation with the tender of my service I rest
>                                    Your honour's
>                                    most humble servant
>                                    WALTER ASTON.
> Madrid. 27 of May.
>    1638 st:lo:

On that very day Sir Arthur Hopton wrote his own letter of departure from Plymouth.[105] The double journey was now beginning in good earnest.

> May it please your honour
> I arrived here on the 16th and found the kinge's ship expecting my comeing and a faire winde, which shee now hath. But they say it is not the use of the kinge's shipes to put to sea but in a setled weather, soe if the winde

shall continue where it is till to morrow morning I thinke wee shall waigh
ancor, for I finde the Captaine and the Master very carefull dilligent men and
in mee they shall find no lett.

I hope I shall not stay here soe long as to write any more. I must therfore
take my leave of Ingland with my humble thanks to your Honour for all your
favours, and to beseech you to continue mee in your good opinion which I
will deserve if I can. God almighty blesse your Honour with all happinesse.

Your honour's most humble servant

ARTHUR HOPTON.

Plimouth May 17 [27 n.s.] 1638.
This morning the 18th the winde stands faire and I am presently going
abroad. God speed us.
Mr. Sec. Coke.

Hopton detested the voyage, the stormy passage of a fortnight with his
ship driven sixty miles too far east. He landed at Corunna on 1 June.[106]
Sometime earlier he had planned, as a nice point of economical arrangement, that Aston should arrive there first, enabling him to make use of
the returning traveller's mules and carriages for his own journey. Aston,
on the other hand, a sick man, did not desire to reach a desolate
uncomfortable port with no proper lodging before his ship came into
harbour; so Hopton before leaving London sent a courier to Madrid to
hire and send the necessary transports into Galicia — where none were
obtainable. These had been waiting some weeks, an expense in itself.
Hopton sent forward his baggage and servants, stayed a night or two in
the Governor's house, chatted with the sergeant-major of Tyrconnel's
Irish regiment, soldiers of the King of Spain fearing shipment for service in Brazil, and then began his own journey. The two ambassadors
met at Villafranca, some days travel inland;[107] Hopton reached Madrid
at the beginning of July, although parts of the baggage straggled behind.
He was pleased to meet old friends, and gradually, he says, recovered
from his journey. The heavy bill, which Mr. David Mathew his 'correspondent' presented to the Secretary of State in London, he excused on
the ground that the mules from Madrid were delayed at Corunna while
he was delayed in England: travelling by way of Santander, as he had
desired, was simple and cheaper. Sir Walter Aston meanwhile landed at
Plymouth and he also wrote petitioning that a pension which he used to
enjoy before he became ambassador might be renewed. He still felt a
sick man.[108]

At a time when war between France and Spain made the overland
journey more hazardous than earlier, and English merchants in San
Sebastian were quitting the town as the French drew nearer, this was the
manner in which one ambassador replaced another in Madrid. At about
the same time the old respect which these men felt for Spanish imperial
power first began to fade. Some who knew Spain at close quarters
suspected after 1635 that the long continued campaigning of the Habs-

burgs in Flanders. Germany and Italy was straining the Spanish economy and constitution as never before. There is a gap between Cornwallis's and Digby's opinion of Spain, compounded of contempt, suspicion and admiration for its universal influence — between such a view and Hopton's words when Catalonia broke out in rebellion and French armies threatened to invade Castile: 'Ill-success would put the affairs of this Crown in a worse case than were fit for the State of Christendom, which begins already to be unequally balanced.'[109] Not the strength, but the weakness, of Spain now appeared more dangerous. A sensible observer, he was anticipating one of the conventional judgments on the balance of power in Europe held later in the century.

# 11. PRIVATE AND COMMERCIAL TRAVELLERS, AND ENGLISH ECCENTRICS IN SPAIN

It will be clear that the difficulties of travel in Spain were sufficient to preoccupy every diplomat bound for Madrid. The difficulties which faced private travellers can have been no less, but in this case the records are scattered and scarce;[1] and it must be concluded that few people, of all the Englishmen who toured on the continent in this period, ventured over the Pyrenees. A journey into Spain with no other purpose than the desire for pleasurable instruction involved notorious disadvantages and discomforts which evidently deterred a majoity; it had none of the prestige attaching to the tour round France or the inspection of Italian cities. An English diplomat stationed in Madrid lamented bitterly to a colleague in the Low Countries that he so rarely saw his own country-men, while elsewhere in Europe they travelled in force.[2] However, instances occasionally appear, showing that a certain number came as far as Madrid where they spent some time. In March 1607 a member of the embassy household reported that Mr. Altham, Sir H. Mildmay and Mr. Tomkys. Fellow of Trinity College, Cambridge had arrived at the capital, having travelled by way of Bayonne. They intended to visit Lisbon, Seville and Barcelona on a tour of the country.[3] In 1617 Cottington states that 'Mr. Carew, son of Sir George Carew, and Mr. Grey (a very rich gentleman from the north)' had reached Madrid.[4] About the same time Nicholas Ferrar, who had already seen something of the Low Countries, Germany and Italy, was also in Spain. In 1622 Aston wrote of Mr. Scott (an English gentleman out of Yorkshire) then in Madrid.[5] About ten years later an aristocratic party, Sir John Dormer afterwards Earl of Carnarvon, Richard Fanshawe, and William Russell heir to the fourth Earl of Bedford, travelled from Paris to Madrid in order to learn Spanish;[6] Fanshawe was in due course to be justly celebrated for his translations from Spanish and Portuguese, as well as becoming first an ambassador's secretary and then ambassor in Madrid. In the sixteen-thirties, also, the sons of Endymion Porter and the sons of Secretary Windebank appeared there. The Windebanks, who did not come to-gether, were certainly engaged on a general tour round western Europe.

In February 1641 Charles Cavendish, brother of the Earl of Devonshire, was reported from Madrid as 'thus farr on his way homeward from a long peregrination whereof I believe he hath reaped good fruite'. Two of the Earl of Kingston's sons were likewise there at the same date.[7] In the winter of 1662 Henry Savile, Robert Lord Sunderland and Henry Sidney, who had all previously seen much of the continent, were in Madrid — 'we have been in this town a week which seems already to be a year; so wretched and miserable a place are we got into', where there was so little to do that they determined to learn Spanish in their own defence.[8] To such parties as these, and there must have been others of whom no record remains, may be added the young men of good family who accompanied extraordinary ambassadors from the English to the Spanish court, and the great but temporary exodus from England in the footsteps of Prince Charles in 1623.

A less ambitious expedient for the traveller to Spain was simply to interrupt a tour round France and spend a few days on the southern side of the Pyrenees. In 1648 an anonymous gentleman made what his companion or servant called 'an incursion into Catalonia' from Languedoc, before going on to Italy. This particular account gives a few details describing the way from France into Spain. Thus, already at Toulouse the travellers thought they detected a Spanish seriousness of demeanour in the inhabitants. They noticed the great fortifications at Narbonne and Perpignan, and crossed over the mountains to Girona and from there to Barcelona, which they found more beautiful than any of the French cities except for Paris. They inspected the sights of the place, especially the Arsenal, and the palace where the Cortes assembled; it is possible to catch a glimpse of the seventeenth-century Englishman collecting stray information about political conditions abroad in the following comment from the journal of these travellers.[9]

> Neither to the King of Spaine, nor to the King of France now, is any other title given than Count of Catalonia, and the Parliament or counsell men did in the presence of the King of Spain, and doe now in the presence of the King of France, put on their hatts. This I was tould by a Catalonian of good condition.

But their journey's end in Spain was a few leagues further on, at Montserrat, where the great treasury guarded by the monks extorted their enthusiasm and admiration; and then they returned quickly towards France, the diarist concluding this section of his account with a few conventional remarks on the differences between the French and Spanish characters. He rather respected the Spaniards in spite of French hostility. At this date, of course, Catalonia was occupied by the French and the journey had not involved the dangers of crossing a frontier in wartime, a difficulty which must have halted many peaceable travellers at or near the Pyrenees between 1635 and 1660.

Not until 1664 is there a respectable and well-known record of a private gentleman's tour into Spain, a record which was published soon afterwards. Francis Willughby the naturalist had travelled round Europe with a party of friends, seeing the Low Countries, Germany, Italy and France. He could not persuade them to accompany him to less familiar territory, and in August 1664 left Montpellier, and took the road leading west and south: 'a very bad way among desolate mountains after many hours riding' was his description of the journey past the Pyrenees into Spain. In the course of a ten weeks' tour he proceeded to visit Barcelona, Valencia, Granada, Seville, Cordova, Madrid and Vittoria. His interests were largely scientific, the plants, minerals and craftsmen's techniques of the countryside through which he travelled. Montserrat he passed by at a distance, and dismissed in a sentence; the religious disposition of the Spaniards was a matter for comment, but not for imitation nor yet for violently Protestant attack. He certainly considered himself a member of a new, forward looking generation which had nothing to learn from Spain; and the Spaniards, he found, took little interest in the intellectual world beyond their frontiers. Here are his comments on the city and university of Valencia:[10]

> As we passed through the Market-place at Valencia all the people shouted at us, and threw parings of melons etc. on our cloaks. It seems they are not used to see strangers and travellers there. This was the first place in Spain where we were searched. In this City is an University. I heard a Professor read Logic. The scholars are sufficiently insolent and very disputacious. One of them asked me, Quid est Ens universale? and whether I was of Thomas Aquinas his opinion: another, Quid est Genus? None of them understood anything of the new Philosophy or had so much as heard of it. None of the new books to be found in any of their Booksellers shops: In a word the University of Valencia is just where our Universities were 100 years ago.

With this, and many similar impressions, Willughby returned to Montpellier.

With him we have obviously passed on to a period when travel into Spain was, for the private gentleman, nothing more than a private adventure, nor was he concerned with the prospects of ultimate political advancement. But in the earlier years of the seventeenth century, Salisbury, Cornwallis and Digby still held to the view that an Englishman in Spain, if he was not a servant of theirs on a political errand or a genuine merchant, required supervision because travel in a country so notoriously uncomfortable seemed to denote special affiliations religious and personal, and these could easily have political consequences.

In the case of Lord Roos, grandson and heir of the Earl of Exeter, and Salisbury's great-nephew, they believed this with added vehemence. Roos, like Lord Cranborne in France a year earlier, prudently kept a journal while travelling through Spain in 1610 and he then sent this to

Salisbury as a proof of his good intentions during the journey. It is also valuable as one of the few accounts of touring a country rarely visited.

In May 1605 Roos had obtained a licence to travel abroad for three years[11] and whether or not this was renewed he spent the greater part of ten years in wandering over the Continent. In that part of their letters reserved for lesser news of the day correspondents would note that Lord Roos was now in Paris, that Lord Roos was coming up from the south of France, that he was in Florence, Rome and Naples,[12] his name continually cropped up in such reports, by which Salisbury kept his eye on the movements of important Englishmen abroad. On 2 November 1609 Lord Roos arrived in Madrid. Cottington, then agent in the absence of an ambassador, was glad to welcome a relative of the Lord Treasurer.[13] Late that same night he wrote to London saying that the traveller could live in his own very commodious house and spend the winter there, learning the language as he wished to do. During the next few months Cottington mentioned Roos regularly in his reports, considering that he had not before 'observed so much gravytie, discretion and sound judgment in so young a man',[14] although the circle of Roos's acquaintances struck him rather unfavorably. At first it was true, Roos refused to talk with any of the English priests or fugitives except Sir John Fearne. Then he met his old friend Toby Mathew who had been with him at Florence and had recently arrived in Madrid with Sir Robert Sherley. Neither Mathew, nor Sherley were viewed approvingly by Salisbury who was alarmed by such intelligence. In February 1610 he wrote ordering his relative to leave Spain at once.[15] However, it was not until July that Roos crossed the frontier at Bayonne, where he and his companions completed a long apology to Salisbury which took the form of an account of Lord Roos's travels in Spain.[16]

It is quite a thoughtful piece of writing. Friends or secretaries, of whom nothing can be traced, may have supplied some of the knowledge but many of the sentences sound like a man recording his own impressions. One page survives written in Roos's own hand, probably a part of the original draft.

The author began by protesting that he was at a loss to understand why he had been ordered to leave Spain. His licence for four years' travel never excluded that country. It was very necessary to visit so important a dominion because hatred of Spain felt by others, and Spanish patriotism, were both excessive. 'The desire and love of truth drewe mee into that contrie, as the sence of my duetie to your Lordship drewe me out of it soe soone. That which happened unto me in the meane tyme which was a mater of seven moneths...I will presume to lay at your Lordships feet.'

Coming from Italy and leaving France after the heats of the year were over, he went from the French fortress town of Narbonne to Perpignan, a citadel built after the pattern of the famous Milanese fortifications.

Few English people entered Spain on this Mediterranean side of the Pyrenees, either going through Bayonne or, from the south, coming by sea from Genoa — like Toby Mathew and Robert Sherley in this same autumn of 1609. Lord Roos arrived at Barcelona and praises the fair, quiet seaside, the thickly populated city and the background of hills gradually rising as they receded inland. Fortifications only fronted the sea, where the galleys lay which scoured the coast against the Turks. He learnt here that were few very rich men and few poor, the government was good, the ground fertile and the glass-works and the glass were second only to the Venetian. On he went, to Lerida, Saragossa — 'the head Cittie of Aragone and a Cittle of great delicacie and Regalo', substantially built of brick with many stately churches and monasteries and hospitals — Alcalá de Henares, well known for divinity schools (Wadsworth, we may remember, spent some time there) and finally, Madrid. Here he spent the winter, chattering with Toby Mathew and making acquaintance with the Spanish court life. He did not think much of the city; nobody did. It was 'a tent for the Court', the houses jumbled together and unpleasing in appearance, which 'men of all conditions have built for ease in following their suits'. One of Roos's difficulties here was his perennial lack of money, troublesome to a man of lavish extravagance. His grandfather had given orders to Van Lore, the well-known merchant in London to enable Roos to draw on a certain Fleming, Maximilian Van Hulft, at Madrid for £178.15, then £100 at Easter and a further £100 at the end of three months. The Fleming however refused to proceed with this arrangement on the ground that no money was coming into Spain from Flanders. Roos appealed to Cottington. Cottington went round the town, discovered that Roos's credit had already sunk very low, but finally borrowed £100 from a friend on bills payable by Exeter's steward, underwritten by Cottington.[17] About this time Salisbury's letter of recall arrived. With a little ready money in his pocket Roos determined to spend it and see the country before returning. His excuses were transmitted to England: before coming to Spain he knew what travel meant, he said to Cottington, and the Lord Treasurer need not fear that he would be too much in love with the country.

Leaving Madrid on 3 March he rode through Merida, Badajos and Elvas to Lisbon. Lisbon he found a very rich city though not so prosperous as in former years; someone must have explained that trade there had seriously declined since the English and Dutch had penetrated to the East Indies. From this pleasant situation on the Tagus he rode southwards for Seville, a monotonous journey, the ways bad and the towns unworthy of notice. But for Seville, 'full' of Nobility, full of business and Merchandise' he reserved the high praise of comparison with Italian cities which at that period provided for a cosmopolitan English nobleman the patterns of good life, 'where men lived continually in the honorable fashion'. At Seville Roos singled out for approval the courtyards of the houses and their fountains of sweet water, and he learnt to think of this city as a ladder by which millions of money descended each year from the Indies and America into Europe; the inhabitants boasted that partial loss or default in the treasure never caused a bankruptcy in their own city while ruining men by the score in Genoa, Lucca, Florence, Venice, Antwerp and Lyon. In passing he went to Cadiz which was far more strongly fortified, they claimed, than fourteen years before when the English sacked the city. He called at San Lucar and Jerez where even in those days the Spaniards marvelled at the poor quality of wines which merchants bought for shipping to England: *Vino por Borrachos*, they said. Then he came to Cordova on the road northwards and admired the royal stables and the splendid jennets they housed; a point of special interest to Lord Roos who paid great attention to horses and the gear of horses, fine cloths and saddles. At Toledo he was told of the silk worms. At Ciudad Reale he breathed with some relief after a wearisome journey, observing that the country looks 'very pleasantly upon a man that hath newly passed the Sierra Morena as I had done'. Always there were the terrible hills of Spain, impeding every journey. At last, after twelve weeks' continual movement, he reached Madrid once more.

Meanwhile news arrived of Henri IV's assassination in Paris, offering another excuse for delay. It was surely better for an English nobleman to observe cities and institutions in Spain than hazard himself in a journey through France where civil war might break out at any moment. The Pyrenean frontiers were closed and Lord Roos rode down to Valencia until trouble in the north had blown over.

He was not to be hurried. Traversing Don Quixote's own landscape after an inspection of the Escurial, La Mancha seemed a reasonably good countryside but offered such inadequate lodgings that 'I was more wondering than angry'. He found his way gradually south-eastward to the coast and then back again into the interior, admiring Valencia itself, pottering among the sepulchres and inscriptions of Murviedro (once the famous Roman city of Saguntum), and gazing at Cuenca from a distance, with its great church perched on a surgar-loaf hill and surrounded by other hills. Here he discovered that Spain, like England, was a land of sheep, with many private gentlemen owning from twenty to a hundred thousand heads. In a very interesting passage he described to Lord Salisbury how he picked up his information; in it Roos and the people he met come vividly to life:[18]

At Quenca I was tolde of a Cavallier dwelling within a league of that place called Don Lewis de Gueman that was said to have betweene 70000 and 80000 sheep, and I went for curiositie sake to see him, whome I found with his wife (who had lived in the Courte 14 yeares) in the midest of some 200 shepheards that they keepe. Don Lewis used me courteously and made me a countrie banquett and discoursed to me the particulars whereuppon that Commonwelth did stande.

Roos now toured very leisurely north and westward, admiring the glorious Roman work at Segovia and Avila, visiting the university city of Salamanca and also Alba, where he divided his enthusiasm between the picture gallery and the arsenal, which housed artillery captured by the Emperor Charles V at Mühlberg and given by him to the Duke of Alba, a Spanish grandee so notorious to all Elizabethan Englishmen. After passing through the old capital of Valladolid — stopping to admire the Piazza, the fairest he had seen outside Italy — and then travelling northwards through Burgos, Vittoria and San Sebastian, he halted at Bayonne. There he dated this description of his experiences in Spain on 27 June 1610.[19]

What was the influence of such a journey upon a man like Lord Roos? It is not easy to say but clearly he liked Spain, admiring those southern cities and their multiplicity of churches and monasteries, while he was unaffected by any assumption that in certain respects it was enemy country. The Inquisition never troubled him as did the Earl of Salisbury's watchful suspicion. He praised Spanish dramatic art; saying of its comedies that among all those he had seen they alone steered a true course, with a lively natural witty and modest representation of historical and human actions, between the scurrility of French and Italian shows and the 'foolish affectation' of the English. He learnt to speak and write the language with a certain fluency. His taste for an elaborate, expensive manner of life probably appealed to the Spanish nobility and when he resided in Naples, a few years later, another English gentleman observed how my Lord Roos loved the Spaniards.[20] That affection was at least based on a modicum of observation and experience.

Next came the commercial men, merchants or their factors. There are two or three examples of this class who left a fair amount of evidence which still survives, in print or manuscript.

Reaching Spain for the first time in 1620, James Howell the letter writer was an English traveller concerned with both litigation and commerce. He excelled his colleagues in refinement and literary art and they probably did better business. A younger son with an Oxford education he found a post in commerce through the recommendation of Dr. Mansell, his tutor at Jesus College, whose uncle was Sir Robert Mansell, sailor, naval administrator and monopolist. Young Howell worked first in Mansell's glass factory in London but was soon sent abroad to purchase materials in Spain and bring to England craftsmen from Venice and Amsterdam. He succeeded in combining the profession of a merchant's agent with the distractions of a gentleman. In the intervals of a pleasant tour he did a little business — or such was the impression he wished to leave with the reader when twenty years later he refurbished his correspondence for the press. Expenses were paid by the glass-monopolists, for he promised not to apply to his father except in the greatest necessity. After a leisurely journey through the Low Countries to Rouen and Paris, and then by sea from St. Malo to La Rochelle and Bordeaux he travelled over the Pyrenean frontier to Barcelona, and spent a year in eastern and southern Spain (1620–1621). He learnt Spanish and bought barilla in Valencia to ship to the glassworks in London. He grew fat on a diet of bread and grapes, visited Roman antiquities, and on leaving for Venice thought himself lucky to escape the pirates who swarmed along that coast line.

Two years later he was in Madrid. This time he was attempting to wring from a former Viceroy of Sardinia the compensation which Spanish courts had adjudged to English owners of the famous Turkey merchant-ship *Vineyard*, confiscated in Sardinia in 1605. Most of the original owners had long since sold their share of ship and cargo to others who speculated in the long dated risks of a claim which the Spaniards might ultimately honour with interest and compensation. These men now sent Howell to represent them, paying his expenses and promising further reward if and when their claims were met. Knowledge of Spanish and previous experience in Spain seem sensible qualifications for such a post, and at first he worked away in high hopes, claiming in letters to his employer that he had interviewed Olivares, had audience of the King, procured warrants, schedules, promises. The Spanish lawyers considered him masterly, so he said. There the matter halted. It may be doubted whether he would have extracted real compensation in any event, but the arrival of Prince Charles in Madrid and the increasingly difficult diplomacy for his marriage to the Infanta made the time-honoured case of the *Vineyard*, so irritating to the Spaniards, an obstacle to more important agreements: one testimony to the drawbacks of Charles's presence in Madrid. Howell was requested by his own countrymen to stop proceedings. The next few months he spent in observing the curious march of Anglo-Spanish politics in Spain and writing some of those witty letters which since their publication have amused readers and alarmed historians. Turning over copies of old correspondence twenty years later in the Fleet Prison, whither the career of a not very respectable royalism had brought him. Howell misdated, erased, inserted and invented with such facility and charm that the genus of 'Familiar Letters' which he was to make fashionable in England, the forerunners of Tatler and Spectator, soon flourished on the borderlands between gossip, history and fine writing. Among other qualifications he had at his command many more Spanish quotations and stories, besides an acquaintance with Spanish history, than were usual among English literary men of a later date.[21]

After peace was restored with Spain in 1630 the English merchants who instituted proceedings in Spanish courts were a constant preoccupation of the embassy at Madrid, but their complaints never led to serious difficulties. In one case, a young man concerned took very sensible advantage of the slowness of proceedings in Spain. Paul Ricaut, in the preface of his translation of Gracian's *El Criticón*, related that after five years at Cambridge he was sent by his father, a flourishing merchant who wished to give him a liberal education, to the Spanish capital in order to help his elder brother in recovering a large commercial debt. Rycaut in fact went to the neighbouring university of Alcalá de Henares, where he found his Latin and poetry held in higher esteem than they had been in Cambridge. The first part of *El Criticón* was then a very recent publication (1651) by a famous writer, and for the sake of the exercise in Spanish Rycaut determined to translate it into English.[22] *The Critick* appeared in print in London thirty years later, the incidental result of a young man's journey into Spain.

Another memorial of the Peninsula compiled by a traveller of this kind is the Spanish section of Robert Bargrave's diary.[23] Much of it is taken up with simple daily entries for a journey during the winter of 1654–5 but Bargrave also explains clearly what he was about in Spain. His ship carried wheat from London and, as the supercargo, he landed first at Alicante in order to find a customer. He waited for the return of a messenger from Valencia in connection with this business, and passed the time pleasantly in hunting and other recreations, 'especially in recounting the Godly predications of Generall Blake given the Merchants for a second Course at a feast on board his shipp, and in converse about those 24 frigatts then in Port with him'.[24] Bargrave next sailed up the coast to Barcelona, where he noted the absence of safe anchorage for shipping, together with the extraordinary risks which beset the landing of cargo there. Only on six days in the course of three weeks, in this particular instance, was the work of unloading feasible. He stressed two points, arising from his personal experience: at Barcelona it was best to sell goods 'to be delivered on board', obliging the buyer to pay the costs of delivery ashore; at Barcelona also it was wise not to deal 'with the army contractors upon bills on the Crowne at Madrid', which only promised delay and financial loss. He gives a most detailed estimate of the potentialities of this port from the English trader's point of view, how many pilchards, how much corn, metal and drugs the market could probably assimilate. He himself apparently sold his corn to private customers and not to the Spanish government, but nevertheless had to go on·to Madrid to receive payment. His ship meanwhile was sent back to Alicante to pick up a cargo of wool destined for Venice. His own journey inland from Barcelona to Madrid occupied the following sections of his diary.

The route from the Catalonian coast to the capital led travellers past Montserrat, which Bargrave visited and described in overwhelming detail, then to Lerida on a tributary of the Ebro, across to Saragossa, up another tributary to the sierras which divide Aragon from Castile, and finally down the valley of the Henares to Alcalá and Madrid. Bargrave travelled on horseback accompanied by a guide and the journey, taken in leisurely fashion in deep winter weather, lasted seventeen days. He found many Catalonian villages desolated by warfare; in Aragon and Castile conditions improved. Food was usually bad and expenisve, though prices varied greatly from valley to valley. Officials searched him on leaving Saragossa for 'fraud of Custome' and confiscated all his gold coins, and they examined him again on the frontiers of Castile.

He formed a low opinion of Madrid as a capital city;[25] the total population was small, the churches inferior, the palaces few in number. His analysis of Spanish government was hardly more favourable. The multiplicity of councils, widespread corruption, the mismanagement of army contracts and the supineness of the military commanders, all argued 'a Declination'. On the other hand he admired the royal palaces. The Escurial was an unparalleled monument to Spain's imperial glory, where the surrounding forest, the gardens, the 'uniform' mass of building — with its gorgeous though unfurnished interiors — provoked his enthusiasm and praise. So did the Buen Retiro and, later on, Aranjuez south of Madrid, which he visited on his way back to the coast.

After securing payment for the cargo of corn Bargrave set out for Alicante. This time he was less than a week on the roads eastward. Food and accommodation tended to be even worse than before, as he crossed over successive ranges of hills from valley to valley. On the frontier yet another examination faced him:

> I came to Rhingéna [he wrote] a little Toune where the King has a Custome house at the Exit of Castilia and entrance of Valentia, and here though I had nothing with me of merchandise yet I should have had sufficient trouble to pass my horse and Pistolls, but yt to prevent such Remoras I armed my selfe at Madrid with a Pass from my Colonell Don Ferdinando Philippe Erberfelt — a Gentleman of Flanders and my peculiar frend, who had owned me formally as one of his Captaines from which authoritie I was dismissed with small Expense, while by theyr Law Pistolls are not to be used but by Souldiers, nor Horses to be exported by any but by Connivance.[26]

What time the traveller could spare from business in Valencia city he spent in sightseeing, with his usual devotion: el Seo the great church, la Lonja de Seda the merchants' exchange, the Colegio del Patriarca and its remarkable relics. And round about the city was the Huerta de Valencia, the fertile gardens and plantations of mulberries, oranges and lemons through which Bargrave rode on his way south to Alicante. Before reaching his journey's end the countryside deteriorated, 'miserable scraggy mountainous land as would (of it were possible) outvie Catalonia', thus preparing him for Alicante itself, which he did not like. Dirty, misgoverned, expensive and superstitious; with the English colony infected by the same faults. On the other had Bargrave again gives a detailed survey of commercial prospects at this port, what goods could be sold there and at what prices.[27] His own business was complete; the cargo of corn had been sold and the money was on board. A new cargo, of wool, had been taken in at Alicante. Their course was set for Venice.

Lord Roos's narrative describes the experience of a few English gentry travelling for pleasure and instruction. Bargrave's account is a summary of many careers in Spain, careers of the numerous English commerical men earning a livelihood for themselves and their employers, merchants at home. And there were the young Catholics who often crossed the sea posing as merchants' factors or as sailors. Sometimes they came to the notice of the English ambassador but if their disguise was successful, they left no trace in official records. In 1610 a youth named Gage, born either in Sussex or Essex, visited Cottington some days after reaching Madrid. (A perfectly innocent Protestant should have called at once.) 'The Gentleman seemes to have many good parts and to be yet well disposed towards his Majestie and our Cuntrey, But beeing a Papist and of soe yong years (for I judge him of about 20 years of age), your Lordship can best understand how easyly they wyll make him a Traytor.'[28] Creswell, the Jesuit father in Madrid, blamed Gage for seeing Cottington at all. It is just possible that here was the future author of the famous 'English-American', on his way south to a Jesuit education in Andalusia before undertaking a more strenuous pilgrimage to fortune in Mexico.[29]

A few weeks later Cottington received a letter hideously written and spelt, in the hand of a boy, a somewhat pathetic insertion in his official transactions:[30]

> to the Rit worshipfull my Lord inbasidour My lord, it is to let you understand that I am a Englis youth, the sone to justis Collines, in Sallimanca in the Convent of Augustines repenting me much of my folley. I was by a lud Preest brogth over in[to] Spaine and mayd a papist wich I do repent much; my lord, I do not know your name but I deseare you as you are a lord, take piti on me and rit to me as son as is possibell what you will do for mee tordes helping me from that Helis Religeon — if to serve of your honor, I am willing, for the rong to my father I have don to him, help me to serve a Protistant to ride wyth him. If yow please to do me aniy good you know my mind.
>
> Your lords to command<br>CHRISTOPHER COLLINES.

While Lord Roos, in his journey passed through Salamanca admiring the colleges Christopher Collins was in restraint behind convent walls.

A sadder case, a wanderer lost on the margin of history, came to Sir John Digby's notice. The ambassador wrote in September 1612:[31]

> Here have likewise this monthe died foure Englishmen in Madrid, two of myne own familie and two other English gentlemen in the Towne, one Osbaston and one Mr. Brett of White stanton in Somersetshire, who being a

man as I understand in England of good fortunes, came here to a miserable end, for having lingred and wandred here up and downe Spaine in a Pilgrimes weed was, at his first coming to Madrid about some seven or eight monthes since releived by myself although I saw him not, yet by his Letters understanding him to be a Gentleman and to be in great wants and distresse, I lent him money to carry him to the seaside, thinking he would have returned for England. About 5 or 6 monthes after he returned again, also like a Pilgrime secreatly to this Towne but neither came nor sent unto my self. But causing an eye to be had of him found that algthough he was furnished with money by the Marchants at Lisbone, where he had beene, yet he lodged and dieted himself here in verie meane and base howses, and so with the yllnes of his lodging and fare, fell into a Fever and for want of attendance and conveniency he was carried into an Hospital where within two or three dayes he died, raging madd.

Another Catholic traveller, somewhat more purposeful, was the sister of Lord Stafford who arrived in Madrid during the year 1621, intending to ask for employment in the Infanta Maria's household: 'so to rayse a fortune if happily the match shold succeed with England.' She also fell sick and was placed in a hospital, comforted by English priests.[32]

Such people found a place in seventeenth-century official records. Sir John Digby, occupied with the problems of English commercial and dynastic policy, considered that the Secretary of State would want to be informed of one Brett's death in a Madrid hospital. Mr. Brett might be a Catholic illegally withdrawing money from his English estates, or an agent in touch with dangerous exiles or with foreign governments. He might be none of these things but at some future date, favoured by his Spanish connection, wish to enter into treasonable conspiracies. He might simply return to England and foment unrest. He might be silly, and die mad. Only in this last case did he not concern a competent diplomat and a watchful government. At the same time the King of England's representative in Spain did his best to protect the King's subjects. The galley slave and prisoner and the harassed merchant, we have seen, owed him a good deal. Sometimes he lent money or gave accommodation to the traveller. A mixture of all these elements may be found in the notorious case of William Lithgow, the one really celebrated British traveller in Spain during this period.

Unwearied by two great previous journeys which had taken him through eastern Europe and the Levant, Lithgow was determined to reach the kingdom of Prester John in Africa by way of Ireland, France, Spain and Egypt, completing his circuit of the whole Christian world.[33] Leaving Bayonne in June 1620 he visited Pamplona in Navarre, and Saragossa, then struck westward to Santiago de Compostela; as a militant Protestant he delighted to view Catholic places of pilgrimage. He mixed with other and more genuine pilgrims, laughing at their superstitions, on the rough roads going along the Asturian ridges. Galicia he found such a poor hungry land that he was tempted into 'twenty days fastidious climbing' in Portugal. Returning to Spain he stopped at Salamanca, regarding the students with much disapproval, carefully examined the Escurial which he ranked above the Seraglio of the Grand Turk in Constantinople, and arrived at Madrid. He was not enjoying the journey with his usual gusto:

> It is miserable travelling, less profitable in these ten Provinces, or petty Kingdoms, hard lodging and poore, great scarcitie of beds and deare: and no ready drest diet, unless you buy it raw: And cause dresse, or dresse it yourself, buying first in one place your fire, your Meat from the Butcher, your Bread from the Baker, your Wine from the Tavern, your Fruits, Oil and Herbs from the Botega, carrying all to the last place your Bed-lodging: Thus must the weary stranger toil or else fast: And in infinite places for Gold or no money can have no victuals; but restrained to a relenting Jejunation.[34]

At Madrid he made himself known at the embassy where they seem to have been aware that Lithgow did not keep his Protestantism to himself, for he says that some of the ambassador's servants[35] testified later to his 'doubtful and dangerous departure from Madrid', words which have some bearing on his adventures further south. Passing through Toledo, which he disliked, but admiring Granada and its exquisite Moorish mosaic work he came to Antequera, fell in with a London merchant travelling from Venice and together they reached Malaga on the coast, late on a Sunday evening. Next day he bargained for his passage with the master of a French ship sailing to Alexandria in Egypt. Everything was in order. The Kingdom of Prester John seemed at any rate not inaccessible. Then, without warning, Lithgow brushed against the force of politics, becoming in that process the self-styled 'martyr of Malaga'.

Lithgow's own narrative has frequently been paraphrased: — An English fleet under Sir Robert Mansell sailed into the harbour roads, on its way to attack the Barbary pirates. He went aboard the ships and fraternized with his countrymen on shore. Some were old friends. On the ships' departure he was returning to his lodging when the Spaniards arrested and brought him before the governor of the town. They accused him of being a spy purposely sent into Spain ahead of the fleet to discover when the American treasure would arrive at Seville, in order to pass on the information to Sir Robert Mansell when he came to Malaga; so that a profitable assault might be made, not against the pirates of Barbary but against Spain. Lithgow protested complete innocence of the charge and was inexpressibly pained when his papers, including King James's safe conduct, his patent as a pilgrim who had been to Jerusalem and his autograph album were confiscated; and then they took all his money, 560 ducats. He was kept close prisoner nor were the English merchants at Malaga informed of his predicament. After forty-seven days they brought him out of the town to a 'Vine press house' standing alone among vineyards and then they tortured him on the rack from four o'clock in the afternoon to ten o'clock at night, mangling and maiming his poor body. And still he would not confess that he was a spy. He remained a close prisoner during January 1621 while an English seminary priest and a Scottish cooper were translating his papers, especially his own notes and observations, into Spanish; whereupon the officials of the Inquisition found evidence of most grievous heresy, and admitting that he had been unjustly charged as a spy — 'as we acknowledge, we were better informed lately from Madrid of the English intention' — they now determined to treat him as a heretic and allotted a span of eight days for his conversion. Lithgow entered enthusiastically into a week's theological controversy, and after every session and many bitter words on Pope and Sacrament 'the fiery faced Jesuits with boisterous menacings left me'. Alternatively, he was offered a pension of 300 ducats a year if he would become a Roman Catholic. Lithgow held firm, and now the ecclesiastical tortures began, tortures of water and strangulation. Only Hazier the Turk, and Ellenor the Indian negro woman, servants of the prison, comforted him in his agonies. At last, fortune turned about. A Fleming overheard the Governor talking of Lithgow's case, informed the English consul, Mr. Richard Wilds 'who conjectured it was I, because of the other reports of a traveller and of his first and former acquaintance with me there'. Wilds sent a letter post haste to Sir Walter Aston who obtained an official warrant for Lithgow's release. He was set free, brought on board the ship *Vanguard*, a spectre in a pair of blankets. The merchants made him a present of clothes, wine, sugar, oranges and eggs and he sailed for England in the *Goodwill of Harwich*, a storeship attached to Mansell's fleet. Fifty days later he was carried into Theobalds Palace on a feather bed, arousing the sympathy of king and court. And now he was a hero and a martyr, claims which he repeated incessantly through another thirty years of vigorous activity.

Soon afterwards Lithgow secured a promise of compensation from the Spanish ambassador and when this was not paid he insulted Gondomar, who struck him, and he retaliated. The Secretary of State thereupon committed Lithgow to the Gatehouse prison in February 1622 where he remained for two years.

This statement of an adventure in Spain has always suffered for standing alone. His battle with Gondomar and his imprisonment are confirmed by official papers but Lithgow's normal reliability, the consistency of the details with one another and with the general history of Sir Robert Mansell's expedition have been the only tests by which to judge the events at Malaga. He himself admits that not everyone believed his story; and in 1626, seeking redress by a petition to the House of Lords he first secured testimonials from Mansell, Aston and Sir Thomas Button, vice-admiral of the fleet. Button's letter was printed by Lithgow in 1632. Fortunately there is another witness, Walter Long, a

Part·10   *By 3. voyages in Europe, Asia, and Affrica·*   455

Garden , and right aboue his Summer Kitchin: Where
there,and then, the Sergeants, and the two slaues, thrust
on euery ancle an heauy bolt , my legs being put to the
full stride, by a mayne gad of iron far aboue a yard long, And here is the
vpon the endes of which the two bolts depended , that emblem e ot
were fastned about my legs. Infomuch, that I could ne- my misery.

19.   The unlucky traveller in Spain: from the *Totall Discourse of the Rare Adventures
and Painful Peregrinations . . .* (1632), in which Lithgow offers 'to the understanding
Gentleman insight, instruction and recreation', with 'a tush for that snarling Crew'
of Papists.

servant of Mansell's who corresponded with the Secretary of State. His
testimony shows that Lithgow was as much the victim of his own character as of a confused historical event.

Sir Robert Mansell arrived in the Mediterranean with one purpose,
distinctly stated in his instructions, to use the fleet against that universal
nuisance the Barbary pirates.[36] The navy had been recently reorganized
and its commanders were eager for employment. Another objective was
to influence and restrain Spanish imperial policy at a moment of crisis in
Europe — troubles in Italy, troubles in Germany — by the presence of
an English fleet in southern waters. The one idea visualized Spain as an
ally and the other as an enemy. On their side the Spaniards feared that
the English fleet might join with the pirates; several of the English naval

captains were known as former pirate-commanders. In southern Spain pirates, the English, the Dutch and the exiled Moriscoes all excited acute alarm. No one knew whom to call friend or enemy.

Lithgow understood very little of these problems, but his experience vividly reveals them. When Mansell's ships dropped anchor after dark at Malaga, he reports, the town mistook them for Turks and raised the alarm. The bells rang backward and the drums beat, sending women into the castle for refuge and the citizens to their weapons. They (with Lithgow, 'a staid Consort') remained on the watch. At daylight, the English colours were recognized and the governor of the town went out to greet Sir Robert Mansell who admits in his letters that he was cordially received. But the Spaniards were clearly nervous, suspicious of everybody. During the weekend several English sailors came ashore, to be welcomed by the factors at Malaga, Mr. Wilds, Mr. Corney, Mr. Rowley, Mr. Cooke and others. Then Sir Robert Mansell divided his ships into three squadrons and sailed for Alicante. Lithgow was arrested.

His account of the next six months has already been given. The testimony of Walter Long is in these words:[37]

I was given to understand by the Inglish marchantes...that upon the fleetes departure from hence heere was search made what men weare leaft beehind belonging unto the fleete, in which was founde a scotsman who stiled him self by the name of the King's traviler. His right name I cannot learne. Hee was in these partes beefore the fleetes arrivale heare and in this search was fownd having aboute his neck a kind of leather budget in which was his papers and observations of his travailes. I know not wheather he had aney observations of this cittie or any drafte of the castle heere but it is likely hee had, beeing in that kinde curious. He was seacretly apprehended, and privilie carried to prison beeing suspected to bee left by the fleete as a speye to informe himself of the strength of the cittie, (and as it was reported) the fleete was suspected to goe and joyne with the Turkes and come against this place ...the marchantes acquainted my Lord Embassador hearewith as soone as this fellow was apprehended, certifing him of the rumor which was heere of the suspition which was had of the fleete but he couldly entertained the newes, thinking it but meere surmises uppon false grownds and retourned them a reprehensive answer...(19 December 1620)

It is supposed the partie of whom I wrote was delivered over unto the inquisition after he had bin put to the rack. My lord Embassador and Mr. Cottington did conceive that all theyre proceedings against him proceeded from his owne ill carriage, who in maney places wheare he had bine had given oute that hee had wrote bookes against the Poape, unto whose better oppinions I am bounde to conforme mine. Yet by the sequel one may judge the contrarey, for upon owre fleets retourne from Argire the former rumors revived [it] beeing openly devulged that wee had made a peace with the Turkes and yt they suspected wee would joyne with them against this place...(5 February (n.s.) 1621).

This narrative contradicts Lithgow: the English at Malaga and the English embassy at Madrid knew from the very first that he was imprisoned. Sir Thomas Button confirms this by saying that Mr. Wilds, the consul, told him the circumstances when his ship came to Malaga. And clearly, in Madrid they thought the man a talkative fool who had been arrested by his own fault. Perhaps Cottington and Aston remembered 'the doubtful and dangerous departure', whatever it was, that speeded the traveller on his way from the capital. Lithgow, they may have thought, had only himself to blame; and so at first they made curiously little effort to help him.

Lithgow, therefore, cannot pose as the mere victim of circumstance. His own bearing as he passed through Spain, had something to do with his imprisonment. On the other hand, he was even more clearly a victim of the imperfect sympathy between the two governments; and although it has seemed important, in previous pages, to show that there was some measure of accord between England and Spain, the fate of Lithgow illustrates their persisting antagonism. The idea of allying against a common enemy was weakened by powerful and mutual fears. Cottington, Aston and Mansell concerned themselves simply with the conduct and supply of a naval expedition against Barbary. So far as they were aware, the navy of King James had been sent to check piracy, working in agreement with the Spaniards. But the Spaniards, the governor of Malaga for example, suspected other possibilities which certain English politicians also visualized. Lord Digby, a moderate man who hardly desired to attack Spain, saw in Sir Robert Mansell's fleet an element in the general diplomatic struggle, including the negotiations for a Spanish match, and he much deplored its final departure from the Straits. To judge from Walter Long's account, English merchants at Malaga considered an alliance between the fleet and the pirates as a distinct possibility. Mansell, in accordance with his instructions, first attempted to negotiate for the return of prisoners when he appeared off Algiers: a fact observed by Spanish sea-captains and soon known to the governor of Malaga. Whether this gentleman suspected that Lithgow had been left behind by the fleet — Button's and Long's story — or knew that he had been in Spain some time, which is more probable, there were at any rate reasons for his nervousness and Lithgow suffered in consequence. The implications of the fleet's presence off the Spanish coast constrained both the governor and his captive. A first appearance of the King of England's navy in the Mediterranean coincided most unfortunately with the arrival of 'the King's traveller' at Malaga. It took Aston several months to convince the Spanish government that the pirates were the fleet's single enemy and thereafter it was easier to agree that Lithgow was no spy. By that time the English seminary priest and the Scottish cooper had brought before the Inquisition a translation of Lithgow's notes — his comments on pilgrims who go to 'St. Jago of Compostella', for example, and 'the damnable delusions of devilish miracles'. It required vigorous remonstrance from the ambassador at Madrid to secure his release. So finally he came, not to the distant court of Prester John, but to Theobalds and old King James, begging loudly for compensation.

A few months later Aston wrote a friendly letter to the governor of Malaga regarding the grievances of another petitioner.[38] He asked him for a sympathetic hearing since otherwise Anglo-Spanish relations would suffer, and proved the assertion by referring to the poor Scotsman recently put to the torture — 'aunque presumo con causa Justificada' — who was clamouring in the court of James I, and pestering the Spanish ambassador there to make good the wrongs suffered by the martyr of Malaga. In the following year Aston quotes the English merchants at Malaga as stating that this governor had 'bin ever so good a frend and so ready to doe cortesys'.[39] This evidence all helps to qualify Lithgow's famous narrative.

Meanwhile, Mansell's final attack on Algiers failed. He kept the seas during the summer months, until growing friction between the Dutch and the English brought about instructions for his recall. Countermanding orders, requesting him to remain in the Straits and sent with the object of putting pressure on the Spanish court failed to reach him before his return.

This has been a long review of an individual case but the fame of Lithgow's book deserves it. The fortunes of a traveller and the duties of consul and ambassador in protecting him have obtained a more minute description than is usually possible.

This survey of the records of English travel in Spain, taken principally from the first quarter of the century, fills in a part of the background to Anglo-Spanish diplomacy during James I's reign. It shows that relations between the two countries remained rather slight, except among traders, or when a particular calculation of political interests forced on the manoeuvring for a dynastic marriage. In some respects the effort made to bring about this Spanish match, and the consequent alliance, was indeed prodigious. The diplomats, with much coming and going along the arduous itineraries linking the two courts, engaged in prolonged negotiation. Certain men like Digby and Cottington, and at a lower level like Porter and Tresham, obviously had or acquired a personal interest in cementing the agreement, standing to gain by its success. The affair culminated and ended in the most notorious of all journeys into Spain, the escapade of Prince Charles and Buckingham to Madrid in 1623, which has been exhaustively treated by historians of varying authority. However, from the vantage-point afforded by our general description of travel in Spain it becomes clear that once this political design was repudiated by the statesmen, intelligent merchants and factors were the only class of Englishmen who acquired a respectable knowledge of the country by residence or travel. After 1630 there was no possibility of a dynastic alliance, but there was peace; and the merchants went doggedly on with their business of exploiting a profitable market, assisted by two or three solitary diplomats.

Such conditions, and reports about them, deterred most English gentlemen on their travels from crossing the Pyrenean frontier. Spain is rich and powerful, it must have been said over and over again, but a poor country. Inns and roads are deplorable. The fanatical,[40] hungry, threadbare population proves an uncongenial host, and strangers are suspect to the Inquisition. There appeared to be no real compensation for these drawbacks, and for this reason above all it was surely wise to keep to France, Italy and the Low Countries where an Englishman knew, also by report, that there was much to learn, enjoy, even to envy. His association with these countries was not simply a matter of politics and commerce: far stronger grounds for becoming acquainted with their peoples and landscapes could be found. Anglo-Italian relations, in spite of the distance separating England and Italy, and Anglo-French relations, in spite of bitter traditional hostility, had always been fruitful. But Spain seemed unsympathetic and remote. Travel there was too much an adventure, too little an education.

# V. ENGLISH TRAVELLERS IN FRANCE AFTER 1630

## 12. THE EDUCATION OF ENGLISHMEN IN PARIS AND THE PROVINCES: THE TRIUMPH OF A CONVENTION

Our survey began with travellers in France, noblemen and their tutors, during the reign of James I, then moving on into Italy, Spain and the Low Countries in the same period and the half century following. It is time to turn back to this great central territory on our way home and examine some record of the Englishmen travelling in France after Charles I and Richelieu made peace in 1630, a peace which except at sea and for a short period after 1666 was preserved as long as the Stuarts reigned, even in the interim years of Charles II's exile. The material which bears on Anglo-French relations in the seventeenth century is of course almost boundless; there are diaries, private correspondence, literary affiliations reflected in poetry and prose, diplomatic reports and the papers left by a crowd of exiles who sometimes spoke as private men and sometimes as statesmen excluded from practical politics. It will be necessary, therefore, to take care and not get lost amid the mountainous accumulations of evidence. An enquirer, for example, can spend a week reading the volumes of Sir Edward Nicholas' celebrated correspondence as Secretary of State between 1642 and 1660 and, for all his pains, find only a single entry which explicitly mentions travel as a means of education:

> My lady of Rochester (writes Sir George Radcliffe to Nicholas from Paris in April 1655) sent her second son Mr. Francis Lee hither to Du Veaux's Academy. He came this week to town. My lady did me the honor by her letter to desire my assistance, if I could serve him by any advice. Mr. Thomas Chichele has a sonne (a proper young man) who came along with him, but he is goeinge to the River of the Loire to learne French this Summer.[1]

Such stray hints, illustrating the main purposes of travel but hidden in the unending sequence of political reports, can only be auxiliary to more circumstantial accounts. Fortunately our main task is already complete: examination of State Papers during the preceding decades, examples from the careers of Lords Clifford and Cranborne and Thomas Wentworth of men performing the conventional tour of France as early as 1610 and 1612, demonstration that in Italy such a tour only became fixed in its programme and itinerary from the time of Charles I, and some analysis of the military and religious aspects of an Englishman's usual experience in the Low Countries. In France after 1630 a number of further illustrations can be found, giving more detail on the tour, on life and education in Paris or Blois or Montpellier, but there is no new step to record in the pattern of men's travel marking a positive departure or change of custom. The foundations of current practice were already laid, and later evidence in the main fills in and fills up the general picture. A fashion, the origin of which has been discussed, can be illustrated in its fully developed form as a means of experience and education.

However, there is a further point. Political conditions seem to have made little difference from one decade to another after Charles I and Louis XIII brought hostilities to a close. In the thirties peace allowed men to travel. In the forties the disturbance of civil war induced some to go abroad in order to avoid becoming involved at home; for others a temporary exile appeared the better part of discretion, or even a fatal necessity. In the fifties travel went on as before; the hastiest glance at lists of the wellnigh innumerable passports, issued by committees of the Commonwealth and Protectorate governments, is sufficient to upset any notion that a majority of Englishmen on the continent at that time were professed Royalist exiles. In France itself the Frondes occasionally drove foreigners from one city to another, without driving them from the country. After 1660, with civil differences appeased in England, travellers ventured over the Channel as they had done before the restoration of Charles II. From their point of view, in fact, the vicissitude of English political history now played a less important part than might be expected. Neither the soldier nor the politician were to restrain the traveller; and we have to do with a custom already deeply rooted. For this reason some of the evidence provides a useful side view of the English revolutionary period. England was not then more isolated from the continent than before, the exiles hardly more cut off from their own country than travellers of the preceding generation; and they merged, sometimes very easily, into the ranks of the ordinary travellers.

First, bearing the diaries of Cranborne and Wentworth in mind, another journal of a French tour written by a young nobleman forty years afterwards is worth examination.

A Bodleian manuscript is catalogued as an anoymous travel diary of the years 1649–1652.[2] In fact it was the work of Robert Montagu Lord Mandeville, later third Earl of Manchester. He was never, even in maturity, a distinguished figure to be placed on a level with his grandfather the Lord Privy Seal, his father the unsuccessful Parliamentary general, his brilliant uncle the influential abbé Walter Montagu, nor with his cousin Edward Montagu Earl of Sandwich, the admiral and Pepys's patron. This journal, which he begain at the age of fifteen, has no particular merit but by following Robert Montagu through France, noting what he noted and comparing his remarks with those of other travellers who took the same road, the usual standards of knowledge and experience will secure a fair definition. Surviving records of this type for youths who left England when they were fifteen or sixteen, an exceedingly common practice in noble families, are not so numerous as the diaries of older men on whom undue reliance has often been placed. By taking Montagu, instead of a more intelligent and mature writer, it is possible to come closer to the average youth who was sent to the continent for his education and experience.

On 23 April 1649 the Admiralty Committee in London sent a message to the admiral commanding the fleet in the Downs.[3] Lord Mandeville, it stated, has a pass to travel abroad and desires their aid and protection in crossing the Channel. The admiral was to arrange to take him, his governor, servants and baggage, the captain of the ship giving Mandeville the respect due to his rank. Five years later, in April 1654, the Admiralty Committee received a letter from Captain Algate of the *Drake* reporting that, in obedience to their orders, he had taken on board at Dieppe Lord Mandeville and the Earl of Bolingbroke, landing them at Rye.[4]

It is not possible to say what happened to Montagu throughout this long period abroad between his fifteenth and twentieth years, but part of the time and of his journey are mapped in the diary which he kept from London through France, Switzerland and Germany until he reached the Tyrol on his way into Italy. As in the case of Wentworth, it was not in use when he settled down in one city or another with a view to study, but while travelling he duly noted down what his elders expected him to observe, a testimonial for parents, on return, of the effects of travel as an instrument of education. In Montagu's diary the practical results of the grandiose programme dear to theorists, who wished him to come back stored with knowledge on the comparative methods of government, histories of nations and characters of kings (as well as the names of cities, churches and monuments) were modest enough.

On 6 May 1649 he arrived in Dover and going in a small boat to the flagship gave Colonel Deane his Speaker's pass. The son and heir of a Parliamentary general enjoyed every privilege even though the 'presbyterian' Earl of Manchester, now Royalist in sympathy, was not in favour with the Commonwealth authorities in power. The guns of Walmer Castle saluted Montagu, and the frigate *Nonesuch* prepared to take him across the Channel. The party went on board, and early on Sunday morning left England. Two miles from Dieppe they transferred to a French shallop and, as Montagu and his servants made for the harbour English naval guns fired an official salute. The first stage of the journey was safely over. Other travellers have left further information about the ordinary crossing from Rye to Dieppe at this period. John Finch in 1651 paid 13s.4d. for the passage and describes the difficulty of entering Dieppe, for 'the haven is a safe road when you are in it but by many circuits you come into the port'; Evelyn a little earlier had remarked on this, while in 1664 Dr, Downes was finally carried ashore on the back of a seaman. Another, more serious difficulty came from privateers. In 1649 many of these sailed under Charles II's flag, though usually they were Dunkirk vessels. In October 1636 a Dunkirk privateer held up the Dieppe boat and robbed a Frenchman, secretary of the English ambassador in Paris, of £100. In 1654 a ship going from Rye to Dieppe was stopped by an Ostender but, after a search made for contraband, allowed to proceed. In the circumstances the most tragic incident of this kind may well have been the robbery by Ostende privateers who boarded a ship carrying Sir Edward Hyde, Lord Cottington, Sir George Radcliffe and Warnsford from Dunkirk to the royal fleet off the Thames a few months before Montagu crossed the Channel — an action which made four exiles poorer by £1700. Robert Montagu could count himself fortunate to enjoy official protection. His voyage had been without incident in favourable weather.[5]

He had little time to look round Dieppe because they were going away next morning 'for company's sake', a characteristic detail of the period, but he noticed or someone pointed out to him the shops filled with trinkets of carved whalebone, ivory and tortoiseshell. Most Englishmen remarked on the examples of fine craftsmanship on sale while some admired also the rich ornament of St. Jacques' church and the picturesque long scarves worn by the women.[6] Sir John Finch managed to see over the castle by procuring an interview with the governor but this was exceptional; they usually commented simply on its apparent strength and complete command of the harbour.

The first day's journey brought Montagu and his servants to Rouen along the time-honoured route southwards. They dined at Tôtes, a little village standing solitary in large fields with tall trees round about where Evelyn had found just one inn; another Englishman was able to associated the name with *le roi d'Yvetot*, then regarded proverbially as a man of great titles and small estate. From Tôtes they came to Malauney through a countryside of apply and cherry and along a 'very deepe and foule way' to Rouen, where accommodation was found in the Quadrant de Mer. Other hostels were the Ville D'Anvers and the Bon Pasteur.[7]

Two days were allotted for visiting the capital city of Normandy. Montagu went first to the cathedral and admired its towers and the great bell, called Georges D'Amboise after the cardinal, and inspected the cathedral treasury. He looked at the bridge of boats over the Seine and the ruins of the old stone bridge, formerly one of the finest in France, and a relic of the destruction caused by civil war three-quarters

PONT·DE·LARCHE.

20. Robert Montagu's journey on the Seine: looking upstream from Pont-de-l'Arche.

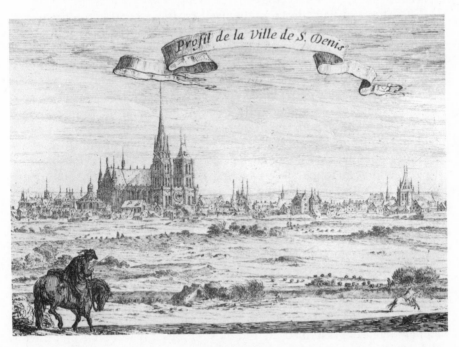

Profil de la Ville de S. Denis

21. The spire of St Denis: seen by English travellers as they approached Paris in seventeenth century but since destroyed.

of a century before; at the palace of the Parlement, the mint, the spot
where Joan of Arc was burnt; finding Rouen grey and melancholy from
the slate roofing of the houses. With slight variations his English contemporaries made the same round the visits here, recording similar impressions. They write that Rouen is an unhealthy city very subject to the
plague. Sometimes they describe the cathedral with more detail than
seemed necessary to a youth, and comment on the aspect of those old
timber houses 'like our merchants of London in the wooden part of the
City'. Everyone duly admired the bell, one of the popular wonders of
western Europe until it was melted down during the Revolution. Others
referred to the large number of Protestants in this neighbourhood.[8]
Peter Mundy's first journey — but he was by no means a gentleman on
tour — had been in his father's ship to Rouen, and his most vivid
memory (writing in 1654) was the tidal bore of the Seine estuary, a fact
more familiar to the many English merchants trading there and com-
peting successfully with the local cloth industries in Normandy, than to
gentleman tourists.[9] Such were the chief features of Rouen as they
appeared to travellers while preparing for the next stage of their journey;
though a few were perhaps tempted to make a short preliminary tour to
Caudebec and Le Havre or westward to Caen, the extreme limit
of the travelling facilities afforded by Louis XIV's posting service in this
direction.[10]

Englishmen usually declared themselves satisfied with the communications between the principal French cities. It was pleasant and convenient to be able to deal with the king's messenger at Rouen who for a
round sum found horses, lodging , food and wine for the journey to
Paris, which took two days with a night's rest at Magny or Vernon.

Robert Montagu's party, however, went by water hiring a boat to take
them up the Seine. 'Coming to Pont de l'Arche I shott the bridge',[11] he
writes with a hint of personal pride; the fort commanding the river there
had been of considerable importance in the recent troubles of the
Fronde. They passed by Gaillan, a palace belonging to the archbishop of
Rouen and sometimes visited by the English who admired its great
gallery,[12] then, by dint of going on through the moonlit night they were
able to dine next day at Vernon. They halted to see the palace and park
of the marquis de Rhosny, of the Sully family. At Mantes Montagu commented that the church, a fine mediaeval building, was large enough,
but built after the old fashion: so much for Gothic architecture! Next
day, 11 May, they left the river and after dining at Poissy took a coach to
Paris, where Hainhofer the tutor found them lodgings with a Protestant
widow at the sign of the Angel in the Rue Anjou.

They remained a month, obediently visiting everything that guides
and guidebooks prescribed. So did most of the early travellers and their
sightseeing had one extremely important result. Montagu, and he was
one of many, learnt a great deal of French history by this Parisian

22.  Richard Symonds
in Paris: taking notes at
the Luxembourg.

pilgrimage. In accordance with the historical approach of his age, he
studied the subject in a piecemeal fashion but as thoroughly as any
English history that would have come his way earlier in life, or even later
on. A branch of knowledge which is so evident in the appraisals of a
good intellect like John Evelyn's, or illustrated on every page of Richard
Symonds' exquisite Paris sketch-book,[13] can be watched growing the
very immature mind of Robert Montagu Lord Mandeville. It is a process
worth observation. The monuments of French history stood before his
eyes, covering an immense span of past history and he surveyed them
one by one, laboriously copying into his journal the appropriate historical detail borrowed from his tutor or his books.

He saw in the Hall of Antiquities at the Louvre a Mercury 'worshiped by the ancient Gaules uppon the hill Montmartir', and he believed the Châtelet to have been built by Julian the Apostate governor of Gaul in order to collect tribute from the people. In the abbeys of St. Geneviève and St. Germain he recognized the work of Clovis the first Christian king and of Childebert his son; at St. Denis admired with something like enthusiasm the foundation of Dagobert, and many gifts and grants from the great Capetian rulers whose names he noted, referring in particular to the achievement of Louis VI, Louis VII and the abbot Suger. Then at St. Innocents he learnt of Philip Augustus who banished the Jews from France, confiscating their property partly to the benefit of this church. The Charterhouse acquainted him with St. Bruno, who had retired with a few friends 'unto that fearefull desert hard by Grenoble'. In connection with all these different foundations he read, or was told of, and he noted, special privileges granted by Pope or King. Then came the constitutional side of French history. At the Palais, which he duly visited, Philip the Fair 'first did settle and establish his Parlement', and in the Parlement it was necessary to distinguish between the different courts which held session there; he mentions the Lit de Justice, the Court of the Aides, the Court of Accounts and the court for the administration of the Edict of Nantes. In regard to the greatness and prestige of the French monarchy, he saw at the Louvre the successive additions to the royal buildings made by many kings. At the palace of Reuil outside the city and in the Palais Royal, formerly Palais Cardinal, he was perhaps able to grasp something of the extraordinary fame of Richelieu, their original owner; the Luxembourg and its gardens demonstrated 'the ingenuitie of this great princesse Marie de Medici'. Finally, at the Hôtel de Ville it was possible to learn the rudiments of Parisian municipal administration, the position held by the Prevôt des Marchands, Echevins and other officials, arrangements for police and price regulation of staple goods, corn, wine and wood. In this short time, therefore, Montagu had surveyed an epitome of French history which M. Hainhofer forced him to transcribe, with abundant if inaccurate detail, into his journal.[14]

This laborious copying betrays not the slightest interest in general questions; and there are no verdicts. But it may be doubted whether anyone could write so much and forget everything, and if this was the ordinary technique employed by student and tutor during the conventional tour, then the travelled Englishman must be given credit for a fair knowledge of French antiquities. Occasionally the deeper historical problems suggested by such a visit to Paris, and the studies which followed that visit, were formulated by the traveller with rather more insight. Sir John Reresby, who came to France in 1654 at the age of the twenty-one, dismissed the buildings of the capital in a few lines but compiled a set of miniature essays on French institutions, the Parlements (which he carefully distinguished from the Estates of the realm and the English Parliament), the Court, the Guards, the Revenue.[15] Reresby had mastered, quite evidently, the contemporary view of French history as reflected in its forms of government, and this knowledge he owed in part to his travels.

On 8 June 1649 Montagu left Paris for the towns of the Loire valley along one of the best roads in Europe, a causeway paved with freestone. Evelyn had compared it favourably with anything in England 'onely' tis somewhat hard to the poore horeses' feete, which causes them to ride more temperately, seldom going out of the trot or *grand pas*, as they call it'. Montagu, like most travellers of the time, took two days to reach Orleans, the second half of the journey leading through thick forest, where wolves and bandits sheltered, into the great valley.

The sightseeing began again: the churches, the statuary on the long bridge over the river, and talk of Joan of Arc and the siege of 1430. But Hainhofer wasted little time and after five days they hired a boat and set off downstream, entering that memorable territory the monuments of which impose on the diaries of all travellers a monotonous simplicity of pattern, with the ever-recurring staircase and stag's horn at the castle of Amboise, the Duke of Orleans' garden of simples at Blois, the Pall-Mall of Tours and St. Martin's enormous wine barrel at the abbey of Marmoutier, filled by the saint from the juice of a single bunch of grapes. On 18 June, six weeks after leaving London, Montagu arrived in Saumur where he was to live for more than a year.[16]

The stay there received only a word or two in his notebook; he found lodgings in the house of a Madame Michon and took tutors in fencing, singing, the guitar, dancing and Latin. Nevertheless, as in the case of Thomas Wentworth, this pause in his travels was of great importance for him. Indeed, in the seventeenth century Touraine and Anjou deserve more attention than Winchester and Eton for the history of education among the higher ranks of English society.

His main task was presumably to learn French, and here a detailed example of current practice, and performance, may be found in the manuscript diary of Thomas Abdy. Abdy made entries in English from the day he left England in July 1633 until he settled in Blois in the autumn, after a journey very similar in all respects to Montagu's. Nothing was recorded during the winter, and then in the new year he set out to make a tour of France very similar to Wentworth's, his first note beginning: 'Je suis parti de Blois 29 Avrill pour commencer l'entreprise du voyage de la France', and from this point the remainder of his journal was written in French. Miscellaneous entries on the last leaf of the same document mention his other activities in Blois during the winter. He had entered a pension on 12 November 1633, and then: 'I began to learn to fence the 15 Novembe...I began to learne the Mathematiques of Mr. Dutemps the 16 November...Hiring a Viol a quart d'escu p. mois from the 17...Began to dance the 10 January.'[17] Three years after Abdy George Courthop came to France with Lord Dacre, and after some weeks spent in Paris Lord Dacre's governor persuaded him to travel down the Loire from Orleans to Tours, Blois, Saumur and Angers 'to see which he liked best and there to stay and learn the language'.[18] Courthop decided to settle at Loudun, Dacre preferred Angers. In 1644, at Tours, John Evelyn made a note that on 8 September two of his kinsmen had arrived from Paris and he 'settled them in their pension and exercises'. A year before Montagu another traveller found Blois too full of English people and preferred to stay for a few months at Tours, surprisingly 'empty' of his countrymen;[19] and somewhat later Charles Bertie divided his time between Saumur and Blois, spending four months in one and over a year at the other. In all these towns travellers busily sought reasonable accommodation. A young Fellow of Queen's College Oxford in 1656 settled his pupils in a private house in Saumur where they had a better chance of learning the language from the French (and ethics from him), as he thought, than in 'those greater Pensions where there is much and so ordinarily bad company'. Joseph Williamson, for it is the future secretary of state, was directed by his patrons to see that their sons learnt to speak and write French properly before going on to Paris and Italy; meanwhile a friend in England wrote to him that his cronies at home made music *à la mode de France* and were dancing 'a Cinquepace in the like remembrance of our travelling Mounsieur'.[20]

Although study of the language and 'exercises' came first, Robert Montagu visited the neighbouring cities. In the course of a year at Saumur he made at least three minor excursions, for which he carefully measured the distance, 27 leagues to Richelieu and Loudun, 130 leagues to La Rochelle, Saintes and Poitiers, 36 leagues to La Flèche and Angers. He took up his diary again, perhaps wearily, and set to work. At La Rochelle he was driven to make a fairly intelligent little sketch of the Huguenots' place in French history; and visited a sugar-refinery. Chinon, it appeared, was the birthplace of Dr. Francis Rabelais, and in Loudun still lived the famous nun from whom the Jesuits had exorcised the devil, a miracle which had greatly impressed his cousin Walter Montagu who came to Loudun with the budding playwright Thomas Killigrew in 1635.[21] But Robert himself was no more impressed than those good Protestants Evelyn, Mortoft and Bertie, and continued placidly on his way. A typical comment from the diary conveys the tone of this usual observations:

Fontenoy Le Conté, a little towne in Poictow where I dined, and the Protestants having in the towne a church I heard a peece of a sermon, it being on a Sunday; this towne is full of Protestants.[22]

Another aspect of the long period of residence in Touraine, naturally, concerns a traveller's circle of acquaintances. Montagu twice visited Thouars, palace of the due de la Trémouille who had close connections

with England through the marriage of Charlotte de la Trémouille with
the Earl of Derby. Montagu met Lord Strange, Charlotte's son, at
Thouars in October 1649 — the only Englishmen of standing mentioned throughout the diary,[23] and he goes on to describe a second visit
to this noble French family in the following terms:[24]

> . . . The Duke of Trimoille receaved me with great courtesy making mee to
> lye in his owne house and to eat with him, as also I had long conference in
> the which he offered to doe me very many favours especially if he did goe
> into Italie as Ambassadour; and in parting permitted mee to hunt in his
> warren which is 5 leagues long, the which permision he gives to very few. I
> saw also Madame la Duchesse his wife who asked mee many questions
> concerning Ingland. I spoek with the Prince of Tarante and with the Earl of
> Laval his two sonnes, with la Princesse of Tarante and mademoiselle the
> Duke's onely daughter, and having stayed heere two dayes I came againe to
> Saumur; and during that yeere I stayed heere I made more particulier
> acquaintence with the Prince of Mecklebourg, his name being John Gorge,
> also with two German Earles of Levenstine, with the Baron of Trawn
> [Traun?] and two other german barons and with severall other gentlemen of
> divers nations.

He hunted also in the woods of Cardinal Grimaldi, uncle of the Prince
of Monaco. A little study, sightseeing and the conversation of foreign
noblemen filled up Robert Montagu Lord Mandeville's time; for an
English peer moved on equal terms with the sovereign princes of
Europe's smaller ruling houses.

It is clear that there were always Englishmen in Touraine; it must be
equally clear that political events in England added to the number. After
all, what was the procedure of Sir Ralph Verney, that perplexed knight
of the sorrowful countenance who felt that he sided with neither party
once they were ranged in decisive opposition, since he was an Anglican
Parliamentarian unwilling to subscribe to the Covenant? He withdrew
with his family from Buckinghamshire and London, going first to Rotterdam, then to Rouen and finally settling at Blois where he lived from
1645 to 1651. He was accompanied by his wife, two of his children and
two English maids, who all with varying success adapted themselves to
unfamiliar surroundings. Verney himself found consolation in books;
some of the works of Prynne, Milton, Lilburne, Ascham, Hooker and
Andrewes were sent out to him. He lived on friendly terms with the local
Protestant pastor. Once or twice he toured down the Loire to Nantes,
La Rochelle and Bordeaux. When Mary Verney returned to England in
the autumn of 1646 — wives were the great intermediaries in the
financial history of the exiles — to deal with the problem created by
Parliament's sequestration of their property, the rest of the family stayed
on in Blois. And intermittently in the Verney correspondence of these
years appear the names of friends and families in a similar situation,
living quietly abroad.[25] If we turn also to some of the surviving letters

addressed to Sir Richard Browne, the King's Agent at Paris, there are a few written from these towns along the Loire which tell the same tale of little resident groups of exiles or neutrals, often barely distinguishable or not distinguished from English citizens travelling in France with whom the Commonwealth government had no quarrel at all, like Lord Mandeville.[26]

At Angers in 1647 was quite a circle of acquaintances known to Browne. Sir Thomas Hanmer wrote from there in December, rejoicing in the good wine and good food and the comforting society of his countrymen: Henry Coventry and his young nephew Sir George Savile (the future Marquis of Halifax had set out on a tour of France and Italy), Sir Richard Percy, Dr. Duncombe,[27] Sir John Armitage and others. Not far off, at La Flèche, were Sir Brian Palmer and Sir Thomas Glenham, who had been Governor of Oxford in the closing stages of the civil war. All waited anxiously on the arrival of news, in the form of rumour, intelligences and diurnals about the state of affairs in England:

> I confesse [says Hanmer] I now long more then ever I did since this warr to hear the next newes, for I expect some very soddaine and furious attempts of the levellers, which nevertheless confesse I feare not, for I think lesse danger to monarchy in their rashnes and violence then in the parliament's more moderate course. If you meete with the Case of the Army, or any of those levelling bookes, and have not occasion to use them I would willingly see them, to compare them with Utopia which certainly resembles them, and is not very irrationall.[28]

Hanmer and his wife were still at Angers in 1649 though disturbed by the local Fronde which had driven many Englishmen away, Lord Willoughby to St. Malo and Lord Falkland to Nantes, about the time Robert Montagu settled in Saumur. Before many years had passed Sir Thomas Hanmer made his peace with the Commonwealth and returned to England.

In accompanying the travellers from England down to Touraine we have followed the most crowded part of the route; so many of them adopted this course, a relatively short stay in Paris succeeded by a lengthy period of residence in Blois, Saumur or Loudun. After that, the road divides: either travellers went on to complete a grand tour of France like Wentworth or, content with what they had already seen of the west, made their way to Lyon and the routes into Italy. John Evelyn, it is well known, spent the summer of 1644 along the Loire and afterwards, 'minding how to shape my course so as I might winter in Italy', passed through Bourges and Moulins to Lyon. A part of this programme was adopted by Hainhofer and Robert Montagu, who never visited Bordeaux or Toulouse. Possibly they were deterred by disturbed political conditions of south-western France. On 1 November 1650 they commenced travelling again and along the approaches to Orleans met Louis XIV and his armies returning from the siege of Bordeaux. On the 9th they reached Paris in time to see effigies of Cardinal Mazarin being carried about the streets with a rope round his neck, and a motto:

> Voicy une Harpie, habilé en Cardinal!
> Qu'on dépende la copie pour prendre l'original!

Next day they left the city and after a visit to the palace of Fontainebleau, involving a laborious description of its main features by the young man, travelled along the ordinary route from Paris to Lyon running south to Briare on the Loire, up the right bank to Pouilly famous for mineral waters ('the cheefest nobility of France come there in summer to drink them, and those that cannot come have them sent in bottels to them with a certain mark on them'), crossing the river at Nevers, to Moulins and Roanne (considered by John Evelyn so delightful a spot for the days of a man's retirement), over the watershed and down to Lyon. They arrived on 30 November, and soon bad weather and severe floods induced the tutor to settle there for the winter.[29]

Lyon was thoroughly explored, its geographical and commercial importance analysed, the libraries, hospitals and the cabinets of rarities belonging to wealthy men visited one by one. Montagu found excellent tutors for geometry and fencing here, even though another Englishman of the period thought Lyon suitable as a residence for merchants rather than gentlemen.[30] Not until May in the following year did he set off once again, travelling through the mountains to Geneva where another long stay was made, for more Latin and dancing, for a survey of the town and its government and the cultivation of new friends. Montagu became acquainted with a Prince of Baden and Baron Windischgrätz, receiving also many kindnesses from Lady Biondi, sister of Sir Theodore Mayerne, a widow who after a lifetime in England had retired to Aubonne, that charming village not far from the north shore of the lake. Geneva, no longer the direct inspiration of militant English Protestantism as in the days of Calvin and Theodore Beza, was evidently the centre of a pleasant social life. Here Milton ten years earlier had been entertained by the Diodati and Cerdagni families. Here lived and studied several of the sons of Richard Boyle the 'great' Earl of Cork, that impenitent English lord of Irish land who had been intent on giving his children a good and godly education, and appointed as their tutor a Huguenot having wife and family domiciled in Geneva. One son Robert Boyle, remarkable author of the Sceptical Chymist, lived in Geneva for nearly two years, practising the usual exercises, reading romances and learning to speak French like a native, before going over the Alps into Italy.[31] Robert Montagu and M. Hainhofer, on the other hand, first travelled through Switzerland to Augsburg before turning south; and having

23.    The metropolis of Lyon: the Rhône is visible on the far left and the bridge over the
       Saône further right. Eastwards, up the Rhône were the routes to Geneva and
       Piedmont, and south were those to Provence and Languedoc.

brought them to the confines of the French-speaking world on the hilly
road from Lausanne to Berne we will leave them. A part of the long
apprenticeship was over.

Such was one alternative after Blois or Paris. The other had been
called by Richard, the wandering brother of Sir Simonds D'Ewes, the
'great route of France', as he travelled along the roads already described
by Wentworth a quarter of a century before. D'Ewes does not appear to
have kept a diary but a few letters home describe his course. After
spending the winter of 1637 in Paris he was in Orleans by the middle of
March, visited La Rochelle Bordeaux and Montpellier, and wrote from
Lyon to his brother in May: 'I shall make all possible speed for Geneva,
oure companie is strong, we shall pass by the Army', Richelieu's army
for the Italian campaigns against the Habsburg. Unfortunately plague
broke out in Savoy and kept him a few months longer in Lyon where,
mindful of his brother's passionate antiquarianism, he discovered 'a
fellow that hath all sorts of Moddals and Roman Coynes, if you please to
send me a note of such as you desire I shall get them'. But the plague
approached Lyon and cities further north so he hastened south to
Marseilles and went to Italy by sea.[32] Thomas Abdy's journal belongs to

the same period and follows the same itinerary. He left Blois at the end of April 1634 and was in Lyon by 20 July having included Geneva in his tour; travelling shortly after the great armed rising in Languedoc, which had ended with the duc de Montmorency's execution in 1632 and the expulsion from France of Monsieur, Louis XIII's brother, Abdy saw everywhere in the south the signs of governmental activity and repression. The intendant Machault, 'Coupe-tête', was busily at work, the castles or fortifications at Béziers, Pézenas and Beaucaire were noted by the traveller as recently dismantled. Apparently the next surviving diary of this tour dates from 1648; after the anonymous traveller of that year, already mentioned, comes Sir Ralph Verney who went with his eldest son from Blois in 1651 through Bordeaux, Toulouse and Montpellier en route for Italy, John Reresby in 1654, then Francis Mortoft in 1658, and Charles Bertie in 1662 and Edward Browne in the same year. Nor are there any deviations from the well-worn track.

However, as time passed the chief interest of many travellers gradually changed. The concern felt by some enlightened men with an academic training for the practical arts of mankind, though coloured by a wealth of literary or classical allusions, as in John Evelyn's work, was an outstanding feature of the second half of the century. A greater emphasis on technology appears in travel literature, while one of the areas where the travellers were most struck by what they saw was southern France. Montpellier, as a celebrated centre for scientific and medical activity, became highly fashionable.

For example, we have already met John Ray, the naturalist who was in Rome in 1665 as the doyen of an important party of gentlemen with scientific interests, Francis Willughby, Phillip Skippon and Nathanael Bacon. Ray, a Fellow of Trinity College Cambridge until he refused to conform in 1662, had previously botanized extensively in different parts of England. He and his friends were now determined to widen their field of study by a more ambitious journey on the continent. Travelling through Germany and Italy they busily collected specimens of plants, fishes, birds, stones and other rarities, and noted the detail of local antiquities, dialects and customs wherever they went. Skippon, into the bargain, was a meticulous observer of machinery and incorporated in his journal sketches of waterworks, sawmills, dredgers, devices for twisting silk and grinding glass and making viol-strings. Their enthusiasms were multifarious and they themselves worthy and characteristic members of the circle of the Royal Society. In August 1665 Ray, Willughby and Skippon reached Montpellier where they spent the winter. They met there a number of Englishmen including Lord Ailesbury, Oliver St. John the Cromwellian exile and young Martin Lister, a medical student. Another resident was Dr. John Downes, afterwards physician at St.

Bartholomew's and Christ's Hospital. Ray's party continued to collect specimens 'although the season for simpling was past', and carefully noted the methods employed in local industries for blanching bees' wax and the manufacture of olive oil. It was unfortunate for them that early in 1666 Louis XIV declared war on England, during in the Second Dutch War, ordering all Englishmen to leave France; and Ray and his friends with many of their countrymen at Montpellier took their way homeward through Lyon and Paris. Afterwards Ray published the results of his labours. In 1673 appeared the *Catalogus stirpium in externis regionibus*, direct outcome of the continental journey; while it is clear that the collections they made abroad also contributed to the writing of Ornithology and *Historia Piscium* of Ray and Willughby (who died before completing his own book), the *Methodus Plantarum Nova* (1682), *Methodus Insectarum* (1705), *Synopsis Methodica Avium et Piscium* (1713) of Ray, and the general advancement of these branches of scientific enquiry towards rational classification of the ever increasing evidence available.[33] All this invites some description of a notebook kept by the medical student, Lister. He was a Fellow of St John's College, Cambridge, becoming later a member both of the Royal Society and the College of Physicians, a physician and scientist of some eminence. At the end of the century he published his account of *A Journey to Paris in the Year 1698*, a highly popular work in its day. On the other hand his first visit to France has been a subject of speculation; it has even been doubted whether he left England at all as a young man.[34] Skippon, however, mentions meeting him in Montpellier, and Lister's own memoranda describe the earlier stages of his tour.

He intended to go by sea from London to Bordeaux but his Yarmouth pink the *Mathew* was stranded at Weymouth, and he transferred to a ship bound for St. Malo. Travelling with the messenger through Brittany he reached Bordeaux on 15 October 1663. The journey had taken ten weeks and in the course of this leisurely progress he wrote letters to his friends and kept up his reading, having looked at a history of the French Academy and the Satyricon of Petronius Arbiter on the way.[35] Early in the new year he left Bordeaux and after visiting Toulouse and Carcassonne arrived at Montpellier, where he usually resided until February 1666. In the summer of 1664 he toured in Provence, but he was undoubtedly in Montpellier by December and again after August 1665 when Ray and Skippon arrived. He lodged with a master-apothecary, excellent apartments and an excellent host for a medical student; but as Ray remarked, there were an unusual number of apothecary shops in the little town, a hundred and thirty, each busily employed in concocting essences known all over France.

With regard to his professional training Lister left a few memoirs, short and fragmentary papers, which confirm the details given by Edward

Browne in his account of lectures and hospitals in Paris at this time, and by Ray and Skippon for the general atmosphere of scientific discussion at Montpellier. At Montpellier as in London even the ordinary English nobleman sometimes followed the fashion by playing a part in or at least encouraging such discussion. Skippon described how he and his friends attended a dissection performed by the great Danish physiologist and geologist Nicholas Steno, but Lister adds that this took place in the rooms of the first Lord Ailesbury then residing in Montpellier. He gives a full account of the occasion, followed by some admirable notes on John Ray's conversation and ideas in December 1665. Very similar discussions were undoubtedly taking place at meetings of the Royal Society in London at that time but the additional experience of Englishmen abroad, like the correspondence with foreign savants which formed part of the Society's proceedings, also had a distinct share in the development of English scientific research.

A few phrases from Lister's account of Nicholas Steno's dissection and then of Ray's table-talk reveal the virtuosi at work in Montpellier:[36]

In my Lord's cabinet we had shewed us the two ductus of his Discovery from the Glandulus on each side the cheeke in an Oxheade...moreover he shewed us yt the make of muscles was not as the Ancients phansied, yt is, the Fibers lay not in a straight line from Tendon to Tendon, but made alternate Angles with the two Tendons etc....[37]

Mr Wray was of the opinion yt never any perfect cure was made of the Pox without Mercurie, which he confirmed him by the generall consent of the best practized doctors he had spoake withall either in England or Italie... That water will make its way through where aire cannot, is manifest from this experiment which Mr Crowne assured me to have tried several times before the Academie of Virtuosi at Gresham and it was there registered, if we blow up a bladder and tye it up...That the specifique and distinguishing virtu of a plant was to be found in the Oily part of yt which was various and different in all, than either in the fix salt or spirit...all fix salts of Plants being alike as alsoe all spirits. This was the result of an Entertein[ment] wherein Mr Wray and Mr Havers were the Antagonists, and where I assisted.

Of the other attractions which Montpellier offered to scientists or philosophers, Skippon gives the name of Monsieur Lort, manufacturer of counterfeit amethysts, topazes, emeralds and sapphires, and he attended experiments in this gentleman's house. Lister almost certainly went there too, as a devotee of the subject; in later life he interested himself in the classification of gems and prepared a detailed Table of Precious Stones and Pearls, which is among his papers. Skippon also thought well of Dr. Joly a Protestant physician, but Lister records a discussion with Joly on the differences between French and English medical practice. Both men must have frequented Monsieur Relle, microscope maker, to examine cheese mites and grains of sand, or eyed the 'perspectives' at three pistoles apiece. Indeed it seems probable that when Ray and his party arrived in Montpellier they were shown round by a fellow-enthusiast and a Cambridge acquaintance. Many of the people and places named in their narratives were more familiar to Lister who had been resident there for two years.

This city, then, occupies a special position in the pilgrimage of Englishmen through France and, as the records tend to show, became prominent at a time when even gentlemen on tour felt anxious to dabble in the sciences. But the best part of Martin Lister's memoranda deals with a slightly different subject, though akin to it. Like Thomas Wentworth half a century earlier he tells us what he was reading while abroad, and it is instructive to compare the two lists. He also might have been content to insert a catalogue of books purchased into the blank pages of his pocket diary — the *Everyman's Companion* published in 1661 — but he was a genuine and conscientious student, and apart from notes of his journey, and the dates of bills of exchange and letters despatched, he kept month by month a list of books read or consulted, calling them Lections Achevées.[38] Some of the items occur repeatedly, testimony to its workmanlike and reliable character and these entries cover the whole period of his residence (October 1663–February 1666). Though often only the barest indication of a title is given, a reasonable catalogue can be reconstructed. What was Lister reading in the course of his stay at Montpellier and during summer excursions to Provençal cities?

He interested himself in three main classes of literature, the authors and poets of classical Rome, scientific books ancient and modern, contemporary letters and history. In the first he mentions Petronius Arbiter, Livy, Tactitus, Suetonius, Pliny's Letters, Martial's Epigrams, Horace, Catullus, Tibullus, Propertius, Claudian, Ausonius, the Noctes Atticae of Aulus Gellius, and Cicero whom he looked at repeatedly, especially the Letters. In the second class he studied from time to time Hippocrates and Dioscorides together with modern criticisms, the Formulae Remediorum of Morellius of which the first published edition came from Leipzig in 1645, a number of recent works on chemistry, fermentation (a favourite subject) and drugs, and Descartes' treatise on light. He had also seen Polydore Virgil's De Rerum Inventoribus. Towards the end of 1665, probably inspired by John Ray Lister was reading books on plants, fishes and snakes. On his arrival at Paris he obtained copies of the *Journal des Savants*, which had recently commenced publication.[39]

In this collection of titles the blend of literary and scientific interests is characteristic of one type of intellectual outlook common in that period. However, contemporary works on literature and history form the most striking group in Lister's notebook. From them much that was passing through his mind at the time can be identified, providing him with the elements of the style and the knowledge required to place a sensitive reader on level terms with progressive thinkers of the day. Reassembling the entries into a coherent sequence, the following is a list of identifiable volumes in this third class, contemporary literature:

N. Faret. *L'Honnête Homme; l'art de plaire à court.*
Eight editions appeared between 1630 and 1660. The most famous of all French courtesy books, Castiglione's courtier brought up to date.[40]

J. de Caillière. *La Fortune des Gens de Qualité. . .enseignant l' art de plaire à cour.*
First edition in 1658. Another work on manners and conduct: in keeping with its later date, perhaps, it is more aristocratic in tone than Faret, less concerned with the preferment of merit than the virtues of preferment.

R. Bary. *La Rhétorique Française.*
Published in 1653. A treatise on language, listing all the appropriate verbs, adjectives and figures of speech permissible in polished conversation. 'Il me semble', says the author, 'qu' on démentirait ses propres luimières si l'on préferait le français de l'Université au français du Louvre, et si l'on aimait mieux s'exprimer en l'homme d'affaires ou de trafic que de parler en homme de Cour ou d'Académie.'

P. Pellisson. *Historie de l'Académie Française.*
Published in 1653. This essay, in the form of a letter, gave information on a subject of great interest to Englishmen after 1650, the reorganization of learning. It is written in a style which Sainte-Beuve considered a model of seventeenth-century elegance.[41]

J. L. G. de Balzac. *Lettres.*
First published in 1624; an English translation appeared in 1634. Further instalments were printed from time to time, and Lister looked at various editions and collections. *Socrate Chrétien* (1652). *Entretiens* (1657). *Aristippe, ou la Cour.*
First published in 1658, an English translation in 1659. A panegyric of Richelieu. The great master of rhetoric, and a dominant influence in the history of French prose style, was Lister's favourite French author, to judge by the number of entries in his reading list.

P. Scarron. *Virgile Travesti* (1648, 1653). *Roman Comique* (1649, 1657).
These examples of their author's burlesque manner were just beginning to fall out of favour when Lister read them but they had exercised great influence in the preceding twenty years. Another title given by him, 'Burlesques', may be the *Receuil des quelques vers burlesques* (1643).

St. Amand. *Œuvres.*
The first comprehensive collection of St. Amand's poetry appeared in 1638: again, verses with too strong a flavour of realism and harsh expression not to attract censure from critics of Lister's generation. 'Lyrian and Sylvia' was translated into English by Sir E. Sherburne (1651).

P. T. de Girac. *Réponse du sieur de Girac à la défense des Œuvres de Voiture faite par M. Costar.*
Published in 1655. The author maintained his previous objection to the letters of the poet Voiture for flippant, ignoble language unworthy of his subjects.[42]

P. Corneille. *Sertorius.*
Published in 1662; usually considered one of his greater plays.

T. Corneille. *Le Geôlier de soi-même.*
　　Published in 1655, an adaptation from Calderon. This work was very
　　successful with the public by introducing in a romantic and sentimental
　　plot a strong element of burlesque.
Bussy-Rabutin. *Histoire Amoureuse de la Gaule.*
　　Lister read this, his final entry, early in 1666. In the previous year Louis
　　XIV had imprisoned the author on account of the book, considered a
　　notorious libel on the ladies of his court. Much of it was based on a
　　classical author very familiar to Lister, Petronius. In a contribution to the
　　Transactions of the Royal Society later on, he mentions that he had been
　　reading both Bussy-Rabutin and Petronius for evidence of the use to
　　which the ancients put a diet of snails.[43]
F. Petrarch. Lister was reading something of Petrarch at Nîmes in March
　　1664.
B. Tasso. *Lettere.*
　　First published in 1549; a work of rhetorical and autobiographical interest
　　by the father of the poet.
G. B. Guarini. *Il Pastor Fido.*
　　First published in 1590. Fanshawe's English translation had already
　　appeared in 1647.

　　The number of French books is increased by the fact that Lister's
classical reading was often in French translation. He mentions using the
text and translation of Phaedrus' Fables prepared for the schools of Port
Royal by de Saci, author of the Port Royal version of the Bible. He read
Arrian on Alexander and Tacitus' Annals in the translation of N. P.
d'Ablancourt who frankly adapted the originals to the taste of his own
day. D'Ablancourt once wrote: 'Je ne m'attache donc pas toujours aux
paroles ni aux pensées de cet auteur, et demeurant dans son but, j'agence
à notre air et à notre façon.' In his scanty theological reading Lister
entered the same literary world; the one ecclesiastical writer named by
him was Antoine Godeau, Bishop of Grasse, one of the original members of the Académie Française and a stylist complimented by Balzac.
Lister often looked at his *Vie de St. Paul* (1647; an English translation by
Edward Lord Vaux, 1654). It seems, therefore, that although the general
characteristics of the seventeenth-century French literary style were
shaped amid the noisy controversy of hostile groups of authors, an
English reader, with every French book that he handled, might participate indirectly in the process of change.
　　All these items formed his principal reading of modern literature, and
of works on conduct and good writing. From the present-day point of
view, with its common acceptance of the distinction between literary and
scientific pursuits, Lister was primarily a student of the sciences, a
doctor of medicine, a naturalist and a mineralogist; the day and hours
which he must have spent at Montpellier reading French and Italian
books of the sorts just described may come as a surprise to us, but it
would have surprised very few of his more intelligent contemporaries.

A collection of titles on history and politics can also be taken from his notes:

P. Sarpi. *Storia del Concilio Tridentino di Pietro Soave Polano.*
The first comprehensive Italian edition appeared in 1629.
A. Correri. *Relazione della Corte Romana Fatta l'anno 1661*
Published in 1662. The reports of a Venetian ambassador to Rome: by its outspoken criticism of the papal court under Alexander VII this book attracted general attention.[44]
F. Pallavicino. *Il Divorzio Celeste, cagionato dalle dissolutezze della Sposa Romana.*
Written before 1643. A pasquinade which enjoyed great popularity in Protestant circles. The author had a talent for scurrility. There is an English translation by J. Howell (1644).
*Le Courrier Desvalizé.*
By the same author in the same vein. An English adaptation by C. Gildon appeared in 1692.
Perefixe. *Histoire de Roi Henry le Grand.*
Published in 1662. A panegyric, and an exhortation to Louis XIV to whom Perefixe had been tutor.
Bassompierre. *Mémoires* (1598–1626).
Published in 1665. Lister secured a copy early in the following year.
C. Bourdeille, comte de Montrésor. *Diverses Pièces durant la ministère du C. de Richelieu.*
Published in 1664–5.
La Rochefoucauld. *Mémoires sur la Régence d'Anne d'Autriche.*
First published in 1662. Greatly valued by contemporaries for elegance of style, and general reliability.
La Châtre. *Mémoires.*
Bound together with the preceding item in an edition ostensibly published at Cologne in 1664, and dealing with the same subject.
L. de Brienne. *Réponse par...Brienne aux mémoires de la Chastre.*
Ostensibly published at Cologne in 1664.
N. Besonge. *L'Estat de France.*
First published in 1663; a general sketch of the monarchy, the household offices and nobility of France. Many editions subsequently appeared, keeping it up to date. English translation, 1691.

These titles, with some miscellaneous exceptions, complete Lister's catalogue of 'Lections Achevées'. One of these exceptions was Sir Henry Wotton's *Elements of Architecture* which with Willis on *Fermentation* are the only English contributions. At Montpellier he had English friends and fellow-students but English books were most conspicuous by their absence. Very probably when Anglo-French hostilities began in 1666 he returned home with a far more vivid knowledge of French than of English literature and history. One reservation there might be; his reading was conservative. Much that he studied was fast falling out of favour in Paris with the progressive critics. Balzac, Scarron, Voiture and

St Amand no longer satisfied the canons of excellence approved by Boileau and his followers. In other respects it is necessary to recognise the substantial knowledge of French literature acquired by an individual English student and scientist in the course of his travels.

This bibliographical excursion must not be allowed to overshadow the grand tour itself. These books were read largely in Montpellier in the days when Englishmen passed through on their conventional journey round France. Lister's papers, as well as the journals of Ray and Skippon, give some idea of the life lived there by travellers who stopped for a while; and they illustrate the significance of another stage in the long itinerary. Montpellier, like every city on the classic route, received the Englishman on his travels, and occasionally he died there. Lister or Ray or Dr. Downes might return safely home, but in 1682 the Robert Montagu of a few pages ago, now third Earl of Manchester, decided to leave England and travel south for his health 'that air being prescribed him for the perfectest cure for his rheumatism'.[45] He came to Montpellier, which he had failed to visit in 1649–1651; and there he died, early in 1683. All the physicians in a school for physicians could not cure him. The younger generation continued on their way, by the ordinary route. Orleans, Bordeaux, Toulouse, Montpellier, the Rhône valley.

However, if there were orthodoxies of travel in the seventeenth century and for that reason men kept to the highroads, and lived in the French cities traditionally known to strangers, heresies come occasionally to light. The other ancient rule, that it is wise to avoid one's fellow countrymen abroad, was sometimes enforced by a zealous parent who sent his children to a quiet place generally neglected by Englishmen, before allowing them to enter the Parisian hurly-burly or Blois Saumur and Loudun, crowded with strangers. Just while Lister and others were travelling in the south Philip Lord Wharton chose Caen, eighty miles west of Rouen, as a suitable centre for the upbringing of his children. The town had been well known to the English royalists, a number of whom lived there before 1660, but this importance was temporary. Wharton's correspondence reveals another example of the now familiar grouping, one or two young noblemen guarded by tutors and servants, but in this case they resided in an unfamiliar district and their tutors, victims of the Restoration in 1660, were likewise unconventional figures in this setting.[46]

After 1660 the fate of ejected Puritan divines was very varied. Perhaps the most fortunate secured the patroage of a powerful family which sent its sons abroad at an early age, according to custom; and nonconforming ministers escaped out of harm's way by accompanying them as tutors. Theophilus Gale, formerly Fellow of Magdalen College Oxford and Abraham Clifford, formerly Fellow of Pembroke Cambridge, who were compelled to surrender their university positions, held this post in the Wharton family between 1662 and 1666. In particular, they taught the son and heir Thomas, later the Marquis and fifth Lord, and Goodwin his brother. The aftermath was curious: Thomas Wharton became a thoroughgoing man of the world who liked best in life party management, parliamentary elections and race meetings; the alliance of the Whig magnates with nonconformity was never more oddly foreshadowed and exemplified. In 1662, however, he was a boy of fourteen, his brother was nine, and a long period of travel abroad preceded this radical transformation.

Lord Wharton's adviser John Gilbert, an influential Puritan who was chaplain at Magdalen 1656–1660, recommended for the post of tutor two of his colleagues Henry Hickman and Gale, the first 'of the more authoritative Presence' and the second 'of the choicer spirit, Grave mild and sweet as well as holy', adding that his own idea of young Thomas Wharton's temperament led him to prefer Gale to Hickman.[47] After this introduction Gale, who welcomed any port in the storm now breaking over Cromwellian Oxford, closed with Wharton's offer of the tutorship of his children 'in order to their intended travel'. Dismissing pupils and getting rid of many books he went to the great country house at Wooburn where Thomas, Goodwin, Henry, Mary and Philadelphia Wharton, aged between eight and seventeen, and their servants Joseph Perkins and James Lefèvre, must have anxiously awaited the new tutor's arrival. Gale, logician and philospher, was soon concerned with children's ailments and elementary Latin. Timetables of lessons devised by Lord Wharton a few years earlier (it may be noted in passing that music, practice on the theorbo, guitar, virginals and harpsicals, with dancing and singing, had taken up many hours each working day in this most Puritan of noble families) were now to be modified since it was planned, in the near future, to send the children abroad in Gale's care.[48]

Several suggestions for a suitable spot on the continent, Saumur, Caen or Grenoble, had been put forward,.[49] Gale himself felt there was no time to lose, nervously anticipating an ecclesiastical visitation in the neighbourhood which would put this awkward question to churchwardens, What private schools were there in each parish? 'I should not care how soon your Honour would put us into a capacity of not being obnoxious unto such guilts and punishments'.[50] It became necessary to compromise between the hesitancies of Lord Wharton on the subject of a godly education and the downright desire of Gale to be gone. The tutor was sent abroad at once to learn French, reconnoitre the ground and make adequate preparation for the children's arrival. He went first to Caen, apparently at the suggestion of Doctor Coxe, an acquaintance of Wharton's, who had sent his sons there some time before. Gale satisfied himself that the journey was short, the lodgings inexpensive, the climate good, the number of resident English inconsiderable (only Mr. Rolls and his tutor, Mr. Beecher, an old man, and Mr. Daniells the merchant who kept a coach) while teachers of riding and other exercises were available at moderate cost. The Protestant church enjoyed the security of public status. Gale had also a personal reason for recommending Caen: his own philosophical system which derived all past history, including classical antiquity and its intellectual achievement, exclusively from Hebrew and Old Testament antecedents was modelled on the writings of the celebrated Huguenot Samuel Bochart, who saw in Semitic Phoenicia the taproot of later historical development; and Bochart was a minister and teacher at Caen. It seemed therefore the ideal place of study and retirement for a non-conforming English divine.[51]

Gale secured another important concession, by persuading Lord Wharton to keep his daughters in England. He had objected that they would require a separate establishment, a French governess, a French servant and a coach to take them to church. In any case 'the coming of English ladies into France for an education is a thing singular'. Furthermore, his own lodgings in the Grande Rue, Caen, with one of the Huguenot elders who spoke both French and Latin, were admirably suited for Thomas and Goodwin:

> Here is a good chamber for them and a large Cabinet or study belonging to it, which for need will hold a bed for Mr Perkins besides their books. Here is also a large room adjoining which will serve for their exercises viz. dancing etc. with a cabinet adjoying which for the summer season will suffice for my lodging.[52]

It may be that here we have a description of typical quarters for an English 'family' resident in France at his period, ready swept and prepared for the Whartons. Meanwhile, let the children and Mr. Perkins practise their French before they come!

In June 1663 Thomas and Goodwin arrived with Perkins and Lefèvre. They remained in Caen until April 1665, then moving to Paris until war broke out between England and France in 1666. For the elder boy it was an important period in his life when first he jolted the tutelage of parent and teachers and began the process of liberation. For Joseph Perkins it was an interlude in twenty years' service as nurse and domestic in the Wharton family; passably educated, he wrote a fair hand and was a most rigid Protestant, terrified of approaching a Catholic church or monastery. For Lefèvre, a Frenchman, it proved the opportunity of finding a French wife. For Gale it meant some intolerable drudgery as governor of the two boys, work for which he was unfitted, combined with leisure for further study, and conversation with Bochart whom he regarded as master-thinker; the first part of his own enormous *Court of the Gentiles* must have been maturing during these years. Communication between this little group and the family in England was maintained by letters and statements of account from the tutor; occasionally Lord Wharton replied, and occasionally the children wrote stiff little complimentary notes to their father, who liked to think that he arranged every hour in their daily timetable and every detail of their conduct. Lefèvre and Perkins also wrote from time to time. Periodically supplies of money were forwarded through Papillon the London merchant and Mr. Daniel at Caen.[53]

Gale, it is clear, was inept. The austere parental programme for their education, the children's allotted periods of private prayer and catechism, the censoring of all friendships which might come their way, were enforced with a humourless severity. Lefèvre's approval of Thomas, who read romances, and his charitable desire to stop teaching the younger boy grammar, Gale condemned outright. Later Lefèvre wrote home to justify himself:

> Master Goodwin speaks as good French and as readily as he can speak English, yet one cannot tell how it came to pass. We never toiled and moiled but I drove that work on insensibly and under pretence of play and merriness, sometimes singing and sometimes fooling together, which some thought an idle boisterousness.[54]

Theophilus Gale disliked such a view of education and, when the school-year began in the autumn of 1663, preferred to send Thomas to the local 'class' in oratory and Goodwin to the grammar class, while he himself spend the day by rising early and working hard at his books and going to bed before the children wished to sleep. He combined severity with neglect, and complained to Lord Wharton. Gale describes prayer and catechism as religious duties for the children which 'could not arise from their own spirits so much as from some external infusions'. He describes dancing and singing as 'pleasing exercises your sons will be alwaies enclined unto, but when once they quit their humanity studies they will not be easily reduced'. When Thomas did well at school, and made friends there, neither Gale nor Perkins considered them fit company for a nobleman and a Christian. By February 1664 the situation was becoming intolerable; and harmony had long since vanished from the Protestant elder's house in the Grande Rue, Caen.[55]

The tutor then wrote a letter which is of some interest for the biography of Thomas Wharton, and led to his own retirement from the family's service. It illustrates what tended to happen when English boys travelled abroad as children, and grew up away from home:

> My Lord, to deal faithfully, I am not without some feares and difficulties as to your sons especially Mr Wharton, in point of Religion and conversation. And because your Lordship commands a particular account of the grounds of our differences I conceive it my duty (though unpleasing) to make some mention, as time will give leave, of particulars. 1st, my Lord, as to Conversation Mr. Wharton judgeth himself fit and capable to choose his company and thinks it too hard an imposition to be tyed up to such as I shall

judge meete; wherupon he has sometimes persons come to him whom I neither know nor can approve of. Also as to times for recreation he is unwilling to be tyed up to rules but sometimes useth violent exercises as fencing etc. immediately after dinner and at other times most proper for study. Again, as to rising it is now usually well nigh 8 of the clock before he is ready, so that oft times we have not sufficient time for praying together, much lesse does he use private prayer. But my cheifest fears are to matters of Religion and a reverent observance of the duties thereof, especially on the Lords Day. I find your sons encline to the French custome of giving themselves liberty (so far as they can get fit occasion) to recreate themselves on that day with musick etc., and I might mention also some neglect of your Lordship's instructions as to your sons' diet, eating fleshe suppers, going to bed late, but these are not so considerable. My greatest feares are lest they should suck in any atheistical or unchristian principles which though they continue civill in their conversations (which, as yet blessed be God they doe) for the present, may at last end in open wickedness. I conceive if your Lordship send fresh instructions to us upon these or the like heads, they might be of great use: for your sons retaine a great reverence of your paternal authority.[56]

It seems, therefore that an English Puritan's progress towards secularism in this instance first involved a period of residence amid the milder Protestant conventions of Huguenot France.

This letter, and many others bearing the same message, perturbed Lord Wharton. Gale honorably confessed that he was unsuited for the post, saying that people in the town thought him too morose, too clumsy in French and Latin conversation and 'those modes of civil behaviour which is necessary for a person in my place'; and he wanted them all to leave Caen, and go elsewhere in France. The father found it advisable to send over Robert Bennet, another ejected nonconformist who enjoyed security in the service of the Whartons, to look into the whole matter. Bennet came, saw and returned to advise that a change must be made. A difficult period followed, in July and August 1664. At Caen Thomas was once present at an evening masque, despite Gale's peremptory veto, and this led to trouble. In England the tutorship was offered to Henry Lever, formerly a minister in the Tyneside, who refused. Gilbert again passed judgment on various candidates, among them Abraham Clifford who was a good scholar from Cambridge badly needing work of some kind. William Moses, sometime Master of Pembroke, commended him. A former Professor of Divinity offered a testimonial: 'he hath ever observed him affecting to go a little (as he thought) too spruce and fine, but sure this will not dissuite him for such an employment'. Clifford accepted an offer with some pleasure. His salary would be £50 rising by £10 yearly to a maximum of £80, his ordinary expenses while travelling included in the general cost of the boys' education. It was a fair wage for an outcast.[57]

The new tutor succeeded, by taking pains to be pleasant with his pupils. His very spruceness and fineness won the day, for he was curiously preoccupied with a 'true and genuine spirit of nobility and grandeur corresponding to their birth and breeding, that they may not be carried away either with things or persons that are below 'em'. He had a lighter touch than Gale though, like him, darkly afraid that Thomas Wharton might be leavened by anti-puritanical principles. For this reason he, too, vehemently requested permission to take the little party away from Caen. Now was the time to go, before the autumn term began, because the boys insisted on attending school as long as they remained, in order to meet their boisterous friends. Moreover the philosophy class which Thomas was due to enter (having acquitted himself so well at oratory) involved a study 'obsolete, nugatory and intricate' for a gentleman. Clifford, it can be seen, bombarded Lord Wharton with reasons for departure.[58]

To his vexation the noble lord first delayed an answer and then ordered them to stay another winter. Gale meanwhile had gone to Paris where he met an old friend John Panton, ejected from All Souls College, now a tutor to Sir John Trott and touring the continent with him. They both lived in the Rue des Boucheries, an address in the Faubourg St. Germain which was passed on to Lord Wharton, and here the travellers came to live when permission to leave Caen was at length granted in the spring of 1665.[59]

The journey proved a delight enjoyed by them all as they went by water up the Seine estuary to Rouen and by coach to Paris. They found themselves in a crowded world of polite society to which they were by no means accustomed. Clifford believed at first that this was simply a halt on the road to Geneva where a quiet and studious life might be resumed. Lord Wharton, however, thought that they could well remain in Paris though secluded from the rout of mutual hospitalities, forbidding them formal suppers or the company of visitors, including other boys and their tutors. Clifford pointed out the sheer impossibility of this course but Wharton, who was obsessed by the dangers of associating with other travellers and following conventional practice, refused to sanction 'a grand tour of France' with periods of residence at Orleans, Saintes or Montpellier. Instead he requested them to commence a long journey through Flanders and Germany to Italy. Clifford's eloquent plea that all experienced travellers recommended the usual itinerary, that not one in a hundred knew anything of the unfamiliar route, that neither Thomas nor Goodwin was old enough or strong enough to profit from so wearisome an adventure, had no effect; and in the summer they left Paris for the Low Countries. This part of their journey has already been described. Outbreaks of war and disease forced them to return to Paris where Thomas Wharton caught smallpox. In the following year, after his recovery, the international situation led to the formal declaration of Anglo-French hostilities and they, like Ray Skippon and Lister, like Sir

John Trott and Mr. Panton who ran into trouble with zealous official-
dom at Dieppe,[60] all came home.[61] Their long education in France was
completed, rather abruptly. Their experience, as Clifford complained
earlier, had not been in accordance either with common practice or with
the advice of the best authors on the subject of travel. On the other
hand this account of their continental adventures shows how much all
English travellers in France had in common. What was usually sought in
Blois or Saumur was equally available in Normandy.

The aftermath, Clifford soon discovered, consisted of a tussle to
secure payment for service rendered.[62] His predecessor was meanwhile
reaping the reward of travel in France, for in 1669 Gale published an
excellent book on *The True Idea of Jansenisme* which he owed partly, says
the preface, to a direct acquaintance with the issues and personalities
involved. Samuel Bochart, of Caen 'in conversation with an English
gentleman' is quoted in this work.[63] In the same year appeared the first
part of Gale's formidable masterpiece, *The Court of the Gentiles*. It may
be doubted whether Thomas Wharton ever read his sometime tutor's
books, since after their return to England fortune led one man to found
a non-conformist academy in London, and the other into the mazes of
Whig political management; but they had come together as travellers
abroad, in uneasy companionship.

Martin Lister's papers shed some light on the development of the
English traveller's intellectual interests in the second half of the century,
by comparison with the attitude of an earlier generation, and the Wharton family correspondence serves the same purpose from a different
point of view. For if the timorousness and caution of Lord Wharton and
his chosen tutors reveal once again that age-old fear of the dangers of
travel, mixed with an admitted appreciation of its necessity and benefits,
their fears are no longer quite the same as those felt half a century
earlier. An anti-Catholic bias is barely perceptible throughout the correspondence; instead, the new menace to the young traveller is defined
as atheism, irreligion, contact with a secular view of the world in its
various forms; and as such its alleged appearance was a portent in the
history of travel, considered as one phase in a man's education, and in
the history of English society.

However, the temptations and the benefits of travel in France would
be felt most keenly in the capital city, Paris itself. In France, men say, all
roads lead to Paris, and to Paris we mut go.

It was a wonderful city owing much to the past and yet full of promise
for the future. Everywhere could be seen the signs of change, or of lively
traditional activity in the old setting. Great palaces were going up, the
Luxembourg and Palais Royal (begun in 1615 and 1636) with their
gardens open to the public. North and east of the Louvre the city walls
were rebuilt to take in more ground, and the city gates widened to cope

with increasing traffic. Marie de Medici opened the Cours la Reine (1628) beyond the Tuileries and along the river, where court and society learnt to enjoy the leisure of fine afternoons with fashionable clothes, carriages and conversation. The Champs Elysées lay to the north of the Cours, and through them ran the roads from Normandy, bringing English travellers to Paris, and from the royal lodge at Versailles and the royal palace of St. Germains. Le Nôtre, who redesigned the famous garden of the Tuileries in 1665 (and was to do the same at St. James and Greenwich) planned a series of orderly vistas on this side of the city to the open country. Meanwhile domes or cupolas, the Sorbonne, the Collège des Quatre Nations, the Val de Grâce and Ste Marie, were altering the skyline seen from the top storey of lodging-houses where travellers slept. The quays on the Seine were being extended, and the first Pont Royal was built, connecting the Faubourg St. Germain directly with the Tuileries; the Jardin des Plantes dates from 1636. There was a growing spaciousness in certain areas. Elsewhere were countless new churches, countless shops and stalls, countless carriages and sedan chairs in the narrow streets, all in some way the concern of a busy, animated and vociferous populace.[64]

Paris in fact was a capital of such outstanding importance, nearer London than the north or west of England, that it is no surprise to find many Englishmen always there after peace had been made in 1630. They did not differ in character from the preceding generation in Henri IV's reign, boys in the academies, embassy officials going backwards and forwards at irregular intervals, and the serious-minded systematically viewing the city. The diary of John Evelyn, kept in Paris in 1643–1644, 1646–1647, 1649–1651, reveals a whole world of folk dining, riding, reading and sightseeing. Other sources simply fill in the picture. Here is Christopher Wren going daily to the Louvre in 1665, where work in progress on column and entablature led him to declare that it was probably the best School of Architecture in Europe; he 'surveys' palaces, buys prints and generally stimulates his genius by direct observation in fresh fields.[65] Here are English medical students (they were much else besides), William Petty, John Finch or Edward Browne attending lectures and operations or walking the great Parisian hospitals.[66] Here is a young man from Essex practising his theorbo in lodgings off the Rue St. Jacques, and there Henry More the Platonist reading Descartes in the gardens of the Luxembourg.[67] Here is one crowd in the Rue Quincampoix where the post for England goes every Wednesday and Sunday at one o'clock and arrives on Tuesdays and Fridays, and another at the English coffee house kept by Mr. Wilson in the Faubourg St. Germain.[68] Here is Thomas Hobbes looking down from a window, on 7 September 1651, as Louis XIV and a great procession pass through the streets to the solemn ceremony which marks the end of the young King's

24.  Paris in the later seventeenth century: a view which includes the statue of Henri IV
     on the Pont Neuf and the more recent additions to the Louvre.

minority;[69] and there John Cosin, in poverty and going blind, struggling
to complete his exposition of the canon of Holy Scripture and Tran-
substantiation from the Anglican point of view.[70]

It seems impossible, and perhaps unnecessary, to analyse so haphazard
a scene. As in the case of Venice, however, what can be done is to distinguish English travellers who helped other travellers, and people who
did most to encourage contacts between the two countries; for the
Englishman abroad was often a lonely figure to whom the society of the
foreigner appeared totally inaccessible. He got lost by day in the muddy
streets of Paris, and at night lay unhappily awake cursing the harsh
chorus of the city cats. He required an intermediary.

First of all, there were the ambassadors and embassies. Sir Isaac
Wake, who figured largely in an earlier chapter, died in Paris in June
1632 and a new ordinary ambassador, Lord Scudamore, did not arrive
at the French court until June 1635. An extraordinary embassage led by
Lord Leicester also took up residence in Paris, and William Aylesbury,

it will be remembered, belonged to his following. Scudamore returned to England in 1639 and Leicester in 1641. They were succeeded by Sir Richard Browne who remained the resident Agent of Charles I and Charles II in Paris until 1660. The households of these men were English footholds in France and could be regarded as information bureaux, places of safety and privilege, and the proper meeting place for friends. John Milton made the acquaintance of Grotius through the kindness of Lord Scudamore. Richard D'Ewes, commissioned by his brother to seek out the house of De Thou the historian, and acquire relics — portraits and papers — of the great man, was helped by James Battyer, Leicester's secretary.[71] In the period before the civil wars in England we know most of Leicester's household: his despatches relate how he was met, on arriving near Paris, by thirty or more English gentlemen including Lord Bayning, a Mr. Russell and Mr. Howard, the son of the Earl of Berkshire, as well as by the whole clientele of du Vaux' academy; and how he began by residing in the Hôtel des Ambassadeurs in the Faubourg St. Germain but moved to a fine place opposite the Louvre in 1639. He rescued young Englishmen who were arrested and sent to the Bastille by Richelieu's officers. He was constantly negotiating with the French court. He appears to have been a busy, sociable man.[72]

Nevertheless, the great patron of Englishmen in Paris, who received and befriended them for a quarter of a century, was Sir Richard Browne. Little is so far known of his early life. He had been a Fellow of Merton in 1624 at the age of nineteen, and a student at Grays Inn in 1627.[73] He was a servant of Sir Isaac Wake at Venice in 1628 and visited Constantinople in 1630, while at home his father maintained very friendly relations with the Warden and Fellows of his College, and the Warden and Fellows brought the young man's name to the notice of Lord Dorchester Secretary of State, hoping for his further promotion.[74] During the next decade, however, he continued to act as servant and secretary to Wake and then to Lord Scudamore in Paris. From time to time he returned to England on official business. In June 1637, for example, he was carrying despatches from London to Paris, and back to London again.[75] In November 1638 he was in England negotiating Scudamore's petition to be called home.[76] He was sufficiently in touch with great men at court to obtain a clerkship of the Council in January 1641, but his real work lay in Paris during the civil wars and the exile. A political agent with a mass of diplomatic business to his credit, he was also the postal official who received and forwarded the correspondence of Royalists from one city to another,[77] the host who gave the passing traveller hospitality and the patron who maintained in his chapel the Anglican service during the interregnum. There John Evelyn was married to Sir Richard's daughter Mary Browne, priests were ordained and sermons preached week after week by Cosin, Earle and others. Evelyn preserved among his papers a printed order of service for use in Paris, the Chapel prayer books, and his own papaphrases of the sermons which he heard there. It is not surprising that Sir Richard Browne was greatly loved: the number of correspondents who thank him for his kindness, or invoke it on behalf of sons and relatives, was very large. He kept an eye on young men at the academies. He gave parties. He lent money.[78]

After the Restoration the first ambassador ordinary was Lord Holles, old, gouty and politically insignificant. Louis XIV, he complained after one interview, took no notice of him 'but with a little nodd of the head as if I had bene a Jack Straw'[79] and the King of France was imitated by Charles II's advisers in tending to disregard this sometime hero of the Long Parliament. But as a host in Paris he did his duty. He came over accompanied by his wife, his nephew Lord Clinton, and by the son and heir of Lord Mohun, and lived in the Rue St. Honoré. He kept in touch with travellers who arrived in Paris, Lady Holland or Lord and Lady Fauconberg or Lord and Lady Ailesbury returning from the spa at Bourbon or Lord Sunderland who fought a duel with a certain Mr. Digby and won; or young Thomas Wharton.[80] Edward Browne related in his diary how he went to the embassy to hear an English sermon, drink English beer and talk to his countrymen in 1664.

Apart from the ambassadors there were also other men who possess-ed great influence in Paris, partly owing to long residence there, and familiarity with important or intelligent people. Probably the most power-ful of these was Walter Montagu, and the most versatile Kenelm Digby.

Montagu's career provides a perfect commentary on that Anglo-French connection which finally ruined the Stuart cause but was also something more than a political expedient. A younger son of the first Earl of Manchester Lord Privy Seal, he went abroad early in life and first found serious employment during the crisis of 1625, before the terms of Prince Charles's French marriage contract were mutually agreed. At one point the Venetian ambassador in Paris ascribed the resumption of negotiations between the weary, embittered French and English minis-ters partly to his own, partly to the diplomacy of Montagu, who was then about twenty-two years old. He returned to London, and set about making Charles 'in love with every hair in Madam's head'.[81] His own friendly acquaintance with the French princess, her sister-in-law Anne of Austria, and the duchesse de Chevreuse had commenced. Thereafter he continued to travel between London and Paris on business of the court. He was in Paris in the spring and again in the autumn of 1626. He was there in the spring of 1627 and again — as a prisoner, captured on his way home from the second of his two missions to Turin in that year — in the autumn. Released after a few months' captivity he was sent to negotiate with Richelieu before the walls of La Rochelle. In 1630 he was in Paris, in 1631, and different visits are recorded every year between 1633 and 1637 and between 1641 and 1643, a phase of his career abruptly terminated by imprisonment in the Tower until 1649. It is not the detail so much as the frequency of his journeys which was significant. When in Paris there were always messages to give and to accept; the faction at the French court opposed to Cardinal Richelieu and the faction round Henrietta Maria in Whitehall opposed to Weston or Windebank kept in touch with one another, thanks to the service of itinerant courtiers like Montagu. He fostered the family alliance which shaped his own career and became all important in the history of Stuart diplomacy. He was himself the English courtier turning Frenchman, an advocate of the French connection as long as he lived.[82]

After his release by Parliament he went into exile, rejoining Henrietta Maria and her other faithful servant Henry Jermyn. As in England, where his brother the general had helped to support him during his imprisonment,[83] so in France the influence of Henrietta Maria and Anne of Austria secured his appointment as head of the religious house of St. Martin at Pontoise, north of Paris; soon the abbé Montagu became one of the few wealthy Englishmen of the exile, and played an important part in maintaining the Catholic faction of the Royalists. Many travellers going from Rouen to Paris learnt to say, with Ormonde in 1659 or Charles Bertie in 1660, that they passed through Pontoise leaving St. Martin's abbey on the right hand, where Mr. Walter Montagu enjoyed the amenities and the profit of his great revenue.[84] It was an enviable position.

It might be thought that Montagu was simply a man whose continental experience led him to acquire political and ecclesiastical influence in the service of the Stuarts and the Bourbons and the Catholic church, one for whom Paris and Pontoise were centres of political and ecclesiastical activity; his attempt to convert the Duke of Gloucester in 1654 was a characteristic venture. However, he did in fact take a broader view, evidently appreciating the advantages of a general education in Paris for young men in the most liberal and farsighted manner, and this can be seen from his correspondence with Edward Montagu Earl of Sandwich, his cousin, formerly one of Oliver Cromwell's advisers and the patron of Samuel Pepys. The diarist noted, in August 1661, that the son and heir Lord Hinchinbrooke, then fourteen years old, and his brother Sydney left England for France. In Paris the abbé Montagu speedily and seriously entered upon the duty, obviously assigned him at some earlier date, of acting as their guardian. He received and transmitted money needed for their expenses. He placed them in a 'preparatory' school before sending them to the well-known academy of Du Plessis. He selected their French governor, M. de Jacquières. He took a sufficient interest in their progress and made visits of inspection: 'il y a quelques jours', wrote Jacquières in 1663, 'que M. l'abbé et m. le comte dalbon [St. Albans] vinrent voir monter à cheval m. le comte [Hinchinbrooke], dont ces messieurs en furent fort satisfaits'.[85] In the summer of the same year Sandwich wrote asking Montagu's advice on the next stage of the children's education. After taking time to reflect he sent the following reply, which takes into account all the factors judged relevant at this period.[86]

> Upon consideration of what you were pleased to propose concerning your sonn my Lord of Hinchinbrook I have conceived this opinion that you shall doe best to leave him this winter still in the academy where he may perfect those exercises which his age is disposed unto, and in the spring you may send him to visit the rest of France and what other forreine parts you shall like best, and to that purpose a discreet compagnon with autority over him will be requisite, one who hath bin in all those parts wher he shall travel. If I can find such a one I shall give you notice of it. . . I will enquire on my part with all the care I can as to the marrying of your sonne. So soon I should not advise it. You are sole judge of the other conveniencys offered to your family but surely it will be greater abatement of part of them, the tying him up so soon instead of giving him that liberty which must now forme and perfect him in all his present propertys.
>
> For this winter I shall not be very hasty in giving him another governor. I shall put a sober discreet valet de chambre about them, who shall have care of theyre persons, and I shall have an eye upon my lord's inclinations in this his self guiding, and fit every remedy to what shall appear requisite. This, my Lord, is my opinion.

In accordance with this admirable advice, the equally admirable 'compagnon' appointed by Walter Montagu received a letter from the Earl of Sandwich on 28 March (n.s.) 1664 requesting him to move the boys from the academy.[87] They found temporary lodgings in Paris, and then awaited the return from England of the abbé who was bringing detailed instructions. During this interim period the accounts of their expenditure, fortunately preserved, contain many items which indicate something of the French style of living which was being gradually imposed on these young boys: clothes, point de Sedan for cuffs, a new suit for master Sidney cut in the French fashion at the abbé Montagu's special request and ordered from a tailor patronized by Monsieur, Louis XIV's brother; diversions, money lost at pall-mall to French noblemen and visits to the Gobelins; books, purchased if not always read, Perefixe on Henri IV, d'Ablancourt's translation of Caesar, an abridged history of France, Rohan's *Parfait Capitaine*, and many others. All these entries testify to a growing familiarity with their foreign environment.[88]

Montagu's responsibility now ceased, for Lord Hinchinbrooke left Paris on a conventional tour of France and Italy. He wintered in Rome where he learnt Italian and 'designing', though his letters home continued to be in French.[89] Afterwards, his career was by no means distinguished but his former guardian should have been satisfied that this was not owing to faulty supervision abroad. With long experience as an intermediary between England and France he had given his relatives the best that Paris offered.

What is true of Montagu applies equally to Henry Jermyn. He also first appeared in politics in the English embassies at Paris in 1624–1625 and, like him, spent forty years in the service of Henrietta Maria in England and on the continent. Little enough has ever been said in his favour, except that while living comfortably in exile he befriended or employed three eminent English men of letters, Crashaw who went on to Italy, Cowley who returned to England in 1656 but came back to Jermyn in 1658, and Sir William Davenant who was in England by 1651 and visited Paris again in 1653. (Musical and dramatic performances which Davenant would have seen in Paris probably influenced him, for he became the first producer who brought English actresses on to the English stage, and the first producer of 'opera' (1656) with a sung recitative in this country.)[90] Moreover, it was Jermyn travelling to France with Henrietta Maria in 1665 who earned the gratitude of Christopher Wren for helping him on the journey and in Paris, doubtless with a sheaf of introductions.[91] He was himself always more interested in court politics than in poets musicians or architects, and his standards of excellence were those of the courtier. Many years later Evelyn remembered him insisting that a young relative in Paris should learn by heart the French rules of polite behaviour, 'the forms of encounter and Court addresses'.[92] For him, these were the supreme qualifications to acquire in France.

The other influential figure of this type in Anglo-Parisian society was Sir Kenelm Digby. Here again it would be an eror to regard him simply as an exile, for in the twenty-five years between 1635 and 1660 he was as often as not residing in France out of sheer preference, collecting and writing books, experimenting, arguing with learned men or dabbling in politics. He came to London from time to time, in 1637 and 1641 and 1653–1655. He was the witty widower, a guest at other men's tables rather than a host, but became so well known in both French and English circles that he was in a position to keep one in touch with the other.[93] In this Digby resembled Sir Richard Browne and the abbé Montagu, though he moved among scientists and philosophers as well as in the company of politicians and ladies of the court. For example, in October 1637 he sent to Thomas Hobbes a copy of Descartes' *Discours de la Méthode*, which had just appeared; both men were at the time in England, but both had been in Paris during the previous summer and it seems possible that Digby first introduced Hobbes to Mersenne. and the group of thinkers who met in this great and good man's cell off the Place Royale, talking religion, science and philosophy.[94] Later, Hobbes was to owe them much, for hospitality and intellectual stimulus, during his last long stay in Paris between 1640 and 1651; one helped to publish his books, another offered him a retreat in Languedoc, and they all helped to spread his reputation in Europe.[95] Kenelm Digby meanwhile flitted from place and place, and person to person. Evelyn met him, Sir

John Finch met him, Sir Balthazar Gerbier's daughters met him,[96] John
Thurloe met him, and all the world knew of his famous Powder of
Sympathy. Coming again to England after 1660 he was one of the original
members of the Royal Society, but his library remained in France.

Here, then, were a number of semi-permanent residents in Paris.
They all had political interests; and they were more than mere politicians. Round them ebbed and flowed the busy life of a vigorous city, in
many respects the most important in Europe. They submitted to its
manifold influence and were themselves middlemen or interpreters,
who introduced other men to the same type of experience. It has been
seen that in several cases their activity in Paris began before the English
civil wars and continued after the Restoration, while even during the
revolutionary period they were often in touch with men who remained in
England or returned to England. At the same time youths kept coming
over the sea to France, whatever the politics of their families. There
were more older men abroad, and there were more women, than would
normally have been the case; but they also tended to return to England,
perhaps at one time or at another but certainly before the official
Restoration. In fact, the intimate ties between England and the continent, forged in the past by dint of many travellers going backwards and
forwards, were preserved without any particular interruption, and there
was no need to reforge them after 1660. The King's execution on 30
January 1649 was at first treated by popular opinion abroad as a defiance
of European tradition; then political necessities quickly asserted themselves, so that France and Spain bid against one another for an alliance
with the Commonwealth. This is true, but also and just as important,
educated Englishmen inevitably continued to look upon the continent
as a place of education, amusement and 'better experience'; western
Europe continued to received them on that assumption. The tour was
performed as before, the academies and universities accepted English
students as before. A few men in special posts of vantage, without giving
this side of the matter much deliberate thought, went on with their work
as intermediaries between France and England.

What were the enthusiasms and interests of travellers arising out of
their experience, and is it possible to observe in any detail their transference to England, particularly during the interregnum? Several instances
can be given and, from the papers of John Evelyn, an attempt made to
catch a glimpse of the consequences at home after the traveller's return.

At this period, for example, the interest which Englishmen had always
taken in foreign books began to develop along new lines. The academic
student was being overshadowed by educated gentry who wanted to buy
books, bind them elegantly, and arrange them according to some approved classification on their library shelves; and they learnt far more in
Paris, a place they frequented, than in Frankfurt the traditional centre of

the book trade. When Richard D'Ewes at length secured entrance to the house of de Thou in 1638, he was lost in admiration of one great press containing 800 manuscripts and wished his brother Sir Simonds had been with him, to see their bindings and 'the contrivance in placing them'.[97] Sir Kenelm Digby, having given away one library in England, was busy collecting another in Paris, having his books gloriously bound and telling his friends to do likewise. 'I presume to send you', he wrote to John Selden, 'a little book of French binding to shew you a pattern for others that happily you would wish so done. In that case let me be your factor. I could not choose a more exactly composed body to putt a faire coate upon than this I send you.'[98] At the same time he gave constant advice to Lord Conway on the purchase of books.[99] Another enthusiast in Paris was Christopher Lord Hatton. One of the prosperous exiles, he acquired books abroad while his son's tutor — Peter Gunning, future Bishop of Ely — was his agent in London. Among his papers may still be seen the copy of an agreement with a French craftsman, dated January 1649, for binding books in morocco and in calf.[100]

Richard Browne was also buying books at this period and having them properly bound. When John Evelyn came to Paris, becoming in due course one of the family by marriage, he quickly and naturally learnt to share this enthusiasm and the two almost conspired together to form that magnificent series of finely bound volumes, some bearing Evelyn's arms and monogram and some bearing Browne's, which were the glory of the Evelyn collection. In fact, this became an abiding passion of the younger man's life. He records his attentive admiration in the Duke of Orleans' library — for the morocco-work and gilding of the books, the green velvet gold-fringed valance of the shelves which held them, the arrangement by size, and the cabinets of medals close at hand to portray the heroes of ancient history memorialized in books — and on his travels he examined other great libraries in Europe. Then, in maturity, he translated Naudé's *Avis pour Dresser un Bibliothèque*, publishing it in London in 1661 with a dedication to Clarendon, himself about to house and furnish his books in a setting of appropriate grandeur. Later on Evelyn poured out his learning and enthusiasm on this subject to guide and stimulate Pepys to raise the Pepysian Library to the standard of the best continental models; and throughout life he was having his own volumes bound (sometimes in Paris) and arranged, catalogued, re-arranged and recatalogued.[101]

Many of Evelyn's books were acquired either in or from Paris. For one thing gifts from his father-in-law began that process which ended in his acquisition by inheritance of all Sir Richard Browne's collections. In 1647 he was given a novel by Cervantes and a *Receuil de plusieurs machines militaires*, in 1649 a very fine copy of the Discourse on Method, a first edition, and there were many more. John Cosin gave him a work by Grotius in 1650. He was also buying on his own account. In 1643 he bought Dupleix on Philosphy for 25 sous near the Ste Chapelle. He first encountered Naudé on Libraries while searching through the stalls of 'the stationers of Paris'. He bought a book from the Mazarin library during one of the cardinal's temporary exiles from the capital. After his final return to England in 1651 such purchases continued. He is translating Lucretius: can Sir Richard Browne find him in Paris a certain old commentary not available here? Will Sir Richard send over Fréart on the Parallels of Architecture, which in fact Evelyn later translated and published? Meanwhile he was reading hard. *Le Jardinier Français* appeared a very useful work to him in 1656, while replanning the garden of his house at Sayes Court, Deptford; two years later he published it in English. In general much of his literary work pays tribute in one form or another, to French influence, even while he criticized sharply men and women who slavishly copied French fashion in dress and manners.[102]

Let us leave the library at Sayes Court, and go into the garden. There a similar transformation was taking place. It is important first to recall two entries in the Diary. In April 1644 Evelyn visited M. Morin and his garden in Paris, 'of an exact oval figure planted with cypress cut flatt and set as even as a wall', with tulips, anemones, ranunculus and crocus of rare quality; monsieur had also collections of shells, flowers and butterflies. On 23 May 1651 he looked once again at the same garden and the same collections, now greatly enlarged. In 1652 he came back to England and determind to settle down at Sayes Court, the lease of which the Brownes and Prettymans were willing to sell. In May 1652 everything there was still in disorder and dilapidation but workmen were soon brought in, the house was altered, while outside indications of vigorous activity abounded. Evelyn wrote to Browne in the autumn:[103]

> Wee are at present pretty well entered in our Gardning, towards which one good supply of Phyleria seedes would infinitely promoate; whilst I am transplanting my Glorious Nursery of neere 800 plantes (two foote high and as fayre as I ever any saw in France) about our Court, and as farr as they will reach (at a foote distance) in our Oval-Garden, the exact designe whereof (together with out other environs) I purpose to send you coppied exactly from the plott, which I have now finished and is the guide of all our designes.

In the same letter he says specifically that he wishes to compare his plan with that of Morin, and by May 1653 he is referring to 'my Morine garden' which, if God prospered him, would surpass the original both in design and contents; and this, Evelyn thought, was a bold claim. Browne's part in the venture was to despatch package after package of seeds or plants and 'whatever else M. Morin recommends'. Cypress lemon orange, alaternus and anemone: Evelyn's demands for fresh consignments echo through ten years' correspondence, and also his thanks for good received. By June 1657 he was satisfied. 'The moyst sommer has made my Oval perfect, and the place most beautiful.'[104]

In addition his collection of specimens began to grow. After discussing a catalogue of plants sent from Paris he once went on to refuse some rare but expensive scarabs which Browne had offered to obtain. His collection of insects and butterflies, he said, was increasing fast from personal bequests, and he was determined not to be robbed by the itch of his own curiosity.[105] Bargains and gifts were enough to occupy the leisure of one virtuoso. The assumption that the accumulation of specimens should be associated with gardening, as medals with books, was of course characteristic of this period.

What else did the tenant of Sayes Court expect from Paris? When John wrote to Mary Evelyn on 8 February 1652, shortly before she left France to join him, he asked her to buy and bring silverware for housekeeping, and listed their requirements. 'The pieces which will aboundantly furnish any appearance here, as the dayes goe now', were 12 plates, 18 spoons, 12 forks, one sottacoppa [sic], 6 porrengers, 6 trenchers, a great salt, salts, candlesticks, chafing dish, sugar-box and boats. On the other hand tankards, basins, skillets and 'such grosse plate' might just as well be bought in England. 'The fashion is the thinge considerable heere', he concluded; 'how playne soever, so made in France is enterteynement enough'. The Evelyn dinner-table, in fact, should conform to the best and most progressive standards of the time.[106]

Since this was in great part the concern of Mrs. Evelyn it may be well to mention here the lively interest which English women, her contemporaries, likewise showed in Paris fashions of dress for which evidence seems to go back to the period of the civil wars. They are wearing coloured sleeves and stomachers in France now, writes Anne Lee to Lady Verney, saying she will make no more new clothes until she hears from her.[107] John Evelyn was quick to inform his sister on these points in November 1649:[108]

And now to speake something of the fashion heere for women, they have in no particular altred, by all the most diligent inspection I can make possibly (and I was last weeke at the frenche court at an Audience which my Friend had) sinc I came last out of France save onely that they dresse their locks so farr backward that the tipps of their eares may be seene, or just as if they were marching against a gentle wind, which they now imagining [sic] gives a grace to their faces. For their Gorgetts, those Crabbats I brought you are now more than ever in fashion; as you may see (without the least alteration) if you have any friend acquainted with my Lade Montague, unto whom (with a Velvet gowne) my Mother sent two by the last Post, but I presume shee will not put it on till Nativity-tyde. The English Ladys heere are like to continue their profound mourning another yeere.

For some time after this fashions did not alter, owing to the long absence of the French court from Paris and the disturbances of the Fronde; but the interest shown by English people in the whole subject is evident.

Experience in France and elsewhere thus had some effect on the way of life in England. There were perceptible modifications of past practice in the library, the garden, the dining room and the wardrobe. Foreign teachers and craftsmen, it is true, worked on this side of the Channel, and books were brought over, but English travellers who had seen something of the continent were so often men of means and power that the development of *their* taste, or the erasure of *their* prejudices, did most to secure acceptance of new standards. Conversely, it came to be agreed that such men, while young, should have this apprenticeship in order to fit them for their place in society. From that point of view this general development was of greater importance than the exile abroad and the return of political refugees, many of whom had been in France and Italy before the civil wars, and were home long before 1660; the truth was, that they merged quite naturally into the large stream of ordinary travellers coming and going across the sea.

This helps to explain the 'Restoration' quality of the life lived in certain circles, illustrated by various types of evidence, during the Protectorate of Oliver and Richard Cromwell. The reappearance of court and monarchy in 1660 simply set a stamp of official approval on these tendencies. Charles II had his French tailors, and the coronation robes were made in France. He had his French gardeners, and they purchased flowers in Paris. He employed French musicians, and sent Pelham Humphreys to France.[109] At Denmark House Henrietta Maria kept her court à la française. St. Evremond, the marquis de Gramont and Lodovic Stuart d'Aubigny[110] all helped to create an atmosphere in the Westminster which English dramatists of the day in their manner, and Samuel Pepys in his, depict so vividly. In many respects it was exaggerated and artificial but it had also an element of permanence, due partly to the genuine potency of French cultural influences in the seventeenth century, partly to royal approval and example after 1660, and partly to the solid apprenticeship abroad of so many English travellers which proceeded without substantial interruption after the war with England and the civil wars in France in the sixteen-twenties. Mr. Spectator, fifty years later still, with his innumerable references to French influence upon the English way of life, was in fact analysing the effects of this apprenticeship.

At the end of 1665 and the beginning of 1666 Englishmen in France were preparing to leave, as Louis XIV prepared for war. The young Whartons, Sir John Trott and Mr. Panton, Lister Ray Skippon and their friends, were all forced to think of departure. Lord Holles the ambassador was a worried man: he felt ill, his wife lay dying and they had no money available to meet the costs of travel. Moreover, 'I thinck all the English in this Towne have already spoken to goe with me not knowing else how to gett over . . . so many English of quality . . . I am sure we shall fill a good shipp.' In time these matters were arranged, and goods loaded into a barge for sending down the Seine to Rouen. The ambassador's desk and his ciphers, gifts of wine for Charles II and his ministers, were put aboard. At last they came home, even the body of Lady Holles for burial in England.[111] But this had been the upshot of ephemeral political manoeuvres, like the attempt to substitute 'Persian' for French fashions of dress at Charles II's court in 1666, and was of no special significance. Soon, in accordance with a conventional practice which had grown up in the course of a century, the English would be back.

# CONCLUSION

The common form of our ancestors, things they were accustomed to do and think without much conscious need to explain what they had in mind, is an important field of historical enquiry. In some respects it presents difficulties more elusive than the unravelling of political incidents, or the compiling and analysis of statistics which denote economic change. In these pages an attempt has been made, first of all, to illuminate the simple seventeenth-century phrases dear to contemporary biographers, that someone 'travelled three years', and 'travelled in Italy, France etc. for his better experience'. Amid a medley of detail the general implication of these phrases has now emerged, and with it the early history of the Grand Tour in western Europe. The Elizabethans had visited the continent, some to study, some to fight, some on special embassies or to gather confidential diplomatic intelligence; a few, in particular, were greatly influenced by Italian example. But after the turn of the century a different and more coherent pattern of travel began to take shape. For private travellers, both the time-table and the itineraries acquired a certain rigidity: a period of residence in Paris or the Loire valley, a tour of southern France during the summer, the tour of Italy in the winter and the following spring, all became conventional. The routes through France had been settled before the death of Henri IV; his sensible government, and improved communications, made travel safe along the main highways. Then, after a tedious interlude of civil commotion, in which English sympathy with the Huguenots forced official envoys to go the length and breadth of the country under difficult conditions, and ordinary travellers hesitated to come at all, the itinerary was resumed after 1630 and thronged year by year. At the same time the tour of Italy, unlike the haphazard journeys between various cities and the varying periods of residence in Tuscany and Venetia characteristic of the reigns of Elizabeth and James I, was also performed increasingly after 1630. The courteous relations of Urban VIII with the English court contributed to the popularity of a *giro* right round the country. The old roads over the Mont Cenis and Brenner passes were now generally neglected, and travellers went in reasonable security from Marseilles along the coast to Genoa, to Florence Rome and Naples, back to Rome, to Venice, and northward over the Simplon into the

Rhône valley. The same academies and the same inns and pensions sheltered one young Englishman after another. To an extraordinary degree these travellers shared a common experience. The convention of the islander's tour of the mainland was common form by 1650, and came into existence during the period of England's enforced retreat from continental politics. Such were the origins of the Grand Tour, and their date.

Now, for a few intensely imaginative men journeys are unnecessary, or a short journey not many miles from home is stimulus enough. As William Blake sang, on coming to the south coast from London:

> Away to sweet Felpham, for Heaven is there
> The Ladder of Angels descends through the air;
> On the turret its spiral does softly descend,
> Through the village then winds, at my cot it does end.
> You stand in the village and look up to Heaven.

Other men, less exceptional, have done well for themselves without going further afield than he did. Yet on the whole a historian must reckon with the fact that ordinary folk require something more radical to influence and stimulate them. The conventional series of vistas unfolded on a tour of western Europe was an answer to this problem, providing a measure of experience, adventure and edification before a traveller 'resolved to be quiet' (the phrase is Lord Clarendon's) and return home again. At first, maybe, his parents hardly recognized some one who came to their door in foreign clothes, and dusty after the long journey; but he was their son, grown a man. They had been willing to adopt an expedient — given the changing condition of Europe and the relative pacification of each country within its frontiers — which was neither impracticable nor very dangerous for their children. The expedient became a fashion; and so Clarendon, writing in old age of his father Henry Hyde, comments on his desire to travel, 'which in that strict time of Queen Elizabeth was not usual except to merchants, and such gentlemen who resolved to be soldiers'.[1] He is assuming that a marked change has come over Europe, and over English society, between 1600 and 1667 when he settled into exile at Montpellier to complete a great indictment of that society as an apologia for himself. In his father's day, as a rule, men of this class did not travel abroad, in his own as a rule they did, and belonged for a while to the considerable army of private gentlemen on their travels.

A historian must also reckon with other facts, which are above or below the notice of the William Blakes of this world. A state has its connections with neighbouring states to adjust; and a large community is rarely self-sufficient, and therefore buys and sells beyond its own frontiers. Citizens travel abroad on business of various kinds. We have observed travellers becoming acquainted with Europe in the course of

official and commercial employments. During this period the diplomatic
service was gradually extended. Besides the embassies at Paris and the
Hague James I usually had a permanent resident at Madrid, Venice,
Brussels and Constantinople. Later on in his reign a resident agent was
placed at Turin, while Henrietta Maria sent Sir William Hamilton to
Rome. Ambassadors and their staffs became indispensable. As travellers,
they were constantly on the move along the principal routes of western
Europe, by sea to Corunna and across Galicia and Castile to Madrid,
from northern France to Paris, Bordeaux and Bayonne, from Paris to
Lyon, Turin, Milan and Venice, from Calais northwards to Brussels
and the Hague, occasionally through Germany to Vienna. There were
special missions to Scandinavia and Russia. There have also been
glimpses, from time to time, of the English merchants travelling abroad.
Factors usually lived in port towns on the coast, making journeys to
cities inland to obtain payments or follow law-suits. There were merchants from Malaga, Seville and San Sebastian who came to worry
Cornwallis and Aston, English merchants of Rouen and Bordeaux with
whom Becher or Doncaster were concerned, merchants going backwards
and forwards between Leghorn and Florence, and many others in many
Italian and Dutch cities. Partly as a result, English consuls became more
numerous.

The itineraries of the three main groups of travellers inevitably
crossed again and again, since the direct routes from court to court
intersected the tour of Europe at various points. Partly as a result, the
travellers assisted one another: merchants negotiated bills of exchange
and transported heavy baggage by sea, ambassadors tried to insist on the
payment of commercial debts owing to Englishmen and the release of
their countrymen unjustly imprisoned in foreign countries, while both
merchant and diplomat gave hospitality to the private traveller. In this
way English society abroad sometimes revealed a very genuine cohesion,
compatriots depending upon mutual service far from home.

Furthermore, many of them often combined business with pleasure,
and pleasure with instruction. James Howell and Robert Bargrave were
representative of the educated commercial men abroad, but the diplomats naturally became the most versatile and the most influential. In
this, personal preference decided the bent of their interests. Some
became intermediaries in bringing works of art from Italy, the Low
Countries and Spain to England, or they collected pictures and statuary
on their own account. Wotton and Fanshawe took advantage of a long
residence abroad to become profoundly acquainted with the literature
and language of the countries they knew most intimately. Richard
Browne was in touch with the booksellers and bookbinders and gardeners of Paris. Members of their households followed this example.
James Mabbe, once on Sir John Digby's staff at Madrid, translated
picaresque novels from the Spanish. Bedell, Sir Henry Wotton's chap-

lain, associated with Sarpi in his ecclesiastical warfare against the Papacy. Bashford, a servant of Wake and Feilding, dealt in pictures. Becher drew on his personal observations in Paris to write an account of Henri IV's amours; and, mixing politics with a pleasant social round, men like Wotton and Walter Montagu and Kenelm Digby learnt to impersonate the fashionable continental influences of their day. These were, at any rate, significant individual achievements.

Such is the outline of the scene discernible in our records during the first half of the seventeenth century. The movement of tourists in Italy and France is one great subject, the travels of the diplomats another, the emigration of Catholic and Protestant recalcitrants to the Low Countries a third, the military volunteers are a fourth, the seasonal journey of convalescents to Spa a fifth (of lesser importance), while peregrinating eccentrics like Lithgow follow their own trail regardless of contemporaries: and taken together they combine, and present an extraordinary spectacle of many different folk rich and poor in different places, in cities and on mountain passes or riding over the Lombard and Picardy plains, their paths crossing with surprising frequency — and then the records multiply — or their isolation in alien territory painfully obvious — when the enquirer must depend on the testimony of a single witness. And yet, it is all something more than merely a spectacle.

In this period English society was breaking the mould which had contained it, with some difficulty, under Elizabeth. The fact was demonstrated in the most fundamental way possible by a collapse of the old constitutional order shortly before the Civil War, and a history of travel illustrates the process from an unusual angle. The connection, which had originally been taken almost for granted, between travel and governmental supervision and preferment in the crown's service, was partially severed. We have seen how important it had been in the reign of James I: diplomats reported the movement of travellers, tutors became diplomatic officials, ambassadors stood a chance of becoming secretaries of state. By the middle of the century, despite the extraordinary powers of a revolutionary government, the significant point was really the free course of the Englishman's travel on the continent. That is why ordinary travellers, increasing greatly in number as they did, tend to disappear from view in the State Papers Foreign, and why tutors and their charges can no longer readily be found as embassy officials and messengers. Men who went abroad still considered themselves, or were considered by their fathers, to be learning to grow into good citizens but not quite in the sense that Shakespeare's Polonius and his Elizabethan contemporaries would have appreciated. The justification of travel as a preparation for the service of the monarchy was no longer viewed from the old, strict standpoint. A conventional itinerary, with a syllabus of studies loosely attached to it, had already become acceptable to many families as an element in the private education of their young men, nobles, gentry, or others. Indeed the 'Grand Tour' began to flourish at a period very considerably earlier than that popularly associated with its heyday in the eighteenth century.

The records of travel throw light, not only on the relation of society to its governing authority, but also on the changing character of that society. In 1650 and 1700, as in 1610, the nobility and wealthier gentry determined to visit the continent. But were their companions of the same type? The history of the educated servant (sometimes the gentleman-servant) class in the seventeenth century is as important and difficult as the history of the yeomen, and still requires much investigation. The view that, while it was always possible to climb from one rung to another on the social ladder, the distance between them was increasing and the intermediate footholds tending to disappear, receives a good deal of support from our studies in biography; certainly the collecting of this kind of evidence is needed to deal with the problem. In the earlier seventeenth century there apparently existed a large class of well-educated laymen, members of which were willing to take to every sort of employment as it was offered by a likely patron; they were forced to adopt this course by pressure of economic circumstances, frequently becoming the upper servants of a great man's family and following. Becher, Woodford, Lorkin, Rooke are all excellent examples. According to the patron's position, as a country gentleman, a gentleman at court, a private traveller, an ambassador, or all these things in turn, so they also undertook various employments as his servants. In particular they welcomed experience abroad because it sometimes gave them an additional qualification as a useful man of business. They might ultimately rise to become patrons themselves. In time, however, the 'family' of educated retainers tends to disappear. The governor who conducted a young gentleman abroad was now more often a Frenchman, or a tutor by profession; or he was a simple clergyman who hoped one day for a living at home. Neither the Frenchman nor the clergyman ever expected to be more than a passing visitor at the English embassies on the continent. Equally, the Fellows of Oxford colleges no longer belonged to the staffs of ambassadors at Paris and Venice. All these activities, educational, clerical, diplomatic, must have become more specialized. Perhaps the Civil Wars gave members of this old 'roving middle-class' their final chance of moving quickly from one kind of work to another, and thereafter they tended to settle down into one vocation or another. The colonies, and commerce, now offered the better opportunities of advancement to ambitious men.[2]

Travellers abroad naturally take with them impressions of home, and they are what their country has made them; therefore they reflect English social and political development. As travellers returning, they have something positive to contribute. Very simply, they bring Knowledge. It may be a working acquaintance with continental politics, continental languages, continental fashions in dress, music, amusements and building. An impression of these things helps to form an educated public. Foreigners also come over to England, perhaps of extraordinary accomplishment as artists or scholars or diplomats; but for their influence to spread they have to begin by satisfying a circle of English patrons and politicians who had been stimulated in the first instance by a period of travel in western Europe. People like Richard Symonds or John Evelyn returned from abroad with heavy portfolios. Ships sailing from Italy carried their purchases of pictures and glass. They had their portraits painted while in Rome or Venice, they chose Delft tiles in Holland to brighten the fireplaces and floors at home, or looked out for cabinets of inlaid stone and polished wood to set beside their own old furniture as a novelty in fashion. Books acquired in foreign cities, occasionally annotated by the traveller and even with faded flowers pressed between the leaves, were sometimes to remain for centuries on their library shelves. These visible tokens were certainly less important, though more easily identified, than the gradual response of the traveller's mind to experience overseas. They learnt history, they learnt geography, they learnt politics. Many vivid images, peculiar to the continent, were imprinted on the memory which would have been poorer without them: the Princes of the Roman Church, the oppressed French peasant, the Venetian mountebank, Carnival, bullfighting, regattas, unusual forms of ceremony on feast days and in foreign courts. Someone like Sir William Temple, recalling the perfume of Asiatic spices heaped in the East India Company's office at Amsterdam, or the glorious oranges growing at Fontainebleau, worked these memories into essays which he wrote, years later, in the retirement of his country house.[3]

It is difficult to say positively what were the general results of this experience, but the testimony of Clarendon is of interest. Here was a statesman whose life and labours coincided with the period under consideration. In the bitterness of two exiles he found much to lament in the trend of English history; the civil wars had been a judgment on the nation, his own downfall in 1667 a further proof that evil was by no means eradicated. Foreign travel, he remarked, increased enormously as the century progressed; and conservatively minded, he might be expected to condemn the practice. In his little dialogue between an old courtier, an old lawyer, an old soldier, an old country gentleman and an old alderman, on the want of respect given to old age, the lawyer courtier and countryman all lay passionate stress on the baleful effects of foreign travel, particularly the custom of sending young boys to France.[4] The results were stated to be perversion to Rome or general contempt for religion, giddiness in dress and talk, and a dangerous ignorance of English institutions. In the French academies the young men learnt only dancing, riding and fencing: what their mentors called philosophy was mere arithmetic, what they called mathematics was a rudimentary study of fortification. Such travellers were of course quite incompetent to play an understanding part in English local government. Yet Clarendon's own opinion emerges in a second dialogue between the same reverend seniors, on the subject of education. Travel is here considered the final phase of a good education, which men who are old enough are recommended to attempt. I must tell you, says the soldier, the custom of this age in visiting foreign countries more than we were accustomed to formerly hath very much lenified that Stubbornness, and filed off much of that Roughness which used to appear in our behaviour and demeanour.[5] Civility, frugality, pleasant and facetious wit, the general rules of policy and wisdom, were not better taught and learnt anywhere than, for example, in Italy. The vices of the Italians were counterbalanced by some experience of the virtue of the Spaniard, the vices of Spain by a period of residence in France and the cheerfulness of Frenchmen. Clarendon hardly permits other speakers to attack the colonel's argument; and if the old and conservative will now grant the travellers so much, it may indeed be granted them.

Education of this kind is necessarily slow and intermittent. Originally, it was thought enquiry might show that the Royalist exile, arising out of the Civil Wars which sent many of the defeated party for several years into foreign parts, accelerated the process. Hence the inclusion of the period between 1660 and 1667 in this survey, to allow the returning Royalists time to settle down at home once more after their experiences abroad. However, the truth is not so spectacular. During the reigns of James I and Charles I foreign travel had evidently become an important and conventional element in the upbringing, sometimes in the adult life, of many Englishmen. If an important minority chose temporary exile after the Parliamentary victory, it was by no means electing to go into the wilderness. They went partly because western Europe was familiar ground; only the circumstances, particularly the poverty, of this second residence abroad, were strange to some of them. In most cases they returned long before 1660, and they were in any case always outnumbered by ordinary travellers. For this reason, that special quality of life often associated with the Restoration and compounded by historians from the diaries of Pepys and Evelyn, contemporary drama and the Philosophical Transactions of the Royal Society, in which foreign and especially French influences are readily perceptible, does not owe too much.to the new court and the returned cavaliers; it owes even more to the steady stream of travellers over sixty years.

In the sphere of politics the biographies of a few travellers cannot be made to prove that their foreign experience affected the trend of events in England. But in the seventeenth century, except during the revolutionary interim, the majority talked and thought of politics in terms of the normal battle for preferment; and undoubtedly the experience and education, as well as the personal connections of different candidates, influenced the issue in this continual struggle. Some travellers, the third Earl of Essex or the second Earl of Bristol or the second Duke of Buckingham, or Sir Thomas Wentworth and Sir Robert Phelips, were men of great property and simply came home with the added advantage of having seen the world; their future was always assured. Others, poorer men, longed 'to be quiet' and enjoy the prosperity which can keep a fire filled with logs, and the flagons with wine. But how could they attain their purpose and what had they to offer? A little French and Italian, a few correspondents in Paris, some table-talk about Titian and Michelangelo, a knowledge of the current affairs which they called 'emergent occasions'. Such were Endymion Porter, Becher, Lorkin, Woodford and Williamson. Between these two extremes were others, whose families enjoyed rather more affluence or influence, Windebank, Wake, Wotton, Carleton, Fanshawe and Richard Browne. Occasionally they fought their way to responsible office in England, sometimes their apprenticeship abroad paved the way to a somewhat easier solution, employment on the continent in the service of the crown as ambassador or agent. Whatever their fate, they provided the personnel needed to fill responsible positions, experienced men who knew the world, and in a number of cases they were formidable, well-educated people. Their struggles for place and prosperity are one element in the English political history of that period.

A few tags of knowledge, whether they led to court appointments or not, and trinkets and prints which are often the only mementoes of a journey, may seem unimportant in the history of a civilized community. There are always young men who wonder, rather pertinently, why the experience of older men in places remote and dangerous appears to have taught them so little. There are always the veterans looking back wistfully to the travels of youth, not because they regret the lack of an intellectual stimulus now beyond their reach, fettered by age and home and work, but because they know that travel assuages ordinary human restlessness. There are always intelligent men who are sensitive and well-informed without this particular form of experience. Above all, there is the fact that any vigorous society has a core of custom strongly resistant to alien influences. These are general criticisms difficult to answer, except that seventeenth-century writers quoted an overwhelming number of authorities who believed in the value of such journeys, on the basis of much reasonable argument. A more specific objection, relevant to this period, was that Englishmen in the reigns of James I and Charles I found nothing of particular significance to study on the continent like the humanistic learning of the fifteenth century, radical Protestant theology in Mary Tudor's time, or even communist theory and practice in the twentieth century. But the European tradition comprises more than theology and classical learning and political theory. A fair degree of acquaintance with the diverse habits and customs of several neighbouring territories and races is another essential element, and that acquaintance is unthinkable without travel. If English society was very much a local growth at this time, because there had been little recent immigration except in London and East Anglia, its governing class at any rate managed to acquire a reasonable familiarity with the wider world of western Europe. Comparison with any culture which fears, and attempts to exclude or to avoid, contaminating influences from outside will demonstrate the historical importance of this fact. The history of travel always deserves, therefore, the attentive scrutiny of an enthusiast here and there among our archives; he will find much to occupy him, while outside, in all winds and weather, the English go on going over the seas for their better experience.

This very day, some of them may be looking for the first time along the reaches of the Seine to Château Gaillard resplendent in the sun, or climbing the steps of Trinità dei Monti towards the Pincian Hill, or sailing out across the lagoon from the Piazzetta to San Giorgio Maggiore. They may rummage in their memories and guidebooks for appropriate fragments of French and Roman and Venetian history to illuminate the scene; but then, if they are wise, they will also reflect that for centuries the traveller has stood on the same ground, with the same prospects before him, and that this experience is an undoubted part of the Englishman's history.

# NOTES

## INTRODUCTION

[1] T. Herbert, *A Relation of some yeares travail, begunne anno 1626...* (2nd ed.) 1638, p. 2.

[2] *Acts of the Privy Council 1617–1619*, p. 126; *ibid., 1613–1614*, p. 457.

[3] T. Palmer, *Essay on...our Travailes into forraine Countries*, etc., 1606, Epistle Dedicatorie.

[4] Bodl. Perrot MS. 5, fo. 3; the opening quotation, from this 'Advice to Travailer', is fo. 6. The whole work is studded with picturesque expressions, a result of the author's unwearied striving for rhetorical effect.

## CHAPTER 1

[1] *Letters of John Chamberlain* (ed. N. E. McClure), 1939, ii. 255. All subsequent references to *Chamberlain* are to this edition.

[2] T. D. Whitaker, *Deanery of Craven* (ed. 1878), p. 363.

[3] In 1610 Sir D. Carleton, travelling through France, which he had last visited in 1605, reported: 'I must needes confess that in regard of sumptuous buildings, of cutting new canals for transport of merchandise, of paving highwayes almost through whole provinces, of building bridges and other public workes France hath a new face.' Carleton to Salisbury 4 October 1610, S.P. Venice, 6/88. Cf. G. Fagniez, *L'Économie Sociale de la France sous Henri IV*, 1897, pp. 174–186.

[4] Edmondes to Winwood, 2 June 1617. S.P. France, 67/126. There is a full account of the Earl of Leicester's journey to Paris in 1636 in the *Sidney Papers* (ed. A. Collins), 1746, ii. 379–380. For the payments to kitchens, butteries, stables, laundries etc. made by an ambassador for the maintenance of his company on the road from London to Paris see Additional MS. 11407. This is the account-book kept by Lord Scudamore's steward in August 1635, and gives the price of goods in two countries in terms of current English money.

[5] T. Coryat, *Crudities* (ed. 1905), i. 152–185.

[6] P. Heylin, *Survey of the estate of France*, 1656. Another issue of this work in the same year has for its title, *A full relation of two journeys: the one into the mainland of France. The other into some of the adjacent islands*. The adjacent islands are the Channel Islands which Heylin visited a few years later.

[7] E. Herbert, *Autobiography* (ed. S. Lee), 1886, pp. 89–90. In all subsequent notes *Herbert* refers to this edition.

[8] The youth has been identified as Francis Manners, later 6th Earl of Rutland. K. J. Höltgen, 'Sir Robert Dallington (1561–1637)', *Huntingdon Library Quarterly*, 47 (1984), p. 159. The full title of the published work (?1605) begins: *A Method for Travell. Shewed by taking the view of France...*; the 'method' was probably written several years after the 'view'.

[9] The earliest of many editions of *La Guide des Chemins de France* had been published by Charles Estienne in 1552–53. A different version, first appearing in 1592, was edited by a man famous in English history, Theodore de Mayerne Turquet, Sir Theodore Mayerne the physician.

[10] Parry to Cecil 26 October 1603, S.P. France, 50/71.

[11] Standen to Cecil 30 November 1603,

S.P. France, 50/125.

[12] Morgan to Cecil 26 April 1604, *ibid.*, 51/150; *The Conversion of Sir T. Mathew* (ed. A. H. Mathew), 1907, p. 10; Duke Charles of Lorraine to James I 27 October 1604, S.P. France, 51/296.

[13] *Winwood Memorials*, ii. 48.

[14] *Hist. MSS. Comm. Salisbury MSS.* xvii. 455.

[15] Nicholls, *Progresses of James I*, ii. 106.

[16] *Ibid*, vols. ii, iii and iv, and the DNB. For the role of the Gentlemen Pensioners, *The English Court from the Wars of the Roses to the Civil War*, ed. David Starkey, 1987.

[17] R. Cocks to Sir T. Wilson 12 July 1605, S.P. Spain, 11/174.

[18] S.P. France, 52/280, 294, 311, 336.

[19] For this phase in Carleton's career see *Cal. of S.P. Dom. 1603–1610*, pp. 265–319; *Salisbury MSS.*, xvii. 447, 533–567.

[20] Carleton to Chamberlain 10 November 1605, S.P. France, 52/342.

[21] T. Birch, *Historical View of the Negotiations...1592 to 1617*, 1749, p. 240.

[22] For Roos, see *Cal. of S.P. Dom. 1603–1610*, p. 220; *Salisbury MSS.*, xvii. 564 and xviii. 117, 130, 157; Carew to Salisbury 16 December 1605, T. Morgan to Salisbury 17 July 1607, S.P. France, 52/372, 53/302; and below, pp. 33, 77, 192, 262.

[23] Carew to Salisbury 18 November 1607, S.P. France, 53/361; V. F. Snow, *Essex the Rebel*, 1970, pp. 37–8.

[24] *Chamberlain*, i. 268, 278; A. J. Loomie, *Ceremonies of Charles I. The Note Books of John Finet 1628–1641*, 1987.

[25] *Hist. MSS. Comm. MSS. of J. E. Hodgkin*, p. 36; Carew to Salisbury 24 April, Becher to Wilson 2 May 1609, S.P. France, 55/73, 80; *Salisbury MSS*, xxi, 19, 35.

[26] *Salisbury MSS.*, xxi, 104–13.

[27] *Hist. MSS. Comm. Rutland MSS.* i, 421.

[28] One can well imagine that, in the course of his travels, Cranborne met no less a student of Roman building than Inigo Jones. In 1609 Jones, as Lord Salisbury was aware, went to France and he undoubtedly inspected Chambord, Nîmes, the Pont du Gard, Arles and Orange (Gordon Higgot, 'Inigo Jones in Provence', *Architectural History*, 26 (1983), pp. 23–34, and a link with the tourists is possible.

[29] *Winwood Memorials*, iii. 84, 154, 175; Carew to Salisbury 9 May and 16 August 1609, Becher to Wilson 25 July and 18 August, Becher to Carew 10 and 24 October, Becher to Salisbury 5 May 1610, S.P. France, 55/82, 160, 140, 162, 208, 214, 56/71. Carew had already been recalled in the previous year.

[30] Becher to Salisbury 13 September 1610, *ibid.*, 56/265.

[31] Harleian MS. 7002, fo. 198.

[32] *Salisbury MSS.*, xiii. 35.

[33] Becher to Salisbury, 13 and 26 September 1610. S.P. France, 56/265, 286.

[34] *Ibid.*, 56/286.

[35] Harleian MS. 7002, fo. 147.

[36] Harleian MS. 7002, fos. 152, 160; see also Lansdowne MS. 91, fo. 190; for Sir Adam Newton see T. Birch, *Henry Prince of Wales*, 1760. The newsletters of the Frenchman, named 'Forboyst', are to be found in Harleian MS. 7015, fos. 240–375, running from 10 February 1612 until 13 December 1613.

[37] Becher to Salisbury 2 November 1610, 3 and 29 January, 28 March 1611, S.P. France, 56/317; 57/1, 31, 111.

[38] Harleian MS. 7002, fos. 199–201. For Lord Roos in Spain, below, pp. 262–6.

[39] Becher to Salisbury 9 March 1611, S.P. France, 57–84.

[40] Becher to Salisbury 26 April, 28 May, 10 June, 9 and 15 July, 7 October, 8 November, 4 December 1611, George Rooke to Salisbury 27 August 1611, S.P. France, 57/154, 188; 58/9, 50, 57, 207, 227, 255, 117. It will be noted that Clifford followed Cranborne's itinerary, but in the reverse direction.

[41] However, Cranborne's expenses in France between March 1609 and March 1610 amounted to £3872–2–7. Hatfield House, Cecil Papers, typescripts, vol. iii. 286, and vol. iv. 8.

[42] Toby Mathew to Dudley Carleton 16 March 1605 (quoted in A. H. Mathew, *Sir Toby Mathew*, 1907, p. 43), S.P. France,

52/73; T. Coryat, *Crudities*, i. 173–176.

[43] A. Berty, *Topographie Historique du vieux Paris*, 1876, iii. 278–281. *Cf.* Herbert's satire entitled 'Travellers from Paris':
　　　　　　　　　all they learn is
　　Toys and the language, but to attain this
　　You must conceive they're cozened, mocked, and come
　　To Fourbourgs St Germans, there take a Room
　　Lightly about th'Ambassadors...

[44] *Hist. MSS. Comm. Downshire MSS.*, ii. 299; Herbert, *Autobiography*, p. 191.

[45] Berty, *op. cit.*, iv. 449–457 and i, Région du Louvre et des Tuileries, *passim*; G. Hanotaux, *Richelieu*, i. 72–74; F. A. Yates, *French Academies of the Sixteenth Century*, 1947, pp. 278, 284; H. de Terrebasse, *Antoine de Pluvinel*, Lyon, 1911.

[46] Becher to Salisbury 26 September 1610, S. P. France, 56/286; Lansdowne MS. 108, fo. 3; *Diary of Sir Henry Slingsby* (ed. D. Parsons), 1836, p. 265; T. D. Whitaker, *Deanery of Craven*, p. 365.

[47] *Hist. MSS. Comm. Portland MSS.*, ii. 126; by then the Academy had moved to the Marais.

[48] *Collectanea Curiosa* (ed. J. Gutch), 1781, i. 213–214.

[49] *Ibid.*, ii. 24–35.

[50] W. Frijhoff, 'Étudiants étrangers à l'Académie d'Equitation d'Angers au xviie siècle', *Lias*, iv (1977), pp. 13–84. There is evidence here that George Villiers, later Duke of Buckingham, attended the Angers academy in 1611. For Buckingham as a horseman, see G. Parry, *The Golden Age restor'd...1603–42*, 1981, pp. 141–2. Details about the scale of charges in a Paris riding school are given by William Hammond (of Wadham College, Oxford) in B. L. Additional MS 59785 (13 January, 1656).

[51] *Lettres Missives de Henri IV*, vi. 181, vii. 85; *Life of the Duke of Newcastle by his Wife* (ed. C. H. Firth), 1907, p. 105; Salisbury to Edmondes 6 April 1611, S.P. France, 57/129.

[52] E. G. Castle, *Schools and Masters of Fence*, 1892, *passim*; Herbert, pp. 327–32, L. Stone, *The Crisis of the Aristocracy 1558–1641*, 1965, pp. 242–50, 770, and

the commentary on this in F. Billacois, *Le duel dans la société française des xvie–xviie siècles*, 1986, pp. 49–59.

[53] S.P. France, 55/21. (23 January 1609).

[54] Herbert, *Autobiography*, pp. 107–108. In the library of Sir T. Lucy, later M. P. for Warwickshire in six Parliaments, were many books of modern history and French literature. P. Styles, *Sir Simon Archer*, Dugdale Society, 1946, p. 46.

[55] Queens College Oxford MS. 372.

[56] K. Lambley, *French Language in England*, 1920, p. 227 and *passim*.

[57] H. Ellis, *Original Letters*, Second Series, 1827, iii. 221–222.

[58] Wentworth's notebook, Strafford MS 30 of the Wentworth Woodhouse muniments, at present deposited in Sheffield Public Library; also MS 21 for his letters 1611–13. In the notebook, fos. 1 to 27 contain miscellaneous jottings, lists of books and notes from books, fos. 28 to 162 are a description of his itinerary and of places visited. Further notes and quotations appear on alternate pages in the early part of the diary proper. Other documents in the Strafford MSS include one entitled '1612. Remarques sur l'estat de France' which commences: 'C'est une vraye et absolue Monarchie, encorque quelques uns se contestent...', and a copy of Sir George Carew's long report on the state of France in 1609, which is printed in T. Birch, *Negotiations...1593 to 1617*, 1745. See also C. V. Wedgwood, *Thomas Wentworth, a Revaluation*, 1961, pp. 24–7

[59] T. Wentworth to his father, London, 10 December 1611.

[60] S.P. Domestic, Jas. I, xiv. 49.

[61] Tanner MS. 74, fo. 115.

[62] 'Me juvet ire per altum/my anger helps me to mount/Richard Marris' construction'. MS. Diary, fo. 13.

[63] The single exception to this general rule was his verdict at Carcassonne: 'the people be courteous and all Catholiks', MS. Diary, fo. 94.

[64] T. Wentworth to his father, Montpellier, 15 September (n.s.) 1612.

[65] T. Wentworth to his father, Orleans, 5 November 1612 and 1 January 1613.

CHAPTER 2

[1] Carew to Salisbury 31 October 1606, S.P. France, 53/190.

[2] Lansdowne MSS. 90, fo. 4, 89, fo. 158.

[3] Becher to Wilson 2 May 1609, S.P. France, 55/80.

[4] Lansdowne MS. 90, fo. 191.

[5] *Downshire MSS.* ii. 307, 310.

[6] *Ibid.*, iii. 439; *Issues of the Exchequer . . . James I* (ed. F. Devon), 1836, p. 155.

[7] Merrick and Becher to Winwood 7 August 1614, 29 January, 23 July and 15 December 1615, S.P. Russia, 2/1, 7, 11, 19; I. Lubimenko, *Les Relations Commerciales et Politiques de l'Angleterre avec la Russie avant Pierre le Grand*, 1933, pp. 151–153.

[8] For Woodford, pp. 31, 48, 64–7 87, 98–105 above.

[9] *Chamberlain*, ii. 97; Edmondes to Winwood 9 October 1616, Woodford to Winwood 10 October 1616 and 9 May 1617, Becher to Secretaries of State November and December 1617, S.P. France, 66/117, 125, 67/109, 214–240; Harleian MS. 1580, fos. 94, 96.

[10] *Cal. of S.P. Dom. 1619–1623*, p. 480; *Acts of the Privy Council 1621–3*, pp. 387, 451; for these clerks, J. Vernon Jensen, 'The Staff of the Jacobean Privy Council', *Huntingdon Library Quarterly*, 40 (1976–77), pp. 11–44.

[11] *Cal. of S.P. Dom. 1623–5*, pp. 241, 276, 373–393; Harleian MS. 1580, fos. 90, 92. For Becher as a royal spokesman in the Parliaments of 1624 and 1625, Conrad Russell, *Parliaments and English Politics 1621–1629*, 1979, pp. 180, 236.

[12] For the modern debate on the intricate topic of Buckingham's intentions, S. L. Adams, 'The Road to La Rochelle: English Foreign Policy, 1610–1629', *Proc. of the Huguenot Society of London*, 22 (1975), pp. 414–429; T. Cogswell, 'Prelude to Ré: the Anglo-French struggle over La Rochelle, 1624–1627, *History*, 71 (1986), pp. 1–21.

[13] S.P. Domestic, Chas. I, lxxii. 22. i. This is Becher's diary.

[14] P. Mervault, *The last famous Siege of the City of Rochel* (English trans.) London,

1679, p. 2; E. Herbert, *Expedition to the Isle of Rhé* (ed. 1860), p. 26.

[15] S.P. Domestic, Chas. I, lxxii. 22. i.

[16] S.P. Domestic, Chas. I, lxxiv. 68.

[17] *Hardwicke State Papers*, ii. 13; S.P. Domestic, Chas. I, lxxviii. 16 and lxxix. 40; Ashmole MS. 824, xvii, fo. 5.

[18] Ashmole MS. 824, xvii, fo. 5.

[19] S.P. Domestic, Chas. I, lxxxiv. 56.

[20] In 1628, as MP for New Windsor and an official spokesman in the Commons he warmly defended Buckingham's conduct of the expedition to Ré, *Commons' Debates in 1628*, New Haven 1977, ii. 413–16, iv, 116, 310, 323 etc.

[21] *Cal. of S.P. Dom.*, *passim*; see especially under November 1636, June–August 1637.

[22] *Lords Journals*, iv. 86, 87, 89; *Hist. MSS. Comm. Montagu MSS.*, iii. 389.

[23] *Cal. of S.P. Dom. 1640–1641*, pp. 433, 458; Additional MS. 15857, fos. 78–86.

[24] *Cal. of S.P. Dom. 1641–1643*, pp. 298, 426.

[25] *Cal. of Com. for Advance of Money*, ii. 1059, i. 333; Sir W. Becher's will, Somerset House, Grey 77; Harleian MS. 6759: the opening words of this manuscript, which is an account of Henri IV's amours with the Princesse de Condé, run as follows (fo. 1): 'this excellent piece of History was writt by S^r William Beecher ffrom whose Naturall Sonne William Beecher my Chamberfellow in the Temple I received the same. I sent it (by Beecher's consent) to the late Archbishop of Canterbury Sheldon in the year 1664'. Old Sir William, writing of Henri and the Princess, says that he was 'in a manner Spectator of the whole Tragedy'. Another essay, which likewise owed something to his experience abroad, was an account of the loss of La Rochelle in fos. 52–58.

[26] O. Manning, *The History and Antiquities of the County of Surrey*, 1814, iii. 297.

[27] Lansdowne MS. 90 fo. 99.

[28] Harleian MS. 7002, fos. 264, 338, 340, 363, 367, 368 *et passim*.

[29] Some of Rossingham's newsletters are printed in *Court and Times of Charles I* (ed. R. F. Williams), 1848, ii. 228–284, and see below, p. 551. Cf. Additional

MS. 11045 for newsletters by 'E. R.' in 1640–1641.

[30] Lansdowne MS. 93, fo. 62.

[31] Additional MS. 4176, fos. 198, 206, 208.

[32] Additional MS. fos. 206, 221, 239, 242, 248, 251, 255; *Court and Times of James I* (ed. R. F. Williams), 1848, ii. 159; *Acts of the Privy Council 1618–1619*, p. 467.

[33] Harleian MS. 7000, fos. 7, 142, 144, 147, 149, 115; Additional MS. 4176, fo. 266.

[34] Harleian MS. 7000, fo. 118. A letter from the Bishop of Bath and Wells shows that Sir Adam Newton had also been active on Lorkin's behalf (Additional MS. 4222, fo. 270).

[35] Harleian MS. 7000, fo. 118, 128, 130; *Hist. MSS. Comm. Bath MSS.* ii. 71; *Alumni Oxonienses* (ed. Foster), ii. 939. In Harleian MS. 7015 is a series of newsletters for November and December 1623 from C. Brese at Paris to Puckering (fos. 109–121); the last is endorsed: 'From Mr. Lorkin and from a Frenchman of his procurement out of France in anno 1623.'

[36] Kensington to Conway 15 March, 7 April, 9 May 1624, Conway to Kenisngton 24 March and 14 April, Lorkin to Conway 23 April, S.P. France, 72/64, 120, 188–192, 80, 137, 157.

[37] Carlisle to the King 27 May 1624, to Buckingham 14 June, to Conway 23 and 29 July, Kensington to Conway 14 June, Kensington and Carlisle to Conway 7 August, Woodford to Nethersole 2 September and 12 November, S.P. France, 72/240, 287, 361, 388, 291; 73/5–10, 128, 303.

[38] Kensington to Conway 18 August 1624, S.P. France, 73/65–68.

[39] *Hardwicke State Papers*, i. 556, 568, 569.

[40] Conway to Carlisle 13 (?) October 1624, Conway to Carlisle and Kensington 4 November, S.P. France, 73/237, 280.

[41] In addition to accounts of the negotiations in English see also J. Goll, *Die französische Heirat*, 1876, pp. 44–49, 88–89.

[42] *Hardwicke State Papers*, i. 535; Carlisle and Kensington to Conway 9 October

1624, S.P. France, 73/229–234.

[43] Lorkin's original letter is in Egerton MS. 2596, fos. 57ff.; it is printed in *Hardwicke S.P.*, i. 542–545.

[44] Carlisle and Kensington to Conway 28 October and 12 November 1624, S.P. France, 73/259, 293; *Cal. of S.P. Ven. 1623–1625*, pp. 487, 496.

[45] Holland to Conway 4, 15 and 31 January, Carlisle and Holland to Conway 15 January 1625, S.P. France, 74/11, 17, 21, 47.

[46] Lipscomb's *Buckinghamshire*, iv. 362; Bishop's Certificates Lincoln, no. 6, and Composition Book 17, fo. 41, in P.R.O. I owe these references to Professor Claude Jenkins.

[47] *Hardwicke S.P.*, i. 565–566.

[48] *Cal. of S.P. Dom. 1625–1626*, p. 154.

[49] After a long search I have failed to find a satisfactory account of Lorkin's end, which remains something of a mystery.

[50] Cf. Harleian MS. 1581, fos. 64–69.

[51] Lorkin to Conway 12 May 1625, Augier to Conway 1/11 October, Conway to Augier 11 October, S.P. France, 75/18, 76/1, 34; P. R. O. French Transcripts 3/62; *Cal. of S.P. Dom. 1625–26*, p. 154.

[52] Lipscomb, *op. cit.*, iv. 362; Bodleian MSS., Bucks Archdeacon Records: Transcritps of Parish Registers, C.234; Bishops' Certificates, Lincoln, no. 7, in P.R.O.

[53] *Hist. MSS. Comm. Digby MSS.*, p. 521.

[54] *Downshire MSS.* iv. 343, 387.

[55] L. Anquez, *Histoire des Assemblées Politiques des Réformés 1573–1622*, 1859, p. 270. The spokesman at Grenoble was the remarkable convert Giovanni Francesco Biondi, born in Dalmatia. For Wotton and Bedell, who first encouraged him in his Protestantism, see pp. 103, 115 above. Biondi was later knighted by James I.

[56] Stowe MS. 175, fo. 58; M. Bouchitté, *Négotiations...à la Conférence de Loudun*, 1862, pp. 270–273. Edmondes encouraged both Catholic and Protestant opponents of the Regent's ministers, while also negotiating to restrain the more militant Huguenots. S. L. Adams, *op. cit.*

[57] *Hist. MSS. Comm., Ancaster MSS.*, p. 422.

[58] Memoirs of Sir George Courthop, *Camden Miscellany*, xi, 1907, p. 105.

[59] *Herbert*, pp. 219, 225.

[60] *Chamberlain*, ii. 391.

[61] Despatches of Doncaster to Calvert from 28 August to 19 December 1621, Woodford to — 5 October, S.P. France, 69/176, 187, 214, 232, 262, 291, 313, 344; 275. Cf. *Mercure de France* for 1621.

[62] Doncaster to Calvert 31 January 1622, and his despatches from 4 May to 26 June, S.P. France, 70/31, 103, 115, 142, 162; L. Anquez, *op. cit.*, pp. 372, 384. For the signs that at this date James I was distancing himself from the Calvinist interest, Nicholas Tyacke, *Anti-Calvinists*, Oxford 1987, pp. 102–4.

[63] The handwriting of Carlisle's despatches from Boulogne, written on his journey to Spain in 1623, is certainly Woodford's. S.P. France, 71/43, 45. A letter from Carlisle to Buckingham, also in Woodford's hand and dated from Hampton Court on 20 November 1625, is in Harleian MS. 1580, fo. 201.

## CHAPTER 3

[1] The account of Venice given by Fox, the servant of Henry Cavendish, during a journey to Constantinople in 1589 faithfully expresses this conventional view in its simplest form. *Camden Miscellany*, xvii, 1940, pp. 12, 13.

[2] R. Dallington, *A Method for Travel* London), p. F.

[3] Bodl. Perrot MS. 5, fo. 21.

[4] A Booke of the Travaile and Lief of me, Thomas Hoby, etc. *Camden Miscellany*, x. 1902.

[5] F. Moryson, *Itinerary* (ed. 1905), ii. 362.

[6] L. P. Smith, *Life and Letters of Sir Henry Wotton*, 1907, i. 330ff. In all subsequent notes *Wotton* refers to this work.

[7] Sloane MS. 682, fo. 8.

[8] A. L. Maycock, *Nicholas Ferrar of Little Gidding*, 1938, p. 44; M. F. S. Hervey, *Arundel*, 1921, p. 75; on Herbert, M. M. Rossi, *La Vita le Opere I Tempi di Edoardo Herbert di Cherbury*, 1947, i. 223.

[9] For the itineraries into Italy see also pp. 94–5 above.

[10] Lansdowne MS. 93, fos. 46, 48; further information about Parvis may be found in the *Cal. of S.P. Ven.* and *Wotton, passim*.

[11] Sir S. Lesieur to Salisbury 28 May 1608, S.P. Tuscany, 2/143.

[12] J. Howell, *Epistolae Ho-elianae* (ed. 1890–1892), i. 87; cf. H. Koenigsberger, 'English merchants in Naples and Sicily in the seventeenth century', *English Historical Review*, 62 (1947), pp. 304–326.

[13] W. Davies, *A True Relation of the Travailes and most miserable Captivitie of William Davies, Barber-Surgion of London*, 1614, p. C.2. This was his second spell of such captivity.

[14] H. Foley, *Records of...the English Province of the Society of Jesus*, 1886, vi. 732; E. K. Chambers, *Aurelian Townshend*, 1912, pp. xiii, xliii–iv; *Wotton*, i. 331.

[15] W. Lithgow, *Rare Adventures* (ed. 1906), p. 38; M. V. Hay, *The Blairs Papers 1603–1660*, 1929, p. 124.

[16] T. Coryat, *Crudities* (ed. 1905) i. 299; *Wotton*, ii. 114.

[17] W. Davies, *A True Relation*, p. C.3; *Wotton*, i. 388.

[18] A. H. Mathew, *Life of Sir Toby Mathew*, 1907, pp. 124–137.

[19] *Wotton*, i. 434; Lesieur to Salisbury 11 June, 25 July, 20 August 1608, S.P. Tuscany, 2/157, 190, 211; Hervey, *op. cit.*, p. 84; Carleton to J. Chamberlain 15 July 1614, S.P. Venice, 16/213; Sir R. Chamberlain to Carleton 26 March 1613, S.P. Sicily, 1/32. For Mathew and Gage, Edward Chaney, *The Grand Tour and the Great Rebellion. Richard Lassels and 'The Voyage of Italy' in the Seventeenth Century*, Geneva, 1985, pp. 264–7. This work is a mine of new information on Anglo-Italian relations. For the Italian version of Bacon's Essays, cf. p. 127 below.

[20] Coryat, *op. cit.*, i. 238; Hervey, *op. cit.*, 75.

[21] 'The seat of Venice when I beheld it in my Gondola as I came from Marghera me thought resembled some flemish painted table of Landskipt or some mathematical demonstration in prospective: the towers and monasteries in the sea and especially of Muran divided from Venice

resembled it so well' (Tanner MS 309. f. 53). S. Powle to J. Chamberlain, 21 September 1587.

[22] Lithgow, *op. cit.*, p. 33; *Wotton*, i. 397. Carleton to Wotton 25 October 1610, S.P. Venice, 6/103.

[23] James Howell.

[24] Pius V had imposed an oath of fidelity to the Church on all doctors who proposed to supplicate for a degree but the Venetian authorities refused to insist on the oath. For the university procedure at Padua entitling William Harvey to his doctorate, Gweneth Whitteridge, *William Harvey and the Circulation of the Blood*, 1971, pp. 9–14.

[25] *Wotton*, i. 300, 434–5; Mathew to Carleton, 19 August 1608, S. P. Tuscany, 2/210; F. Moryson, *op. cit.*, i. 316, 355; R. Dallington, *Survey of...Tuscany*, 1605, pp. 16, 30 — a work which gave offence in Florence when it was published in London (A. M. Crinò, *Fatti e figure del seicento anglo-toscano*, 1957, pp. 41–8).

[26] Harleian MS. 6867, fos. 27–40 (partially printed in *Papers of the Brit. School at Rome*, vi. 482ff.); G. Sandys, *Relation of a Journey begun An: Do: 1610* (second edition, London, 1621), p. 309; *Ferrar* (ed. J. E. B. Mayor), 1855, pp. 16, 191–192; G. Cavendish (?), *Horae subsecivae, Observations and Discourses*, 1620, p. 411.

[27] Wotton to Salisbury August 1610, S.P. Venice, 6/66.

[28] Carleton to Salisbury 12 April 1611, *ibid.*, 7/183. For the connections of Hore and the Dormer family with Exeter College see *Registrum Collegii Exoniensis* (ed. C. W. Boase), 1894, pp. 88, 279.

[29] Carleton to Salisbury 13 March 1612, S.P. Venice, 9/120.

[30] Carleton to Salisbury 26 June 1612, *ibid.*, 10/62.

[31] *Discourse of Rome* in G. Cavendish, *op. cit.*, pp. 325–417.

[32] *Inigo Jones on Palladio*, ed. B. Allsopp (1970). It appears that Jones referred to notes made on the spot when he commented, later, on buildings viewed in Italy.

[33] Chamberlain to Carleton 26 March 1613, S.P. Sicily, 1/32.

[34] Tanner MS. 74, fo. 115; Sir R.

Chamberlain to Carleton 16 July 1613, S.P. Sicily, 1/37; Harleian MS. 7002, fo. 365; Lithgow, *op. cit.*, pp. 309–311, 347–348; W. Lithgow, *Poetical Remains*, 1863, p. 39.

[35] Lansdowne MS. 108, fo. 175.

[36] For Harrington see *Cal. of S.P. Ven. 1607–1610*, pp. 407, 513, 687, 716; Lansdowne MS. 91, fos. 35, 37, 39, 115; Lansdowne MS. 108, fos. 156, 158, 175; *Wotton*, i. 441, 445, 462. The fortress-town of Palmanova, northwest of Trieste, dates from 1593.

[37] For Cranborne see *Cal. of S.P. Ven. 1607–1610*, p. 393, and *ibid.*, *1610–1613*, *passim*; numerous letters in S.P. Venice during 1610/1611; The Italian section of Cranborne's diary is printed in *Salisbury MSS*, xxi. 238–44.

[38] Harleian MS. 7021, fos. 329, 330: an apparently anonymous document but in Puckering's hand; its dating and references agree exactly with dates and references in the series of letters from Carleton to Puckering in Harleian MS. 7002, fos. 239, 304, 259, 266, 274, 292, 354, 365– the chronological sequence between November 1612 and November 1614.

[39] *Cal. of S.P. Ven. 1613–1615*, pp. 191, 195, 205; Carleton to Chamberlain 6 September 1614, S.P. Venice, 17/127.

[40] Another outstanding tutor was Henry Oldenburg who looked after Richard Boyle, a young nephew of Robert Boyle the chemist, on a tour abroad in 1657–8. Oldenburg's introduction to scientific circles in Paris was a wonderful experience for the future first secretary of the Royal Society. *The Correspondence of Henry Oldenburg* i (1965), pp. xxxvi–viii, 214 ff., 378.

[41] For recent discussions of this dark corner in the career of Hobbes, see Noel Malcom, *De Dominis (1560–1624: Venetian, Anglican, Ecumenist and Relapsed Heretic*, 1984, pp. 49–51, 120, and Chaney. *op. cit.*, pp. 302–3. We must wait for Dr Malcom's biography of Hobbes.

[42] Carleton to J. Chamberlain, 2, 6 September and October, 1614, S.P. Venice, 17/106, 127, 270, and Harleian MS. 7002, fo. 315.

[43] For Coke and Arundel, Hervey,

*Arundel*, and David Howarth, *Lord Arundel and his Circle*, 1985, pp. 16–20, 34, 52, 228; *Hist. MSS. Comm. Cowper MSS.*, i. 23–109.

[44] Jones himself was in Vicenza and its neighbourhood in September 1613 and August 1614. His prior ownership of a copy of *I Quattro Libri dell'Architettura di Andrea Palladio*, ed. 1610; his scrutiny of Palladio's buildings in this area, as of the classical remains elsewhere; and his subsequent dense annotation of Palladio's text and plates, combined to influence his architectural and theatrical designs. Cf. *Inigo Jones on Palladio*, ed. Allsopp; A. A. Tait, 'Inigo Jones — architectural historian', *Burlington Magazine*, 92 (1970), p. 235.

[45] Lord Maltravers, also, did not reach home, catching smallpox and dying in Brussels. His younger brother is the Maltravers mentioned above, p. 148. The cause and date of Coke's death elude me.

[46] *Wotton*, i. 410–412, 436.

[47] *Memoirs of Sir Henry Slingsby* (ed. D. Parsons), 1836, pp. 269–273; *Acts of the Privy Council 1613–1614*, p. 104; Carleton to Chamberlain 17 June 1614, S.P. Venice, 16/119.

[48] Carleton to Salisbury 19 July 1611, S.P. Venice, 7/375.

## CHAPTER 4

[1] *Acts of the Privy Council*, James I, *passim*.

[2] *Wotton*, ii. 365.

[3] W. A. B. Coolidge, *The Alps*, 1908, pp. 150–199.

[4] *Wotton*, ii, 96.

[5] *Ibid.*, ii. 94–95.

[6] *Chamberlian*, i. 303–304.

[7] Carleton to Salisbury 24 September, 20, 25 October and 3 November 1610, Carleton to Wotton 25 October, S.P. Venice, 6/87, 91, 101, 112, 103.

[8] Carleton to Wotton, Wotton to Carleton, November 1610, *ibid.*, 6/110–120.

[9] Expenses of the journey, *ibid.*, 6/153.

[10] *Wotton*, Appendix III.

[11] G. C. Brodrick, *Memorials of Merton College*, 1885, pp. 276, 277. The Warden, Savile, had himself visited Venice as

a young man thirty years earlier (M. Feingold, *The mathematicians' apprenticeship...1560–1640*, 1984, pp. 125–9).

[12] Carleton to Chamberlain 17 June and 15 July 1614, S.P. Venice, 16/119, 213; miscellaneous accounts, *ibid.*, 20/229–232.

[13] Wake to Conway, *ibid.*, 23/113.

[14] R. Browne to Wake from Constantinople, 24 July 1630. (Browne's copy in the Evelyn MSS. at Christ Church, Oxford.) See above, pp. 311–12, for the later career of Sir Richard Browne.

[15] Carleton to Salisbury 17 May 1611, S.P. Venice, 7/251.

[16] On such occasions Englishmen first familiarized themselves with the use of the word *Regatta*. In a letter of 9 July 1613 (to Chamberlain, S.P. Venice, 13/110), the ambassador describes a festival devised in honour of the Duke of Modena's son: 'On Sonday last there was a *Regata* performed unto him which I cannot describe better unto you then in this unproper terme, a horse-race of botes, and truly, considering the circumstances of the windows well furnished through the whole Canal Grande, the multitude of gondolas on both sides, with certaine large botes of ten ores which were guilded and painted, and the rowers all in liveries, which carried gentlemen in them who had the marshalling of the sport, it was the best entertainment I saw since I came to Venice.'

[17] *Wotton*, i. 498; Carleton to Chamberlain 17 June and 15 July 1614, S.P. Venice, 16/119, 213.

[18] *Despatches of Sir Henry Wotton*, Roxburghe Society, 1850, pp. 47, 48, 61.

[19] W. Munk, *Roll of the Royal College of Phyicians*, 1878, i. 125; Whitteridge, op. cit. for a full discussion of Harvey's debt to Fabrizio of Acquapendente and other European scholars.

[20] cf. above, p. 351.

[21] e.g. Eleazar Hodson, who became a well-known London practitioner, graduated M.D. at Padua on 30 June 1612 (*ibid.*, i. 172). He was soon on his way homeward and in November of the same year dined in the English embassy at the Hague where he met Carleton's secretary, Isaac Wake, also bound for England on

urgent political business (Wake to Carleton 18 November 1612, S.P. Venice, 11/100); and Laurence Wright, later Oliver Cromwell's physician, matriculated at Padua on 22 August 1612 (Munk, *op. cit.*, i. 181) and was chosen a councillor of the English nation in the Law Faculty there in 1615 (J. A. Andrich, *De Natione Anglica et Scota... Patavinae*, 1892, p. 51).

[22] *Wotton*, i. 486.

[23] Sloane MS. 682, fos. 46–47. This section of the MS. has been published by A. Favaro in *Attie Memorie della R. Accademia di scienze, letter ed arti in Padova*, N.S.XXXIV (1918), 12–14. In the printed Index to the Sloane MSS. it is suggested that Sir Thomas Lucy was possibly the author of the diary but there seems to be no real evidence to support this view. On the other hand the diarist evidently left Brussels (fos. 2–4) at the very time when Trumbull reported to Salisbury that Sir Thomas Berkeley, heir of Lord Berkeley, had left Brussels on his journey to Italy (18 April, S.P. Flanders, 9/358), and on 20 August Sir John Digby wrote to Carleton that his kinsman Thomas Berkeley was now in Venice, requesting the ambassador's good offices on the young man's behalf (S.P. Venice, 6/70).

[24] A. Wood, *Ath. Ox.*, ii. 539.

[25] Additional MS. 18639, fo. 38. This is the first volume of the series of Isaac Wake's letter-books (Additional MSS. 18639–42, 34310–11) and much the most useful of them, since it contains copies of letters of friends and fellow-diplomats, as well as duplicates of despatches to the Secretary of State, the originals of which are in S.P. Venice, S.P. Savoy, etc.

[26] Additional MS. 18639, fos. 95–96. Domenico Tintoretto also appears to have painted a portrait of John Chamberlian. 'I shall have more of your company then you thinck, having violently robd Tintoret of a picture of yours he retained, which is (I assure you) a master piece' (Carleton to Chamberlain 30 July 1613, S.P. Venice, 13/150). An English courtier in touch with Tintoretto was John Finet (pp. 46–7, 126 above): 'I have sent Mr Finet a letter from Signor Tintoret' (Carleton to Cham-

berlain 3 April 1612, *ibid*, 9/166).

[27] The anonymous traveller who discussed Galileo also had a high opinion of Wotton's pictures. Sloane MS. 682, fo. 21.

[28] *Wotton*, ii. 119.

[29] Carleton to Chamberlain 7 February 1612, S.P. Venice, 9/62.

[30] R. T. Gunther, *Architecture of Sir Robert Pratt*, 1928, p. 23.

[31] A work of much greater practical importance was the publication by Robert Peake of Holbourne in 1611 of *The First Book of Architecture made by Sebastian Serly, translated out of Italian into Dutch and out of Dutch into English* – a folio of elevations, sections and detail drawings of ancient buildings which 'could not fail to influence English designers ... the effect upon English designs of the early seventeenth century in popularizing the Italian manner was profound'. (N. Lloyd, *History of the English House*, 1931, p. 87.)

[32] Sir H. Wotton, *Elements of Architecture* (ed. 1624), Preface and pp. 51, 89, 98, 99.

[33] E. S. Shuckburgh, *Two Biographies of William Bedell*, 1902, p. 8.

[34] Shuckburgh, *op. cit.*, p. 229.

[35] Shuckburgh, *op. cit.* p. 10. A Hebrew Bible acquired by Bedell in Venice is now in the Library of Emmanuel College, Cambridge.

[36] Bedell also looked on his work at Venice as a means to preferment: 'Possibly Sir Henry [Wotton] may be not unwilling to mention me to his Majesty for some Prebend ere his departure...whereto he might have some pretence from those slender services I endeavoured to performe in Venice, in translating the Booke of Common Prayer, his Majesty's Booke [*Triplici nodo triplex cuneus*, London 1607], Sir Edwin Sands his booke [*Speculum Europae*, 1605] the third Homily of Chrysostome touching Lazarus, and some other thinges into the Italian toung.' Bedell's application was not successful. At last, in 1627, he was appointed Provost of Trinity College, Dublin, though he will hankered after Venice: 'I hope and lately understand, there is hope more than heretofore of doing some good at Venice.' Shuckburgh,

*op. cit.*, pp. 253, 266.

[37] For this topic, John L. Lievsay, *Venetian Phoenix: Paolo Sarpi and some of his English Friends*, 1973; and for a modern view of Sarpi contrasting with that formed by his English contemporaries, David Wootton, *Paolo Sarpi. Between Renaissance and Enlightenment*, 1983.

[38] Wood, *Ath. Ox.*, iii. 333; Carleton to Chamberlain 15 July 1614, S.P. Venice, 16/213.

[39] G. Cozzi, 'Fra Paolo Sarpi, l'Anglicanismo e la "Historia del Concilio Tridentino,"' *Revista Storica Italiana*, 68 (1956), pp. 559–619.

[40] *Correspondence of Sidney and Languet* (ed. S. A. Pears, 1845), pp. 9–10.

[41] The translation was by Lewis Lewkenor, later a Master of Ceremonies at the Stuart court. In the preface to this *Commonwealth and Government of Venice* Lewkenor regrets that he himself had never visited the city: — 'my education hath been in the wars; this I onely doe to beguile time', but the fame of the place was such that the labour seemed worth while. Another author known to English people was Sabellicus, *De Venetis Magistratibus*, first printed in 1488. Both Contarini and Sabellicus are recommended to a prospective traveller in the Advice to a Traveller, Bodl. Perrot MS. 5, previously quoted.

[42] For the following account of George Rooke, the sources consulted were: *Wotton*, i. 328, 381, 401, 450, ii. 478; *The Genealogist*, 1st series, iv. 195–204; J. A. Andrich, *De Natione Anglica...Patavinae*, pp. 48, 104; *Chamberlain*,i. 315, 382, 451, 539; *Salisbury MSS.*, xviii. 33, 34; *English Historical Review*, lxxii. 309n.; *Cal. of S.P. Domestic 1603–1611*, p. 390; Carleton to Chamberlain 17 September 1612, Carleton to Williams 26 April 1613, S.P. Venice, 10/293, 12/230; Rooke to Salisbury March–August 1611, S.P. France, 57/116, 173, 58/59, 95; Rooke to Salisbury 20 November 1608, 26 July and 18 October 1610, 14 January, 12 and 13 February 1611, S.P. Switzerland, 1/155–170.

[43] By the terms of his will Rooke bequeathed a book, 'the meditations of Monsieur du Plessis Mornay in two small volumes which he gave me himself at my last being at Saumar.' This may have been the journey during which Rooke 'retrieved' his French.

[44] He possessed a copy of J. Bassantin, *Discours Astronomiques*, fol. Lyon, 1557.

[45] D. Mathew, *The Jacobean Age*, 1938, pp. 132–136; but see also J. A. Gotch, *Inigo Jones*, 1928, pp. 72–76 for a more tentative interpretation of the scanty evidence, and D. Howarth, *op. cit.*, pp. 39–50 for a recent summary.

[46] See J. Temple-Leader, *Sir Robert Dudley*, 1895.

[47] T. Coryat, *Crudities* (ed. 1905) i. 215–228. For further information on the passes into Piedmont see Victor de St. Genis, *Histoire de Savoie*, Chambéry, 1868, i. 486–487, and ii. 476–479. The Mont Cenis route to Italy appears to have been most widely used by English travellers in the seventeench century from 1600 until the terrible period of plague and war in northern Italy commencing in 1628; and again after the Peace of the Pyrenees, after which communications were greatly improved. During the war years, the sea-route from Marseilles to Genoa and Leghorn came into favour.

[48] Additional MS. 18639, fo. 50; on the quarrel between Foscarini and Muscorno see *Cal. of S.P. Ven. 1610–1613, 1613–1615, passim.*

[49] Additional MSS. 18639, fos. 199, 213; 18641, fos, 16, 38.

[50] *Letters...illustrating the Relations of England and Germany* (ed. S. R. Gardiner), Camden Society, 1865, i. 170, 172, 202, 208; Additional MS. 18641, fo. 85.

[51] Wake to Conway 14 January and 9 May 1625 and an undated letter, S.P. Venice, 26/10, 122, 219. In order to secure the patent for Rowlandson, the ambassador also wrote to Balthazar Gerbier, Buckingham's confidante: 'Par le commandement de Monseigneur le Duc j'ay pris pour Secretaire Italien le sieur Tomas Rolanson qui mérite certes un charge plus relevé; mais par ce qu'il est natif de ceste ville et qu'il a icy ses soeurs et parents il désire de s'accomoder icy. Il a quitté tout à fait le service du Duc de

Savoye...' Tanner MS. 72, fo. 68, Wake to — (the name of the addressee has been torn out since the compilation of the Tanner MSS. Catalogue). He says also, that failing the patent Rowlandson felt tempted to join the wars; and from an earlier letter the impression is left that he took part in the Duke of Savoy's campaigns in 1614–1615 (Additional MS. 18639, fo. 50).

[52] Signet Office Docquets (P.R.O.), February 1629, April 1635; Feilding to Weston 13 February, Feilding to Coke 27 February 1635, S.P. Venice, 35/34, 49; *Hist. MSS. Comm. Denbigh MSS.*, V, ii. 40; *Hist. MSS. Comm. Cowper MSS.*, pp. 73, 103; *Cal. of S.P. Ven. 1629–1639, passim; Cal of S.P. Dom, 1635*, p. 467.

[53] *Cal. of S.P. Ven. 1629–1632*, p. 510; *Cal. of S.P. Ven. 1632–1636*, pp. 172, 568; *Cal. of S.P. Ven. 1636–1639*, p.22.

[54] *Cal. of S.P. Dom. 1595–1597*, p. 168, 173; *Winwood Memorials*, iii. 236.

[55] In a letter to Carleton dated 22 August 1610 Sir John Digby adds his entreaties to what he understands is Carleton's own inclination that Wake shall be his secretary. Wake's best friends 'have written unto him with all convenient speede to make his repayre unto you at Venice'. Digby says also that he is related to Wake, another reason for supporting his appointment. S.P. Venice, 6/70.

[56] Wake to Carleton 18 November 1612, S.P. Venice, 11/100.

[57] Wake to Carleton 25 November, 2, 24 and 31 December 1612, *ibid.*, 11/125, 153, 191, 208.

[58] Wake to Carleton 2 December 1612, *ibid.*, 11/153.

[59] Carleton to Chamberlain 4 February and 16 April, 1613, *ibid.*, 12/73, 202.

[60] *Cal. of S.P. Ven. 1613–1615*, p. 214.

[61] Carleton to Somerset 14 October 1614, S.P. Venice, 17/221; *Cal. of S.P. Ven. 1613–1615*, pp. 210, 222, 224.

[62] *Ibid.*, pp. 275, 278, 282, 292–332. Morton to Winwood 26 December 1614, 3 January and 3 February 1615, S.P. Savoy, 2/133, 158, 178. Carleton had received these instructions at an earlier date, with the proviso that he was not to

act upon them till he received word from Turin; Morton, the resident agent, having returned from London and conferred with the Duke, advised Carleton to proceed.

[63] Carleton to Chamberlian 19 February 1615, S.P. Savoy, 2/186.

[64] *Cal. of S.P. Ven. 1613–1615*, pp. 381, 387, 417 and *passim*. Carleton to the Secretary of State 8 March, 12 April, to J. Chamberlain 17 March, to the King 16 March, 1615; Morton to the King, to Somerset, to the Secretary of State 16 March 1615; Wake to Carleton 4 April, S.P. Savoy, 2/243, 245, 264, 268, 270, 272, 298.

[65] Additional MS. 18639, fo. 38.

[66] Additional MS. 18639, fo. 38 *passim*.

[67] *Chamberlain*, ii. 161.

[68] *Ibid.*, ii. 198, 200, 229, 232.

[69] *Ibid*, ii. 225.

[70] *Ibid.*, ii. 425.

[71] *Chamberlain*, ii. 540, 558. Lady Wake took with her to Italy a young man named Peter Moreton whose letters are in Additional MS. 33935 Moreton's struggle for perferment by gaining experience abroad follows a familiar pattern. First, friends apply to his relative Sir Albertus Morton, and to Lady Wake whom he accompanies to Italy (fos. 52ff.). Then Wake sends him on a tour of the country to learn the language (fo. 73), saying that he had done the same himself; he lends him money. Next, on Sir A. Morton's appointment as Secretary of State, the young man expects to be called home for perferment (fo. 79). The Secretary dies, and his own prospects are dashed. He falls back on the less promising patronage of Wake (fo. 149) and finally becomes Agent at Turin (see S.P. Savoy).

[72] *Cal. of S.P. Ven. 1629–1632*, p. 598; Egerton MS. 2597, fol. 64.

[73] *Wotton*, i. 426, 454, 484, and *passim*.

[74] *Chamberlain*, i. 355, 359, 363.

[75] *Ibid.*, i. 369, 382, 385; Wake to Carleton 25 November and 9 December 1612, S.P. Venice, 11/125, 158.

[76] *Proceedings in Parliament 1614 (House of Commons)*, ed. M. Jannson, Philadelphia, 1988, pp. 311, 314–17. cf. *Commons Debates 1621* (ed. W. Notestein), 1935, vii. 644.

[77] J. Forster, *Sir J. Eliot* (ed. 1872), i. 333: 'And indeed you would count it a great misery if you knew the subjects in foreign countries as well as myself; to see them not look like our nation, with store of flesh on this backs, but like so many ghosts and not men, being nothing but skin and bones with some thin cover to their nakedness, and wearing only wooden shoes on their feet; so that they cannot eat meat or wear good clothes but they must pay and be taxed unto the King for it.' It was not necessary to travel abroad to hold this view of continental despotisms, but it is interesting to compare this speech with some of Carleton's observations to Lord Salisbury, written while he was actually travelling through France in October 1610: 'I must needes confess that in regard to sumptuous buildings, of cutting new canals for transport of marchandise, of paving highwayes allmost through whole provinces, of building bridges and other publike workes France hath a new face; but in respect of tirannie of Landlords, of excessive tailles, and imposts raised uppon these publike pretences, such a poore face of people and such extreme miserie that as happines is onely knowne by comparison...' etc., S.P. Venice, 6/88.

[78] *Salisbury MSS*, vii. 392; *Cowper MSS*, i. 18, 24-6; *Cal. of S.P. Dom. 1603-1610*, pp. 366, 390, 403. RalphWinwood, another of James I's Secretaries of State, had been given a passport to travel abroad in 1954; in October 1594 he enrolled at Padua (*Hist. MSS. Comm. Buccleugh MSS*, p. 26, and J. L. Andrich, *op. cit.*, p. 134.). Subsequently he was for number of years in the embassies at Paris and the Hague, but never in Italy.

# CHAPTER 5

[1] We can take our choice of memorials to this: the building of Santa Maria della Salute in Venice, Manzoni's account of Milan in *I Promessi Sposi*, or the excellent modern works of Monique Lucenet, *Lyon malade de la Peste*, 1981, Antonio Brighetti, *Bologna e la peste del 1630*, 1968 and Carlo Cipolla on Prato in *Cristofano and the Plague*, 1973. It was a phase of unusual misery in western Europe.

[2] In 1630 Thomas Hobbes brought his charge Sir Gervase Clifton's son as far as Geneva, only to find that conditions beyond the Alps made a journey into Italy quite impracticable; on the other hand they had previously met at Lyon two Englishmen who were on their way down the Rhone to the Mediterranean and hoped to reach Italy by the sea route. *Notes and Records of the Royal Society of London*, vii. 201.

[3] For another treatment of this theme, G. B. Parks, 'The decline and fall of the English Renaissance admiration of Italy', *Huntingdon Library Quarterly*, 31 (1967), pp. 341-57.

[4] 'The common course is to go first into France, and then into Italy, and so home by German, Holland and Flanders, as I did once; but my opinion is that it is better for a Young Man to go first into Italy, and returning by Germany, Holland and Flanders, come into France to give himself there the last hand in breeding,' R. Lassels, *The Voyage of Italy*, Introduction. The author admits the primacy of France but declares a preference for Italy, 'that Nation which hath civilized the whole world, and taught Man Manhood'.

[5] H. Blount, *A Voyage into the Levant*, 1636, p. 1.

[6] *Camden Miscellany*, xi. 105ff.

[7] The diary of Nicholas Stone, Junior, in the Appendix, *Walpole Society*, vol. vii (1919), pp. 167, 172. For further information on the life of William Paston see Additional MS. 27447.

[8] 'In Siciliam quoque et Graeciam trajicere volentem me, tristis ex Anglia belli civilis nuntius nuntius revocavit: turpe enim estimabam, dum mei cives domi de libertate dimicarent, me animi causa otiose perigrinari,' *Defensio Secunda, Works* (ed. 1933), viii. 124. The first six words may well have been true, even if the reason given for the failure to go further occurred to Milton at a later date.

[9] *The Diary of John Evelyn*, ed. E. S. de Beer, 1955, ii. 451-2. In subsequent notes *Evelyn* refers to this edition.

[10] G. Albion, *Charles I and the Court of Rome;* L. Pastor, *History of the Popes*, xxix.

318; *Burlington Magazine*, xc. 50–51. The argument is carried a stage further in H. Trevor-Roper, *Catholics, Anglicans and Puritans* 1987, pp. 110–119.

[11] Tanner MS. 93, fos. 58–60. Neither MS. nor calendar give any hint as to the writer, but he was Thomas Raymond, author of an autobiography in part printed from Rawlinson MS. D 1150 by G. Davies in *Raymond and Guise Memoirs 1622–1737*, Camden Society, 1917. It seems to have escaped notice hitherto that the Rawlinson MS. is continued by Tanner MS. 93, fos. 46–60. The handwriting is the same, and although the top of fo. 46 is torn the opening words obviously complete the description of Mass celebrated in St. Peter's Rome which begins on the concluding page of the Rawlinson MS. There are some useful details about the Rev. William Petty (the Earl of Arundel's agent) in the unprinted portion of the latter.

[12] *Milton*, vill. 124.

[13] Rawlinson MS. C799, fo. 7; this section of the MS. printed in *Gentleman's Magazine*, 1836, p. 604. J. Bargrave, *Alexander VII and his Cardinals*, Camden Society, 1867, pp. 57–58. Cf. the testimony of Sir John Finch in 1653: 'From Milan wee went after wee had been ther 4 dayes towards Parma with one Lodovico di Calurno, president of the Inquisition at Como, and a Dominican Friar. He was extremely civill to us in our Journy and when wee parted at Parma told us wee being strangers might possibly not know yt all bookes were had unlicensed by the Inquisition were forfeited and the persons carrying any such to be fined, he desired us to send him a catalogue of what bookes wee had and he would license them, which wee sent and accordingly he subscribed.' Additional MS. 23215, fo. 16.

[14] D. Masson, *Life of Milton*, i. 800; *Milton*, viii. 124.

[15] Tanner MS. 93, fo. 53; H. Foley, *Records*, vi. 614. There are equally appreciative accounts of the kindness shown to English Protestants by the English Jesuits at Rome in 1638–1639 in Harleian MS. 383, fo. 158, and *Camden Miscellany*, xi. 135.

[16] *Evelyn*, ii. 213; H. Foley, *Records*, vi. 629.

[17] T. Gage, *The English-American, his Travail by Sea and Land* (ed. A. P. Newton), 1928, p. 390.

[18] S.P. Domestic, Chas, I, ccccxiv; H. Foley, *Records*, vi. 618.

[19] H. C. Foxcroft, *Character of the Trimmer*, 1946, p. 7; *Letters of the Earl of Chesterfield* (ed. 1829), p. 10; J. Bargrave, *op. cit.*, pp. 11–12; Travels of Banister Maynard, Rawlinson MS. D 84, fo. 14; Commonplace book of Robert Southwell, Egerton MS. 1632, fos. 21–23, 53, 54.

[20] *Travels of Sir J. Reresby* (ed. A. Ivatt, 1904, p. 86; Rawlinson MS. D 84, fo. 17; *Works of Sir Thomas Browne* (ed. S. Wilkin), 1836, i. 88, 89.

[21] *Milton*, viii. 124; *Evelyn*, ii. 164–71, 95; J. Raymond, *Itinerary . . . through Italy*, 1648, p. i; Rawlinson MS. D 120, fo. 16 (Anon.); *Francis Mortoft, His Book*, Hakluyt Society, 1925, pp. 33, 34, 37; Abdy's Diary, Rawlinson MS. D 1285, fos. 95–102. Naturally, after the conclusion of hostilities in Piedmont, some travellers still used the Mont Cenis route but they appear to have been a distinct minority. In 1664 Edward Browne found himself 'forc'd' to go this way by reason of the plague in Provence (*Works of Sir T. Browne*, i. 71). Richard Symonds reached Genoa via Turin in September 1648, Lady Whetenall and Richard Lassels in December 1649; the latter party found Piedmont devastated by recent warfare (*Travels of Peter Mundy*, Hakluyt Society, 1907, i. Appendix, p. 233); *Notes and Queries*, 12 Series, 143.

[22] *Evelyn*, ii. 173; J. Smith, *Catalogue Raisonné . . . Rubens*, 1830, ii. p. xxiii (note). R. T. Gunther, *Architecture of Sir Roger Pratt*, 1928, p. 37. A number of the diaries end abruptly after completing the record of journeys through France, Switzerland or Germany: viz. those of Sir John Finch, 1651–1652 (*Hist. MSS. Comm., Finch. MSS.*, I. 59–73); of Charles Bertie (*Hist. MSS. Comm. Lindsey MSS.*, pp. 275–372); of Robert Montagu (Rawlinson MS. D 76).

[23] F. Mortoft, *op. cit.*, p. 46, note 1; R. North, Lives of the Norths (ed. 1826), ii. 327.

[24] e.g. Richard Symonds, preparing to leave England in the autumn of 1648 packed a separate trunk for use in Italy: 'In the box which Mr Hodgson sends to Livorno/My silk suit, cloake, stockings, garters and tops./Florio's Dictionary, Thomas' Dictionary/This box Mr. Hodgson sends in July by Mr Thomas Trenchfield, master of the ship Northumberland to be delivered to Mr. Francis Greeve (?) there for my use.' Similarly, in December 1651, while in Venice, he sent another package to Leghorn for despatch to England. Harleian MS. 943, fos. 21, 112.

[25] Banister Maynard was detained a month at Leghorn by the profuse hospitality of Messrs. Ashby, Sidney, Browne, Dethick and Joseph Kent. Rawlinson MS. D 84, fo. 12.

[26] Rawlinson MS. D 84, fo. 14. This servant, Robert Moody, states that he had previously spent three years at Rome and knew the language and the city well.

[27] *Walpole Society*, vii. 191; Additional MS. 15857, fo. 23; Pastor, *op. cit.*, xxvi, chap. v; xxix, chap, vi; Mario Praz, *Panopticum Romanum*, 1967, pp. 157–171.

[28] Rawlinson MS. D 120, fos. 20, 22.

[29] *Walpole Society*, vii. 176.

[30] Dr de Beer, in his great edition of Evelyn's diary has shown (i. 69–101) that strictly speaking this statement is incorrect. The original notes of his tour abroad do not survive but he used them to compile his manuscript diary at a later date; borrowings from books published after Evelyn's return to England were also included. It remains true that the chronology and content of his early notes are preserved in the final version. For Fynes Moryson's somewhat similar practice, see above, p. 39. One guidebook which Evelyn was to use extensively was J. H. Pflaumern, *Mercurius Italicus*. He bought a copy of this (ed. Lyon, 1628, 637 pages) in Rome on 14 November 1644; it is now in the British Library (c.97.a.22).

[31] The Bodleian MSS. show that Abdy entered Rome on 20 November 1634, left for Naples on 9 January, returned on 8 February, and left Rome for Loreto on 20 April (Rawlinson MS. D 1285, fos. 130–133). The anonymous traveller of 1648–1649 entered Rome before 7 January, saw Naples and Loreto and reached Venice before 27 April (Rawlinson MS. D 120, fo. 35). Maynard entered Rome on 23 December 1660, left for Naples on 6 March and returned on 25 March, leaving for Loreto and Venice on 15 May (Rawlinson MS. D 84. fos. 13–17).

[32] J. Raymond, *op. cit.*, p. 142; *Evelyn*, ii. 331–7; R. Lassels. *Voyage of Italy* (ed. 1686), p. 165. Lassels also allowed his traveller in Naples one day for visiting 'the shops of silk stockings and waistcoats'. Chaney, *op. cit.*, p. 180.

[33] In January 1639, however, Richard D'Ewes visited both Messina and Malta (Harleian MS. 379, fo. 181), and there must have been a few others.

[34] Lassels, *op. cit.*, p. 120; Mortoft, *op. cit.*, p. 143; Raymond, *op. cit.*, p. 167.

[35] Raymond, who did not take this road, nevertheless remarks: 'Those that make the circuit in Italy, *far il Gyro*, as they say, goe to Venice by the way of Loreto' (p. 268).

[36] *Evelyn*, ii. 402.

[37] A copy of one of these instruments of exchange runs as follows: 'Three months after date of this my third bill of exchange, my first and second being not paid, pray pay unto Mr Braye Chowne or his assigns the summe of one hundred and five ducketts by Banco at the rate of fifty three pence per duckett, at the day pray make good payment placing it to account as per avizo, and so God keep you. Ry. Symonds. [Venice, 7 September, 1651.] To Mr. John Symonds in London or elsewhere. This bill is due 3 months after date.' Harleian MS. 943, fo. 119.

[38] Rawlinson MS. D 84, fo. 19; Rawlinson MS. D 120, fos. 35, 36; Rawlinson MS. C 799, fo. 163; Raymond, *op cit.*, p. 233.

[39] Sloane MS. 118, fo. 62. There is an exceptionally good account of this part of the journey in Harleian MS. 379, fo. 171, a letter from Richard D'Ewes to Sir S. D'Ewes, 29 June 1639. Lord Arundel's *Remembrance of Things worth seeing in Italy given to John Evelyn 25 April 1646*, ed. John M. Robinson, Roxburghe Club, 1987; this sensible, brief guide for Venetia

and Lombardy was given to Evelyn in Padua before he set out on the next stage of his journey.

[40] Although the rigidity of this itinerary and time-table must not be exaggerated, it is significant that even a traveller like Heneage Finch, later the second Earl of Nottingham, who went direct from Marseilles and Leghorn to Venice, left the latter city on 28 February 1659 and travelled via Loreto to Rome where he arrived on 15 March. He began his return journey on 23 April and was back in Venice on 5 May. He returned to England by way of Germany. *Finch MSS.*, i. 75–76.

## CHAPTER 6

[1] J. Howell, *Instructions...for Forren Travell*, 1650, p. 5.

[2] R. Lassells, *Voyage of Italy*, 1670, Introduction.

[3] Rawlinson MSS.: D 120 (Anon.), fos. 35, 36; D 84 (Maynard), fos. 1. 2; D 1285 (Abdy), fo. 157; D 445 (Alington), fo. 1. J. Raymond, *Itinerary*, p.175.

[4] Rawlinson MSS., Letters 47, fos. 1–13; *English Historical Review*, xl. 235–240.

[5] Warcup, *op cit.*, p.33. Edmund Waller was in Padua during January 1646 (H. F. Brown, *Inglesi e Scozzesi all' Università di Padova 1618–1775*, 1921, p. 154).

[6] The full title of the editio princeps ends with the words: '...in quo, tamquam in Theatro, Nobilis adolescens, etiam domi sedens, praestantissimae regionis delicias spectare cum voluptate poterit'. This idea, at first subordinate to the older purpose of providing pilgrims with a guide to places of religious significance, gradually overshadows it in the later editions, viz. F. (and sometimes A.) Scoto, *Itinerario overo Nuova Discrittione de' Viaggi Principali d'Italia*, Vicenza 1615, Roma 1650, etc. For guidebooks to Rome, H. Schudt, *Le Guide di Roma*, 1930.

[7] *Walpole Society*, vii. 197; *Works of Sir T. Browne*, i. 77; Harleian MS. 943, fo. 13.

[8] Chaney, *op. cit.*, (cf. above, p. 116) has transformed our knowledge of Lassels' life and works.

[9] J. Howell, *Survey of Signory of Venice*, 1650, pp. 38–39.

[10] For the early travels of Neville and Harrington, Chaney, *op. cit.*, pp. 285–6; for Neville's Italian letters, A.M. Crinò, *Fatti e figure del seicento anglo-toscano*, 1957, pp. 173–208; and his responsibility for the translation of Machiavelli, F. Raab, *The English Face of Machiavelli*, 1964, pp. 267–9. In 1656 Andrew Marvell was described as 'a notable English Italo-Machavillian' (H. Kelliher, *Andrew Marvell Poet and Politician*, 1978, pp. 55, 62, and p. 216 above). It should be noted that Harrington's account of French and Venetian politics was 'written in the tone of a student and theorist rather than a traveller reporting what he had seen' (J. G. A. Pocock, *Political Works of James Harrington*, 1977, pp. 2–3).

[11] For the life of Henry Cogan see *Wotton*, Appendix III — the Bodleian copy of *The Court of Rome; and a Direction for such as shall Travel to Rome*, 1654, was purchased by John Lee of Merton College for 1s. 8d. in 1655; the original version by Martinelli is described in Pastor, *History of the Papacy*, xxix. 517. For Honywood see *D.N.B.* There are notes on Lodge in the *Vertue Note Books*, Walpole Society (1930 and 1932), i. 120–121, ii. 89, etc.

[12] *Diary*, etc (1575–79) of Sir John North in Bodl. Additional MS. C193.

[13] Booksellers, rather than tourists, had Italian books brought to England. The catalogues (1633, 1635, 1639 and 1640) of the London bookseller, Robert March, are described in J. L. Lievsay, *The Englishman's Italian Books*, 1969, pp. 42–8.

[14] *Evelyn*, ii. 300, 307–9; for his notion of 'Gothic' see editor's comment, *ibid.*, vi. 1–7.

[15] J. Raymond, *Itinerary*, p. 243.

[16] Langlois, *Livre des Fleurs*, Paris 1620 (Ashmole 1741 in Bodleian Library).

[17] The influence of Italian gardens on our travellers, a topic neglected here, is described in John Dixon Hunt, *Garden and Grove. The Italian Renaisance Garden in the English Imagination: 1600–1750*, 1984.

[18] These prints and their publication in Rome and abroad, deserve enquiry: for De Rossi we must wait for Francesca Consagra's forthcoming study, and meanwhile there is relevant material in Cesare d'Onofrio, *Roma nel Seicento*, Rome, 1969.

[19] *Le Fontane di Roma* (1618) by Giovanni Maggi: cf. Pastor, *History of the Papacy*, xxvi. 437. This work's much more distinguished successor was *Le Fontane di Roma* (1655) by Giovanni Battista Falda.

[20] *Walpole Society*, vii. 197–199.

[21] *Galleria Giustiniana del Marchese V. G.*, Rome, 1631, folio (with 322 plates).

[22] *Walpole Society*, vii. 165.

[23] *Walpole Society*, p. 170.

[24] R. T. Gunther, *The Architecture of Sir Roger Pratt*, 1928, *passim*, but especially pp. 3, 10.

[25] H. F. Brown, *op. cit.*, 153; J. L. Andrich, *op. cit.*, p. 40; H. Foley, *Records*, vi. 625; Evelyn, ii. 77, iii. 340; a letter from Evelyn at Rome to a correspondent at Leghorn, dated 25 November 1645, ends: 'Present my service to Mr Pratt' (Evelyn MSS. at Christ Church, Oxford).

[26] R. T. Gunther, *op. cit.*, pp. 23, 24, 60.

[27] *Ibid.*, pp. 289–300, 202; *Diary and Correspondence of John Evelyn* (ed. H. B. Wheatley, 1906), iii. 340. For another architect, James Smith (c. 1645–1731), whose early Italian travels may have been no less thorough and no less important than Pratt's, Colvin, *British Architects*, 'Smith, J.'

[28] Harleian MS. 943, fos. 100–110, 114–116; H. and M. Ogden, 'A seventeenth century collection of prints and drawings', *Art Quarterly*, ii (1948), pp. 42–73.

[29] Bryan's *Dictionary of Painters and Engravers* (ed. 1921), art. 'Lanfranco'. Another version of the Testamentum appeared in 1649, the year Symonds arrived in Rome, drawn by Nicolas Chapron. The copy of this in the Bodleian Library apparently belonged to Sir Joshua Reynolds. A third version appeared in 1674 (Francis Douce's notes inserted in Douce Prints, c.6).

[30] Evelyn, ii. 229, 247. This is a work by Correggio which he mistakenly attributed to Annibale Carracci.

[31] E. K. Waterhouse, The Althorp Collection (Catalogue of T. Agnew & Sons), 1947; J. P. Kenyon, *Robert Spencer Earl of Sunderland*, 1958, pp. 5–7.

[32] For Frizell, *Burlington Magazine*, 89 (1947), pp. 70–75; and for the arrangements made by Gerbier in 1621 for transporting a large Titian canvas and other purchases across the Alps, with 8 men carrying them over the Mont Cenis, *ibid.* 99 (1957), p. 156.

[33] Bashford was apparently employed by Sir Isaac Wake to carry letters from Italy to England in 1629–1630. Additional MS. 34311, fos. 389, 394, 397, 427.

[34] *Hist. MSS. Comm., Appendix to 4th Report*, 1874, pp. 257, 258; M. Hervey, Arundel, pp. 336–410 and *passim; Denbigh MSS.*, V. 67, 75.

[35] This painting is probably the great 'Vendramin Family' in the National Gallery, (London). Cecil Gould, *National Gallery Catalogues. The Sixteenth-Century Italian Schools*, 1975, p. 287 and plates, nos. 224–5.

[36] Additional MS 15970, f. 38, now printed with many other Arundel letters in Francis Springell, *Connoisseur and Diplomat*, 1963. For the similar correspondence of Hamilton and Feilding, 'Documents for the History of Collecting', *Burlington Magazine*, 128 (1986) pp. 114–52, ed. P. Shakeshaft, who points out that the depressed economy of Venice in the 1630s made it that much easier for Petty and Feilding to operate on behalf of their patrons.

[37] *Cal. of S. P. Venetian 1640–42*, pp. 2–7. For the problems of Baker's identity, and of Bernini's share in the work of which he is the subject, see the *Burlington Magazine*, 95 (1953), pp. 19–22, 138–41 and J. Pope Henessy, *Catalogue of Italian Sculpture in the V. and A. Museum*, 1964, pp. 600–6.

[38] See chapter 9 above.

[39] Egerton MS. 1635, fo. 75; Sloane MS. 179 A, fo. 86; the reference to the academy at Florence comes from Byran's Dictionary but is not confirmed. Chaney, *op. cit.*, pp. 321–2, and S. Stevenson and D. Thomson, *John Michael Wright. The King's Painter*, 1982, pp. 13–15, 56.

[40] *Evelyn*, iii. 339; Egerton MS. 1635, fo. 75.

[41] Egerton MS. 1636. Another notebook kept by Symonds in Italy, Rawlinson MS. D 121, contains some charming sketches of his. Mary Beal, *Study of Richard*

*Symonds: his Italian Notebooks and their Relevance to 17th century painting Techniques,* 1984, is now indispensable for its subject.

[42] Egerton MS. 1636, fos. 11, 18, 23, 28, 32.

[43] Egerton MS. 1636, fos. 96ff.

[44] Sloane MS. 179 A, fo. 86. I suggest tentatively a member of the Cavendish family because Dr. Downes, among whose papers this inventory is to be found, was certainly a few years later in the service of the Earl of Devonshire (fo. 83). Among the purchases was a portrait of Sir Richard Willis, for whom see Appendix, *Letter-Book of John Viscount Mordaunt,* Camden Society, 1945.

[45] A. Malloch, *Finch and Baines,* 1917, pp. 51, 77.

[46] J. Bargrave, *Alexander VII and his Cardinals,* Camden Society, 1867, p. 139.

[47] Harleian MS. 374, fo. 168. He explains that there were two good reasons for getting a picture painted at Venice rather than elsewhere: the best painters lived there, and it was easy to send the pictures to England. His own portait arrived safely (Harleian MS. 379, fo. 178). In 1653 John Finch, residing in Venetia, thought that he was more likely to find a competent portrait-painter in either Florence or Rome than Venice (M. H. Nicolson, *Conway Letters,* 1926, p. 73).

[48] *Works of Sir T. Browne,* i. 92.

[49] *Mortoft,* pp. 43–44, 48, 105, 118, 136–143, 158–159.

[50] *Evelyn,* ii. 232–4, 277, 388–9. He also purchased at Rome, in 1645, *Basso Madrigali a Cinque di Gio. Bernadino Nanini,* Libro Terzo, Rome 1612. This copy is now in Christ Church, Oxford.

[51] Evelyn, ii. 449; for the whole subject, S. T. Worsthorne, *Venetian Opera in the Seventeenth Century,* 1954, but especially pp. 31–2.

[52] Rawlinson MS. D 84, fo. 13.

[53] *Letter-Book of John Viscount Mordaunt,* p. 19.

[54] Rawlinson MS. C 799, fos. 173–174.

[55] Rawlinson MS. C 799, fos. 162–163. Bargrave later on makes an interesting reference to a well known musician. He was at Innsbruck: 'I went to receive a most pleasing enterteinment of Musique from Mr William Young, Groome of the bedchamber and cheife Violist to the Archduke, espetially on an Octocordall Viall of his own Invention, apted for the Lira way of playing, farr beyond those with six strings only; to which favour he added his promise to give me his Lessons composed for that Viall, and his Aires for two Bases and a Treble, which he intends to publish' (fo. 180). For Young, see Grove's *Dictionary of Musicians.*

[56] Lassels, *Voyage of Italy,* p. 102.

[57] The Intronati merged with the Filomati in 1654. Some Italian orations addressed by Sir Kenelm Digby to the Filomati about the year 1620 have been preserved: Gabrieli, *op. cit.,* pp. 28–36.

[58] *Evelyn.* ii. 364–5; *Diary and Correspondence* iii. 309–12, 454–6. It has been argued that the Royal Society was a gentleman's club while it also contained a serious group of experimentalists: some of the early Fellows, like Digby, were well aware of the social attractiveness of Italian academic meetings. Cf. p. 158 above.

[59] E. M. W. Tillyard, *Milton,* 1934, p. 97.

[60] D. Masson, *Life of Milton,* 1881, i. 735–834; Tillyard, *op. cit.,* chapter viii; H. R. Trevor-Roper, 'The Elitist Politics of Milton', *T.L.S.,* 1 June 1973; Chaney, *op. cit.,* pp. 244–5, 282, a sceptical view of the evidence. My own intention here has been to bring out the *conventional* elements in Milton's journey by a comparison with other travel records.

[61] *Works of Sir T. Browne,* i. 89, 91, 97.

[62] Sloane MS. 118, fos. 56–58, 64–68.

[63] H. F. Brown, *Inglesi e Scozzesi,* etc., p. 153; Munk, *op. cit.,* i. 331.

[64] Sloane MS. 118, fo. 69.

[65] Sloane MS. 118, fos. 78, 82, 83, 85, 90.

[66] See the letters from Joseph Binns and Anne Giffard to Colston in Sloane MS. 118 *passim;* especially fo. 88.

[67] See A. Malloch, *Finch and Baines,* 1917, and M. H. Nicolson, *Conway Letters,* 1930. Cf. above, p. 337, note 40.

[68] *Evelyn,* ii. 473–6.

[69] Sloane MS, 118, fo. 59, La Misura della Basilica di S. Pietro di Roma, etc.

[70] *Works of R. Boyle,* 1744, i. 6–15; J. Aubrey, *Brief Lives* (ed. Clark), i. 120.

[71] For Killigrew see A. Harbage, *Thomas Killigrew Cavalier Dramatist 1621–1683,* Philadelphia, 1930.

[72] Bargrave, *Alexander VII and his Cardinals,* Camden Society, 1867; D. Sturdy and M. Henig, *The Gentle Traveller,* 1983.

[73] Rawlinson MS. C 799, fos. 163, 181; H. F. Brown, *op. cit.,* p. 155.

[74] Egerton MS. 1632. For Southwell's travel abroad see also *Hist. MSS. Comm. Egmont MSS.,* i, part ii. 603–610 and Crinò, op. cit. pp. 115–6.

[75] Egerton MS. 1632, fo. 53.

[76] Egerton MS. 1632, fo. 27.

## CHAPTER 7

[1] *The Protectorate of Oliver Cromwell,* etc. (ed. R. Vaughan), 1839, ii. 174.

[2] Autobiography of Sir W. Trumbull. All Souls College, Oxford, MS. 317, fo. I.

[3] W. Spelman, *A Dialoge or Confabulation between Two Travellers,* Roxburghe Club, 1896, pp. 2–7.

[4] Tanner MS. 433. It will be recalled that Tanner, while Bishop of Norwich, made large collections pertaining to this area.

[5] The argument must not be pressed too far because Harwich, not Yarmouth, was the normal point of departure for the Low Countries and the gentry would therefore tend to travel up from London to the more southerly of the two ports. This Yarmouth register may, however, be compared with that kept at Rye a little earlier (S.P. Domestic, Chas. I, ccccxviii. 21): here many gentlemen are mentioned, and the same names occur later on in embassy reports from Paris and the university register at Padua.

[6] *Travels of Sir William Brereton... 1634–1635,* Chetham Society, 1844; J. S. Morrill, *Cheshire 1630–1660* 1974, pp. 24–5.

[7] *Ibid.,* p. 83.

[8] Rawlinson MS. K, Hearne's Diaries 177, fos. 77–106: Hearne states that he has epitomized 489 pages in 30 small folios.

[9] *Evelyn,* ii. 30ff., 569–71.

Here again it must be borne in mind that Evelyn filled in his notes later with additional material taken from guidebooks. I have tried to disentangle the original material.

[10] 'The Busse' was English for Bois-le-Duc ('s Hertogenbosch).

[11] *Life of Marmaduke Rawdon,* Camden Society, 1863, pp. 5–8, 92–110.

[12] Moryson, *Itinerary* (ed. 1907), i. 89–118. The number of the Countess's children, and the date, vary. For this and other enjoyable lore Marjorie Bowen, *The Netherlands Displayed, or the Delights of the Low Countries,* 1926.

[13] *Epistolae Ho-elianae* (ed. J. Jacobs, 1890), i. 25–40.

[14] *Travels of Peter Mundy,* Hakluyt Society, 1924, iv. 60–81.

[25] Harleian MS. 7002, fos. 199–201; see above, pp. 52–53.

[16] Rawlinson MSS. Letters 54, fos. 53, 54.

[17] Rawlinson MS. D 84, fos. 34–36.

[18] Journal of William Nicolson, Queen's College, Oxford, MS. 68. Neither Mundy nor Nicolson seem to have been aware that few of the larger Dutch ships came nearer to Amsterdam than the Texel.

[19] *Ibid.,* under the heading 'Amsterdam'.

[20] The work of Owen Feltham, *Three Weeks Observations of the Low-Countries, especially Holland,* printed in 1652, during the first Dutch War is of no particular interest. William Penn's *Account of Travels in Holland and Germany in 1677, 1694,* is more rewarding. Cf. the Haistwell Diary in *Short Journal and Itinerary Journals of George Fox* (ed. N. Penney), 1925, pp. 237–255.

[21] *Hist. MSS. Comm., De Lisle and Dudley MSS.,* iii. 397.

[22] *Hist. MSS. Comm., Downshire MSS.,* iv. 54, 81.

[23] *Sidney Papers,* ii. 324.

[24] *Sidney Papers,* ii. 320.

[25] Richard D'Ewes who came to the Middle Temple a few years before Evelyn, also preceded him in Holland, France and Italy. In 1636 he joined the army campaigning in the Low Countries; his letters to his brother, at this time, form an interesting series (Harleian MS. 379, fo.

153; MS. 374, fo. 97; MS. 383, fo. 135; MS. 374, fo. 92: the last is from Sir W. Boswell, the bearer D'Ewes).

[26] *Autobiography*, pp. 110–126. For Herbert and Howard in France, above, pp. 20, 23.

[27] *De Lisle and Dudley MSS.*, iv. 217.

[28] *Autobiography*, pp. 142–151, 176–178, 183 and above, pp. 00–00.

[29] Additional MS. 29549, fos. 33–37.

[30] *Autobiography*, p. 153.

[31] *Wotton*, ii. 110–124.

[32] *Hist. MSS. Comm., Portland MSS.*, II. 110ff.

[33] *De Lisle and Dudley MSS.*, iv. 70.

[34] F. Peck, *Desiderata Curiosa*, 1735, ii, Bk. xii.

[35] The numbers present at this siege (1629) who played a role in the English Civil War (1642–6) is noteworthy.

[36] *Fairfax Correspondence* (ed. G. W. Johnson), 1848, i. xxxi–liii, 160–165, 318–322.

[37] G. Holles, *Memorials of the Holles Family*, Camden Society, 1937, pp. 34, 73–86, 116, 184, 193–194.

[38] *Raymond and Guise Memoirs*, Camden Society, 1917, pp. 30–44: a very animated description; *Hist. MSS. Comm. Denbigh MSS.*, v, p. 74.

[39] *Cal. of S.P. Dom.* 1623–1625, p. 6.

[40] Life of Sir John Digby, *Camden Miscellany*, xviii, 1910, p. 7.

[41] E. Walsingham, *Britannicae Virtutis Imago*, 1644.

[42] E. Walsingham, *Alter Britanniae Heros*, 1645.

[43] *Acts of the Privy Council, 1621–1623*, p. 191.

[44] *Cal. of S.P. Dom. 1627–1628*, p. 527.

[45] For his plan of assisting Charles I in 1639 with an army of 5/6000 infantry and 400 cavalry see *Correspondance de la Cour d'Espagne sur les Affaires des Pays Bas* (ed. Cuvelier and Lefèvre), 1930, iii. 247, 305, 312, 321.

[46] *Cal. of S.P. Dom. 1603–1610*, p. 610.

[47] Harleian MS. 7002, fo. 200.

[48] The following details are based on the accounts given in E. Arber, *Story of the Pilgrim Fathers*, 1897; H. M. and M. Dexter. *The England and Holland of the Pilgrims, 1906*; W. Steven, *History of the Scottish Church at Rotterdam*, 1833; C. Burrage, *The early English Dissenters*, 1921; and R. P. Stearns, *Congregationalism in the Dutch Netherlands*, 1940.

[49] For the fullest modern account of an English church in the Netherlands in this period, A. C. Carter, *The English Reformed Church in Amsterdam in the Seventeenth Century*, 1964. The records of its membership (pp.. 116–23) should be compared with the passport registers described on p. 173 above.

[50] W. Bradford, *History of Plymouth Plantation 1606–1646* (ed. W.T. Davis), 1908, p. 38.

[51] W. Steven, *op. cit.*, p. 319.

[52] *De Lisle and Dudley MSS.*, iii. 173, 368–374, 442.

[53] W. Stevens, *op. cit.*, p. 289; cf. a remark in the *Cornwallis Letters* (ed. Lord Braybrooke), 1842, pp. 289–290, written in May 1639: 'Your Frends, Mr. Laurence and his wife are in good health at Arnhem, the ayer of which place is very agreeable unto them as to the rest of the good sosietye that live there'; and also the interesting letter printed in C. Burrage, *op. cit.*, i. 299.

[54] Cf. below, pp. 287–8, and R. P. Stearns, *The Strenuous Puritan, Hugh Peter, 1598–1640*, 1954.

[55] T. Cawton, *Life and Death of that Holy and Reverend Man of God Mr. Thomas Cawton*, 1662, p. 52; W. L. Hull, *Benjamin Furly and Quakerism at Rotterdam*, 1941.

[56] Cf. F. O. Dentz, *History of the English Church at the Hague*, 1929.

[57] This was less clearly the case in the 1630s than earlier. Archbishop Laud, with some help from the Dutch authorities and with some success, sought to supervise the English congregations in Holland. After 1640 the Anglican clergy in exile likewise accentuated a more conservative tendency.

[58] The following account is based on J. Gillow, *Bibliographical Dictionary of the English Catholics*, 1885–1902; H. Foley, *Records of the English Province of the Society of Jesus*, 1875–82; the volumes of the Catholic Record Society, and P. Guilday, *The English Catholic Refugees on the Continent*, 1914. A. C. F. Beales, *Education under Penalty*, 1963, surveys the schooling

of English Catholics both at home and abroad in the seventeenth century; for the recusants of one county and their reliance on the Continent, see J. T. Cliffe, *The Yorkshire Gentry*, 1969, pp. 189–209.

[59] *Salisbury MSS.*, xvii. 626.

[60] Catholic Record Society, *Miscellanea*, 1917, xi. 1–92.

[61] H. Foley, *Records*, vii. 1147ff.: Annual Letters of the Belgian College of the English Province.

## CHAPTER 8

[1] *Nicholas Ferrar*, ed. J. E. B Mayor, 1855.

[2] *Salisbury MSS.*, XV. 54.

[3] *Downshire MSS.*, ii. 348, 373, 390.

[4] Calvert to Salisbury 17 October and 18 November 1610, 28 February 1611, S.P. France, 56/100, 330, 57/58.

[5] D.N.B.

[6] *Downshire MSS.*, ii. 103. At the same time Overbury was also sending short notes recommending himself and describing the political situation, to Salisbury, S.P. France, 55/126, 144. Trumbull, to whom (and to his descendants) we owe the magnificent material of the Downshire papers still appearing under the aegis of the Historical Manuscripts Commission, first served in Sir Thomas Edmondes's embassy at Brussels, and then as resident Agent there for a great many years. *Cf.* below, p. 353, note 9.

[7] *Downshire MSS.*, iii. 31, 44, 46.

[8] *Histoire de Belgique* (ed. 1927), iv. 414.

[9] Chaworth's narrative and other papers of his are in the *Losely Manuscripts* (ed. A. J. Kempe), 1836, pp. 418–487.

[10] It seems that the price was subsequently lowered to £1500. Chaworth's narrative, *op. cit.*, p. 485.

[11] See especially Temple's Life by his sister Lady Giffard in *Early Essays and Romances of Sir William Temple*, ed. G. C. Moore Smith, 1930 and K. H. D. Haley, *An English Diplomat in the Low Countries*, 1986.

[12] *Works of Joseph Hall* (ed. 1837), i. xix–xxiii.

[13] *Downshire MSS.*, i. 5, 66ff., 104, 320.

[14] *Ibid.*, iv. 105, 107, 138. Among those

who went to Spa after Heidelberg were Sir Robert Drury and his attendant John Donne: R. C. Bald, *John Donne*, 1970, p. 242.

[15] *Ibid.*, iv. 351, 434, 441, 469–470.

[16] *Cal of S.P. Dom. 1619–1623*, pp. 286, 412, 420, 421, 586, 587, 596; *ibid.* 1623–1625, pp. 6, 195, 285; *ibid. 1629–1631*, p. 312; *ibid.* 1641–1643, pp. *47ff.*; *ibid. 1649–1650*, p. 139.

[17] *Ibid. 1663–1664*, p.376. In E. Dean. *Spadacrene Anglica the English Spaw, or the glory of Knaresborough*, York, 1654, the credit for the discovery is given to Wiliam Slingsby 'about 55 years ago who, because he was a well travelled man, first realized that these Yorkshire waters and those of Spa in Belgium possessed similar properties.

[18] For what follows see W. N. Sainsbury, *Original Papers Relating to Rubens*, 1859, pp. 9–65.

[19] Cf. a letter from Sir Thomas Overbury to William Trumbull, 15 September 1612. He asks the Agent to try and acquire for his patron Rochester pictures and hangings of fine quality, if and when any of the Flemish nobility should chance to die and their property was sold. *Downshire MSS.*, iii. 369. See also *Correspondence of Jane Lady Cornwallis*, 1842, pp. 50–51.

[20] *Losely Manuscripts*, pp. 456, 457.

[21] Another Englishman also commented on the Dutch, at about this time: 'Their greatest Vanity, that draweth on a Charge, is in Pictures and flowers, every Man's House is full of Pictures as they are the greatest part of their Moveables.' The Politia of the United Provinces, *Somers Tracts*, fourth series, vol. ii (1752) p. 394.

[22] Cf. Robert Bargrave's description of an inn at Dordrecht in 1656; 'a faire salone (or great Hall) in the same tavern; the two ends whereof are adorned with incomparable Pictures of the Magistrates and Burghers of the City all in full proportion and in exquisite postures'. Rawlinson MS. C 799, fo. 191.

[23] W. N. Sainsbury, *op. cit.*, Appendix D.

[24] *Ibid.*, pp. 307, 308.

[25] *The Agrarian History of England and Wales*, v. ii (1985), pp. 545–6, 549–50.

[26] I would gladly be proved wrong on this point, which made it impracticable to expand the remarks of Evelyn and others on Leyden. But see *The Oxinden Letters*, ed. D. Gardiner, 1933, pp. 31–2. and D. Thomson, *op. cit.*, pp. 9–13, 31–40. An analysis of E. Peacock, *Index to English Speaking Students . . . at Leyden University*, 1883, shows that approximately 950 English speaking men were matriculated at Leyden between 1575 and 1675: 110 before 1600, 45 in 1600–9, 60 in 1610–19, 95 in 1620–9, 145 in 1630–9, 300 in 1640–9, 70 in 1650–9, 85 in 1660–9, 40 in 1670–5. The reason why no correspondence remains is, probably, that few resident students belonged to a class whose family papers had much chance of survival. The most important were certainly the medical students, and biographical studies of members of the Royal College of Physicians (W. R. Munk, *op. cit.*) show that Leyden shared first place with Padua as a foreign centre for learning physic. After 1680 English medical men went infrequently to Padua, but they continued to take the Leyden degree.

[27] See *The Relation of Sydnam Poyntz 1624–1636*, Camden Society, 1908.

## CHAPTER 9

[1] Repeated in D.N.B. This chapter was in the first place an attempt to correct and amplify the article on Aylesbury in the D.N.B. from papers in the P.R.O., the Clarendon MSS. and the MSS. of T. Cottrell Dormer, Esq., at Rousham.

[2] Leicester to Sec. of State 9 February 1638, S.P. France, 105/75, 102.

[3] For the handwriting of Leicester's despatches cf. a letter written and signed by Battyer himself to Sir T. Roe (*ibid.*, 105/327) which contains references to the Earl of Arundel, the purchase of drawings in Paris, and Inigo Jones.

[4] Browne to Scudamore 18 March (n.s.) 1639, Additional MS. 11044, fo. 86.

[5] Cf. addresses of letters in Clarendon MS. 19 *passim*, also Clarendon's *Life* (ed. 1857), i. 24.

[6] Clarendon MSS. no. 1473.

[7] Already in March 1640 the Earl of Northumberland, evidently at Leicester's request, was trying to obtain for Aylesbury the command of a company in the army. *Sidney Papers*, ii. 640.

[8] No. 1466.

[9] No. 1516.

[10] *Cal. of S.P. Dom. 1640–1641*, p. 558.

[11] No. 1517.

[12] No. 1583.

[13] H. Foley, *Records*, vi. 623.

[14] Evelyn MSS. in Christ Church Library, Oxford.

[15] *Sidney Papers*, i. 130.

[16] *Life and Times of Anthony Wood* (ed. Clark), 1891, i. 83.

[17] *Lords Journals*, vi. 60.

[18] *Ibid.*, 163.

[19] A. Wood, *Fasti Oxonienses* (ed. 1815), i. 476; Lords Journals, viii. 552.

[20] *Cal. of the Com. for Advance of Money*, p. 528.

[21] Evelyn MSS.

[22] *Cal. of S.P. Dom. 1644–1645*, p. 604.

[23] Aylesbury to Sir R, Browne, Additional MS. 15857, fo. 23.

[24] H. Foley, *op. cit.*, vi. 629.

[25] *Ath. Ox.*, iii. 1157–1158: the D.N.B. (art. on Woodhead) rejects Wood's evidence on chronological grounds, rather unconvincingly.

[26] R. Flecknoe, *Relation of Ten Years Travells in Europe*, 1656, p. 95; H. Foley, *op. cit.*, vi. 629–632.

[27] *Times Lit. Supp.*, 5 June 1924, modified by Chaney, *op. cit.*, pp. 347–50. Some authorities question Marvell's authorship of the Elegy for Francis Villiers, but not his presence in Rome early in 1646.

[28] *Commons Journals*, iii. 369, 395 and iv. 216; *Cal. of the Com. for Advance of Money*. p. 528.

[29] *Denbigh MSS.*, v. 79, 80.

[30] *Lords Journals*, viii. 552–553.

[31] *Commons Journals*, iv. 716, 723; *Lords Journals*, viii. 567.

[32] *Commons Journals*, v. 296, 325.

[33] *Lords Journals*, viii. 609.

[34] See the flyleaf and title-page of the *Historie of the Civill Warres of France*, London, 1647.

[35] A dedicatory letter to Charles I, which prefaces the second volume, is dated 1 January 1648 [9] and subscribed by both

Aylesbury and Cotterell. The king naturally found much of topical interest in a study of the French civil wars. For this, and for William Dobson's symbolical painting on the same theme, *Burlington Magazine*, 90 (1948), pp. 97–9, and Malcolm Rogers, *William Dobson 1611–1646*, 1984, pp. 73–4.

[36] John Evelyn to Sir R. Browne 25 October 1647, Evelyn MSS.

[37] No. 2734.

[38] *Hamilton Papers*, Camden Society, 1880, p. 158.

[39] No. 2732.

[40] S. R. Gardiner, *Great Civil War* (ed. 1893), iv. 87; *Hamilton Papers*, p. 175. Goff was a doctor of divinity (*D.N.B.*).

[41] C. Oman, *Henrietta Maria*, p. 135; *Letters of Henrietta Maria* (ed. A. E. Green), 1856, p. 152.

[42] Clarendon, *Life*, i. 214–218.

[43] No. 2847.

[44] No. 2819.

[45] No. 2822.

[46] *Life of the Duke of Newcastle by his Wife* (ed. C. H. Firth), 1907, p. 50.

[47] No. 2823. Another letter to Aylesbury from the Hague, dated 30 July 1648, states that the armes and pistols' were ready for shipment to London but, in view of Buckingham's recent defeat, would not be sent 'unless I hear further from you'. No. 2848.

[48] No. 2805.

[49] Nos. 2769, 2813, 2821.

[50] No. 2901.

[51] Nos. 2769, 2813, 2821, 2826, 2829, 2884.

[52] For the administration of the Villiers interest see nos. 2551–2739 *passim* (viz. Clarendon MS. 30), and the *Cal. of the Com. for Compounding*, p. 2182 *et passim*.

[53] S. R. Gardiner, *op. cit.*, iv. 58.

[54] *Hamilton Papers*, p. 238.

[55] No. 2833.

[56] Nos. 2814, 2816, 2828, 2831–2833, 2843.

[57] Nos. 2836, 2839, 2844, 2888.

[58] No. 2895. Woodhead here refers to his position as Fellow of University College, Oxford.

[59] No. 2902.

[60] No. 2884.

[61] Nos. 2890–2891.

[62] No. 44 (in *Cal. of the Clarendon S.P.*, vol. ii).

[63] No. 53.

[64] No. 45.

[65] No. 51.

[66] No. 18.

[67] Clarendon MS. 137, fo. 10. This is the diary kept by Hyde's secretary, William Edgeman, on the journey from the Low Countries to Spain. For Hyde's letters written during this journey, Richard Ollard, *Clarendon and his Friends*, 1987, pp. 126–8, 134–6.

[68] Clarendon MS. 129, fo. 27.

[69] Letters from Hyde to Lady Hyde in *Hist, MSS. Comm. Bath MSS.*, ii. 80ff.

[70] cf. Ollard, *op. cit.*, p. 142.

[71] Letters from Hyde to Lady Hyde in *Hist. MSS. Comm. Bath MSS.*, ii. 89.

[72] The evidence in this and the three following paragraphs comes from the MSS. of Sir Charles Cotterell preserved at Rousham. I am deeply indebted to Mr. Cottrell Dormer for his courtesy and kindness.

[73] I omit here consideration of the two questions which interest historians of art, What were the precise contents of the Buckingham collection of pictures? and, What were the pictures sold at Antwerp? The Cotterell MSS. might be of some use of these topics.

[74] These instructions are signed, and the clauses occasionally amended, by Buckingham himself.

[75] Also involved was Hugh May, Charles II's architect at a later date. Colvin, *British Architects*, 'May'.

[76] *Thurloe Papers*, *1742* v. 374; also v. 154, 170; *Narrative of General Venables*, Camden Society, 1900, p. 110.

## CHAPTER 10

[1] Rawlinson MS. C 178, fo. 47: Ordinances of the Company trading to Spain, 30 August 1605.

[2] Bodl. Perrot MS. 5, fo. 23.

[3] *Ibid.*

[4] *Ibid.*

[5] L. Lewkenor, *The Estate of English Fugitives under the King of Spain*, 1595.

[6] In 1609, English ships were chartered to carry banished Moriscoes to the African

coast at 7 ducats a head. Cottington to Salisbury 15 October 1609, S.P. Spain, 16/203.

[7] Quoted in S. de Madariaga, *Rise and Fall of the Spanish Empire*, 1947, ii. 180-182.

[8] See S. Gaselee, *Spanish Books in the Library of Samuel Pepys*, Samuel Pepys Club, 1925, ii. 117-157.

[9] For the early Hispanists in England, F. de Rojas, *Celestina or the Tragick-Comedie of Calisto and Melibea*, ed. G. Martinez Lacalle, 1973, pp. 7-17. It is interesting to find that William Trumbull (p. 200 above) first learnt Spanish in Nottingham's household 'of a couple of gentlemen Spaniards that were taken by his Lordship at sea.' *Hist. Mss. Comm. Downshire MSS*, v (1988), no. 410.

[10] For Nottingham's embassy and its journeys see *Winwood Memorials*, ii. 62-91; S.P. Spain (P.R.O.); R. Treswell, *A Relation of such things as were observed to happen in the Journey of...Nottingham*, London, 1605; *The Royal Entertainement of...the Earl of Nottingham* (printed by Valentine Sims for William Ferbrand), London, 1605; Bodl. Lister MS. 18, a contemporary English translation of the Spanish account by Antony Coello, stationer of Valladolid; and M. Hume, *Court of Philip IV*, 1907.

[11] Nottingham to Cranborne 5 April 1605, S.P. Spain, 11/34.

[12] Treswell, *op. cit.*, p. 12.

[13] *Ibid.*, p. 16.

[14] Lister MS. 18, fo. 19.

[15] *Winwood Memorials*, ii. 74.

[16] Sir George Buck to Cranborne 30 April 1605, S.P. Spain, 11/48.

[17] Lister MS. 18, fo. 19.

[18] Lister MS. 18, fo. 21.

[19] 'With much reverence and decencie in 'the procession' (fo. 29), and, 'Some of the English gentlemen, desirous to see fashions went in the procession with great reverence' (fo. 43).

[20] *The Royal Entertainement*, etc. p. 11. In Henry Clifford's *Life of Jane Dormer, Duchess of Feria* (ed. J. Stevenson 1887), p. 68, the author states that Nottingham told him in 1605 in Spain that the Duchess of Feria had been the fairest lady of Queen Mary's court. For Cornwallis's unfavour-able opinion of Clifford, see *Winwood Memorials*, ii. 213.

[21] Nottingham to Cranborne 28 April 1605, S.P. Spain, 11/45.

[22] *Letters of Sir T. Bodley to Thomas James* (ed. G. W. Wheeler) 1926, p. 118.

[23] *Winwood Memorials*, ii. 73.

[24] Treswell, *op. cit.*, p. 48.

[25] *Ibid.* pp. 51-3; Lister MS. 18, fos. 57-65.

[26] Carleton to Chamberlain 2 June 1605, S.P. Spain, 11/123.

[27] Nottingham to Salisbury 28 April and 2 June 1605, S.P. Spain, 11/44, 124.

[28] Nottingham's Spanish pension soon lapsed. C. H. Carter, 'Gondomar: ambassador to James I', *Historical Journal*, 7 (1964), p. 196.

[29] R. Cocks to Sir T. Wilson 12 July 1605, *ibid.*, 11/174.

[30] See the notes on fo. 1 of Lister MS. 18.

[31] *Winwood Memorials*, ii. 97.

[32] Cornwallis to Salisbury 13 May 1607, S.P. Spain, 14/10.

[33] M. Bruning to (?) Sir T. Wilson 26 March 1609, *ibid.*, 16/54. Digby, Cornwallis's successor, wrote to Carleton on 14 September 1611: 'I am beholding to them heere for giving mee the fayrest and pleasantest house in Madrid, having the commoditie of gardens and all other conveniences. And yf it had not bene for that I think wee had been halfe of us dead by this tyme.' (*Ibid.*, 18/184).

[34] Cornwallis to the Council 18 September 1607, *ibid.*, 14/142.

[35] Cornwallis to the Council 10 July 1607, *ibid.*, 14/77.

[36] E. R. Adair, *Exterritoriality of Ambassadors in the 16th and 17th Centuries*, 1929, pp. 182-183.

[37] Cf. *Winwood Memorials*, ii. 74-75: 'How manie of this Companie that attended his Excellencie have since our comeinge into these Partes made Declaration of themselves to be Papists, I shall relate unto your Lordship, my Lord Admiral himself having taken upon him to doe it.'

[38] Digby MSS. (P.R.O. Transcripts) fo. 394. An experienced traveller wrote of the Spaniards in 1664: 'At the Ave-Mary Bell they all fall down upon their knees;

whereas in other Countries they are contented only to pluck off their hats.' Francis Willughby in J. Ray, *Observations*, 1673, p. 464.

[39] Wadsworth to Cornwallis 8 September 1605, to Salisbury 14 September, S.P. Spain, 12/23, 41.

[40] Cottington to Salisbury 29 June 1610, *ibid.*, 17/111.

[41] Cottington to the Secretary of State 12 and 22 May 1616, *ibid.*, 22/36, 44.

[42] For the Wadsworths see also the articles in *D.N.B.*

[43] *Winwood Memorials*, ii. 95.

[44] It was probably suspicious that Sir Thomas Palmer had desired, early in 1605, to precede Nottingham's embassy into Spain. Zuñiga to Anaya 3/13 February 1605, S.P. Spain, 11/6.

[45] See M. J. Havran, *Caroline Courtier. The Life of Lord Cottington*, 1973.

[46] Ousely had probably been a merchant in Spain and became a spy sending intelligence from Spanish ports in the period before the Armada of 1588. He was on good terms with Howard, Drake and Walsingham. *State Papers . . . relating to the defeat of the Spanish Armada*, ed. by J. K. Laughton, Navy Records Society, 1895, i. 301, ii. 62.

[47] *Winwood Memorials*, ii. 391.

[48] Cornwallis to the Council 3 February 1609, S.P. Spain, 16/26.

[49] Matt. Bruning to — 26 March 1609, *ibid.*, 16/53.

[50] Cornwallis to Salisbury, 7 April, 1610, *ibid.*, 17/60.

[51] Once he travelled over to Sardinia in connection with the famous lawsuit of the ship *Vineyard*, was captured by Turks and taken to Algiers. J. Howell, *Epistolae Ho-elianae*, i. 152, 162. Howell addressed one letter to him, *ibid.*, i. 204.

[52] J. Jude to — 4 March 1609, S.P. Spain, 16/46.

[53] R. Cocks to Sir T. Wilson 6 December 1605, S.P. Spain, 12/139. Cocks lived the last years of his life in Japan (*Diary of Richard Cocks*, Hakluyt Society, 1883).

[54] Neville Davis to Salisbury 22 October 1605; Cornwallis to Salisbury 30 October 1605, S.P. Spain, 12/90, 104.

[55] *Travels of Peter Mundy*, Hakluyt Society, 1907, i. 14.

[56] *Winwood Memorials*, ii. 390, 432, 439.

[57] A. Montesino, *Epistolas y Evangelios* . . . (edited by Roman de Vallezillo), Madrid, 1603. Bodley pressmark: M.10.7.Th. The inscription is on the verso of the title page.

[58] There are letters from Davis to Salisbury between 1605 and 1610 in S.P. Spain.

[59] *Original Letters . . . of Sir Richard Fanshawe*, 1701, p. 153. For the limited period during which a notion of 'the line' had some currency, G. Mattingly, 'No Peace beyond what Line?' *Transactions of the Royal Historical Society*, 1963, pp. 160–1.

[60] Fanshawe to Coke 2 June 1638, S.P. Spain, 40/85.

[61] G. Gage, *The English-American, his Travel by Sea and Land* (2nd edit.), 1655, p. 202.

[62] J. Stone to — 11 August 1620, S.P. Spain, 24/20. For conditions in Lisbon early in the century see M. Brearley, *Hugo Gurgeny, prisoner of the Lisbon Inquisition*, 1947.

[63] Cornwallis to Salisbury 11 April 1606, S.P. Spain, 13/66.

[64] Although in the same year a traveller passing through said that there was not a single English merchant or factor in Barcelona (*Epistolae Ho-elianae*, i. 58). For the English at Malaga, below, pp. 383–6, and at Bilbao, D. Mathew, *The Social Structure of Caroline England*, 1948, p. 95.

[65] Cottington to Winwood 20 May 1617, S.P. Spain, 22/144.

[66] Digby to Salisbury 12 October 1611, *ibid.*, 18/210. The young man, Tibbald Gorge, spent the winter in Madrid and returned through France in the spring after visiting 'some townes of Spaine'. Digby to Salisbury 4 January and April 1, *ibid.*, 19/2, 58.

[67] *Memoirs of Ann Lady Fanshawe* (ed. 1907), pp. 125–40. On the consequences of the 1667 treaty, J. O. McLachlan, *Trade and Peace with Old Spain*, 1940, pp. 1–22.

[68] E. B. de Fonblanque, *Lives of the Lords Strangford*, 1877; Dorothy Townshend, *Endymion Porter*, 1897; Gervas Huxley, *Endymion Porter*, 1959.

[69] Nottingham to Salisbury 28 April 1605, S.P. Spain, 11/45; and *Winwood Memorials*, ii. 76.

[70] *Cal. of S.P. Spain. 1580–1586*, p. 456.

[71] Arthur Wilson, *History of Great Britain*, 1653, p. 229.

[72] *Winwood Memorials*, ii. 327; Cornwallis to Salisbury 19 September 1607, S.P. Spain, 14/154.

[73] G. Porter to E. Porter, 5 January 1607–8, S.P. Spain, 13/142.

[74] Cottington to Salisbury 19 January 1610, *ibid.*, 17/7.

[75] *Downshire MSS.*, iii. 261, 284, 302; J. Figueroa to G. Porter 19 February 1612, S.P. Spain, 19/40.

[76] J. Howell, *Epistolae Ho-elianae*, ii. 55–56.

[77] Digby MSS. (P.R.O. Transcripts), fo. 473; *Hist. MSS. Comm. Skrine MSS.*, p.156.

[78] Cottington to Porter 24 January 1630, S.P. Spain, 34/150, and J.H. Elliott, *Olivares*, 1986, pp. 206, 606.

[79] *Downshire MSS.*, ii. 27, 78, 404, 464, and iii. *passim*. Cawleigh's name was also spelt Calley, Caley, etc.

[80] Cottington to Salisbury 16 November 1609, S.P. Spain, 16/239.

[81] Hopton to Cap. Mennes 9 August 1638, *ibid.*, 40/178.

[82] *Hist. MSS. Comm. Various Collections*, iii. 133, 147.

[83] R. Cocks to Sir T. Wilson 13 July 1605, S.P. Spain, 11/176.

[84] Harleian MS. 1581, fo. 362. In this document Tresham is described as a Gentleman of the Privy Chamber.

[85] Tresham to the 'Duke' 25 September 1617, S.P. Spain, 22/190. Among his travelling companions were Thomas Lorkin, young Kenelm Digby, and Sir Robert Phelips. The latter, the prominent MP on many occasions, wrote a rather critical account of this embassy (*Hist. MSS. Comm.*, Appendix to the First Report, 1874, pp. 59–60). For a list of Digby's gentlemen-servants in 1617, see S.P. Spain, 22/241.

[86] *Ibid.*, 26/249.

[87] *Hist. MSS. Comm., Montagu MSS.*, p. 87.

[88] *Chamberlain*, i. 612, ii. 277, 318. The second visit was to old Lady Tresham.

[89] Memorandum on the posts through France to Spain, 1605, S.P. Spain, 12/186.

[90] Jude to Sir T. Wilson 14 September 1609, S.P. Spain, 16/186.

[91] Cornwallis to Salisbury 13 September 17 October and 13 November 1609, *ibid.*, 16/184, 208, 234.

[92] *Downshire MSS.*, iii. 27.

[93] For Sanford, *ibid.*, *passim*; for Mabbe, P. E. Russell, 'A Stuart Hispanist: James Mabbe', *Bulletin of Hispanic Studies*, 30 (1953), pp. 75–84.

[94] *Chamberlain*, i. 326, 397.

[95] Digby to Salisbury 8 and 10 May 1611, S.P. Spain, 18/75, 79.

[96] *Ibid.*, 18/105. Payment was made by the end of the year, *ibid.*, 18/248.

[97] An ambassador to Spain enjoyed a few other sources of income. He was permitted to import free of custom his own household supplies. The allowance was generous and he could sell the surplus very handsomely to the English merchants, who thereby obtained stock a little more cheaply than if full custom had been paid. Secondly, he might hope to a make a profit out of successful commercial cases in the Spanish Courts. Digby was to be paid £500 for his share in dealing with the famous *Vineyard* case (the papers on this case in the Digby MSS. (P.R.O. Transcripts) are of great interest). Digby respected the central courts of justice in Spain — 'Tribunals of much delay but great sincerity and justice.' He opposed the alternative policy of issuing letters of marque to aggrieved merchants.

[98] Digby to Salisbury 5 July 1611, S.P. Spain, 18/124.

[99] Cottington to the Secretary of State 12 February 1616, S.P. Spain, 22/7.

[100] Cottington to the same 12 and 22 May 1616, *ibid.*, 22/36, 45.

[101] Coke to Aston 20 February 1638, *ibid.*, 40/24.

[102] J. Chandler to Hopton, and merchants' petition to Charles I, *ibid.*, 40/68, 70.

[103] Aston to Windebank 12 May 1638, S.P. Spain, 40/73.

[104] Aston to Coke 17 May 1638, *ibid.*,

40/75.

[105] Hopton to Coke 17 May 1638, *ibid.*, 40/77.

[106] Hopton to Coke 4 June 1638, *ibid.*, 40/87.

[107] Hopton to — 9 June 1638, *ibid.*, 40/91.

[108] Hopton to Coke 7 July, 8 August, Aston to Secretary of State 3 July and 4 August 1638, S.P. Spain, 40/123, 174, 115, 166.

[109] Hopton to Windebank 23 September 1640, *ibid.*, 42/51.

## CHAPTER 11

[1] For example, the meagre references to Marvell's period of residence in Madrid in 1646–7. *Notes and Queries*, January 1972, p. 17.

[2] *Downshire MSS.*, ii. 394.

[3] J. Jude to Robert Wilson [sic] 30 March 1607, S.P. Spain, 13/199. Thomas Tomkys is known as the author of a drama. *Albumazar*, performed at Cambridge in 1614. He wrote from Italian models (*D.N.B.*). For Altham see also his own letter to Cornwallis 25 July 1608. S.P. Spain, 15/87.

[4] Cottington to Winwood 4 November 1617, *ibid.*, 22/204.

[5] Additional MS. 36449, fo. 24.

[6] *Memoirs of Ann Lady Fanshawe*, pp. 28, 339–343.

[7] Hopton to Vane 17 February 1641, S.P. Spain, 42/133.

[8] J. Cartwright, *Sacharissa*, 1901, pp. 170–171. Joseph Colston, of London, who spent several years in Italy and France, realised a bill of exchange for £40 in Madrid on 15 June 1644 but there is no evidence to suggest that he studied in Spain as he had done in Italy, or practised such accomplishments as fencing, which was his pastime in France. Sloane MS. 118, fo. 83.

[9] Rawlinson MS. D. 120, fo. 12.

[10] J. Ray, *Observations*, 1973, p. 474. For a more favorable view of these matters, M. Grice-Hutchinson, 'Some Spanish contributions to the early activities of the Royal Society of London', *Notes & Rec. R. Soc. Lond.* 42 (1988), pp. 123–132.

[11] *Cal. of S.P. Dom. 1603–1610*, p. 220.

[12] T. Morgan to Salisbury 17 July 1607; Becher to Wilson 25 July 1609, S.P. France, 53/302, 55/140.

[13] Cottington to Salisbury 2 November 1609, S.P. Spain, 16/228.

[14] Cottington to Salisbury 20 January 1610, *ibid.*, 17/21.

[15] Cottington to Salisbury 4 March 1610, S.P. Spain, 17/45.

[16] Roos's narrative 27 July 1610, *ibid.*, 17/119–154; see also *Hist. MSS. Comm. Rutland MSS.*, i. 422.

[17] Cottington to Salisbury 4 March 1610, S.P. Spain, 17/45, 68.

[18] Roos's narrative, *op. cit.*, fo. 126.

[19] One reason for Roos's leisurely return was that he wanted to avoid the company of other English travellers on their way home. Cottington to Salisbury 11 May 1610, S.P. Spain, 17/85. Possibly he owed them money.

[20] Sir R. Chamberlain to Carleton 26 March 1613, S.P. Sicily, 1/13.

[21] J. Howell, *Epistolae Ho-elianae*, i. 55–61, 151–212.

[22] Sonia Anderson, *An English Consul in Turkey: Paul Rycaut at Smyrna, 1667–1678*, 1989, gives a full account of this remarkable man.

[23] Rawlinson MS. C 799, fos. 102–157.

[24] Rawlinson MS. C 799, fo. 105. Admiral Blake, commanding the fleet of the Protectorate, was starting from Alicante on his memorable Mediterranean expedition which continued into the following year.

[25] Rawlinson MS. C 799, fo. 135.

[26] Fo. 151. Rhingéna is Requena. On his journey from Barcelona to Madrid Bargrave explains that, on the frontier between Aragon and Castille: 'every Passenger must take a Manifest of all he carries with him (espetially his horses) before he can pass further: the Direcho for every horse, whether imported or exported being 115 Ryalls (about 14 Crounes) which I saved for mine by pretending I had a returne the same way' (fo. 125).

[27] Fos. 155–156.

[28] Cottington to Salisbury 18 April

1610, S.P. Spain, 17/68.

[29] Cf. above, p. 246.

[30] Collines to Cottington? April, 1610, S.P. Spain, 17/78. The date of this appeal is uncertain.

[31] Digby to Lake 13 September 1612. See also Digby to Salisbury 4 January 1612, *ibid.*, 19/149, 2.

[32] E. Wilson to — 12 May 1621, *ibid.*, 24/176.

[33] W. Lithgow, *The Totall Discourse of the Rare Adventures and Painefull Peregrinations.* London, 1632; modern edition, Glasgow, 1906.

[34] W. Lithgow, *op. cit.* (1906 edition), p. 388.

[35] At this very time Aston was having trouble with one of these servants. A certain Cheyne Roe was detained by the Inquisition, and in October 1620 the ambassador wrote on his behalf to the Inquisitor General saying that he had only gone to Salamanca to learn the language: certainly he was 'indiscretissimus', and would be sent back to England. Rumours about this affair had reached England by December. Additional MS. 36451, fo. 23; Additional MS. 36444, fo. 250. The person in question was very probably the Cheyne Roe who was a Fellow of Trinity College, Cambridge, later became Vice-Master of the College, and was ejected by the Parliamentarians.

[36] The classic authorities on this expedition remain Gardiner's *History* and J. Corbett, *England in the Mediterranean*, 1904. The fleet consisted of six royal and twelve private ships. Mansell was Blake's precursor in the Straits of Gibralter.

[37] Long to Secretary of State, S.P. Spain, 24/69–70, 99.

[38] Additional MS. 36451, fo. 42.

[39] Fo. 63. This volume of Aston's papers contains much valuable material, not to be found in S.P. Spain (P.R.O.), on the general duties of an English ambassador in Spain at this date.

[40] Cf. the judgement of Sir Thomas Wilson: 'For although Englishmen were so discreet to give noe scandale yett will the Spaniards both men and wemen be continually urging them, yea some of the cheefest of them in the port townes have said unto my self, yt lett ther Kinge doe what he will in other matters, but for religion they will lose life and goodes and abandon ther contry and goe dwell in the Indies rather then they will suffer heresye (as they cale it) to creepe in amongst them or heretiques nestle ther. I itterate this point for yt I knowe it will comber most of any, by reason of the blynd perversnes of the comon. Albeit the great ones yt governe the state doe not much regard it.' Wilson to (?) Cranborne 22 January 1605, S.P. Spain, 11/5.

## CHAPTER 12

[1] *Nicholas Papers*, Camden Society, 1892, ii. 263.

[2] Rawlinson MS. D. 76.

[3] *Cal. of S.P. Dom. 1649–1650*, p. 105. Apart from the date of this entry which agrees with the date of the travellers' departure in the diary, proof that the writer was Lord Mandeville is the name of his governor, M. Hainhofer (fos. 37, 51): they spent the winter of 1650–1651 at Lyon, and from there on 31 January (n.s.) Hainhofer wrote a letter to the Earl of Manchester which is printed in the Duke of Manchester's *Court and Society from Elizabeth to Anne*, 1864, i. 375. For Montagu's diary see also M. Wiemers, *Der 'Gentleman' und die Kunst*, 1986, pp. 13–27.

[4] *Cal. of S.P. Dom, 1654*, p. 86, 101.

[5] *Hist. MSS. Comm. Finch MSS.*, i. 59–60; Evelyn, ii. 124; Sloane MS. 179 A (Journal of Dr. Downes), fo. 93; *Camden Miscellany*, xi, p. 104; *Memoirs and Travels of Sir John Reresby* (ed. 1904), p. 1; Clarendon, *Life* (ed. 1857), i. 214–218; Rawlinson MS. D 84, fos. 1, 2.

[6] *Hist. MSS. Comm. Lindsey MSS.*, p. 275.

[7] Cf. Rawlinson Letters, MS. 54, fo. 14.

[8] As above, with *Francis Mortoft: His Book*, Hakluyt Society, 1925, p. 2.

[9] *Travels of Peter Mundy*, Hakluyt Society, 1907, i. Introduction, p. xix.

[10] E.g. in Rawlinson MS. D 1285, fos. 69–70, *Evelyn* ii. 121–7.

[11] Rawlinson MS. D 76, fo. 3.

[12] Rawlinson MS. D 1285, fo. 71.

[13] Harleian MS. 1278.

[14] Fos. 4–25.

[15] Evelyn *The State of France*, 1652, is very similar in substance.

[16] Fos. 26, 27.

[17] Rawlinson MS. D 1285, fos. 75, 157; cf. *Hist. MSS. Comm. Ancaster MSS.*, p. 423.

[18] *Camden Miscellany*, xi. 105.

[19] Rawlinson MS. D 120, fo. 4.

[20] S. P. Domestic, Commonwealth cxxiv. 60, 70, 95; cxxxi. 99. One of the pupils in Saumur in 1656 was William Paget, forty years later William III's impressive ambassador at Istanbul, and another tutor there was Andrew Marvell (Kelliher, *op. cit.*, p. 62). Williamson and Marvell, in their tutorial capacity, are interesting: the former had been teaching at Oxford, and his contacts with pupils and their families developed into a commission to take them abroad. Marvell was first appointed to look after Cromwell's ward Dutton at Eton College; from Eton he accompanied him directly to Saumur.

[21] Ashmole MS. 800 no. 3.

[22] Fo. 30.

[23] Fo. 29.

[24] Fos. 36, 37.

[25] *Verney Memoirs* (ed. 1904), i. 300ff.

[26] Additional MS. 15858, fos. 11–14; cf. fos. 135, 192.

[27] This may be Dr. Eleazar Duncon, Prebendary of Durham. See *Correspondence of John Cosin*, Surtees Society, 1869, i. 280.

[28] Additional MS. 15858, fo. 13. There is also a letter from Hanmer to Browne, dated 25 March 1648 at Angers, in the Evelyn MSS. He says that Dr. Duncombe, Sir G. Savile and others left for Paris in the previous week.

[29] Fos. 38–40.

[30] *Finch MSS.*, i. 68. Charles Bertie took the opposite view in 1662: 'Here is a good Academy in this town of Monsieur Forestier's, which is esteemed the best in France after some in Paris' (*Lindsey MSS.*, p. 366). William Hammond carefully observed the technique of silk manufacture in a workshop at Lyon (Additional MS. 59785, letter 27, 23 March 1658).

[31] *Lismore Papers* (ed. Grosart), 1st Series, v.80, 112ff.; 2nd Series, iii. 219; iv. 96–203. Shortly after returning to England Boyle wrote to his former tutor in Geneva: he referred for the first time to the 'invisible college' in which he had become involved. Charles Webster, 'New Light on the Invisible College', *Transactions of The Royal Historical Society*, 1974, p. 19.

[32] The sequence of documents for this part of R. D'Ewes' travels, through the trackless wilderness of Sir Simonds D'Ewes' correspondence, is as follows: — Harleian MS. 374, fo. 116; MS. 383, fos. 151, 152; MS. 379, fo. 57; MS. 383, fo. 183.

[33] J. Ray, *Observations Made in a Journey*, etc., 1673, *passim*; especially pp. 454–465; *Churchill's Collection of Voyages and Travels* (ed. 1732), vi. 359–736; Sloane MS. 179 A, fos. 2–40, for Dr. Downes; E. Browne, *Journal of a Visit to Paris 1664* (ed. G. Keynes), 1923; *Works of Sir T. Browne* (ed. S. Wilkin), 1836, i. 70, 100–106; C. E. Raven, *John Ray Naturalist*, ed. 1986, pp. 129–40.

[34] For the doubt, *D.N.B.*; for what follows the principal sources are Bodl. Lister MS 19, a pocket diary, and Lister MS 5 entitled 'Adversaria'. For additional material, R. P. Stearns (ed.), *A Journey to Paris in the Year 1698 by Martin Lister*, Chicago, 1967, pp. xxiv–lvi, and the *Dictionary of Scientific Biography*.

[35] Lister MS. 19, fos. 15–17, i. 49.

[36] Lister MS. 5, fos. 225–227; fos. 215–227 are all of interest.

[37] The whole of this significant entry has now been printed in G. Scherz, *Nicolaus Steno and his Indice* (Copenhagen, 1958). p. 291. Lister says of Steno, 'I observed in him very much of the Galant and honest man as ye French say, as well as of ye schollar.' For Steno, contacts with the English in Montpellier provided an introduction to the Royal Society.

[38] Fos. 44–49.

[39] Cf. Henry Compton to Sir Joseph Williamson 14 January 1666: 'The journal de savans is licensed afresh, which informs us of all the new books of the times. I have sent you the last to give you a taste, that you may pass your judgment upon the

design, which is renewed weekly.' S.P. France, 122/16.

[40] M. Magendie, *La Politesse Mondaine ...1600 à 1600* (n.d.), i. chap. x.

[41] In the Causeries de Lundi, vol. xiv.

[42] *Ibid.*, vol. xii.

[43] *Philosophical Transactions*, no. 50, p. 1013.

[44] L. von Ranke, *History of the Popes*, Appendix 132.

[45] *Hist. MSS. Comm. Montagu MSS.*, I. 336.

[46] The following paragraphs are based on the Wharton papers in Bodl. Rawlinson Letters. MSS. 49, 52, 53, 54 and 104. There is a general account of these in *Congregational Hist. Soc. Trans.*, x, 55ff. by A. G. Matthews. Cf. John Carswell, *The Old Cause*, 1954, pp. 33–39.

[47] MS. 52, fo. 98.

[48] MS. 52, fos. 101, 11; MS. 53, fo. 2; MS. 49, fos. 3–5, 11–18.

[49] MS. 49, fos. 11–17; MS. 52, fos. 91, 113, 114. The passport obtained by Lord Wharton for his children, Gale, Perkins, Lefèvre and two servants is dated 6 August 1662 (Carte MS. 117, fo. 213).

[50] MS. 49, fo. 17.

[51] MS. 49, fos. 22–24; MS. 54, fo. 1; MS. 52, fo. 108. Gale's expenses at Caen between 23 October and 8 January 1663 amounted to £10 sterling (MS. 104, fo. 2).

[52] MS. 49, fo. 24.

[53] MS. 49, *passim*.

[54] MS. 49, fo. 66.

[55] MS. 49, fos. 32–45, 82.

[56] MS. 49, fo. 45.

[57] MS. 49, fos. 48–55; MS. 53, fos. 53, 55, 57; MS. 54, fo. 8.

[58] MS. 54, fo. 2; MS. 52, fo. 98; MS. 49, fos. 67–78. Clifford himself uses the word 'antipuritanical' (MS. 52, fo. 98.).

[59] MS. 49, fos. 79, 21, 46; MS. 54, fo. 38. For Panton see *Calamy Revised* (ed. A. G. Matthews). Gale says of him here: 'He has been in France about one year and half, and made the great tour of France, staying some while at Geneva.' MS. 49, fo. 46.

[60] S.P. France, 126/76, 102.

[61] MS. 54, fos. 36, 32, 14, 35, 13, 18, 17, 12, 30, 27, 10, 24, 26, 25, 23, 28, 38, 15, 31, 29, 34, 37: the chronological order

of the documents from the time Clifford left Caen. For the Whartons in the Low Countries, above p. 183.

[62] MS. 54, fo. 8; also MS. 104, fo. 15.

[63] *True Idea of Jansenisme*, p. 97.

[64] M. Poëte, *La Promenade à Paris au 17e siècle*, 1913, and *Une Vie de Cité*, 1932, pp. 105–221, J. F. de Castelnau, *Le Paris de Louis XIII*, 1928; P. de Crousaz-Crétet, *Paris sous Louis XIV*, 1922; E. Magne, *Images de Paris sous Louis XIV*, 1939.

[65] S. Wren, *Parentalia*, 1750, pp. 261–2; *Sir Christopher Wren*, R.I.B.A. Memorial volume, 1923, pp. 175–28; M. Whinney, 'Sir Christopher Wren's visit to Paris', *Gazette des Beaux-Arts*, 6th series, 51 (1958), pp. 229–40. The Great Fire of London, occuring a few months after Wren's return home, providentially offered him opportunities to put into practice what he had observed abroad: the construction of domed buildings, the organization of building operations on a very large scale, even radial street-planning.

[66] *Aubrey's Lives*, ii. 140; Additional MS. 15875, fo. 109 (on Petty); M.H. Nicolson Conway Papers, 1930, p. 59; E. Browne, *Journal of a Visit to Paris 1664* (ed. G. Keynes 1923) *passim*.

[67] Harleian MS. 943, fo. 47; *Conway Papers*, p. 118.

[68] Sloane MS. 179 A, fo. 8; E. Browne, *op. cit.*, p. 9.

[69] Evelyn, iii. 41. *Leviathan* had just been published, the climax of ten years' work in Paris. At the end of 1651 Hobbes returned to London and submitted to the Commonwealth government. It proved to be the close of his last period of residence across the Channel.

[70] *Correspondence of John Cosin*, Surtees Society, 1869, i. 230ff.

[71] Harleian MS 374, fos. 117, 119.

[72] *Sidney Papers*, ii. 379–80, 461–2, 466, 606–7; *Conway Papers*, p. 29.

[73] *Al. Ox.* and *D.N.B.*

[74] Document endorsed 'my Ld. of Carlisel's and my Ld.'s proposition to the Senate at Venice, 28 August o.s. 1628'; Browne to Wake from Constantinople 24 July o.s. 1630; Browne to Sec. of State from Paris 21 June 1631; five letters from Peter Turner to C. Browne July 1629–

March 1632, Evelyn MSS. in the Christ Church.

[75] Leicester to Windebank 5 June, Scudamore to Coke 9 June, 1637, S.P. France, 103/342, 366.

[76] Scudamore to Coke etc. 24 November–21 December 1638, *ibid.*, 106/329, 333, 341, 388.

[77] E.g. in *Hist. MSS. Comm., Ormonde MSS.* N.S., i. 163, 209, 216, 230, 263.

[78] Additional MS. 15857, fos. 192–3; Sir B. Gerbier to Browne 20 May 1644, a document endorsed 'Compte de M. Aylesbery, 1 May 1645, and Evelyn to Jane Glanville, 27 November 1649, in the Evelyn MSS.

[79] Holles to Secretary of State 20 September 1665, S.P. France, 121/91, 92; also 12 August, *ibid.*, 121/41.

[80] Holles to Secretary of State 28 September and 12 October 1664 and 13 September 1665, *ibid.*, 119/110, 126, 120/194; E. Browne, *op. cit.*, pp. 7, 9, 34; Rawlinson Letters, MS. 54, fo. 35.

[81] *Hardwicke State Papers*, i. 528. This undated letter was assigned by the editor (subsequently followed by the *D.N.B.*) to the autumn of 1624. From internal evidence it was written between the middle of March and the middle of April 1625 (cf. the details given in *Cal. of S.P. Ven. 1623–1625*, pp. 615–621).

[82] His conversion to Catholicism was made public in 1635; he informed his father 'that the greatest part of my life capable of distinction of Religions hath been in places, and conversant with persons, opposite to the faith I was bred in'. *Coppy of a Letter sent from Mr. Walter Montagu to his Father the Lord Privie Seale...*, 1641, p. 11.

[83] *Cal. of S.P. Dom. 1657–8*, p. 215.

[84] Manchester, *Court and Society*, 1864, ii. 13; *Lindsey MSS.*, P. 276.

[85] Bodl. Carte MS. 223, fo. 76; fos. 63, 69.

[86] Carte MS. 223, fo. 65.

[87] Carte MS. 223, fo. 79.

[88] Carte MS. 223, fos. 80, 85–88, 105.

[89] Carte MS. 223, fos. 90–97, 113–130.

[90] For Davenant, the opera in Paris, and his own reference to 'recitative musick', E.

J. Dent, *Foundations of English Opera*, 1928, pp. 46–7, 64. Cf. M. E. Bukofzer, *Music in the Baroque Era*, 1948, pp. 186–7.

[91] S. Wren, *Parentalia*, p. 261.

[92] *Diary and Correspondence of John Evelyn*, iii. 458.

[93] As an instance of his French connections see Additional MS. 41846, fos. 1–13, for an exchange of letters with P. Hilaire, Reader in Theology at Tours, where they had been introduced by Mde. de Chevreuse. Digby refers feelingly to his subsequent reflections 'durant la froide mais claire nuit que je passais à cheval en venant de Tours à Paris, où ce nombre infini d'estoiles en un ciel très serein (ces autres mondes, beaucoup plus grands que le nostre) me donnait occasion de contempler la quasi· immensité des substances intellectuelles....' etc.

[94] Hobbes's contact with the circle of people round Mersenne, a decided stimulus to his scientific and mathematical interests, began with his journey to Paris in 1634, and his stay there before and after further travels to Italy. *Correspondance du P. Marin Mersenne* (ed. de Waard), iv. 381–2, vi. 101–2.

[95] *Mind*, 1890, xv. 440–447 and Q. Skinner, 'Thomas Hobbes and his Disciples in France and England', *Comparative Studies in Society and History*, 8 (1965–6), pp. 153–167.

[96] H. R. Williamson, *Four Stuart Portraits*, 1949, pp. 47–50.

[97] Harleian MS. 374, fo. 116.

[98] Bodl. Selden Supra MS. 180, fo. 78.

[99] Evidence about Conway's activity as a collector is summarized in D. Mathew, *op. cit.*, p. 107.

[100] Bodl. MS. (Bodl.) 878, fo. 87: Accord pour la Relieure..., etc.

[101] G. Keynes, *John Evelyn, a Study in Bibliophily*, 1937; *Evelyn*, i. 69, iii. 438ff.

[102] Evelyn's notes on the title-pages, etc., of his books, and his letters to Sir R. Browne of 29 November 1656 and 6 March 1657, in the Evelyn MSS. For the sale of Cardinal Mazarin's books in 1651 see *Finch MSS.*, i. 63.

[103] Evelyn to Browne, September 1652.

[104] Evelyn to Browne 2 May 1653, 18 October 1656–June 1657. Phillyrea and

alaternus are both evergreen, ornamental shrubs. The text of J. Evelyn, *Directions for the Gardiner at Sayes-Court*, ed. G. Keynes 1932, is a charming example of the way in which an English gardener's language was sown with French words and names.

[105] Evelyn to Browne 18 October 1656.

[106] Such importations would help to explain the popularity of Huguenot silversmiths in London later on. A household account book of the Ailesbury family (*Hist. MSS. Comm. Ailesbury MSS.*, pp. 184–185) shows that in 1689 they sold a great many specimens of 'French plate', worth £107 18s. 5d. out of £770 18s. 5d., the total of the sale; one wonders whether these had been acquired by the first Lord and Lady Ailesbury during their long residence in France soon after 1660.

[107] *Verney Memoirs*, i. 340.

[108] Evelyn to Jane Glanville 27 November 1649; also 2 May 1650 and 17 June 1651, Evelyn MSS.

[109] For tailors, gardeners and musicians after 1660 see L. Charlanne, *L'Influence Française en Angleterre au 17e siècle*, 1906.

[110] For d'Aubigny see chap. vi of R. Clark, *Strangers and Sojourners at Port Royal*, 1932.

[111] Despatches of Holles 12 Dec. 1665–16 May 1666, S.P. France, 121/199 to 122/184. Richard Cromwell, who had been drawing and reading in Paris for a year or more, made his way southward to Geneva or Italy (*Cal. of S.P. Dom. 1665–1666*, p. 299).

## CONCLUSION

[1] Clarendon, *Life*, ed. 1827, i. 3; cf. Clarendon, *Tracts*, 1747, p. 336: 'We can all remember when very few Men travelled beyond the Seas, except it was to be a Soldier, which is a Profession we have learnt too much of without Travel: Now very few stay at Home, or think they are fit for good Company if they have not been beyond the Seas.'

[2] However, due notice must now be taken of 'the sheer carrying capacity' of the professions at home during the following period, described by Geoffrey Holmes, *Augustan England. Profession, State and Society 1680–1715*, 1982.

[3] *Works of Sir William Temple*, 1740, i. 181, 282; the essays 'Of health and long life' and 'Of gardening'.

[4] Clarendon, *Tracts*, 1747, pp. 285ff.

[5] *Ibid.*, p. 340.

# BIBLIOGRAPHY

## A

The following are lists of the manuscript travel diaries, and of the printed account of journeys, consulted in writing and revising this work. Both are given in their approximate chronological order.

Bodl. Additional MS. C 173. Sir John North in Flanders, Germany, Switzerland and Italy, 1575.

P. R. O. State Papers, Spain, 19/119–154. William Cecil, Lord Roos in Spain, 1610.

B. L. Sloane MS. 682. Catalogued as anonymous, but probably written by Sir Thomas Berkeley or a member of his party (see p. 339 above). Flanders, Germany, Switzerland and Italy, 1610.

Sheffield Public Library, Wentworth Woodhouse MSS. Thomas Wentworth in France, 1612.

B. L. Harleian MS. 7021, fos. 329–330. Catalogued as anonymous, but certainly the work of Sir Thomas Puckering (see p. 337 above). Venetia, 1614.

B. L. Harleian MS. 6867, fos. 27–40. Anonymous Catholic pilgrim in Italy and France, 1622. This is partially printed in *Papers of the British School at Rome*, vi. 482–486.

Bodl. Rawlinson MS. D 1285. Probably Thomas Abdy, in France and Italy 1633–1635. His name is on the flyleaf but there is no other evidence to show that he was the writer.

Bodl. Rawlinson MS. D 1150 ⎫ Thomas Raymond in Holland and
Bodl. Tanner MS. 93, fos. 46–60 ⎭ Italy, 1632–1637 (see p. 343 above). This is not, properly speaking, a diary but reminiscences compiled long afterwards.

B. L. Sloane MS. 118. Joseph Colston in France, Italy, etc., 1641–1645. Fragmentary diaries interspersed with the letters of relatives sent from London and miscellaneous memoranda.

Bodl. Rawlinson MS. C 799. Robert Bargrave in Spain, Italy, Germany, etc., 1646–1653.

Bodl. Rawlinson MS. D 120. Anonymous, in France, Catalonia and Italy 1648–1649.

B. M. Harleian MSS. 943, 1278
B. M. Egerton MSS. 1635, 1636
Bodl. Rawlinson MS. D 121

— Richard Symonds in France and Italy, 1649–1652. For the authorship of the Rawlinson MS. see *Bodleian Library Quarterly*, vii. 176.

Bodl. Rawlinson MS. D 76. Catalogued as anonymous, but certainly the work of Robert Montagu Lord Mandeville, later 3rd Earl of Manchester (see p. 357 above). France, Switzerland and Germany, 1649–1651.

Bodl. Clarendon MS. 137. William Edgeman, accompanying Sir Edward Hyde and Lord Cottington through Flanders, France and Spain, 1649–1651.[2]

B. M. Egerton MS. 1632. Commonplace book of Robert Southwell at Rome, 1660–1661.

Bodl. Rawlinson MS. D 84. Robert Moody, servant of Banister Maynard, in France, Italy, Germany and the Low Countries, 1660–1662.

Bodl. Lister MS. 19. Martin Lister in France, 1663–1666.

B. M. Sloane MS. 179 A. John Downes in France, 1664.

Queen's College Oxford MS. 68. William Nicolson in the Low Countries and Germany, 1678.


Moryson, F. *An itinerary...containing his ten yeeres travell...*(London, 1617; 4 vols. Glasgow, 1907–1908).

Davies, W. *A true relation of the travailes and most miserable captivite of William Davies, barber surgion of London* (London, 1614).

Treswell, R. *A relation of such things as were observed to happen in the journey of the earle of Nottingham...*(London, 1605) and also in *Somers Tracts*, Fourth series, vol. ii (1752), pp. 96–127.

Anon. *The royal entertainment of...the earl of Nottingham* (printed by V. Sims for W. Ferbrand, London, 1605).

Herbert, E. *The life of Edward Lord Herbert of Cherbury written by himself,* ed. H. Walpole (Strawberry Hill, 1764) and ed. S. Lee (London, 1886).


[1] Two other manuscripts (which I have not seen) should be placed here: B.M. Additional MS. 28010, fos. 55, 59, etc, described by D. Gardiner, 'Some travel notes during the Thirty Years War' in *History*, new series, xxv (1941), 14–24; and B.M. Additional MS. 4217, described by M. Letts in *Notes and Queries*, 12th series, i (1916), pp. 141–144. The first concerns France and the Low Countries in 1644–1646, the second is a journey from Flanders to Italy in 1649–1950.

[2] In Catalogue no. 6 of 1945–1946, issued by Messrs. Hodgson & Co. of Chancery Lane, London, lot 88 was an MS. written by Sir John Cope which described a visit to France in 1654.

Coryat, T. *Coryats crudities, hastily gobled up in five moneths travells in France, Savoy, Italie*...(London, 1611; Glasgow, 1905).

Mundy, P. *The travels of Peter Mundy*...*1608–1667*, ed. R. C. Temple, vols. i and iv (Hakluyt Soc., second series, xvii, xlvi, 1907–1924).

Lithgow, W. *The totall discourse of the rare adventures and painefull peregrinations of long nineteene years travayles*...(London, 1614, 1632; Glasgow, 1906).

Cecil, W. *Hist. MSS. Comm. Salisbury MSS.*, vol. 21 (1970), pp. 104–13, 237–49. Viscount Cranbourne in France, Italy, Germany, etc., 1609–1610.

Sandys, G. *A relation of a journey begun an: do: 1610*...(London, 1615).

Phelips, R. *Hist. MSS. Comm. Appendix to First Report* (1874), pp. 59, 60. Sir Robert Phelips in Spain, 1617.

Chaworth, G. *The Losely Manuscripts*, ed. A. J. Kempe (London, 1836), pp. 418–487. Sir Gilbert Chaworth in Flanders, 1621.

Heylin, P. *A full relation of two journeys*...(London, 1656).

Brereton, W. *Travels in Holland, the United Provinces, England,*...*1634–1635*, ed. E. Hawkins (Chetham Soc., i, 1844).

Blount, H. *A voyage into the Levant*...(London, 1636).

Stone, N. *Diary of Nicholas Stone, Junior*, 1638–1640, ed. W. L. Spiers (Walpole Soc., vii, 1919, Appendix).

Gage, T. *The English-American, his travail by sea and land*...(London, 1648) and ed. A. P. Newton (London, 1928).

Boyle, R. 'An Account of Philaretus during his Minority', in R. E. W. Maddison, *Life of the honourable Robert Boyle, F. R. S.* (London, 1969), pp. 26–45.

Evelyn, J. *The Diary of John Evelyn*, ed. E. S. de Beer (6 vols, Oxford, 1955).

Raymond, J. *An itinerary contayning a voyage through Italy in the years 1646–1647* (London, 1648).

Willoughby, R. *Hist. MSS. Comm. Ancaster MSS.* (1907), pp. 418–424. Robert Lord Willoughby in France, 1648–1649.

Reresby, J. *Memoirs and travels of Sir John Reresby*, ed. A. Ivatt (Dryden House memoirs, London, 1904).

Finch, J. *Hist. MSS. Comm. Finch MSS.*, vol. i (1913) pp. 59–76. Sir John Finch in France and Switzerland, 1651–1652, etc.

Lassels, R. 'Description of Italy' (1654), printed in E. Chaney, *The Grand Tour and the Great Rebellion*, pp. 147–231.

Lassels, R. *The voyage of Italy* (Paris, 1670).

Mortoft, F. *Francis Mortoft: his book*...*1658–1659*, ed. M. Letts (Hakluyt Soc., second series, lvii, 1925).

Bertie, C. *Hist. MSS. Comm. Lindsey MSS.* (1942), pp. 275–372. Charles

Bertie in France, 1660–1662.

Browne, E. *Journal of a visit to Paris in...1664*, ed. G. Keynes (London, 1923).

— *Works of Sir Thomas Browne*, vol. i, ed. S. Wilkin (London, 1835).

Ray, J. *Observations...made in a journey through part of the Low Countries, Germany, Italy, and France...*(London, 1673).

Skippon, P. Churchill's *Collection of voyages and travels* (ed. London, 1732) vol. vi. 359–736.

Lauder, J. *Journal of a foreign tour in 1665 and 1666...by Sir John Lauder...*, ed. D. Crawford (Scottish Hist. Soc., xxxvi, 1900).


B

I.  Some sources for the study of seventeenth-century travel:

*Acts of the Privy Council*, 1600–31; *Privy Council Registers*, 1631–1645; and *Calendars of State Papers Domestic*: entries in the indexes under 'passes', 'passes to go abroad', etc.

Anstruther, Godfrey, *The Seminary Priests*, vols. ii and iii (Great Wakering, Essex, 1975–6).

Andrich, G. L. *De Natione Anglica et Scota Iuristarum Universitatis Patavinae 1222–1738* (Padua, 1892).

Brown, H. F. *Inglesi e Scozzesi all'Università di Padova dall'anno 1618 sino al 1765* (Venice, 1921 and 1922).

Colvin, Howard, *A Biographical Dictionary of British Architects 1600–1840* (London, ed. 1978).

Davenport, F. G. 'Materials for English diplomatic history 1509–1783', *Hist. Mss. Comm. 18th Report* (1917), pp. 357–402.

Firth, C. H. and Lomas, S. C. *Notes on the Diplomatic Relations of England and France 1603–1688* (Oxford, 1906).

Frank-van Westrienen, Anna, *De Groote Tour: tekening van de educatiereis der Nederlanders in de seventende eeuw* (Amsterdam, 1983).

Frijhoff, W. 'Étudiants étrangers a l'Académie d'Équitation d'Angers du xviie siècle', *Lias*, iv (1977), pp. 12–84.

Innes Smith, R. W. *English Speaking Students of Medicine in the University of Leyden* (Edinburgh, 1932).

Mączak, Antoni, *Życie codzienne w podróżach po Europie w xvi i xvii wicku* (Warsaw, 1978). An English translation of this important study of European travel is expected shortly.

Mączak, A. and Teuteberg, H. J. (eds.), *Reiseberichte als Quellen europäischer Kulturgeschichte (Wolfenbütteler Forschungen, 21)*, 1982.

Matthews, William, *British Diaries, An annotated bibliography of British diaries written between 1442 and 1942* (Berkeley, 1950), pp. 7–52.

Peacock, Edward, *Index to English Speaking students...at Leyden University* (London, 1883).

Pine-Coffin, R. S. *Bibliography of British and American Travel in Italy to 1860* (Florence, 1974), with a supplement in *Bibliofilia*, 83 (1981).

Schudt, Ludwig, *Le guide di Roma* (Vienna, 1930).

Schudt, L. *Italienreisen im 17. und 18. Jahrhundert* (Vienna, 1959).

Sells, A. Lytton, *The Paradise of Travellers. The Italian influence on English travellers in the seventeenth century* (London, 1964).

Stagl, J. 'Die Apodemik oder 'Reisekunst' als Methodik der Sozialforschung von Humanismus bis zur Aufklärung', *Statistik und Staatsbeschreibung in der Neuzeit...*, ed. J. Stagl and M. Rassem (Paderborn, 1980), pp. 131–87.

Stone, Lawrence, *The Crisis of the Aristocracy* (Oxford, 1965), chap. xii.

Wiemers, Michael, *Der 'Gentleman' und die Kunst, Studien zum Kunsturteil des englischen Publikums in Tagebuchaufzeichnungen des 17. Jahrhunderts* (Hildesheim, 1986).


II. Some books and articles referring to individual travellers:

Beal, M. R. S. *A Study of Richard Symonds. His Italian notebooks and their relevance to seventeenth-century painting techniques* (New York, 1984).

Brearley, Mary, *Hugo Gurgeny: prisoner of the Lisbon Inquisition* (London, 1947).

Chaney, Edward, *The Grand Tour and the Great Rebellion. Richard Lassels and 'The Voyage of Italy' in the seventeenth century* (Geneva, 1985).

Cozzi, G. 'Fra Paolo Sarpi, l'Anglicanismo e la Historia del Concilio Tridentino', *Rivista storica italiana* 68 (1956), pp. 559–619.

Crinò, A. M. *Fatti e figure del seicento anglo-toscano* (Florence, 1957).

Gabrieli, Vittorio, *Sir Kenelm Digby: un inglese italianato nell'età della Controriforma* (Rome, 1957).

Havran, M. J. *Caroline Courtier: the life of Lord Cottington* (London, 1973).

Höltgen, K. J. 'Sir Robert Dallington (1561–1637): author, traveler and pioneer of taste', *Huntingdon Library Quarterly* 47 (1984), pp. 147–177.

Howarth, David, *Lord Arundel and his Circle* (New Haven, 1985).

Huxley, Gervas, *Endymion Porter: the life of a courtier, 1587–1649* (London, 1959).

Jacquot, J. 'Sir Charles Cavendish and his learned friends', *Annals of Science* 8 (1952), pp. 13–27, 178–91.

Kaufman, H. A. *Conscientious Cavalier: Colonel Bullen Reymes 1613–1672* (London, 1978).

Kelliher, W. H., *Andrew Marvell: poet and politician, 1621–78* (London, 1978).

Lievsay, J. L. *Venetian Phoenix: Paolo Sarpi and some of his English friends* (Lawrence, Kansas, 1973).

Malcom, Noel, *De Dominis (1560–1624): Venetian, Anglican, ecumenist and relapsed heretic* (London, 1984).

Malcom, N. 'Hobbes, Sandys and the Virginia Company', *Historical Journal*, 24 (1981).

Ollard, Richard, *Clarendon and his Friends* (London, 1987).

Raven, C. E. *John Ray Naturalist* (Cambridge, ed. 1986).

Rogers, Malcom, *William Dobson 1611–46* (London, 1968).

Rossi, M. M. *La vita, le opere, i tempi di Eduardo di Chirbery* (Florence, 1947).

Strong, Roy, *Henry Prince of Wales and England's lost Renaissance* (London, 1984).

Skinner, Q. 'Thomas Hobbes and his disciples in France and England', *Comparative Studies in Society and History*, 8 (1965–6), pp. 153–167.

Snow, V. F. *Essex the Rebel: the life of Lord Devereux, the third Earl of Essex 1591–1646* (Lincoln, Nebraska), 1970.

Springell, F. C. *Connoisseur and Diplomat; the Earl of Arundel's embassy to Germany in 1636...*(London, 1963).

Stevenson, Sara, and Thomson, Duncan, *John Michael Wright the King's Painter* (Edinburgh, 1982).

Thomson, Duncan, *A Virtuous and Noble Education* (Edinburgh, 1971) (the travels of Robert and William Kerr, 1651–7).

Whitteridge, Gweneth, *William Harvey and the Circulation of the Blood* (London, 1961).

Wedgwood, C. V. *Thomas Wentworth Earl of Strafford: a Revaluation* (London, 1961).

Whinney, M. 'Sir Christopher Wren's visit to Paris', *Gazette des Beaux Arts*, 6th series, 51 (1958), pp. 229–40.

III.   The English Background:

Adams, S. L. 'The road to La Rochelle: English foreign policy and the Huguenots, 1610–1629', *Proceedings of the Huguenot Society of London*, 22 (1975), pp. 414–429.

Aylmer, G. E. *The King's Servants: the civil service of Charles I, 1625–42* (London, ed: 1974).

Barcroft, J. H. 'Carleton and Buckingham: the quest for office', *Early Stuart Essays*, ed. H. S. Reinmuth (Minneapolis, 1971), pp. 122–136.

Beales, A. C. F. *Education under Penalty, English Catholic education from the Reformation to the fall of James II* (London, 1963).

Cliffe, J. T. *The Yorkshire Gentry from the Reformation to...the Civil War* (London, 1969).

Jenson, J. V. 'The staff of the Jacobean Privy Council', *Huntingdon Library Quarterly*, 40 (1976–77).

Lambley, Kathleen, *The Teaching and Cultivation of the French Language in England during Tudor and Stuart Times* (Manchester, 1920).

Lee, M. 'The Jacobean diplomatic service', *American Historical Review*, 72 (1967), pp. 1264–82.

Lievsay, J. L. *The Englishman's Italian Books, 1550–1700* (Philadelphia, 1969).

Loomie, A. J. *Ceremonies of Charles I: the note books of John Finet 1628–1641* (Fordham, New York, 1987).

Loomie, A. J. 'The Spanish faction at the court of Charles, I, 1630–8', *Bulletin of the Institute of Historical Research*, 59 (1986), pp. 37–49.

Mathew, David, *The Social Structure in Caroline England* (Oxford, 1948).

O'Day, Rosemary, *Education and Society 1500–1800; the social foundations of education in early modern Britain* (London, 1982).

Parry, Graham, *The Golden Age restor'd: the culture of the Stuart court, 1603–42* (Manchester, 1981).

Stone, Laurence, ed: *The University in Society*, vol. i (Princeton, 1975).

IV. The English abroad, and European influences:.

Billacois, François, *Le duel dans la société française des xvie-xviie siècles* (Paris 1986).

Bowen, Marjorie, *The Netherlands display'd, or the Delights of the Low Countries* (London, 1926).

Cozzi, G. 'Bacone, la Riforma e Roma nella versione Hobbesiana d'un carteggio di Fulgenzio Micanzio', *English Miscellany*, viii (1957), pp. 195–250.

Carter, A. C. *The English Reformed Church in Amsterdam in the Seventeenth Century* (Amsterdam, 1964).

Hunt, J. Dixon, *Garden and Grove: the Italian Renaissance garden in the English imagination: 1600–1750* (London, 1986).

*Inigo Jones on Palladio*, ed. B. Allsopp (Newcastle-upon-Tyne, 1970).

Raab, Felix, *The English Face of Machavelli: a changing interpretation, 1500–1700* (London, 1964).

de Rojas, F. *Celestine* (trans. James Mabbe), ed. Guadalupe Martinez Lacalle (London, 1972).

Stearns, R. P. *Congregationalism in the Dutch Netherlands: the rise and fall of the English Congregational classis 1621–1635* (Chicago, 1940).

Worsthorne, S. T. *Venetian Opera in the Seventeenth Century* (Oxford, 1954).

# INDEX